Encyclopaedia of Indian Theatre - 9

CONTEMPORARY THEATRE

(EAST & NORTH-EAST)

In this series..........

Encyclopaedia of Indian Theatre – Series

1.	Bhasa (2000)	Biswajit Sinha
2.	Major Sanskrit Dramatists (2001)	"
3.	Kalidasa (2002)	"
4.	Dictionary of Music, Dance and Drama (2003)	"
5.	Rabindranath Tagore (Two Parts) (2004)	"
6.	Folk Theatre (2004)	"
7.	Sanskrit Theatre	"
8.	Contemporary Theatre (South India)	"
9.	Contemporary Theatre (East and North East)	"
10.	Contemporary Theatre (West, North and Central India)	

Encyclopaedia of Indian Theatre - 9

CONTEMPORARY THEATRE

(EAST & NORTH-EAST)

Biswajit Sinha

Raj Publications
New Delhi - 110002 (INDIA)

[Encyclopaedia of Indian Theatre – 9] : Contemporary Theatre

First Published in 2008

ISBN 13: 978-81-86208-59-5
ISBN 10: 81-86208-59-3
ISBN (Series): 81-86208-18-6

Published by : **Poonam Goel**
Raj Publications
108, 4855/24, Ansari Road
Daryaganj, New Delhi - 110 002

Tel. : 011 - 30120939

Laser Typesetting by : Tamalika Computers, Delhi

Printed at : Balaji Offset Printers, Delhi

PRINTED IN INDIA

CONTENTS

PREFACE

In the Constitution of India, tribals are named as janjati (tribes) which is wrong. A modern scholar outbursts 'Adivasi' do not belong to any cast, they are neither *janjati* nor *vanvasi* - they are Adivasis. It is the dream of modern Adivasi arts and literature that the social system should be free from classicism and casteism and they would not accept those life-values which never belonged to them. Mankind's history is the history of successive displacement and ruin of Adivasis by the so-called civilized class. In India, they are alienated from the mainstream of the society even today. In the *'Oxford Companion to Indian Theatre'*, excluding Manipuri, not a single line is devoted either to their folk traditions or the modern urbanized theatre. I find such work, a threat of marginalization. Not a mere rant, when one considers the problematization of Adivasi culture, art, its language and literature, in the age of globalization. Already works broughtout by the premier publishing houses or theatre institutions are sign enough to suggest that there would be little scope for different Adivasi theatre to develop and duly reckoned in near future.

In the present volume, I have moved away from their rich past-traditions (folk arts) and have documented only the new stream, theatrical endeavours in modern context comprising languages such as Bodo, Garo, Khasi, Khortha, Kokborok, Lepcha, Mahali, Manipuri, Mizo, Nagamese, Nagpuri, Santali, etc.

The focus of my present venture is to highlight the north-eastern and eastern zones and I have culled materials for the purpose from all possible literary sources, with a zeal to awaken the consciousness of the mainstream Indian theatre, so that a new beginning for art appreciation is made forthwith.

I

BODO

Introduction

Assam State of India, has multiracial and linguistic groups of people with different cultures of whom the Boro Kacharis or the Bodos from a very important section of these groups and are believed to be among the earliest settler of Assam. At one time they built a powerful kingdom with their capital at Dimapur and then at Maibong and Khaspur. They spread over the Brahmaputra Valley, North Bengal and Bangladesh and constitute a very important group of Indo-Mongoloid people of the East. Those who live in scattered hamlets along the foot hills of the Himalayas in the North East as well as in scattered areas of the Brahmaputra Valley, have now been mixed up with the neighbouring peoples. But they still call themselves 'Boro or Bodo', although they are otherwise known as 'Kacharis' in the Assam Valley. The Bodo group of speech community includes Bodo proper, Dimasa, Rabha, Tiwa, Kok-Borok, Deuri-Chutiya, Koch-Hajong, Garo etc. Bodo belongs to the Bodo sub-section of Bodo-Naga section under the Assam-Burmese group of the Tibeto-Burman group of the Sino-Tibetan family of languages. The Bodo speech community is now well-spread throughout the North-Eastern states of India, not only Assam but also Arunachal Pradesh, Meghalaya, Nagaland, Mizoram, Manipur,

Tripura and Northern parts of West Bengal, Bihar and adjoining areas of Bangladesh, Nepal and Bhutan. Among the districts in Assam, the highest proportion of Bodo speakers is noticed in Kokrajhar, followed by Bongaigaon, Nalbari and Darrang. Bodo is a full fledged language, recognized under VIII schedule of Indian Constitution. It has attained the state of a major Indian language. They have a rich cultural life. Their culture is manifested in various aspects of their life. Their artistic sense and lore of beauty are found in their various festivals, dances and songs, enchanting music and in their arts and crafts.

Though the folk segment is very rich, the written Bodo literature is only recent phenomenon.

Bodo Dancers

The Christian missionaries were the first to publish books on religion, tales, rhymes and songs. But they are not accepted as proper Bodo literary productions by the present Bodo scholars. According to them, the appearance of '*Birbar*', the mouthpiece of Bodo Chhatra Sanmilani in 1924 under the editorship of late Satish Chandra Basumatari, the Bodo literature proper came into being. Another Bodo journal '*Alonbar*' was launched in 1936 under the editorship of late Pramod Chandra Brahma. These journals were the breeding grounds for young Bodo writers who were infact the harbingers of the first renaissance of Bodo literature, be it fiction, shortstories, drama, essay or other genres.

In 1952, the Bodo Sahitya Sabha was established and its house journal '*Bodo*' was broughtout under the editorship of Satish Chandra Basumatari. This journal had a catalystic role in moulding new consciousness among the new generation of Bodo writers.

Bodo language and oral literature may be very old. But the modern history of Bodo language and written literature is not very old. As stated earlier, it all began in 1952 when the first conference of Bodo Sahitya Sabha was held and the able stewardship of late Satish Chandra Basumatary and Sri Jogen Basumatary who untiring labour brought Bodo language as the medium of instruction in primary and secondary level respectively. The Bodo language was recognised as the medium of education in the school level from 1963 and as one of Modern Indian Languages from 1977 under Gauhati University in Assam. Later on it was recognised as M.I.L. subject under North-Eastern Hill University (Shillong), Assam University (Silchar), and Dibrugarh University (Assam). The language was recognised as the Associate State Language of Assam from 1985. This language was recognised as M.I.L. for Post-graduate Certificate Course in 1985, Diploma Course in 1994, language subject from M.A. degree in 1996. T.D.C. Elective in 1999 and is going to be introduced as M.I.L. for Major course very soon. Eventually it was approved as a state languages by the Cabinet Committee for inclusion in the 8th schedule of Indian Constitution in 2003 itself. Thus the leaders of Bodo Sahitya Sabha in later period should also deserve praise for their continued effort to develop the language. Late Sri Bireswar Brahma's leadership that helped in the process for recognizing the Bodo language in the VII schedule of the Indian Constitution.

Bodo Sahitya Sabha at Kokrajhar is the apex body of the Bodos to develop the Bodo language, literature and culture. Meanwhile, there had been a rising trend of political movements too among the Bodos in Assam for establishing their all-round identity. The 1974 movement for Roman script for Bodo Language added a new dimension to the world of Bodo literature. A batch of promising writers particularly of poetry and fiction made their mark, but very few emerged as playwrights.

Since times immemorial, the Bodos living in the districts of Goalpara, Darange and Kamrup have composed Bodo songs, poems and dramas in the Assamese alphabet and the first Bodo journal, the '*Bibar*', was itself published in the Assamese alphabet in 1923. From the Assamese as well as the Roman alphabets Bodos have, now stwiched over to Nagari script in Bodo literature.

The Bodo is a developing language. It is developing very rapidly, covering every aspect of literary field. Amongst various genres of modern Bodo litarature, the most frtile field is, however, the shorter fictions. '*Mulugni Solo*', is a collection of world famous short stories translated into Bodo by different translators, published by the Bodo Sahitya Sabha in 2002. Modern Bodo short stories, a compilation of Bodo short stories by eleven renowned Bodo writers, selected and translated by Joykanta Sarma was published by the Sahitya Akademi, New Delhi in 2003. It includes the stories of Janil Kumar Brahma, Heramba Narzari, Bandhu Ram Basumatari, Mangal Singh Hajowari, Ishan Mushahari, Haribhushan Brahma, Manoranjan Lahari, Siken Brahma, Nil Kamal Brahma, Ranjit Kumar Bargayari, and Jhareswar Basumatary.

Other contemporary creative writers in Bodo language are :- Jaraphagla/ whose collection of short stories in Bodo '*Dantharu*' was published in 2004 by Danali Publications. Gopinath Bargayary wrote the book 'Ālāsi', also a collection of short stories in Bodo, broughtout by Sri Sansumwi Basumatary, Mainao Nwgwr, Simbargaon, BTAD, Assam in 2004. '*Khanthaini Ikebana*' is the title of the anthology in Bodo, published by the Bodo Sahitya Sabha, Kokrajhar in 2005 which comprises of over 450 poems by diverse poets in Bodo language. An invaluable publication in recent time is 'Mwsoudaan' a Bodo version of Munshi Premchand's Hindi classic 'Godaan' by Gobinda Narzary and published by Bodo Sahitya Sabha, Kokrajhar in 2005.

Bodo Dramatic literature

Bodo language is now developing as language of literature. The genre of drama has also evolved in it and publication of drama books has started. Few notable modern playwrights in Bodo languages are :- Madhu Ram Baro, Kamal Kumar Brahma, Manoranjan Lahary, Dwarendra Narayan Basumatary.

Madhu Ram Baro

Bodo playwright, novelist, short story writer, poet and critic, Madhu Ram Baro was born in 1938 in Kalitakuchi, Hajo in District Kamrup of Assam. He obtained his B.A. degree from Gauhati University and later pursued M.A. from Poona University. Madhu Ram, after doing his M.A. in Linguistics followed research for several years in Deccan College at Poona. After coming back to Assam, he started writing Grammar, Vocubulary and Dictionary on Bodo language along with the text-books prescribed for different levels of education. Madhu, however, did his research in Mizo language from the Poona University. From that he gathered experience, which he applied in the Bodo language later on He did research on the Bodo and Assamese language in the light of the modern linguistics. He is the first Master's Degree holder in Linguistics not only among the Bodos but in Assam as a whole Madhuram started his teaching career from Saniadi High Madrasa and after serving many schools he joined Gauhati University and worked there till his retirement in 1998. He was a faculty member of Deptt. of Linguistics. Before this job, he served in various schools for a long period.

Madhu Ram Baro's first experience as a writer was the feeder of the text books. He has also written some reference books in the field of languages, literature and culture. These include some creative writing too.

Madhu Ram Baro

Author knows Assamese, Hindi, Bengali, English, French and German. He is credited with more than 70 books in Bodo, English and Assamese—most of them prescribed as text books from lower level to Master's Degree level. In the field of linguistics, his well known books in English are: *Historical development of Bodo language, the Bodo structure, Assamese and Bodo: a comparative and constructive study.*

Madhu Ram Baro's creative writings include poems, short stories, dramas novels, biographies, in Bodo language based on the real facts. Most of these writings reflect his own experience, which carry the true picture of the everyday life of the community. He has contributed over five hundred articles in several leading journals of North East India. Edited "*Sampad Saptahik*", a multilingual news weekly including Assamese, English, Bodo and other tribal language of N.E.- India and *Asomar Janajati*, a multilingual Assamese magazine.

For his creative and scholarly works, Madhu Ram has received several awards and prizes. He was felicitated as Ideal teacher/Litterateur/Artist (vocal music) by Dadara, Damdama Anchalik Hajo Sahitya Sabha and also as Centenary Litterateur/Educationalist by Hajo Anchalik Journalists' Association during the Golden Jubilee Celebration of Indian Independence. He also receive literary pension from Assam Government. In the year 2002, Sahitya Akademi, New Delhi Conferred the *Bhasa Samman* on Dr. Madhu Ram Baro for his unique contribution to Bodo language and literature.

Kamal Kumar Brahma

Sri Kamal Kumar Brahma was the President of the 31st & 32nd sessions of the Bodo Sahitya Sabha held at Basugaon, Kokrajhar and Tangla, Darrang respectively. Sri Brahma has edited the prose collection '*Raithai Bihung*', now prescribed by the Dibrugarh University for its B.A. (T.D.C.) Bodo (M.I.L.) Paper II.

In its 36th Annual Conference of Bodo Sahitya Sabha, Shri Kamal Kumar Brahma was awarded the '*Rangsar Literary Award*' of 1996-1997 for his full-length drama in Bodo entitled '*Horbadi Khwmshi*', published by the Bodo Sahitya Sabha, Kokrajhar.

Dibrugarh University for its B.A. (TDC) Bodo (M.I.L.) 1994-1995 session onwards prescribed the drama text '*Raja Iragdao*' by Sri Kamal Kumar Brahma.

Manoranjan Lahary

Manoranjan Lahary was born in 1936. A poet, playwright fiction writer, Essayist Sri Lahari retired as Principal of Kokrajhar Govt. B.Ed. College. He has written a good number of plays in Bodo language. His praiseworthy dramatic composition is '*Anari*'.

Dwarendra Narayan Basumatary

Writer and Playwright Dwarendra Narayan Basumatary's book '*Raja Nilambar*' was published by Bodo Sahitya Sabha. His well received dramatic composition is '*Sonani Maibong*'.

Syllabus for Elective Bodo for the Bachelor of Arts (B.A.) Three Years degree Course (1+1+1) of the Dibrugarh University in its Ist year Course has a paper on Drama (Drama text to be read) which comprises of the plays of *Dwarendra Basumatary, Manoranjan Lahary* and *Kamal Kumar Brahma* entitled '*Sonani Maibong*', '*Anari*' and '*Horbadi Khwmshi*' respectively.

In its third year syllabus, a section on Western Literary Criticism (Items to be read) includes drama, novel & short stories and poetry.

Another section on Folk Performing Art contains Subung Phaothai, Subung Dengkhw, Subung Mwsanai.

As a part of Tagore Festival at the Prithvi Theatre Festival in Mumbai, in the year 2006. Kalakshetra, a Manipuri theatre troupe of Heisnam Kanhailal produced a multi-lingual play '*Dakghar*' written in Bengali by Rabindranath Tagore and presented it in Manipuri, *Bodo*, Tripuri, Rabha, Assamese and Bengali language, with minimal dialogues, folk songs in Bodo, Tripuri and Manipuri and ripple-less dance movement.

Bodo drama is only at a developing stage with young writers making endeavours for improved style and content.

II

GARO

The Garos and the Khasis are the main tribes who inhibit the state of Meghalaya. Garo belongs to the Bodo group of the Tibeto-Burman family (type Sino-Tibetan) of languages. It was believed that the Bodos, at one time, formed the most predominant section of the population of the region, having established powerful kingdoms. It course of time, they gave way to other races and languages. Besides the Garos in Meghalaya, we find them scattered in the various places in Assam and Bangladesh.

Garo Literature

Garo was the second important language to be reduced to writing by the missionaries in the North East. It was T.J. Keith, one of the first missionaries who established contacts with the Garos in the plains and did an outstanding preliminary work in the development of the language. Be brought out '*Dictionary of the Garo language*: *Garo-Bengali-English*' from Jalpaiguri in 1873, followed by *An Outline Grammer of Garo Languages* from Sibsagar in 1879. The language was put down to writing in the Bengali alphabet and the translation of the Gospel was taken up, followed by the publication of the Gospel of St. Matthew in 1875 and a primer by T.J. Stoddard were first books to appear in print. The New Testament was published in 1894 and after the long years of labour culminated in the publication of the Old Testament in 1924. Apart from Bible, a bulk of Christian hymns and treatises were translated During this first stage of growth, E.G. Phillips wrote and prepared the first school text books which included works of grammar, extracts from Christian scriptures, morals, hygiene, reader and arithmetic etc.

Towards the last decade of the nineteenth century, the American Baptist Mission found it difficult to continue in Bengali script and finally decided to switch over to the Roman alphabet. At the American Baptist Mission Conference of 1893 held at Tura, a general action was taken resolving that 'in the opinion of this conference the Roman alphabet is the best for the Hill tribes about Assam, that have no written language....... "The Italian system of pronounciation of the Roman character should be adhered to. Both Garo and Khasi show the similar trends of growth in the development of the alphabet, translation of Bible and publication of text books that followed.

The second stage of the growth of Garo literature, i.e. from 1900-1927, we witness the transliteration of the existing publication into Roman alphabets. resulting in more and more involvement of the local writers in the field of education.

The introduction of the British administration, followed by the advent of the American Baptist Mission, brought about social change of far-reaching consequence. The first baptism of the Garos occurred in 1863. Conversion of the Garos took place with the establishment of churches in Garo villages located in the Goal para plains of Assam.

Thought the Garo literature was started by the missionaries during the second half of the 19th century when they started their mission and the school in Garo Hills. However the Garo literature during this mission period was mainly confined to religious literature and school textbooks leaving a gap in the collection of Garo indigenous religious rites, mythological stories, recording of their socio-religious festivals, legends etc. The Garos possess extensive tradntional accounts, mythology, fables and others forms of oral literature.

The modern literature on cultural milieu based on several indigenous oral literature, be it ballads, folk-tales, musical incantations, chants and ethical adages came up from 1927 onwards.

In the course of time literature thus developed itself on lines of the indigenous background as culled from the rich folk-lore, oral poetry, wise saying, ethical lessons, musical arts and prayers and proverbs which are in circulation in the society.

Scholars like D. Marak, Samson R. Sangma, Dewan Singh Rongmuthu and others had a great share in the revival of the folk literature.

On Garo folklore, the first compilation was by Jobang D. Marak and Samson in 1927. Initially the indigenous tales echoed and told through ages became significant, invoking, stirring and provided a constant source of power to poetry, drama and novel. From the forties and onwards, most of the creations were adoptations from other literatures. The renderations of Greek mythological stories, Arabian Nights and Cindrella, Aesop's fables, Hans Andersons, Treasure Chest etc. found a place. English literature and the other western classics has greatly influenced the growth of the literature of the Garos and since sixties we find some original creativity works emerging on modern lines. It is pertinent to mention here that 'Tales from Shakespeare', was broughtout in 1971.

Once there was the regeneration of the folk literature, the seeds were also sown by some writers for the growth of original works in the form of novel, drama and other literary genres. The Garo literature is fast developing in the last few years and is now one of the Courses of studies in the post-graduate classes in the North Eastern Hill University, Tura Campus, Meghalaya. Also mentioned above, one of the leading figures in Garo literature is Llewellyn R. Marak who was honoured by the *Bhasa Samman* of the Sahitya Akademi, New Delhi in 1999 for his unique contribution to Garo language and literature. Earlier the author received the award of the Government of Meghalaya for his book, the *Dikki* Part I & II in 1983 and for *Beberaani Bimik* in 1987. In 1991 he was bestowed with the prestigious '*U Tirot Singh Award for Art and Literature*' from the Government of Meghalaya.

Llewellyn R. Marak was born in 1937 at Tura, West Garo Hills, Meghalaya. His was one of the first educated families among the Garos. His father, a teacher, was the Church Leader and President of Garo Baptist Convention, another of English Garo Dictionary, Assamni Katta, Indiani Katta and Editor of Achik Lipeng, the journal broughtout by the Garo Baptist Convention. Sri Llewellyn R. Marak

Llewellyn R. Marak

himself is a prolific writer and editor in Garo. He was the chief editor of Achik Kurang, a journal published by Garo Literature Society, Tura. He was also the publisher of *Chadambe*, a bi-monthly journal of Garo Youth Club, Tura. Sri Marak has written over 10 books and more than 50 articles in Garo and English.

An important cultural forum, *'The Garo Literary and Cultural Society'* was formed in 1982 at the initiative of Sri Milton S. Sangma (b. 1934). The association brings out its journal *Do' Kua* which he edited for five years. It has played a vital role in the promotion and preservation of modern Garo literary and cultural pursuits.

The Garo Literary and Cultural Society was founded with the main objectives of promoting and encouraging Garo literature, collecting reproducing and preserving specimens of early Garo literature and the revision of Garo textbooks as well as Garto dramas and other creative pieces.

In the year 1963 (21.8.63) this society was setup by twelve educated and literary minded Garo elders with the main object of enriching the Garo literature in its all genres.

Many cultural societies and clubs flourih in both districts of Garo Hills. Their main activities cover the fields of music and drama.

The twelve cultural organisation which receive grants from the State Education Departments and Bangsi Chitu Women's Association, Bangsi A'pal; Dainadubi Chitak Dadram Luckystand Youth Club, Dainadubi; Upper Nagarpara Youth Club, Dainadubi; Araimile Socio-Economic Organization, Araimile, Tura, Miapara Union Cultural Club, Mendipathar–Resubelpara; A'gipeniggrae Youth Club, Selsella; Bangkhang Sangma Community Centre; Dibragre Matgrik Club Centre; Satesing Koch Mahila Samity; A'dugre Social Club, (Khongpara) Bouhuri; Children Musical Club, St. Xavier's Compound, Tura.

Garo Drama

Though there have been more contributions in poetry, drama as a genre is gradually evolving. In the realm of drama, three most outstanding playwrights in the contemporary period are Prof. Kennet, Momin, Arjison G. Momin and Redin Momin.

In 1969 Prof. Kenneth Momin's drama *Nokdang* (*Dakmesokani*) appeared in print. A short drama it focusses attention on the social process working on and the form of social reconstruction obtained from the role of ideal families.

The play '*Kamni Bite*' is authored by Arjison G. Momin, a modern social drama in which five characters are represented, two males and three females. It enshrines with its beauty through the interludes and naive dialogues.

Redin Momin's magnum opus '*Khalsin Aro Sonatchi*' in two parts is an exhaustive work that revolves around Khalsin, the hero and Sonatchi. The heroine which exudes from love persuits and adventure among them, interspersing with the thrills of travel, climax of love and the pathetic pangs of separation which finally culminate into the lasting joy of marital union presented in a Bengali style.

Drama, as a form of literature obtains itself from the works of a few dramatists, but works to fit in with traditional, modern, ultra-modern and historical themes are scanty but what little has been done in drama, shows that the path is being trodden to evolve the more and more works fit in with both the modern social and the traditional background.

Garo Performing Arts

Since ages, performing arts in the form of music and dance have been a part and parcel of the Garo society and it came to be used on all occasions. It became the main means of expressing their feeling of sorrow, joy, of thanks giving and adoration; it was used to invoke their gods and to appease them. Stories and events of their glorious past, heroes and heroines have been related through songs in ballad from. These have been passed down from generation to generation in oral tradition, as there were no written scripts then. There is a tradition of epic story narration or epic story moulding known as Katta agana or Katta doka respectively in ballad form. Scholar Iris Watre Thomas gives us an accounts of this performing art. The naration is done by the *Katta agangipa* (native poet-cum-minstrel) who chants out romantic epic themes of ancient days, and of events long past, recounting in an elevated grand style the varied lives and mighty deeds of heroes and heroines like Dikki, Bandi, Giting and So. re; of the manners, customs, ways of living and thinking, love and hate, peace and war, of the colourful past of the Garos, when man possessed supernatural powers. *Katta agana* is of different varieties depending on the tonal manner of singing or modulated chanting. These varieties of *katta agana* are known as *Dikkotchua; Ring badria; Katchi doka* or *Katchi ring a; Dilamandea* or *A.beng Katta; Ruga katta; A.we katta; Saling ring.a or Chisak katta;* and *Ring.dikgita*. There is a legendary belief among the *A.chiks* that, the genuine, unalloyed and most superb *Katta agana*, known as *Katta janggi* or *Saling bireng asol*, can never be taught or sung to anyone who is below fifty years of age; that there must be limited number of listeners, who must be above fifty years. The Garos believe that violation of this restriction bring about total blindness to both the singer and the listener. These poems are not composed extempore but have been handed down from generation to generation by oral tradition. Their origin supposedly dates back to the mystic past. The language is archaic, and when translated, loses its depth and beauty. The "Epic Story Naration" is sung to a modulated tune by a minstrel. At intervals the singer stops and keeps silence, to find out whether his listeners have fallen asleep, because singing generally takes place at night. When a listener responds, saying "Hi", the singing is resumed. Two minstrels may also be engaged in narrating the story responsively.

The Garos are very rich in their art and culture. Music and dance form an integral part of the life of the Garos, though the Christianity has brought about a major in their life and culture. The Christian Garos have practically abandoned all aspects of the Garo culture and religion dance, music and rituals. Traditional music is substituted by the Christian hymns and folk community dances by the western dances. But still there exist different kinds of folk dances, seen on festive occasions. Styles and forms of dance vary according to the nature of the festival. Wangala is considered to be the most significant of all the Garo festivals, held to propitiate *Misi sajong* the God of agriculture and other Gods at the end of the *jhum* cycle, usually in October and November. *The Hundred Drums Wangala Festival*, organised by the Government of Meghalaya every year at Asananggiri in the Rongram Development Block presents a rich and varied part of the cultural heritage of the Garo.

Garos have a vaiety of musical instruments, like drums (known as *dama, kram nadil* and *nagra*), trumpets (called adil and *singga*) and flutes. Most of their musical instruments are made of forest products. They have a very rich folk musical legacies. Agat A. Sangma, a very talented artist was accoladed with the prestigious Sangeet Natak Akademi Award for the year 1999-2000 for his immense contributions by way of nurturing and enriching Garo folkmusic.

In the realm of theatre, the Garos have staged a few playlets from time to time Dr. Hamlet Bareh reminisises : The one I saw once at Gauhati, staged by the students, centred round the first of the Christian conversions, featured with its naive characteristics, simple dialogues — typical gestures of an extempore nature — although much less audible, and focussed on a series of the first contacts opened to the modern age.

A contemporary dramatist in Garo, Keneth Momin drama '*Nokdang*' (family) was first performed in 1961 and was published only in 1969.

This play in Roman script and its English translation is included in the volume '*Garo Literature*' documented and tr. into English by Caroline Marak; broughtout by the Sahitya Akademi, New Delhi in 2002 under the series 'Indian literature in tribal languages'.

References

Bareh, Hamlet. The language and literature of Meghalaya. — Simla : Indian Institute of Advanced Study, 1977.

Momin, Keneth. Nokdang. *In* Garo literature/ edited by Caroline Marak. — New Delhi : Sahitya Akademi, 2002. (Indian literature in Tribal languages). Pp.123-176.

Includes the English translation entitled 'Family'.

Reading in history and culture of the Garos: essays in honour of Miltan S. Sangma/ ed. by Mignonette Momin. — New Delhi : Regency Publications, 2003.

III

KHASI

Introduction

Like the other states on the North East Frontiers of India, Meghalaya was long an enigma, veiled in a pale of mystery. Very little was known about the region before the advent of the British. The Country's Independence led to a series of constitutional and political changes in the region with the ultimate formation of the seven States of North Eastern India, i.e., Arunachal Pradesh, Assam, Manipur, Meghalaya, Mizoram, Nagaland and Tripura, lovingly called the 'Seven Sisters'. The seven sisters have many links and common bonds. One of the Seven Sisters was named 'Meghalaya', (a Sanskritised word) as the areas were proverbially associated with clouds and rain. Literally the word denotes the 'Abode of the Clouds'.

No less than 64 major tribes, which consist of many sub-tribes, with distinctive ethnic and cultural identity live in the region. The inhabitants are as varied and charming. The predominant ethinic groups are: the Khasis, the Jaintias and the Garos. The Khasis inhabit the eastern part of Meghalaya and are now mostly Christians. But before that, they believed in a Supreme Being, the Creator - U Blei Nongthaw and under Him, there were several village deities.

Here in Meghalaya, Khasis first settled in Jaintia Hills and in course of time many of them moved westward to the present Khasi Hills.

The land was ruled by the traditional rulers known as Syiem, Lyngdoh and Sardar who enjoyed complete independence in their respective states or hima.

The East India Company had its office and military establishment in Sohra (Cherrapunji) which became the birth place of Khasi creativity. By 1841, the rulers of the Kasi principalities were peaceful, but one of the Jaintral Hills rebelled against the Company in 1860-61 on house-tax issue which prompted, the British Government to takeover the administration of the Khasi and Jaintia affairs from the Company in 1858. In June 1864 it decided to shift the district headquarter to Shillong and in 1874 the Government created a new province, namely, the Assam and East Bengal Province, and Shillong became the Capital of the province and many villages in the Khasi Hills were brought under the district control of the British Government. The region was brought under the direct occupation and sovereignty of the British during the 19th Century and Subsequently included in the province of Assam.

It was on 21st January, 1971 that Meghalaya came into being as a separate State. Before Independence, most areas constituting Meghalaya were underdeveloped. After-Independence, particularly on attaining the long cherished political aspiration, of the Hills people, i.e. the Statehood, Meghalaya has been steadily progressing in every field.

P.R.T Gurdon and Peter Schmidt attempted to trace the family to which the language of the Khasi people belongs, ie., Khasi language. They assert that it is a branch of the Mon-Khmer group of language. E. Kunt made a comparative study of the Khasi and Mon-Khmer languages, and found many words in them which carry the same meaning.

Meghalaya has its rich traditions of different art forms — decorative arts, performing arts and utilitarian crafts and architecture. The Khasis have two important festivals — Nong Krem Dance and Shad Suk Mynsiem which are an expression of the ethinic art forms and culture, as manifest through their dances, music and their colourful festive dresses and ornaments.

Khasi is rich in performing art traditions. To quote Bareh : the people are music loving and express in songs their proverbs, folk-tales and epics. In the past, victories in wars were celebrated by folk-songs or community singings when the victorious men returned. Folk songs are sung to nature, to the wonders of creations and to the exhilarating scenes. There are fertility action songs which represent the various modes of cultivation and action songs which depict the scenes of war. It is in the harp in accompaniment of drum-beats that the richest poetry is born, the indigenous measure and accent being obtained from the mode of a thrumming of strings and by the pause which follows at the bar. On the harp, poetry richly inspired in music comes down to the listner's ears which throbs their hearts and opens out their imagination to the world of music. Elegy, legends, romance and comedy, both epic and ballad are supplemented by the harpist singing on his harp.

Dirges and lamentations are played by a pipe called sharati during the funeral assemblages side by side with the women mourners who express lamentations in verbose rhythms."

In the past, the Khasis had no written literature of their own. According to a tradition and indigenous script was lost during an incendiary at Nongkseh, but another legend says it was lost in the flood. It tells us that two survivors managed to escape the flood by swimming across. One swimmers was a Khasi and the other was a Hindu man known as "*u dkhar*". Both carried with them only the bundles of their respective scripts. The dkhar managed to retain his script while swimming but the Khasi swimmer swallowed his. The swallowed script got mingled with his flesh and bones, his mind and heart which helped in turn to build up the fabric of an oral literature which freely expresses itself in the songs, folk-tales, epics, poetry and incantation. However, real spiritual development was dependent on literary. Realising this Missionaries spent much of their time in creating written forms of the languages spoken by the hills peoples of North East India among whom they began working in the middle of the nineteenth century. The first tribal language for which this was done was Khasi.

Modern Khasi literature was, however, born in 1841 when Khasi was reduced down to writing in the Roman alphabet. The pioneer was Thomas Jones I who set up three schools which taught the new alphabet to the pupils. It was

Thomas Jones who wrote the first Khasi Reader 'Ka Kot pule Ba Nyng Kong', an alphabet written in 1841 and printed 1842 at the Calcutta Baptist Press.

Before coming down to drama, it is utmost important to mention that 'The Khasi hand their own poetry and developed their own indigenous art of forming regular poetic creations. In the words of Hamlet Bareh: Such poetic addresses are put in verses in a couplet used to be chanted by a group or exchanged amongst two groups of people on important occasions of sports, festivals, ceremonies, archery and are used during warfare occasions. They convey different meanings or lessons. They are called *phawar* or *kynnoh laho* : in reality they form rhyming couplets, each couplet has four rhyming correspondences. Till today they are chanted by the hunting expedition on return with their hound or by archery team on returning from the archery festival. They constitute a real poetry form handed from generation to generation. They are highly ethical though humorous... These were the old poetic creations which preceded the modern poetry form written on the western line of prosody.

As early as in 1813 that the task of translating the New Testament into Khasi though stupendous was carried out in Bengali script with great zeal and devotion, and by 1817 copies of it were distributed to those Khasis living nearest to Bengal, who could read the Bengali script.

It was in 1827 the Khasi New Testament, the firstly truly significant work in Khasi appeared in print, used in the Baptist Mission at Cherrapunji in 1833. Once Khasis had their own alphabet significant tasks carried out in successions were:

(1) to compile oral verses, idioms etc. still in their pure and natural form.

(2) Renderation of the Bible

(3) Translation of many hymns from the Welsch and English hymnals.

(4) Khasi grammer books

(5) Translation of paratbles, short stories having moral bearings etc.

Now the demand was slowly drawing for the original creations which would represent and revive indigenous idea and thought in modern perspectives, distinct from the approach and style of the early Christian writers.

Jeeban Roy (1838-1903) was an influential native during the British Raj who played an important role in the development of Khasi language and literature. He was the first Khasi to start his career as Interpreter and ended it as magistrate. He felt that education a good means for the natives to improve themselves intellectually and economically. A social worker and leader of public opinion, he fought hard for the establishment of a High School at Shillong and that was during 1875-76. To put Khasi culture on record it was must that people should read and write Khasi and English. In the year 1899, U Jeeban Roy Mairom wrote the book '*Ka Kitab Khasi Kaba Lai*' which contains some dialogues, may be reckoned as the immediate forerunners of drama. These includes:

(1) Uwei u briew bad ka Khnap Kulai;

(2) U Julahap bad Khliehbieit;

(3) U Kylli bad u Thuh;

(4) U Sumar bad u Pathat;

Another outstanding writer was Sib Charan Roy. His literary career was from 1902 to 1919. His contribution were mainly in the field of culture and had not contributed to the genre of drama. Yet he left a strong impress on Khasi literature during his times. Sib Charan Roy wrote a number of books which had a direct bearing on Khasi Cultural awakening such as :

(1) Ka Jingpyni ka kamie bad ki khun (1911)

(2) Ka Kot tohkit Tir Tir (1913)

(3) Ka Niam Ki Khasi (Religion of the Khasis, 1919)

(4) Ka jingiakren pule shaphang ka niam (a treatise on religion).

Sib Charan's other important publications are:

(5) Bhagavata Gita in Khasi (1903)

(6) Lekshor (1912)

(7) Lekhor (1913)

(8) Ka jingrwai niam khasi

(9) Ka Bui-Hok-Tynrai

(10) Chankya Niti-Darpane.

In all left behind 13 publications.

Literature, be it poetry, drama or fiction, it reflect and interpret life. The history of Khasi drama is to some extent the history of the intellectual development of the Khasi society. Khasi drama has taken its present shape through education and the history of formal education in the Khasi Society dates from the early years of the nineteenth century. It was as early as in 1813 that the Christian missionaries started their work in the Sohra and Shella areas. Prior to the adrent of Christianity there was no literary tradition in the Khasi language. Scholar H.W Sten informs "Khasi words and forms of speech were put into writing only in 1813 when Krishna Chandra Pal translated the New Testament into the Shala dialect of Khasi language, but that was done in Bengali script. The present written form was introduced at Sohra after 1841 by Thomas Jones of the Welsch Presbyterian Mission. What the people had before the years 1813-1841 was oral literature. Khasi oral tradition found expression in the phawar or rimed couplet, folktales, stories and homilies. There was a branch of this tradition which is known as '*puriskam*' or fables, and '*parom*' or stories. The paroms and of two two categories: the short one like short stories, and the lengthy ones like the novel.

Khasi Drama

Sten of the North Eastern Hill University tells us that Drama was not known among the Khasis in those early days. This is borne out by the fact that the language has no accepted term for drama. It was only in 1937 that E. Elias proposed the word '*sawangka*' for drama. It is inappropriate in many respects as he could not distinguish the different forms of a drama. Moreover, written language follows the usage, and therefore what is Khasi understands is the word 'Drama' itself as the English introduced it.

Theatre was brought to Shillong from the then East Bengal [now Bangladesh] by the educated, the elite, upper class who came to Shillong as civil servants of the British Government. They settled in Jail Road, Thana Road and Police Bazar.

When in 1874, Shillong was made Capital of the then Province of Assam, Assamese started settling in Leban. Khasis borrowed a great many theatrical elements from these two communities, which elements all went to the making of the Khasi theatre of the pre-Christianity years of influence.

It is pertinent to mention here that much before the influx of Bengali elites in Shillong, the Khasis maintained trade relations with their close neighbours of Sylhet, Mymensing and other places of the then East Bengal. During trade contacts, they had witnessed a number of theatrical performances in towns along the border like Jaintiapur, Pathepur, Angarjur, Panduah and even Sylhet. Such artistic activities cast a strong spell on Khasis skirting the border line who did make an effort to initiate their dramatic arts.

Khasi audiences have shown a preference for plays, including skits, as a form of entertainment for a very long time. Many of the earlier plays, commissioned perhaps for particular occasions, were little more than improvisations, albeit skilful ones. The Catholic Mission arrived in Assam and Khasi Hills in the year 1890. Theatrical activities spread from Jaintiapur to Jowai, then to Nongkrem, Mawngap, Mawphlang etc. and finally to Shillong. Even in Mawsynram, there used to be dramatic productions as told by Bhah J.S. Shangpliang who recalls: In his boyhood days when he was in the crowd, helping himself to theatrical performances at Mawsynram, based on the myths and legends of the plains.

The cut-out date for Khasi literature is 1841, that was the year it was born when the Khasi language adopted the Roman script introduced by rev. Thomas Jones who arrived in Sohra on 22 June that same year. Bah Bajubon R. Kharlukhi in his article '*Formation and development of Khasi drama*' stated that after 1841 there was a number of theatrical clubs around the country which vied with one another for excellence.

Bah J.S. Shangpliang reminisces that earlier plays were most based on the myths and legends of the plains, but it was only in 1957 that in Don Bosco Technical School, Shillong he bumped into the Western drama. It was then that he noticed the difference between the two traditions.

From the beginning, Khasi literature owed much to translation. H.W. Sten observed: We have heard of dramatic performances or *ialehke* to have been popular in the different localities of Jowai, and the occasional performances by Christian teachers and their pupils in the evening of either the Christmas Day or the New Year Day, but none of such plays have been published in book form, and it is possible that the manuscripts are lost. The first to experiment in this genre was John Roberts, one of the founders of Khasi literature. He rendered one of the Acts of Shakespeare's *Julius Caesar* into Khasi and his version was included in the Khasi Fourth Reader, broughtout in 1895.

John Roberts renderation of Julius Caesar is one of the earliest fragmentary compositions. The aim of Roberts appeared to be to set example for the natives to produce more plays. The choice of Shakespeare's and not those of any other playwrights was evidence of the esteem in which Roberts held that great English dramatist of the Elizabethan age.

Ka Seng Khasi

Rolong Kharkang SDB aptly points out that the three streams converged in Shillong to eventually usher in '*Ka Seng Khasi*', a moment of Khasi cultural renaissance which sought expression in traditional dances, music and songs. Soon, this socio-cultural institution become a platform which patronised and promoted the dramatic activities. Some Seng Khasi leaders even went further to form a separate club for the furtherance of performing arts and named it '*Khasi Native Club*', the immediate forerunner of the *Shillong Panora Club*.

A need was felt by the Ka Seng Khasi to have a permanent auditorium and in 1899, on the Mawkhar Road, a hall was made. Sri S. Bhattacharya informs : The Pioneering work was done by magnates like Chandranath Roy, Hormu Roy Diengdoh, Hazam Kishore Singh, Mohan Massas. Unlike the Bengali clubs which imported artists from Calcutta and Guwahati, *Ka Seng Khasi* employed local talents to prepare the stage, the scenaries, etc.

During the viceroyalty of Lord Curzon, as a result of '*Bangabhanga*' [the partition of Bengal], Shillong which was the Capital of then then Province of Assam since 1874 was shifted to Dacca in 1904. U Morendro Doonai informs some Khasi young men mused on the change. They got together and put all their musings into a play '*Ka Leit Dacca*' which they staged in the Mission Girl's School.

At Quinton Road, an auditorium was built where the first dramatic impulse was witnessed. It was named after Sir Quinton, who was once the Chief Commissioner of Shillong. It was established by the joint effort of Bengalis, Assamese and Khasis of that time. The major contribution in form of finance and organisation came from Bengalis. It was later converted into the Singhania Talkies.

Assamese art lovers, began to look for a public hall of their own to chiefly preserve and disseminate their culture. So in 1896 the Syiem of Mylliem was approached with a request for a piece of land at Laban. The Assam Club of Laban started putting up performances since 1899.

The Khasi drama cannot be said to have been created in the nineteenth century or with the translation of Roberts. Though dramatic composition has been a favourite form of literary expression with Khasi writers. But it took many years to see original Khasi compositions. It was only in the second decade of the present century that the first drama in Khasi language appeared in print in 1910. A Mahabharata play entitled '*Ka Savitri*' was authored by Sri Haricharan Roy, the son of Sri Jeeban Roy.

Two prominent playwrights worthy of mention are those of Jeeban Roy's sons - U Hari Charan Roy Dkhar and U Dinonath Roy Dkhar. The former wrote *Savitri* (1910) and the latter composed *Srommotimai lane Ka Hok*' again a renderation from Sanskrit, U Arbnai and U Tipsngi etc. In the prefatory note, Sri Haricharan stated that he borrowed his theme from the epic without changing the spirit of the original. He finds that the story has good aim to give good counsel and to broaden the mind of the people, and that they should live circumspectly in the world holding fast righteousness and truth." A critic observes: Thirteen of the character in the play '*Ka Savitri*' bear the stamp of the original, but the playwright's literary faculty prompted him to create characters with Khasi names, perhaps, to give the work a native flavour and relevance. The play was originally intended for the stage, and the stage direction has also been printed along with the text. It could be successful because the dramatist was careful in the selection of events which could be presented on the stage. The play takes devotion to duty, honesty and good conduct as its theme. The heroine, Savitri, was a devout Hindu lady who loves her husband and was devoted to him. It was essentially a morality play.

Before the advent of Hari charan Roy with his drama '*Savitri*', it must be remembered that though no original drama was yet created, but many villages in the state possessed playlets for the stage which were, however, not subservient for literature.

It was in the month of February 1911 that Rev. Fr. Herribert Winkler, a German by nationality arrived in Shillong. Born on 8 October 1875 H. Winkler was a member of the then very young Society of the Divine Savious (SDS). Fr. Herribert was the First Principal of St. Anthony's M.E. School (presently where the St. Anthony's Junior School Stands). Modern scholar, anthropologist and theatre historian Rolond Kharkang inform : "Fr. Herribert had the rare knack of entertaining. Khasi youth flocked to him and learned from him music and dramatics. They had no stage, but just a platform raised two feet above the ground. They had no costumes either. They were improvised from guny bags. Finally, they had an audience of 30-40 people only, all poorly accomodated in a small room in St. Antony's School. Performances used to be held only between 3.00 and 5.00 in the evening and not later.

It was Fr. Herribert who divided and tapped the rich deposits of qualities and aptitudes of Khasi youth. Incidentally, it was he again who laid the foundation for the Catholic Cathedral Band. The setback came when he had to leave for Europe with the rest of the German missionaries in 1915 after the outbreak of the first World War. Herribert who gave a push to performing arts in the soil died on 13 july 1967 at the ripe age of 92.

Dino Nath Roy

After '*Savitri*', the next Khasi play to come out in print was '*Srommotimai*' or 'Ka Hok' (alternative title meaning Righteousness) by Dino Nath Roy, also the son of Jeeban Roy. This play was broughtout in 1912. divides the sequences into scenes only, but in the second play, '*Tipsngi*' he divide the play into acts and scenes. Both follow a simple plot and the simpler theme, ie, to live honestly in this world.

Dino Nath Roy Dkhar also wrote '*U Arbanai*' in 1912 that was published in book form in 1979, from '*Ka Ri Khasi Prem*'. The play dealt with the theme of honesty in adversity like his wellknown drama *'Ka Srommotimai lane Ka Hok'* that came out after the first original dramatic composition.

The Salesians of Den Bosco (acronym 'SDB') are acknowledge as the father of Khasi dramatics and theatrics. They came to Shillong in January 1922, seven year after the departure of the Salvatorians as the members of the Society of the Divine Saviour (SDS) were called. The Salesians took up the task to inculcate in hill people the importance of dramatic art.

A galaxy of people like Fr. Igino Ricaldone, Bro. Santino Mantarro, Fr. Giulius Costa, Fr. George Vanni, Fr. Usai, Bros. N. Valeri and V.S. Mathew etc. rendered invaluable services to th growth and enrichment of Khasi drama, particularly after the demise of the Shillong Panora Club headed by Bah Peace Pariat, when the indigenous theatre almost phased out.

In the year 1924, Dino Nath Roy's '*U Tipsngi*', an original Khasi drama having close affinity with William Shakespeare's "As You Like It" came up. Hamlet Bareh in his '*A short history of Khasi literature*' comments: The theme of the play is—honesty as adversity fixes the righteous persons to the great rigours at the first stage, but honesty as victory crowns them with the untold blessing finally. Being adaptation of other language, the play did not contribute directly to the awakening but inculcated literary arts of a drama among the readers." 'U Tipsngi was a didactic play, the plot well constructed and interlaced with subplots and conflict. The play was a reflection of the traditional way of life of the then society. It also visualised a new generation with a new social order. For "*U Tipsngi*" Dino Nath used the local setting and local characters and this can therefore be acknowledge as the first true Khasi drama. '*U Tipsngi*' was in two acts, comprising of seven scenes in the first act and eight scenes in the second, in all fifteen scenes, Playwright Dinonath Roy was very traditional in characterisation. It was put on boards in 1924.

Haricharan Roy and Dino Nath Roy wrote their plays with a mission: a concern for the traditional values of the Khasis.

Here we may quote H.W. Sten who points out "One fact has to be borne in mind. All the three plays [Mentioned above] were composed for the stage of the Seng Khasi at Shillong, and the creative and imaginative powers of the authors also were controlled by the stage at their disposal. Being morality plays, these works demand a greater attention to the spoken words than to the scenary and action. They mark a considerable advance in the progress towards the modern drama."

In 1920 the play '*U Mihsngi*', written by U Mondon Bareh appeared. But he could not finish the play as he died. This play was a commentary on the dubious life-style of church leaders of the time. The play was studied and completed later in 1962-64 and eventually published by Mrs. B. Bareh in 1966. U Mondon Bareh served as the Deputy Inspector of Schools, for Khasi and Jaintia Hills. In his letter No. D dated 3.1. 1930, he informed the then Registrar of the Calcutta University about his translation of Shakespeare's, '*Measure for Measure*' which was near completion. But since then, the work could never be traced.

Rash Mohan Roy Nongrum (d. 1962) wrote two plays, namely '*Ka Damayanti bad u Nol*', a play culled from the ancient Sanskrit literature appeared in 1924. His extinct drama is '*U Saimaka Ka Duitara*'.

In 1932, on the Thana Road, Shillong a public auditorium was built, owned by the Giti Natya Samaj Named 'Opera Hall', it was frequented by the theatre buffs of the town comprising of different linguistic communities. The performance of Bengali plays involved also Assamese and Khasi players and the spectators, though predominanty Bengali, also was a mixed crowd.

In the thirtees Primrose Gatphoh wrote a radio drama '*Kamai ia Ka Hok*', a short piece for the All India Radio, Shillong. Later in 1933 he included it in the school text book '*Sawdong Ka Lyngwiar Dpei*' the drama upholds the view that dishonesty does not bring lasting prosperity.

Some Khasi poets have chosen *dramatic monologue* a medium of their poetic creation. Soso Tham is the first dramatic monologist among the Khasis. In his book '*Ka Duitara Ksiar I*' (1936), there are two monologues namely '*U Dieng Bilat High School*' or '*the High School Eucalyptus*' and '*U Sib*' or '*Sib*'.

In the same year Bronath Thangkhiew' published a collection of his fiftyseven poems entitled '*Ka Tienrwai Khasi*' (Khasi Poetry). One of those poems, '*U Nongtem Duitara*' or '*The Harprst*' is the dramatic monologue.

Hopewell Elias Sohliya penned the book *'Kar Pansngiat Ksiar Ki Saw Aiom'* (The Golden Crown of the Four Seasons) The book is divided into four sections. Its third part contains poet's major poems in which we find his four dramatic monologues. The first, second and the third sections have jointly been reappeared since 1963 under the title *'Ka Hamsai Ki Por* (The Musing of Times). The theme for all the four dramatic monologue are *'Na Waikhyri*, *'Ka Dymmiew - Ryngnni'* and *'U Lum Lawbah'* and *'U Lapongnai - Ksiar'* is patriotism. These are the socio-political history of the ancient Sutnga, Shillong, Sohra and the Madur-Maskut empires.

According to H.W. Sten 'While *Thangkhiew* and *Elias* concern themselves directly with the Khasi society and make their first person speakers preach direct sermons, Tham makes his speak about themselves. Tham's monologues end with a pleasurable relief, while those of the other two engage the mind of the readers with some pessimistic note. Tham is, therefore, a better monologuist than Thangkhiew and Elias'.

In the thirtees, appeared a comedy in Khasi entitled *'U Diengduh u Kni'*, written by A. Correngia, SDB. This was a translation from the English *'Uncle's Walking Stick'*.

Khasi Native Club

In was during the Second World War, the Khasi Native Club gave a serious of performances in various auditorium of the Shillong like the Seng Khasi Hall, the Opera Hall and the Quinton Hall. Few major production of this club were *Kathryn Bon Bora, Ka Romily and Ka Maryngod*. Though the title of the first play rings back to Lutheran times. But it was very much Khasi in content, style and theme. The drama is stated to be a commentary on the social institutions, traditional and contemporary Peace Roy Pariat acted in the last two mentioned plays, the plays that are no more extant. Prof. Lyngdeh recalls that "as a young boy he had been a spectator at the performances of these plays. How they touched his young heart, how he wept."

During the World War times, there sprang up *'Synjuk Samla Riatsamthiah'* a theatrical troupe that gave a series of dramatic performances such as *'U Uberto bad U Adarno'*.

In about 1942, the *Jaiaw Cultural Club* was formed. To its credit goes the premier production of V.G. Bareh's play '*U Tirot Sing*' that made a history.

In the forties, Khasi theatre got a new lease of life in the hands of Peace Roy Pariat.

Shillong Panora Club (SPC)

After the *Khasi Native Club*, it was the *Shillong Panora Club* that dominated the Khasi theatre from 1943 to 1950s. So far the Khasi Native Club was putting up non-Khasi dramas in the Khasi language and Khasi setting and for Khasi audiences.

Bah Peace, a complete theatre person of rare gift wanted to compose, act and direct his own plays. Eventually he left the troupe to form '*Shillong Panora Club*'. It made its mark with some intense productions with an impressive acting team. It included artists like Bah Opindro Benedict Lynrah, Bah Shanbor Kharjana, Bah Heledi Warjri, Bah Bijoy Khain. Bah Peace Pariat was its first President, Bah Lalit Chandra Umdor, the first Secretary. After Bah Lalit died in 1942, Bah Opindro Lynrah succeeded him as Secretary. He used to be the promoter for the club. Bah Mungor Jana was a very talented actor. It is said that there had never been a man in Khasi theatre as good a Comedian as Bah Mungor. Bah Iowelton Suting was an active member. Club's stage manager was Bah Horen Khar Kongor who managed and oversaw the preparation of the stage. The Club used to appoint one or two 'Arranging Managers' who were in charge of stage preparation. Two strikingly realistic set designers were Bah Esindro Sohkhlet and Bah Nando Beri.

Pariat knew how to turn a play into crowd-puller. He wanted to communicate with the largest number of people possible and introduce them to good theatre. The Shillong Panaro Club used to time their productions to coincide with the second day of the Weiking festival for two reasons: first, it was a practical need, and secondly it brought them good and quick buck. Villagers from all around the country used to come to this annual event. They arrived on the second day. Many of them did not know where and how to spend their time. A night at the Shillong Panora Club in Opera Hall was by far the best option they could have.

The Club had its own stage props, wigs, sarees, local dresses and whenever a play was being prepared, ladies were called to dress male actors if they had to play female roles.

Females were not admitted into the Club or on the stage together with male. In later years, the Club included in the cast a certain lady to play the female role in a certain play.

Peace Roy Pariat with the members of the SPC, at Pynursla, on their way back from Mawshun [Courtesy: Roland Kharkang SDB]

The troupe made its debut with the play '*Ka Romily*' staged on 3rd March 1943 at Quinton Hall. The play received overwhelming response and after this successful venture, it took up in 1944 '*Ieit, ieit, yon, dei Jingieid Shet Khiew Jakai*' that ran for a year. Soon it became a strong rival of the Khasi.

Babu Roland Lyngdoh who had been a teacher of Bah Peace after witnessing the play expressed his great astonishment at what boys were able to do. The performances of the entire crew was so brilliant especially after Act II that the audience had to weep to their heart's content. Emotions were carried over even to outside the stage and the hall, and people hurled abuses at the protagonist, ie, the stage Manager of the Club (Bah Horendro Kharkongor), as if he was the one responsible for the fact in actual life.

This oft repeated production was last performed by them in the Seng Khasi Hall in 1950.

In the year 1951, the Shillong Panora Club staged the play '*Ka Maryngod*', also ascribed to Bah Peace Pariat. But the latter in an interview stated that as a boy he had witnessed this play being staged, which was later restored and re-written.

The Club even posed a threat to a local club of the time called '*Ka Synjuk Wahingdoh*'. The troupe's rich and varied repertoire include plays like '*Ka Bor Ksuid Pyrshah Bor Blei*', *Ka Kyrsan Ka Rhah, Na Nongkyndong Sha Sor, Ka Maryngod, Shangkhawiah' Ki Rang, etc.*

'*Shangkhawiah Ki Rang*' is a social play which clearly mirrors to society one of its deep seated evils—low moral and loose living.

In the year 1945, the Shillong Panora Club premeried the play '*Ka Bor Ksuid Pyrshah Bor Blei*' in the Opera Hall. The play received wider acclamation and eventually travelled extensively to Mawngap, Nogkhlieng, Mawshun etc. The people of Mawngap invited the troupe to stage the play in autumn season and agreeed to pay a fee of Rs.500 over and above all other expenses. The play was an instant hit. Villagers watched the production enthusiastically, reacting and with loud appreciative cheers.

After the production village elders approached Peace Roy Pariat with the request to present a play that vividly portrays the village life. Back home, he worked on the script and a new play '*Ka Kyrsan*' was born. The next time, in the same year when the troupe went to Mawngap with this production, he made history.

An efficient organiser and advertiser, Bah Peace himself used to advertise his own play R.S. Lyngdoh reports: It was market day, Iewduh (Barabazar), Shillong, and, in the morning, as the people spilled on to the road to go to Shillong, two young men, one dressed as a maiden, met them. The young man sang overtures to the maiden who — would you believe it ! — scornfully spurned his advances. The play was sold that evening to a full-capacity audience".

Next year, Bah Peace Pariat was invited to Nongkhlieng for the first time in the spring to put up the play *'Ka Bor Ksuid Pyrshah Bor Blei'*, which the people of that region remembered as 'U Almacava bad Ka Wesselina'.

The people of Nongkhlieng took the troupe to a festival at Mawshun (below Pynursla, on the way to Dawki) where they were invited to perform.

Initially Bah Peace was not ready for such an off-hand invitation, but subsequently he had to oblige the request of the people of Mawshun on behalf of a woman. At Mawshun, at the opening of *'U Almacava bad Ka Wesselina'*, Bah Peace himself took the prosecnium and, much to the merriment of the audience, sang serenades to the young lady who had won him over into accepting to perform there that night. The rest was an easy performance. Tha play was appreciated so much that they pestered him to present another work and from the prolific pen of Bah Peace emerged the play *'Ka Rhah'* with Bah Mungor Jana in the central role who with his humour and wit, kept the crowd laughing till their sides split and their jaws hung loose from ache and exhausion, stated a theatre historian. Song of all kinds added mirth to the night. While returning back to Nongkhlieng, this play was staged again, after which the Shillong Panora Club finally came back to Shillong.

Bah Peace was one of the earliest to try realistic set-designing and costumes. When in the spring of 1947, Na Nongkyndong was played in Shillong, the stage preparation was very real and true to life. The Shillong Panora Club achieved an admirable degree of realism. In their production "*Ieit, ieit, ym dei Jingieid Shet Khiew Jakai*, the *Ward Lake bridge* was reproduced on the stage in miniature form that looked so much like the original, that people used to say that the Club transferred the bridge from the lake to the stage. Even a horse had been hired and brought from Mawtawar, a village on the northern side of Mawlai. A live horse on the stage points to the great effort towards theatrical realism. However, the glare of the lights so scared the animal that the horse leapt straight for the audience. No one was hurt, but it taught them a lesson.

If a barber or a cobbler was played on stage, professional barbers and cobblers were consulted and called in to advise the actors and train them in those profession and their trade accessories would also be hired for authenticity.

The Shillong Panora Club also staged the play '*Ka Tiewlarin*'. Bah Peace had borrowed this play for his group from his uncle who had written it for the Khasi Native Club, of which the uncle was a member. For this production, they had prepared paper snakes to come out of a woman's mouth. It wasn't, however quite real; they were booed out of the stage. In the next show, Bah Peace dropped the scene.

Perhaps its magnum opus, *Shangkhawiah Ki Rang* which might have been written earlier was first made its debut in the Opera Hall in April 1948. It is said that a spring was produced on the stage that seemed almost real.

Once again Bah Peace advertised this production in his own unique manner. In the evening (the scheduled premiere night of the play was in the opera Hall,) of a market day in Barabazar, Bah Peace dressed up two young men, one as a young maiden, as if they were a courting couple. He displayed them onto an equally well draped pony cart. The young man sang love songs to his make-believe lover who shyly coaxed him to take her to the Opera Hall. On the pony cart the couple went to all the key points and junctions of the town. That night spelt a huge success for the Shillong Panora Club.

The cast composed of the following artistes.

Jan	:	Peace Roy Pariat
Jani	:	Morel Lyndem
Saporo	:	Bowel Kharpuria
Thakur	:	Heledi Warjri
Suraiji	:	Dijendro Basaiawmoit
Medina	:	Horen Kharkongor
Samarkan	:	Renol Nongkynrih
Dost	:	Justman
Kumar	:	Bijoy Khain
Noren	:	Pishon Diengdoh
Pukir	:	Mitshon Kharkongor.

Ka Synjuk Wahingdoh

Another group that shot into prominance was *Ka Synjuk Wahingdoh* a rival of the Shillong Panora Club. There was often clashes disturbances between two theatrical clubs that flourished during the second world war period.

Roland Kharkang reports : At Mawlai, theatrical performances were not unknown even in the 1940s; they became better organised and popular with the coming of Seng Savio... Popular theatre here had very humble beginnings in a small shed. Soon the club became quite wellknown, and was invited to Marbisu, Raliang, Jowai, to name but a few places... Some tribute must be paid to Mawlai and Mawkhar Seng. Savio for the contribution they made to the theatre in Shillong from the early 1950's to about 1966. However their major hits were either translation from English or Italian originals by Fr. A. Correngia and others.

In the year 1946, the *Jaiaw Orchestra*, a forum for music and drama was founded which enrolled youths from many other localities of Shillong outside Jaiaw.

In late fortees Bashai Rai Dohling, a celebrated Cartoonist, animator, painter, playwright who was associated with the Shillong Panora Club composed a shadow play entitled '*U Borsing Bad U Borkusain*'.

'IPTA' in Meghalaya

In 1943, when the artificially induced famine stalked Bengal and claimed the lives of five million peasants, the IPTA (Indian People's Theatre Association) troupe in Bengal took to the stage, toured all over India revealing and denouncing the crime of native hoarders and profiteering black-marketeers. They took up production that outlined the horrifying and gruesome realities of greed and avarice which brought about the 'cataclysmic Bengal famine'.

A nation-wide progressive theatrical movement, therefore started from Bengal focussing on the plight of the down-trodden and the exploited.

Bah Justman Kharmih, editor of *Ka Pansara*, a monthly from Jowai reminisces : IPTA visited Jowai in August, 1947 and played the drama '*U Kiang*

Nangbah' in shadow play form. Bah Justman himself was present at the performance.

The General Secretary of the IPTA too, Shri Niranjan Sen, came along. From Jowai the IPTA troupe moved on the Sohra where they played in Shadow play form again the drama '*U Tirot Sing*'.

The extinction of Shillong Panora Club affected the Khasi theatre very badly. The dramatic activities, however continued in the centres and boarding schools and hostels run by the Catholic missions at Laitumkhrah, Mawkhar and Mawlai.

The Catholic Dramatic Society

Late Fr. Giulius Costa, a Salesian of Don Bosco played a key role in promoting theatrics in the Khasi Hills. In the year 1939 he was, however transferred from Shillong to the Garo Hills which gave a serious blow to his dramatic society. When he was again shifted back to Shillong in 1953, his club experienced revival and a series of plays were performed under his able direction.

Thus in Laitumkhrah *The Catholic Dramatic Society* was formed in the year 1954-55 by Fr. Giulius Costa. Some important members of this club were Bah Silvester Satrodin Basaiawmoit (himself a gifted actor), Bah Robert Lostingson, Oswin Synnah, Alfred Shallam, Fidelis Lit Khyriem, John Lyngdoh, Bah Gregory Suting (a fine actor), Bah Cyril Lyngdoh (Lyricist and musician).

Fr. Costa made immense contribution to the development of Khasi Theatre. His two major productions were *Talisman* which was enacted soon after its founding. A well received production, still remembered by many who had witnessed the show.

The second successful venture was an operetta entitled '*Francis of Assisi*'. The lead role of St. Francis was portrayed by Bah Gregory Suting. Late Bah Cyril Lyngdoh wrote the lyrics and rendered fine music. On the whole, the operatta remained the talk of the town for a long time.

A contemporary of Fr. Costa was Fr. Vanni who unlike the former was a born actor. He actively involved himself with the Catholic theatrical activities. A complete theatre person he improved upon what Fr. Costa had started and left behind.

The Catholic missions however tookup mostly translated works. The indigenous theatre revived only when the *Rympei Theatrical Centre* sprang up under the leadership of *Bah Kenny* in the early seventies, who established a powerful theatre in the land with his brilliant sense of the theatre and Khasi Culture.

In 1952, the All India Radio, Shillong broadcast the play '*u Tirot Sing*', written by Bashai Rai Dohling.

Perhaps in September 1954, the first historical drama in Khasi, ie, '*U Tirot Sing*' by Victor G. Bareh was performed by the *Jaiaw Recreation and Cultural Club*' at the Dinam Hall, Shillong. The play was witnessed by then Governor, Doulatram. This play actaually appeared in printed form in 1956-57. This play deals with U Tirot Singh who fought with the British from 1829 to 1833. He was a foremost hero who fought with the British from 1829 to 1933. He skillfully organised offensive and defensive alliances, in handling the war-front situations, in he direction of the operations and in conducting a mass guerrilla warfare. The sacrifices of girls such as Ka Oiñ Tip mei tip pa, Ka Oiñ ieit Ri and others (in English Miss Smarty Rose, Miss Paitriot, Miss Dutiful and Miss Virginia) and their contributions to the struggle are vivid reflections. The loyalties, tenacious adherences and priceless sacrifices of the great masses are other recollections, the mode of the guerilla warfare, an organised one, in the Khasi fashion unfurls itself. Ka Phan Nonglait, a typical heroine, plays a great role; Kohlehnoh is a portrait of freedom-loving soul U Monbhut of Stalwart physique is a typical warrior chief. The climax is reached at Tirot Singh's arrest and imprisonment at Dacca which throws of pathetic scene. The play saw the light of the day in 1957 and English version appeared in 1963.

In the fifties, there was a boom in dramatic writings and about twelve plays on varid themes enriched the modern Khasi literature during this decade. A Correngia, SDB's play '*U Doloi ha Sor*', a comedy got published in 1952. In 1954 his '*Ka Tiket Khalai Nusib*' appeared, again a comedy based on the English '*Lottery Ticket*', followed by '*Ka Dohnud Ksiar*' a quas religious play focussing on the virtues of a good-hearted man. In 1955, Correngia's opera on god Vishnu entitled '*U Blei Vishnu*' appeared in print.

Another eminent dramatist B.C. Jyrwa wrote '*Drama Shaphang Ka Nabon*' and biographical 'U Hakim', both published in 1955. Next year he added four more plays, namely '*U Herod Syiem Barunar*', historical work on King Herod of the Bible, *U Damon bad u Pythias*' (mythological drama) translation of Shakespeare '*Merchant of Venice*' and '*U Sandy*', a biographical drama.

In the year 1956, A Correngia, SDB's two works based on religion namely '*U Slatlai ha Pynthabah*' and '*Ha Ka Eriong* was broughtout. This year the play '*U Tirot Sing*', which strikes a chord of profound patriotism was produced in the Dinam Hall by the Jaiaw Recreation and Cultural Club.

During this time, a socio-cultural organisation named '*Ladies and Children Recreation Centre*' housed in Stoneyland, Shillong - 793002 Meghalaya was established in 1956. It receives grant from the government and public. Though it takes part in welfare work amongst women and children like that of backward classes and communities. The Centre organises children's meet, film shows, exhibitions, festivals of art, music, literature, variety shows and plays. Fr. Giulius Costa was once again transferred from Shillong in 1964, a setback for Khasi dramatic activities.

Sixties saw some remarkable translations of Shakespeare's dramas such as '*Ka Drama Katba Phi Mon*', (As You like it), U Romes bad Ka Juliet (Romeo and Juliet) and Ka Temding ia ka Shla Briew (The Taming of the Shrew), broughtout in 1961, 1963 and 1964 respectively. All these dramas were rendered into Khasi by the eminent dramatist Sri F.M. Pugh. His original social drama '*Ka sawangka ki san-ngut ba iap*' cameout in 1967 which highlight some social vices like liquor addiction. F.N. Pugh's play '*Ka sawangka ki san-ngut ba iap*' ends in a tragedy but leaves a moral lesson to reshaping family and social values and making education play its useful role.

His '*Ka sawangka ki saw ngut ba iap mynsaw*' is a traditional drama, a lenthy one comprisings of about 250 pages.

Ka Sawangka La ki Sawngut Ba Iap Mynsaw, focussing on the insidious effects of incestuous relationships and the inevitability of divine retribution. Pugh, a dramatist of repute, focuses his spot-lights on social evils: drunkenness, broken family relationships, etc., and points to them as fatal cancers of society. It is in these plays that Pugh consciously and deliberately differs from his masters. In his introduction to *Ka Sawangka Ia Ki Saw ngut Ba Iap Mynsaw*, he explains himself. Therein the author makes at least three points.:

a) Unity of place and of time, that is, the plot and action are meaningfully confined to *here* and *new*. He, however, seems to suggest a kind of *extended here and now*, that is, the plot should indicate a time-period of a few years at most, and the locale that is at once large and small enough. In this he wants to differ from Bernard Shaw's '*Candida*', whose plot does not admit of the immediate *before* and *after*, and which is restrticted to a very few actors.

b) Realism in both setting and life situations. So Pugh eliminates in his plays things like the fairies of Shakespeare's 'Midsummer Night Dreams', and the witches in 'Macbeth'.

c) Even in the process of writing the plays, the playwright stands in the shoes of his spectators, and attempts at seeing, understanding and reacting to the world, as they would."

A critic writes: F.M. Pugh's play 'Ka sawangka ia ki saw ngut ba iap mynsaw' is a probe into kinship allegiance and keeping of taboo, how neglect or violation of such sacred laws could lead the family or society to disastrous consequences : for the exagamous laws have their efficacy so that their violation or discard is like opening of Pandora's box. U Hain who pivots an unclean marriage has more dominant role, he is the source of all complications that characterise this drama.

In this period we come across a drama which had the germ of social drama. Written by Mondon Bareh '*U Mihsngi*' appeared in 1966, the drama is largely connotative of conditions during the twenties of the present century. It serves as a satire on degrading moral conditions depicting a characterisation of clownish, then pecked and dubious husbands as also domineering and self-centred women and how both play their part leading to a total collapse of family, while it does not lose sight too of elegant, noble and constructive characters who play their role too in uplifting moral standards. Sub-plots centre also love rivalry and excess. The plays leaves a moral that artificialness is a root of social evil. In family and social setup, jealousy plays too much to upset things. The dramatist however, provided no solution to counteract the social evils.

Sixties also witnessed a number of good plays written in the language such as F.M. Pugh's 'Ka Dialok' (dialogue in Khasi).

This decade introduced to the world of Khasi theatre, another playwright of eminence. Webster Davies Jyrwa promarily composed playlets for the All India Radio, Shillong. He started off with Leo Tolstoy's writing and wrote '*I Phliah ding ba iehnoh Khlem akor i pynpluh ia ka iing* in 1961.

In 1962, W.D. Jyrwa's '*U Kpieng Mawlynnai*', based on Guy de Maupassant's work appeared in print. In 1967 he broughtout the Khasi version of Shakespeare's work entitled '*U Nongkhaii Ka Venice*' (However, the Reception Committee of the Sahitya Akademi in 1977 mentions a translation of this play by B.C. Jywra dated in 1956). In 1968, he adapted Kalidasa and composed '*Ka Sakuntala*'. In 1950 his biblical play '*U Haman bad ka Diengphasi*' got published. All these five playlets appeared in the book '*Ki drama Lyngkot*' n 1981.

In 1961, a tragedy based on the English '*The Price of Blood*' appeared in Khasi, penned by A. Correngia under the title '*Ka Dor Ka Snam*'.

A wellknown play on war and history entitled '*Ka Drama U Tirot Sing*' by V.G. Bareh was published in 1963.

In 1965, A Correngia SDB's play '*Ka Phatok*', a tragedy on njustice was published. F.M. Pugh rendered Shakespeare's '*Macbeth*' in the same year, appeared as '*Ka Shemlanot*'.

In the year 1963, the Don Bosco Past Pupil's Association, Mawkhar Unit presented the play '*Ka Ri Umsham*', a play by Bah John Syntar Shangpliang. At that time the play was in four parts. Later the play was revised and made into four parts that appeared in print much later in 1984. In between it was staged several times between 1974 to 1979.

During this flowering period in the history of Khasi dramatic literature, S.J. Duncan wrote '*Ka Tiewlarun*', a play based on a folk theme, enriched with metaphors and dictions. Words captivate the sense and imagination with lucidity and force. Because of diverse moods, Duncan finds room to express in poetry some exciting as also serene events. Such interludes enrich the scenes they depict. This family drama appeared in print in 1968. Though melodramatic, the play exhibits his masterly craftmanship. It works on the traditional theme of a home being blessed with children. *Het Rande* is eager to see his younger sister, *Ka Shatai*', having a family adorned with children of her own.

In the year 1968, a drama also based on folk tale came out. Entitled 'U Baieit Donshkor' by D.S. Khongdup, the play has successfully inculcated dramatic interest and art. The plot doesnot suffer because characterisation abounds in contrast which makes reading interesting. The playwright makes use of diction which bear on the imagery and reflect different shades of meaning. This play in Khasi though melodramatic, but perhaps the best of the published ones so far. Devi Sing Khongdup started writing this play way back in 1944, in his second year of college and then dropped in. Again in April 1966, after over twenty years of gestation, revised what he had written so far and then proceeded to finish it. He completed the play only in August 1967 and appeared in print in the coming year. An edition of this play was also broughtout from Shillong in 1979.

O.M. Wahlang wrote a tragedy based on the folklore of U Sier Lapalang entitled '*Ka Sur Pangnud Ka Kmie*' in 1968. But this is not a drama proper, but only a dialogue.

The playwriting was given a push in the seventh decade of the last century. J.S. Shangpliang wrote a historical drama '*Ka Ri Umsnam*' in 1971. B.C. Jyrwa's quasi-historical, based on the life of king U Tirot Sing appeared under the title '*Ki Sngi Khatduh u Tirot Sing*' in 1972.

Rympei theatrical Centre (RTC) cameout with two dramas '*Ka Ngiew*', a detective play, and '*Ka Pla I Nab*, a satire on modern life, in the year 1973.

From the seventies, there were some significant developments in Khasi theatre. There emerged various cultural troupies producing plays with a growing awareness in different theatrical devices, lighting, music, acting and body movements etc. This brought about an upsurge in the land, particularly in Shillong. Leading theatre groups of this period are:

(1) The Rympei Theatrical Centre

(2) The Khasi Cultural Society

(3) The Hynniew Trep Cultural and Welfare Organisation

(4) The Royal Theatrical Society

(5) The Dienjat u Hynniew Trep

Seventies was a landmark in the history of Khasi drama and theatre. Kenny Shympa who had himself took intensive training in histrionics from Catholic missionaries was now dreaming about doing something new and fruitful. He first threw open invitations to young boys and girls around Laitumkhrah, Malki and Nongthymmai, if they were interested in taking training lessons in the art of dramatics and theatrics. This was on 20 December, 1972.

Rev. Fr. George Vanni, the then Parish Priest of the Cathedral Parish of Laitumkhrah allowed them to use the Parish Hall for this purpose. The aspirants were given both theoretical and practical trainings that lasted for about five months. The production they took up in the workshop was '*Ka Ngiew*'.

This event paved the way for the formation of the 'Rympei Theatrical Centre', born out of the genius of this man and the name of the newly established club was suggested by Bah Billy Domes, and that name—perpetuated the defunct Rympei Catholic Club of Laitumkhrah, founded by Rev. Fr. G. Vanni SDB.

Rympei theatrical centre's first registered office was at the residence of Bah Kenny Shympa which was situated at Hopkinson Road. The group was registerd under the Societies Registration Act, XXI of 1860 and inaugurated by the then state Finance Minister on 15 June 1973, in the Don Bosco Hall.

On this solemn accasion, as said above the group premiered its first production '*Ka Ngiew*'. Scholar Rolond Kharkang tells us that the Minister, B.B. Lyngdoh, had come only to inaugurate and bless the new venture, but the quality of stage performance was such that he could not but sit through the entire play. The same drama was later staged in the State Central Library Hall in aid of U

Soso Tham Memorial Fund. *Shillong Times* of 13 October, 1973, comended the performance as follows : "*The actors proved beyond doubt their ability to act on the stage. It was all the more creditable for them to hold the packed auditorium spell pound all through*" Even *Amrita Bazar Patrika* and the *Assam Tribune* were generous in their praise.

The Executive Members of the troupe comprised of Bah Kenny (Chairman), Bah Alfond Suting (The General Secretary) and Bah Mihsuk Nongrum (Treasurer).

Still Functioning, The chief aims and objects of the group are as follows:

(1) to preserve the rich cultural herigate of Meghalaya, and that of the Khasi in particular;

(2) to educate the people through the media of stage acting and inculcate in them the importance of dramatic art;

(3) to organise social, cultural and recreational activities.

To promote literary and performing arts, it envisaged

(1) to organise play-writing contests.

(2) to organise one-act play competitions for schools

(3) to organise annual singing competitions for all.

(4) to conduct beat contests etc.

Bah Kenny of Rympei Theatrical Centre also proved his excellence as a playwright. Among his original compositions, mention could be made of *Kaei Ka Daw*, *To Ia Map* and *Ka Lak Ka Putit*. He was equally proficient in translations. He rendered the English play '*Terror*' as '*Ka Ngiew*', *Thok Sa Lanot*', translations of English plays '*Breaking Point*' and '*Mouse Trap*'.

Ka Ngiew play of Kenny Shympa is though an adaptation of the English play. Except for the English names, Director and translator Kenny Shympa came close to the heels of Poet Soso Tham in making his characters localise the English drama.

In the late sixties, original works of Bah Kenny Shympa namely, Kaei Ka Daw, To Ia Map was played at Mawmluh.

The Rympei Theatrical Centre staged the drama *Ka Lak Ka Putit*, composed by Late Bah Kenny was played at the State Central Library.

In the seventies, the Rympei Theatrical Centre premiered the following productions: *Ka Ngiew, Ka Pla I Nah* (1973); *Namar Ka Ri* (1974); *Steshon Shongtyrut, Arngut Ki Hippies* (1975); *Laingut Shipara* (1976); *U Tasam* (1977); *Ka Ksiar Ka Jingkordit, When The Picture Falls, Half-an-Hour's Life* (1978); and T.P. Nongrum's *U Khun Sarong Awria* and *Remy Phankon's Ka Dak Bangla* (1979).

Member of Rympei Theatrical Centre collectively wrote some dramas in Khasi, namely Namar Ka Ri (bilingual tragedy; 1974), Arngut Ki Hippi (satire; 1975), Laingut Shipara (Opera depicting modern social life and its problem; 1975) and Ka Rel Tyrut (detective play; 1976).

(2) The Khasi Cultural Society

This is a renowned cultural centre which has produced many significant plays on the theme of freedom struggle such as '*u Sngap*', '*U Tirot Singh*' and many others. Apart from staging dramas, the society has developed audio-visual transparency and a short documentary film etc.

(3) Hynniew Trep Cultural and Welfare Organisation

Hynniew Trep Cultural and Welfare Organisation was formed on 7th September 1978. The Head of the Organisation is its President and the Principal Executive being the Secretary. The posts are occupied by Sri S.R. Khonglamet and M. Kharjana respectively. The aims and objects of the organisation is to uplift and to preserve the culture of the Khasi society. To materialise these aims and objects the organisation started conducting a Khasi Folk Songs Competition right from 1981 once a year for the public and once a year for the students. On many occasion it staged variety shows. From time to time it put up dramas. Special mention should be made of its plays for the affected people caused by natural calamities.

Since its inception this association put up some remarkable plays to infuse consciousness for corporate growth and progress. Hynniew-Trep Cultural and

Welfare Organisation took up the much acclaimed political drama in Khasi '*Ka Ri Umsnam*' by Bah John Syntar Shangpliang in the year 1979. This off-repeated play, earlier produced by the Don Bosco Past Pupils Association, Mawkhar Unit, way back in 1963. Hynniew-Trep's script was a revised and enlarged version in five parts was performed in the Shillong State Central Library at Sohra.

Hynniew Trep Cultural and Welfare Organisation's address of Communication is as follows: Mahari and Sons, Motphran, Shillong-793002, Meghalaya.

(4) The Royal Theatrical Society

The centre has made a niche for itself by presenting some dramas which inculcate moral values.

(5) The Dienjat u Hynniew Trep

This cultural centre made an addition by presenting traditional dramas on stone dragging and installation Shad nguh Meikha and making efforts to develop them.

Other Theatre Troupes

Apart from this leading dramatic organisations, other centres, schools and colleges that made contribution to the development of theatre in Shillong are theatrical club of Mawlai and Mawkhar Seng Savio at Mawlai, Don Bosco Technical School, Caroline Club, Synjuk Samla Riatsamthiah, Jaiaw Cultural Club, Jaiaw Orchestra, Green Age Club, Langsning Social and Cultural Club, Mawpat Catholic Theatrical Club, Kharbuli Young Men's Organisation, St. Anthony's High School, Dos Bosco Past Pupils Association (Mawkhar Unit). In the seventies the Ever-Green school which is known for its musical and art activities, experimented with the genre of dance drama. The Khasi-jaintia Presbyterian Girls High School also enacted a Coronation of Syiems which was well appreciated.

Thus numerous cultural centres and clubs are existing and rendering invaluably services to the growth of Khasi theatre in Shillong.

The Jaintia Clubs

Roland Kharkang reports that when the Pnars (or the Jaintias) came over from Jowai to Shillong, they occupied an area now called Qualapatty. They were mostly from the Iongpiah, Lumkyrwiang and Shilliang Raid corners of Jowai, bringing with them their arts and skills. So in Shillong, we had three leading *Iongpiah Club*, *the Lumkyrwiang Club* and *the Shilliang Raid Club*, the counterparts and extensions of the respective clubs by the same name that had already been existing in Jowai.

(I) Lumkyrwiang Club

An established theatrical organisation whose bestknown stalwart in Shillong was Bah Nando Wankhar. This troupe reported to have been the first to use *Roll-up Scenes*. Its wellknown productions, staged in the Lung Waliehs (White Houses) of the locality and *Maya Hok*, Maya B.A. and U Railong. One of its talented artist and composer was Bah Kenning Laloo.

(II) Shilliang Raid Club

Though not so active like Iongpiah Club, this club also made a niche for itself. Excelled in theatrical art, they had a close contacts with Jaintiapur Bah Patty Nikhla, known as Bah Longdong, of the Shilliang Raid Club was a gifted artist.

(III) Iongpiah Club

This is the most renouned club that gave theatrical performances only after the Seng Khasi in Shillong had taken the lead. One of its founding members, the first President was *Bah Lakhon Shullai*. He was also a great playwright. The group made its debut with his composition, '*U Kiang Nangbah*' staged in the Lung Walieh (White House) of the locality. The second play was penned by his brother-in-law, Bah Shaimon Pyrbot. Though Bah Lakhon Shullai wrote a number of plays on varied themes, but he himself acted only in two. The subject matters of his dramas were like the Chieftain U Niang Raja, Ka Li Dohkha etc. One of the better known and preserved plays of this troup was about a certain Daiophi.

Iongpiah Club admitted members both from the rank and file and common and ordinary people. One of its educated and amazing actor was Bah Sahin Shullai. Other wellknown names to quote are Bah Tamon Shullai and Bah Roston Syntem, who also served as its Secretary. Female roles were enacted by the men, one of whom who made name was Bah Denning Passah. Bah Khroo Laloo was a comedian, a playwrighter and a composer for this club. An off-stage workers was Bah Nehare who used to prepare trailers and advertisements of the club.

Rolong Kharkang SDB reminisces: "When Bah Lakhon Shullai, the President of the Club, came out on the fore stage to welcome the audience and introduce the play and the case, he used to be greeted with loud and long cheers from the spectators who where keyed up for the curtain to rise".

Apart from the above mentioned three clubs, it had one of the earliest *Ka Panaliar Club* which had a big hall and enjoyed large membership; *Ka Lulong Club*; A break-away group of Lulong called '*Ka Tpep-Pale Club*', *Ka Lumiongkjam Club, Ka Iawmusiang Club* and *Ka Sein Jaintia Socio-cultural organisation*. The latter was a forum for both theatre and music. It staged a play in Shillong entitled '*U Kiang nangbah*', not to be confused with the play composed by Bah Remy Phank bearings the same title.

Theatre Happenings, 1974–

In the seventies, a number of well received dramas emerged, composed by playwrights like O. Lamare, H. Mylliemngap and Webster Davies Jyrwa. In 1974, J.S. Shangpliang penned 'Ka Khet ne phatok' (a tragedy), H.O. Mawrie's drama '*Hei! Nga bat ho ia ka Nia*' (on Cultural Survival), and again, Rympei Theatrical Centre's '*Namar ka Ri*' (bilingual tragedy). In 1974 appeared the play '*Ka Kut Iapngar*' penned by O. Lamare. The play (historical tragedy) based on a folk tale '*Ka Iaw Saring*' as playwright heard it told to him and not as a narrative that has appeared in books. The play, therefore, marks a departure from a traditional approach of other playwrights. It is an immense contribution because it is on the unique and pristine tradition, folk culture, institution and community character that it lays emphasis. Hamlet Bareh comments: Influence from English literature appears more limited in this play, the plot, form and fashion are indigenous; the play is an adaptation of a pure Khasi folktale which in obviously independent, not being influenced from outside. It has a stamp of originality and carries its cultural landmarks, a historical drama with social significance. This is a full length drama comprising of about 254 pages.

Bareh further states: In this play '*Ka Kut Iapngar*' Lamare succeeds to throw reflection upon the sitting of Durbars, coronation, community way of life, war and stratagem, village feast and festival, village gates and watchmen, crime and punishment, administration and judiciary, hobbies and recreation, other landmarks which time have carried them to oblivion.

A very successful drama, '*Ka Ri Umsnam*' of John Syntar Shangpliang was played again in 1974 and eleven times after that, both in and outside Shillong. A patriotic play, it tries to express that the hard-won freedom can be maintained and defended only by the power of the sword.

Rympei Theatrical Centre cameout with a satire entitled '*Arngut Ki Hippi*', in 1975. The same year it broughtout an opera '*Laingut Shipara*', focussing on modern social life and its problems.

The North-Eastern Hill University published a book entitled "Improved Instruction in Khasi = Ka jing pynrolbad jingpynriewspah ia ka jinghikai ia ka khasi". The book is a compilation of the learned papers presented by experts at the '*Symposium on Khasi Literature*' held on May 26-27, 1975. In the field of Fine arts and literature, the important papers were:

(1) Art and Literature/ by Mrs. A.D. Tham;

(2) Literature and Music/ by V.G. Bareh; and

(3) Inadequacy of drama/ by E.M. Reade Syiem.

In the year 1976, a detective drama '*Ka Rel Tyrut*', composed by the Rympei Theatrical Centre appeared in print.

At Nongkrem, on the occasion of Pomblang Festival, the play '*Ha Ka Hima Jong ka Jingieid*', penned by H.O. Mawrie was staged in 1976. The play should not be confused with the novel '*Ka Hima Jingieid*', written by S. Quotient Sumer. The play was produced on stage by the Kharbuli Young Men's Organisation.

Bah L.G. Shullai comments: This play could be included in the text books, both at school and college level. The playwright had trimmed the legend about Manik Raitong of all the non-Khasi elements that the legend culled along the way in its passage through time and place, from one generation to the next. This legend has a certain historical background to it, which fact made Bah Shullai reach the conclusion that "Drama and History are two different sciences; History can help Drama, but Drama cannot help History."

1977 saw two plays in Khasi, written by A. Jala, namely, '*Ka Tupia u Sahep*' and '*U Seiniong*', both commentary on social life.

In the year 1978, appeared the play '*U Androklis bad u Sing*' written by S.J. Duncan. This is a Khasi version of George Bernard Shaw's 'Androcles and the Lion'. A critic comments : Duncan was inspired into going through with the translation by his desire to familiarise his readers with the English playwright, acquainting them with Shavian wit and humour and to unveil to them the wonderful art of playwriting.

On the occasion of U Mondon Bareh Birth Centenary Celebrations, a noted Khasi litterateur, programes were held in 1978. In its second phase on November 6, 1978 organised a drama competition. In this drama festival, six High Schools from the East Khasi Hills participated. This school dramatics were thought evoking on family and social trends.

Students who received prizes in drama competition were from Synod English School, Mawkhar Christian High School, St. Joseph's High School, St. Anthony's High School at Shillong, St. Anthony's High School at Pynursla.

Rympei Theatrical Centre produced the play '*U Khun Sarong Awria*' for the first time in 1979 and repeated it several times later. The play is a story of misdirected youths which is squandered and frittered away in fervent pleasure-seeking only to learn at too-late a time that one has been marching to the grave singing one's own funeral song.

H. Mylliemngap broughtout a play in Khasi entitled '*Ka Synjat ba la shem pat*' in 1979 and in the next year came out his another play '*Ka Rangli*'. H. Mylliemngap's wrote a traditional drama for an old legend which was broughtout in 1979 Bareh Comments 'I donot know whether the legend as dramatised is indigenous or adaptation but Mylliemngap has been capable of focalising the cultural traits... Mylliemngap makes impression of his lucidity, vividity and naivety in the play.

In the year 1979, the amended version of '*Ka Ri Umsham*', written by Bah John Syntar Shangpliang, now presented in five parts was produced at Sohra in the Shillong State Central Library, under the banner of the newly formed Hynniew-Trep Cultural and Welfare Organisation.

Jyrwa, Webster Davies

Contemporary dramatist, translator and writer in Khasi, Webster Davies Jyrwa broughtout some classics from other literatures into Khasi in his volume '*Ki Drama Lyngkot*' which was published in 1979. The translations were basically in the form of excerpts from the best scenes of the original chosen dramas namely The Merchant of Venice, Haman, A Spark neglected burns the house,Sakuntala and Diamond necklace. Jyrwa has very skillfully condensed the subject matter to bringout moral significance and presented beautifully with clarity and appropriate words. Literary Critic Hamlet Bareh while reviewing this book said:

"... the plays have outlived the passage of time still throwing their effulgence, no matter the rapid change of ideologies, impact of science and technology and other developments we are now witnessing. I am particularly interested in the *Merchant of Venice, Haman* and *A Spark Neglected burns the house* because of their plot construction, the contrast of characters, the episodes skillfuly wedged and the variety in moods, temperament and theme. The plays serve the purpose of recreative reading because of their clarity and moral significance. *Esther* itself is an episode of fast changing events with a natural tendency to dramatization."

A landmark in the domain of translation is the effort of Webster Davies Jyrwa. In his book '*Ki Drama Lyngkot*, published in 1979 contains Khasi versions of the Merchant of Venice, Haman, A Spark neglected burns the house, Sakuntala and Diamond necklace. Hamlet Bareh rightly said that 'there should be more efforts to create more effective plays from the indigenous background which could be helpful in disseminating interest in cultural heritage, this publication of Webster Davies Jyrwa is nevertheless welcome for inculcating the art of Drama.. Jyrwa has been able to present it in beautiful and appropriate words... He has the translations condensed so as to reflect the most instructive themes only and infact most of them serve as excerpts from the best scenes of the original plays.

Some contemporary dramatists who made a mark for themselves are U. H. Wamphaign Sten, U Webster Davies Jyrwa, U Hamarbabiang Mylliemngap, U.D.S. Khongdup, U Antony Jalla, U Donbok T. Laloo, U Remy Phankon and U Reginald Nongkynrih.

In the year 1980, *Ka Saia Nongum*, a Khasi literary piece in dialogue form came up. The author of this borderline drama was Phrangsngi Kharlukhi.

This year, the Rympei Theatrical Centre premiered four short plays entitled "*Ka Elekshon, Ka Kti ka Jingim*, a highly patriotic *Sngi Khatduh U Tirot Sing' and Ka Tung Rymbai*. It also produced two new productions, *Ka Nga* and *Ka Kynhun Kheinduh.*

In 1981, the Rympei Theatrical Centre presented three dramas, namely, *Ka Ruh Nar, Ka Kput Kylliang and Last Day of Tirot Sing*.

The year 1982 was very fruitful for the Rympei Theatrical Centre. It's five fresh productions include *Ka Bniat Namar Ka Bniat*, *O Jerusalem*, *Ka Tyrut Kynsha*, *U Kiang Nangbah* and *Tip ia la ka Kam*.

St. Anthony's High School presented a short dramatic piece '*Ka Pop Jongno*?', written by Bah Syntar John Shangpliang and produced on 8th April 1982.

The Caroline Club

It was Bah John Syntar Shangpliang who established '*The Caroline Club*' comprising of his own children. They performed many a children's programmes such as one exhibition show of *Da Kumne Pleng* ? staged by the troupe on 12th April 1982.

In the same year, appeared a significant dramatic publication entitled '*Ar Tylli Ki Play*'. It comprised of two dramas of D.S. Khangdup, namely, *Ai Pat Ka Spah Jong Nga*, a one-act comedy and *Ka Nabon*, a historical tragi-comedy.

Prof R.S. Lyngdoh contributed an illuminating essay entitled '*A Short resume on the development of Khasi drama* in Khasi literature, which was published in the souvenir of the Rympei Theatrical Centre; covering a period from 1973 to 1982. It appeared in the year 1982.

In the year 1983, Prof. H.W. Sten broughtout '*Ka Mahadevi*' a well received drama that has enriched the modern Khasi literature. The year 1983 was a great loss for Khasi theatre. At the close of the year, ie, on 29th December 1983, thespian Kenny Shympa died exactly eleven years after he had formally established the pioneer theatre group 'The Rympei Theatrical Centre'.

Prof. Anthony Jala of St. Anthony's College has proved his calibre as the author of stageworthy dramas in Khasi. He has initiated further development in the quality of drama, and also of theatre. He has profound knowledge about the know-how of dramatic composition, and of the stage. Prof. Jala twice tested his plays on stage, in 1982 and in 1984. In the year 1984, he cameout with brilliant tragedy '*Haba Ka Kupar and Jot Ka Dawa*'.

In the 17th National Short Play Competition held at Allahabad, the Rympei Theatrical Centre bagged the President's Award in 1984 for its grant production '*The Inspection Bunglow*'.

Scholar and playwright Bah D.T. Laloo broughtout a book entitled '*Shi-har Ki drama*' in 1985 which comprises of his two short plays '*Wad Ia Ka Daw*' and '*Ka Jingstad u Basan Nongkseh*'.

The Rympei Theatrical Centre won the President's Award for its play '*U Kiang Nangbah*', adjudged the best one-act historical play at the 18th National Short Play Competition, Allahabad in the year 1985.

On 15 August 1986, a local weekly 'Apphira' selected Bah Mihsuk A Nongrum as the best Khasi actor of 1985 for his lead role in the drama '*U Kiang Nang bah*' and gave him the '*Bashai Rai Dohling Award*'.

Reginald Nongkynrih bagged the prestigious State Award for his drama '*Ka Bniat Namar Ka Bniat*' in 1986. He was adjadged the best dramatist.

A significant event in the performance history of Khasi theatre is that the Government of Orissa invited the Rympei Theatrical Centre to stage its play '*U Kiang Nangbah*' as a part of the Golden Jubilee celebrations at Balasore of the formation of Orissa State.

The play '*Sngi Khatduh U Tirot Sing*' was declared the best Regional Play at the 19th National Short Play Competition, Allahabad in 1986. It was enacted by the Rympei Theatrical Centre that was accoladed with the '*President's Award*'.

In the 20th National Short Play Competition held at Allahabad in 1987, The Rympei Theatrical Centre's production '*Tip ia la ka Kam*' bagged the '*President's Award*'.

On 15th December 1984, Mawpat Catholic Theatrical Club was formed by twelve youths, at the instance of John Rance from Umpling who was also the first President of the Club. its first Secretary was Reginald Susngi. Perhaps its premier production was '*U Sner Rupa*', enacted on 13th February 1988.

The year 1988 also brought home the much coveted '*President's Award*' at the 21st National Short Play Competition Allahabad. The award winning play '*Laingut Shipara*' was produced by the Rympei Theatrical Centre.

The eighties of the last century witnessed some significant works by two outstanding playwrights. They were Remy Phankon and Pascal Malngiang. The former wrote a drama in two acts '*U Koidi*' comprising of eleven scenes in all and the latter broughtout a short dramatic piece '*Sha Ka Khlemrain*', both appeared in print in 1988.

The Rympei Theatrical Centre once again bagged the 'President's Award' for its production '*Kaei Ka Daw*' at the 22nd National Short Play Competition held at Allahabad in 1989. The Govt. of Meghalaya acknowledge the singular and unparalled contributions made by the Rympei Theatrical centre and subsequently selected their prominent dramatic centre to represent at several state sponsored cultural events including the Republic Day parade at Polo Grounds on behalf of the Education Department of the State. In the year 1987 and 1989, this troupe presented the much acclaimed drama '*U Kiang Nangbah*'.

Roland Kharkang in his M.A. programme in Anthropology, 1986-88, prepared his dissertation on '*The Origin and development of the Khasi Theatre in Shillong*', presented to the Department of Anthropology, North Eastern Hill University. Later the dissertation appeared in book form as '*Theatre: art and life*', broughtout by the Omsons Publications, New Delhi in 1994.

A–Z

B

[U] Baieit Donshkor

This play in Khasi by D.S. Khongdup is an absorbing play where he makes use of dictions which bear on the imagery and reflect different shades of meaning. Based on a folk story with varied characterisation. For instance, while king Sympa is thoughtful and kind, king Kharai on the contrary, is over-confident, wordly and intriguing. Underestimating the capacity of others, he thus loses his throne in a bet with a stranger. But Sympa is not strong and shrewd enough so that his daughters take advantage of him which leads to stagnation in court affairs. The hero is u Baieit Donshkor. It is his creativity and witty mind which impress his audience. He makes accurate evaluation and plays exact stratagem to fish from the troubled waters, first to confound the situation and then usurp the sovereignity of two kingdoms into his hands. His flashing and infallible mind creates wonders. His first step is to supplant a princess of Kharai by taking advantage of the weak king and authorities concerned. Then he wins over her and uses her as his instrument for carrying that scheme with audacity. Yet before he appears into his true colour he was no other than a simple, dumb cow-herd to amuse Kharai court. These episodes form the climax. The wise rules at the cost of exploiting the weak. U Baieit's romance with the princess is full of thrills conveyed in beautiful metaphors. He has wrought wonders that kings have to bow down before him; he thus marvels the world. It is an art of no small achievement. This play in Khasi based on folk tale appeared in 1968. The play makes an indeliable mark for its fine characterisation.

Bareh, Hamlet

A modern scholar Hamlet Bareh in his '*A Short history of Khasi Literature*', published in 1979 devoted over thirteen pages to describe 'drama and stage development' in the land (Pp. 88-100). He put the finishing touch to his father's drama '*U Mihsngi*'.

Bareh, Mondon

Mondon Bareh is a modern Khasi playwright whose magnum opus '*U Mihsngi*' is a social drama which throws light on the conditions during the twenties of the last century. A satire on the degraded moral values, the work appeared in 1966. His son U Victor Bareh wrote the play '*U Tirot Singh*'. His another son Hamlet Bareh Ngapkynta completed the unfinished manuscript of Mondon's play '*U Mihsngi*'.

Studies

Bareh, H. 'U Mondon Bareh' *In* Soso Tham Birth Centenary Celebration Souvenir. — Shillong, 1973.

U. Mondon Bareh Birth Centenary Celebration Souvenir. — Shillong, 1978.

Bareh, Mondon *see also* 'Introduction' and 'U Mihsngi'

Bareh, Victor G.

A wellknown Khasi playwright Victor G. Bareh is credited with a historical play, a first of its kind in the land entitled '*U Tirot Singh*'. It appeared in print in 1957 and an English version of it was published in 1963. This is a play on war and history centering on U Tirot Sing. His another work 'Ka drama U Tirot Sing', also appeared from Shillong in 1979. The latter is especially an appreciation of the drama.

Bareh, Victor G. *see also* Introduction and 'U Tirot Singh'

Bhattarcharya, S.

Author contributed a paper in English '*The Origin and development of theatre in Shillong*, which he presented in the eight session of a Seminar held in Kohima College from 27th to 29th October 1978, organised by the North East India History Association. '*The Origin and development of theatre in Shillong*: [Khasi and Assamese Theatre], later got published in '*Mayukh*', Shillong in 1982.

C

Cajee, Terence

Terence Cajee contributed an illuminating essay '*Problems of tribal literature, drama and fine arts in Meghalaya*'. It was published in the Rympei Theatrical Centre: 1973-82 Souvenir, (Shillong) 1982.

Correngia, A., SDB

Modern writer and translator in Khasi, A. Correngia has written a number of plays, both original and translations. He made his debut in the domain of dramatic literature with his comedy '*U Diengduh u kni*' which he translated from the English '*Uncle's Walking Stick*' in 1936. His other wellknown works are: *U Doloi ha Sor* (Comedy; 1952), *Ka Ticket Khalai Nusib* (Comedy based on the English Lottery Ticket; 1954), *Ka Dohnud Ksiar* (quasi-religious dealing with the virtues of a good-hearted man 1954), *U Blei Vishnu* (Opera on Hindu deity Vishnu, 1955), *U Slatlai ha Pynthabah* (religious drama, 1956), *Ha Ka Eriong* (religious drama, 1956), *Ka Dor Ka Snam* (Tragic drama based on the English '*The Price of Blood*'; 1961), *Ka Phatok* (Tragic drama on injustice, 1965).

Costa, Giulius

A Salesian of Don Bosco (SDB) Fr. Giulius Costa is an anthropologist per excellence is also an established name in the history of Khasi theatre. He was born in Italy in 1902 and came to India in the late 1920s and served in the missions in the Khasi and Garo Hills for 34 years. He did extensive research on the customs and lives of the hill peoples of the state and wrote several books and articles on the subject. It was he who founded and patronised the *Catholic Dramatic Society* at Loitumkhrah in 1954-55. But in the year 1964, he was transferred from the Shillong that gave a serious blow to the theatrical activities in the region. Though not an actor himself, his credit lies chiefly in stage direction. His two notable productions are *Talisman* (1954-55) and *Francis of Assisi*. Fr. Giulius Costa died in April 1970 at Mendal, Garo Hills at the age of Sixtyeight.

D

Dance-drama

A major contribution to this genre of performing arts was made by the Ever Green School, which gave a series of performances in dance drama style, the first of its kind in Khasi.

Dienjat U Hynniew Trep

This is one of the wellknown theatrical clubs that was more preoccupied with staging dramas with traditional themes.

[*see* 'Introduction]

[U] Dieng Bilat High School [The High School Eucalyptus]

U Dieng Bilat High School or the High School Eucalyptus is a dramatic monologue in Khasi, penned by the renowned poet Soso Tham. It appeared in 1936 in the volume 'Ka Duitara Ksiar I'. In this monologue, the speaker is a pensonified tree by that name. The readers know the name of the speaker from the title of the poem because it does not disclose its name, the auditors are the populace of Shillong. In the "Eucalyptus" the tree tells that it suffers the heat of the sun and the fury of the wind which might have once broken its branch. Besides this, it stands alone in the compound of the high school as there are no other trees nearby. The speaker does not complain against the elements of nature for being unking to it. It simply states the fact of its suffering. What the tree wants the auditors to know is its own philosophy of a successful life. It tells that though the elements of nature are unfavourable, it stands there firmly and proudly with its branches shooting skywart and its roots piercing deep into the earth. It does not mind being alone because it has many ideas in its mind waiting for an opportunity to be expressed...

Howsoe'er wise a man,
    Nobody can deny;
Without giving a chance,
    How can he make a try?

The voice of the speaker in the poem is the voice of human reason. If an intelligent auditor is moved by his sympathy for the Eucalyptus, he will soon realize that he makes a mistake because he has to take that sympathy from the speaker and transfer it to the poet. In the second movement of the poem, the speaker draws the attention of the auditors to its view of an ideal leader. Such a leader is a trustworthy gentleman. He is concerned for the welfare of the people, and the latter in turn love him. Such an ideal leader, the speaker finds, has a strong will power. Like the wind which as the speaker hints, once broke its branch, destructive elements in the society may attempt to dislodge the leader from the social status he enjoys; but those adversaries would find that their attempt is futile because the ideal leader enjoys the confidence of the masses. Finally, the speaker decides firmly to follow the example of such a gentleman no matter if its conviction leads to a fall for its knows that the fall will shock the entire locality.

[U] Dieng Bilat High School *see also* Tham, Soso and Introduction (Dramatic Monologue)

Dkhar, Dino Nath Roy (1879-1930) *see* Introduction

Dkhar, Hari Charan Roy (1863-1913) *see* Introduction

Dkhar, Streamlet

The scholar did his Ph.D. thesis on the topic '*The Concept of Love in Khasi Drama*'.

Dohling, Bashai Rai

A Cartoonist, painter and theatre person, Bashai Rai was born on 29 November 1923. He was closely associated with the Shillong Panora Club of Peace Roy Pariat. He used to paint signboards for this group. Later in life, he proved himself an accomplished playwright. By profession, he was a cartoon-filmmaker from the Kashi Hills. He served in the Cartoon Film Unit, Film Division, Ministry of Information and Broadcasting of the Government of India for a long span of 23 years. After a brief stint with the Institute of Arts, Calcutta in 1945 he was appointed in the Cartoon Film Unit, Information Films of India Bombay as Animator where he worked only till 1946.

After his return to Shillong, he started composing plays. His wellknown works are '*U Borsing Bad U Borkusain*', a shadow play which he wrote for the girls of Khasi Jaintia Presbyterian High School. His '*U Tirot Sing*' was a 'stage and radio' play for the All India Radio, Shillong in 1952.

Bashai Rai Dohling died on 14 January 1982 at the age of 58.

Duncan, S.J.

An eminent dramatist in Khasi language, S.J. Duncan's early work '*Ka Tiewlarun*' was published in 1968. In the year 1978, his wellknown drama '*U Androklis bad u Sing*' a Khasi version of Geroge Bernard Shaw's 'Androcles and the Lion' came out. It was he who first introduced Khasi readers with this English dramatist, acquainting them with Shavian wit and humour.

An outstanding modern playwright, his '*Ka Tiewlarun*' is a comedy borrowing its theme from folktale, enriched with metaphors and dictions.

Duncan, S.J. *see also* 'Introduction' and 'Ka Tiewlarun'

E

Elias, Hopewell

This wellknown Khasi poet of the modern period is credited with four dramatic monologues, namely, *Na Waikhyri, Ka Dymmiew—Ryngnni, U Lum Lawbah and 'U Lapongnai—Ksiar'* in which the poet allows imagination to have a free play, though the pieces depict the socio-political history of the ancient Sutnga, Shillong, Sohra and the Madur-maskut empires. These were first broughtout in 1937 in the volume entitled '*Ka Pansngiat, Ksiar Ki Saw Aiom*' (The Golden Crown of the Four Seasons) and since 1963 appearing in print under the title Ka Hamsaia Ki Por (The Musing of Times). The theme of Elias's monologues, is patriotism. He devised the same structure for all the four monologues. Each speaker begins with eulogising the achievements made by his predecessors or by himself; and each speaks of the glory, pomp and prowess of the ancients which emanated from the unity and a high sense of responsibility for the common welfare. The prides of each speaker soon yields to pessimism as he envisions the future when the people will bend towards materialism and self-interest which will destroy their own strength. In the process of change, the people will worship new gods, as the speaker in the first monologue says, and will be in good terms with the devils including Ren and Jom as the speakers in the other three monologues foresee. These shows that the moral strength of man has degenerated from time to time. In spite of the degeneration, the commemorative works of the ancients like lakes, ponds, monoliths, the rivers and mountains as well as the beauty of nature stand as living witnesses of the glorious past of the Khasis. Hopewell in his four pieces used a prologue and an epilogue where the poet speaks in his own person. In each monologue the poet used an ancient king to speak to the subjects. Because some events in the history are focussed in the speech, each speaker is a prophet par excellence when he speaks of the political events which are to happen in his kingdom.

·Folklore saw a blossoming in the hands of H. Elias whose 'Ki Khanatang ụ barin' is a colection of 44 folktales. H Elias is renowned more as a poet that prose writes. As versifier, his position is undisputed.

G

Gatphoh, Primrose

Born in 1900, Primrose Gatphoh wrote a short play '*Kassai ia Ka Hok*' for the All India Radio, Shillong, underlying the message that dishonesty doesnot bring lasting prosperity. In 1933 he included it in the school text book '*Sawdong Ka Lyngwiar Dpei*'. In its 5th edition, 1977, the play is incorporated in lesson 18.

H

Ha Ka Hima Jong ka Jingieid *see* Introduction and Mawrie, H.O.

The Harpist *see under* U Nongtem Duitara

The High School Eucalyptus *see under* U Dieng Bilat High School

I

In Ka Synjat Ba La Shem Pat

This Khasi drama, came out in 1979. A traditional drama based on an old legend, but written in modern times by H. Mylliemngup, a detailed account of the plot, as given by Hamlet Bareh in presented below. The principal character is U Kurup Singh a newly crowned king who succeeded the throne. The plot suffers because of the immaturity of both the king and myntris. Not having love experience earlier, the prince found it difficult to build up a balanced patnership with his newly wedded wife; this plight made him intuitional, misled and confounded so that he relied more on the advice of a maid servant than on the queen. He became radically changed into an ill-tempered man liable to make rapid decision but he never went into the core of any problem. And worse, his own mother, devoid of insight and sagacity, was far from other clever and prudent women of the past. As such she laced the power of judgement and calculation and thus failed to provide her son now enthroned, incentives either to face or avert such calamities which befell him. Thus he fell himself a victim to a conspiracy hatched by his own maid servant against the queen. Engrossed in State affairs, he did not care to investigate but instead dismissed the queen. This caused long years of separation, separation of the queen from the king and separation of children from the mother and the father into their respective spheres as destiny and imposed. The episodes obtained from the separation and then the re-union after a long gap, are touching. But the lng years of separaton caused too deep a pang. But why this separation? it was the role of jealousy intrigue and conspiracy hatched by a maid servant. The scenes shift from the warm stately place to seclusion and vagabondage but the long years of parting culminate into a re-union, a climax of the play. Among other vices, jealousy has too much dominance; it creates distortions and adds to the gloom of life. But it plays a temporary role and in the long run, virtue comes out triumphantiy.

Iongpiah Club *see* Introduction (Jaintia Club)

J

Jala, Anthony

Prof Anthony Jala is a modern scholar, academician, author and playwright in Khasi. He is credited with some well received stageworthy plays,. Jala who serves in St. Anthony's College wrote the tragedy '*Haba Ka Kupar-Jot Ka Dawa* in 1984. His plays were produced on Khasi stage in 1982 and in 1984. A critic comments: More typical of the theatre as a forum in Bah (Prof.) Anthony Jala's play '*Haba Ka Kupar-jot ka Dawa*'. The playwright discusses the popular philosophy of fatalism as an attitude of life. The closing lines are very telling : *"Balei ..."* ? (Why ? ,,, Why ?).

A modern Khasi writer and playwright, A Jala's drama '*Ka Tupia in Sahep*' and '*U Seiniong*' focus on social life.

Julius Kaiser

This is the title of the Khasi renderation of the Shakespeare's 'Julius Caeser', Act II, Scene III, translated by John Roberts and published in the Khasi Fourth Reader in 1891. The play is reproduced in *Ka Kot Pule Khasi* (Klass VIII) edited by W. Manners and published by K.J. Presbyterian, Synod Church House, Shillong in 1980 (Pp. 53-69).

Jyrwa, B.C.

An eminent playwright in Khasi, Sri B.C. Jyrwa wrote a number of plays of which *Drama Shaphang Ka Nabon* (1955), *U Hakim* (1955), *U Herod Syiem*

Barunar (historical drama based on King Herod of the Bible; 1956), *U Damon bad u Pythias* (mythological drama; 1956), *Merchant of Venice* (translation of Shakespeare's "*Merchant of Venice*"; 1956), *U Sandy* (biographical drama; 1956).

Jyrwa, W.D.

Scholar wrote '*Ki Drama Lyngkot*', appeared from Shillong in 1981. A much acclaimed play, a critical exposition of this work appeared in '*U Kritik*' as 'Ki Drama Lyngkok' *U Kritik'*, 1982, 11(5) HSLC and II(9), 1982.

'*Ki Drama Lyngkot*' of Webster Davies Jyrwa contain the Khasi renderation of the Merchant of Venice, Haman, A Spark neglected burns the house, Sakuntala and Diamond necklace, published in 1979. A critic states: I find the plays could serve thepurpose of recreative reading because of the clarity and moral significance. Although stress is laid on the social setting, it is obvious that Webster Davies Jyrwa has equally been impressed by the moral conveyed through these dramas, the episodes drawn from them and equally the different characters. The book could provide incentives towards learning things scientifically especially in respect of tackling burning problems one is subject to. The plays have outlived the passage of time no matter the rapid changes of ideologies, impact of Science and Technology in our midst. Naivety and lucidity are the main traits in this adaptation by Jyrwa. What are their impressions? briefly I suggest that in *Merchant of Venice*, one could note that sagacity reflects itself as a great liberating force of mankind from the bondage of evil forces and it needs not too many hands or even revolutions to upturn the world. But Esther another wise woman personage plays a similar role to Portia, in pleading for the cause of her people, victims to bondage with audicity and mature reasoning. In both, the same story repeats itself of the triumph of virtue over vice which leads to a drawning of new order of things. In the next series, we see how the evil devises its instrument to bring about ruin. In *Sakuntala* once could perhaps recall that truth does not deviate from its path. The *Diamond Necklace* seems to emphasise upon us that we do not take heed of what is happening around us: blind to them, we even fail to draw a calculation between a genuine valuable and an imitation one.

Jyrwa, Webster Davies *see also* 'Introduction'

K

Ka Bniat Namar Ka Bniat *see* Nongkynrib, Reginald

Ka Dymmiew-Ryngnni *see* Introduction (Dramatic monologue) and Elias, Hopewell

Ka Kut Iapngar

This Khasi drama is authored by O. Lamare and published in 1974. based on folk story. The plot of this Khasi play is given below:-

Iaw Saring was queen of Iapngar, who does not appear to be sagacious, charming or capable because she lacks insight and power of judgment, and would have plunged her kingdom into anarchy, but the situation was saved by the timely intervention of her counsellors, the Marpan and Rymbai Basans. The finest character is U Thaken, originally an expatriate but later became a naturalised citizen because he contributed immensely to the state, being witty, tactful and shrewd. And by the dint of his labour, the fame of Iapngar spread far and wide. For even Jaintia and Shillong were trembled to see it rose. Time came when this kingdom suffered adverse repercussion because of the queen's arrogance for she managed to hide her wickedness as bese as she could by making such countenance, but one day she burst out into true colour when she picked up a quarrel with a poor fruiterer, Ka Luh Shadap. Not being pacified even by her counsellors and elders, she challenged her in a bet but she was defeated by Ka Luh who now was installed as queen of Iapngar in place of Iaw Saring according to the conditions offered in the bet, whereas the people were jubilant over this drastic change because they were discontent. But Iaw Saring was contemplating a revenge to the whole kingdom, it is here that the drama is confined to the shift of loyalty. Iaw Saring therefore played foul trick with Iapnagar's enemy: treachery and betrayal come into glare before it emerges to an end. She found an opportune occasion when she hatched a conspiracy with the Jaintia spies or reconnaisance party lurking in the jungle on the capital's outskirt and who had come intentionally to study the situation. Another climax ensues when Iapgnar was taken by surprise at the dead of night during a dance festival held by Luh Shadap. Merry making people faced the disaster. Thaken as true citizen made notable contribution. He constructed the Iapngar fortress and surpassed others in accomplishing this feat. His fiancee was Ka Hirmai, a woman of courage and sweet temper. The climax is their simultaneous death during the defence of Iapngar. The two corpsee lying side by side are touching upon the Jaintia General who carries this impression-*War has its victory but love has its glory*. Iaw Saring was rescued but while deserting the village, she carried all her wealth and buried it inside a stone cave called *Mawliehpoh*.

Ka Nabon

This is the title of the Khasi drama, written by D.S. Khongdup and included much later in the book '*Ar Tylli Ki Play*'. A historical play in two acts, based on the story of a lady who was the first among the Khasi Pnars to embrace Christianity at the hands of Rev. William Lewis and his wife, Mrs. Lewis. His *Ai Pat ka spah Jong Nga* is a comedy in one-act, while Ka Nabon is a tragi-comedy of two acts. A critic points out two inaccuracies in the historical play as mentioned below:

(1) First U Bor Manick Syiem was not the king of Sohra as the play alleges. This mechanism is a device called '*dens ex machina*' brought in for sake of the plot of the play.

(2) The Nongsawlia village of the play is not under the king of Sohra.

Ka Pla I Nah

An outstanding translated play in Khasi, *Ka Pla I Nah*, rendered by Bah Kenny Shympa from the English '*Three Top Hats*' was first titled '*Ka Tupia Sahep*'.

Later he made some changes in it for the Rympei Theatrical Centre and the revised script was given the title 'Ka Pla I Nah'. The play shows a particular aspect of the modern Khasi way of life: avarice and interitance. This Khasi play was first premiered by the Rympei Theatrical Centre in 1973. It was an instant hit. Sometimes after the performance of this play, a sort of seminar was organised at the State Central Library where Bah. C. Wolflang, Director of SCERT, Meghalaya commented *'If you want to know the modern Khasi culture, yon should see the play' Ka Pla I Nah'.*

Ka Ri Umsnam *see* Introduction and Shangpliang John Syntar, Bah

Ka sawangka ia ki saw ngut ba iap mynsaw

This is the title of the Khasi drama composed by the eminent playwright and translator Sri F.M. Pugh. A full length traditional drama comprising of 250 pages, the plot of which runs as follows:-

Ka Bliap Bliap is a dominant woman character, of active disposition, swift as wind, fast as lightning, witty, inquisitive who sees the world out of its normal course, full of lying, mischief and jealousy. A contrast is U Nik, an inexperienced lad and because being ignorant of the world round him, he is deceived and exploited. A climax is a gruesome murder of four persons but the plot discovers the role of a jury in which a Syiem, his myntris and sirdars play to tackle criminal cases, how prompt and ingenious are they to detecting the crime using different levels of intelligence to compile facts and figures and assess such clues and evidence and in quite an indigenous conception and practice.

Ka sawangka ki san-ngut ba iap

A social play in Khasi written in modern times, Ka sawangka ki san-ngut ba iap is a composition of F.M. Pugh that was broughtout in 1967.

The playwright seeks to focalise social vices that have their effect upon deteriorating family life. Liquor addiction at its worst, plays foul role to exterminate completely the family and social values. If it has developed as a hereditary habit, the results are worse, the budding genertion of the house being its worst victims. Pugh's conception also elicits itself both on a constructive and destructive roles of education, for without creating first a strong moral character, the service of education in the sharpening of faculties and intelligence cannot be made effective. A promising religious theologian such as u Kyrtong and a witty lawyer, U Kynjai, the characters depicted, could have played significant roles but weak as they are, they just take themselves to liquor addiction, this is because home and school education have not been properly balanced. A note of dissent is struck at a wrong conception of education. Thus village students returned home from Shillong for briefing during holidays, completely neglect the old values, they refuse to uphold the dignity of labour, they isolate themselves from village society and commit acts of juvenile delinquency harmful to themselves and neighbours. Taking things at face value is detrimental. Evils from towns spread very quickly into villages and have their impact in upsetting the community character; they breed superior complexity, thus life is made superficial and cheap. U Kynsai and u Kyntong, the two brothers, during a holiday instead of joining the village in a christmas celebration, set fire to it in mad frenzy and finally meet their fatal end. So also Kyrtong and Kynjai died in a jeep accident being likewise drunken. Female counterparts do not appear morally sound. Weightage is given to superficial and vulgar characters to fit in with the plot. Gossips not wholesome, feature in the conversation. On the other hand, social evils, inherent in villages have not been laid stress in any of such books as came until 1979.

Ka Tiewlarun

This play of S.J. Duncan borrows its theme from a folk story. U Het is beyond compare, a brother faithful affectionate and pitiful on his sister. Ka Shatai, is wholesome, graceful and sober but betrays her weakness being baffled by the empty charms which emerge in her immediate confinement. U Madur Syiem is a fine character who by his tact, shrewdness and intelligence creates a wonder in that he could transform the story from its grim or pathetic tone into a joyous culmination. The play thus sees its climax. The folk-tale itself because of the episodes it abounds, has the natural tendency to dramatisation both in play or verse. Duncan adds u Klon, a jester whose presence makes like rich rather than desolate. But Madur displays his skill with great insight, imagination and infallible judgment. The story presents the snake as a symbol of evil but it is the gods that liberate the victims from its clutches. Though the drama draws its theme from a folk story, but the playwright make innovations here and there with varied characters.

Kharkrang, Roland

Fr. Roland Kharkrang SDB, a wellknown modern Khasi scholar is the author of a treatise on Khasi Theatre which appeared under the title '*Theatre: art and life*' in 1994. He is a member of the Society of the Salesians of St. John Bosco, a religious, educational organisation. He did his graduation from the University of North Bengal in 1971 and later pursued his B.Ed in 1977, M.Ed in 1981, M.A. in 1988 and M.Phil in Anthropology in 1992, all from the North-Eastern Hill University. Roland Kharkrang served as the Headmaster of Sacred Heart Boys High School, Shillong (1982-89), Rector of the Residential Section of Don Bosco College, Tura, (1989-93) and then as Parish Priest of St. John Bosco Parish, Cherrapunjee. Fr. Roland has to his credit some books in Khasi and a number of articles and papers in Khasi and English.

Kharlukhi, Bajubon R.

Author wrote an article entitled '*Formation and development of Khasi drama*' which appeared in the mimeographed publication '*Essays on some important aspects of Khasi literature*', Shillong, 1977. Scholar Bajubon Kharlukhi's essay, *Formation and Development of Khasi Drama*, comprises of five pages giving a short account of the genesis and growth of Khasi drama.

Kharlukhi, Pharangsngi

Pharangsngi Kharlukhi is credited with the Khasi drama '*Ka Saia Nongum*', published in 1980. Ths is not a drama proper, but a piece in dialogue form which should not be confused with the poem by the same title, written by Victor G. Bareh. Both the poet and the playwright were inspired by one of the folktales of Rabon Sing Kharsuka contained in his book 'Ka Jingiathuhkhana Puriskam, 18 October 1908.

The Khasi Cultural Society

This theatrical and cultural group associated itself with freedom struggle during the freedom movement.

[*see* 'Introduction']

Khongdup, Dewi Singh

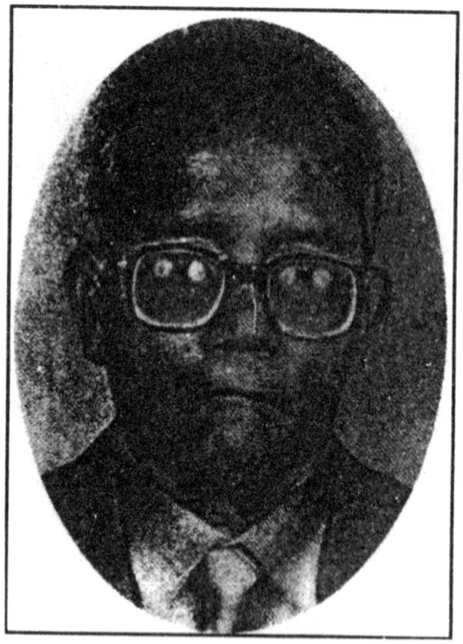

Shri Dewi Singh Khongdup, an eminent scholar and writer in Khasi was born into a very poor family in the village of Mawshun, Assam. Due to penury, he was unable to attend school in early childhood. It was only in March 1936, he got admission in class IV at M.E. School, Mawkher, Shillong. From then on, he stood first in all classes. Dewi Singh had a brief stinct at teaching and in 1952, he was selected to Assam Civil Service and eventually rose higher in the echelons of Civil Service. In 1967, he was encadered in the Indian Administrative Service. In 1997 he took voluntary restirement while serving as Secretary of the Meghalaya Legislative Assembly.

Sri D.S. Khongdup wrote a comedy in Khasi entitled '*U Baieit Donshkor*', published in 1968, basing its plot on Khasi folk-story. An important addition to modern Khasi dramatic literature for its imagery and characterisation abounds in contrast. The play is written with a huge cast. The dramatis personae are as given below:-

Ki Nongiashim bynta

U Syiem Sympa Singh

Maibon Rani : Ka Mahadei jong u.

Shitala Koina
Kortimai : Ki khun kynthei jong ki.

Syntiewbon

Jiang

Husiar : Ki Myntri u Syiem

Mawleiñ Sympa Singh

U Baieit Donshkor.

Meirisan : Ka Kmie u Baieit Donshkor.

Risa Ka Shakri ling u Syiem Sympa Singh.

Jngum : Ka khun jong ka.

Phangaiñ & Thaiñ : Ki nongiarap kam ia ka Risa.

Rnong, Syntai & Mohon : Ki nongap masi u Syiem Sympa Singh

Sliang Mawpun : Shi mynsiem bad ka Shitala Koina.

Jriaw : Ka kmie jong u.

Pyllaw : U shakri u Sliang Mawpun.

Kyrtong : U Rangbah Shipai u Syiem Sympa Singh.

U Syiem Kharai.

U Sngap Lyngskor.

Aibuit & Khanglad : Ki Myntri u Syiem Kharai.

Stem : U Rangbah Shipai u Syiem Kharai.

Puka : U trai shnong ka hima Kharai.

Swoiñ : Ka tnga jong u.

Ki Shipai, ki Briw Syiem, ki Paitbah, Kynthei bad shynrang.

Modern writer in Khasi, D.S. Khongdup broughtout his two short dramatic pieces entitled '*Ai Pat ka Spah Jong Nga and Ka Nabon*'. Written much earlier, the plays were revised, published and appeared in book form in 1982 under the title '*Ar Tylli Ki Play*'.

Apart from play, Khongdup has written poems, shortstories and fiction in Khasi language. He single-handedly enriched Khasi literature through his fictional '*U Don Putit*' series running into fire books in ten years from 1968 to 1978.

U BAIEIT DONSHKOR

(*Drama*)

Secretary, Sahitya Akademi.
with respects.
[illegible] 15/7/88

U DEWI SINGH KHONGDUP

La pynmih
da
U Nongthoh

First Edition

LA SHON HA RI KHASI PRESS, SHILLONG
1968

Ka dor Rs. 2.50

Shri Dewi Singh Khongdup has also rendered the old Testament into Khasi common language. The Khasi language finds the felicity of its expression through Dewi's works.

In the year 1997, the Sahitya Akademi conferred on him '*The Bhasa Samman*' for his peerless contribution to the development of Khasi language and literature.

Studies

Rymbai, R.T. Ar Tylli Ki Play. *U Kritik*, 1982, II (40); P.6.

Khongdup, D.S. *see also* 'Introduction' and 'U Baieit Donshkor'

Ki Drama Lyngkot *see also under* Jyrwa, Webster Davies and 'Introduction'

[U] Koidi *see* Phankon, Remy

L

Laloo, D.T. Bah

Researcher and Modern author in Khasi, Bah D.T. Laloo has tried his hand in playwrighting also. An erudite scholar into Khasi culture, his best known short plays entitled '*Wad Ia Ka Daw*' and '*Ka Jingstad u Basan Nongkseh*' were included in his publication '*Shi-har Ki Drama*'.

Lamare, O.

O. Lamare is the author of a historical tragic drama in Khasi named '*Ka Kut Iapngar*', broughtout in 1974. Best known drama of this playwright is '*Ka Kut Iapngar*' which got published in 1974. This work is accepted as a significant contribution in the domain of modern Khasi literature because of its unique and pristive tradition, folk culture, institution and community characters that it lays emphasis. Some opine '*Ka Kut Iapngar*' is not a drama proper. A scholar simply termed it as literary dialogue.

Lamare, O. *see also* Introduction and Ka Kut Iapngar

[U] Lapongnai-Ksiar *see* Introduction (Dramatic monologue) and Elias, Hopewell

Lumkyrwiang Club *see* Introduction (Jaintia Club)

[U] Lum Lawbah *see* Introduction (Dramatic Monologue) and Elias, Hopewell

Lyngdoh, R.S.

Prof. R.S. Lyngdoh is regarded as one of the best authorities and commentators on Khasi culture and language. Prof. R.S. Lyngdoh contributed an article entitled '*A Short resume on the development of Khasi drama in literature*', appeared in *Rympei Theatrical Centre Souvenir*, (Shillong), 1973-82 (Pp. 9-11). Lyngdoh served as the Head of the Department of Khasi in St. Anthony's College. Prof. R.S. Lyngdoh was the founder - Professor of the Department of Khasi in the North Eastern Hill University. He was a member of the Sahitya Akademi, the National Academy of Letters, New Delhi. Prof. Lyngdoh passed away on 19th December, 1990.

M

Malngiang, Pascal

A contemporary playwright in Khasi language, Pascal Malngiang wrote a short social play '*Sha Ka Khlemrain*', comprising of seven scenes. The play is about something which young men and women often come across. The dramatist feels that it will benefit not only the school or college goers, but also later in life when they would acquire responsible positions in the society. The underlying message is that if the country has to progress, corruption must be wiped out. This play appeared in print in 1988.

Mawrie, H.O.

H.O. Mawrie, a modern author in Khasi language has penned a drama on cultural survival entitled '*Hei ! Nga bat ho ia ka Nia*', published in 1974. '*Hei Nga Bat Ho Ia Ka Nia*' is actually not a drama proper, but better be classed as 'literary dialogue'. His best known drama is '*Ha Ka Hima Jong ka Jingieid*'. The play focusses on all the non-Khasi elements that the legend Manik Raitong had gathered from the time immemorial.

This play was put an board by the Kharbuli Young Men's Organisation in 1976 at Nongkrem during the Pomblang Festival.

Studies

Shullai, L.G. Ha Ka Hima Ka Jingieid. *U Kritik*, Vol. II, No. 35, 16th September 1982.

[U] Mihsngi

This is a modern drama in Khasi authored by the playwright Mondon Bareh. *U Mihsngi* is an incomplete play. U Mondon Bareh's son, U Hamlet Bareh Ngapkynta, put the finishing touch to it and brought it out in 1965-66. The play depicts a characterisation of clownish, henpecked and dubious husbands as also domineering and selfcentred women and how both play their part leading to a total collapse of family, while it does not lose sight too of elegant, noble and constructive characters who play their role too in uplifting moral standards. Sub-plots centre also on love rivalry and excess. U Mihsngi is a hero who sinks down in moral life, being not self-consistent, too much baffled of Ka Hiu, a vulgar woman and being henpecked to her. He indulges in artificialness. Because of this temperament, family standards have become heavily sabotaged. What is worse Ka Alis, daughter by his first demise wife becomes victim to her unruly step-mother's treatment. Alis is of noble disposition and shares in a more realistic temperament and outlook with Dr. Liaw, her fiance. Being brutally treated at home, Alis one day seeks refuge in Lar Sing's home. Lar Singh is a contrast of Mihsngi and keeps with the moral values. Hui's temper knows no bounds when she learns of Alis' proposed marriage to the extent that a conspiracy is hatched to poison her. The conspiracy is averted by the immature death of Mihsngi. And against all the pathos from the play, Alis and Liaw are happily settled. The play depicts other vulgar characters at the background.

Mylliemngap, H.

A contemporary writer who has made a niche for himself for his lucid style, vividing and raivety in his dramas. His master piece being '*Ka Synjat ba la shem pat*' appeared in print in 1979. This seeks to inculcate traditional drama for an old legend. His another significant publication is '*Ka Rangli*' broughtout in 1980.

Mylliemngap, H. *see also* 'Introduction and '*Ka Synjat ba la shem pat*'

N

Na Waikhyri *see* Introduction (Dramatic monologue) and Elias, Hopewell

Nongkynrih, Reginald

Reginald Nongkynrih of the Rympei Theatrical Centre was given the state Award for his play '*Ka Bniat Namar Ka Bniat*'. Reginald's drama *Ka Bniat Namar Ka Bniat* is in full length, having double heroes and is a mixture of history and fiction. The play was first premiered by the Rympei Theatrical Centre in 1982. Nongkynrih's another wellknown drama '*Ka Tyrut Kynsha*' was brought by the Rympei Theatrical Centre which was then revised by U Mihsuk A. Nongrum and premiered by the troupe in 1982.

Nongrum, A.M.

Scholar is credited with an unpublished paper '*Ka Drama*' presented at *Ka Seminar jong Ki Nongthohkot Katholik*, Shillong in 1982.

Nongrum, Mihsuk A. Bah

Bah Mihsuk A. Nongrum was the first treasures of the Rympei Theatrical Centre. A great dramatist and organiser, Nongrum was adjudged the best Khasi actor for the year 1985 by a local weekly 'Apphira'. For his lead role in '*U Kiang Nangbah*' he was given the 'Bashai Rai Dohling Award' in 1986. Mihsuk A. Nongrum's play '*Ka Kput Kylliang*' and '*Tip ia la ka Kam*' were premiered by the

Rympei Theatrical Centre in 1981 and 1982 respectively. The same year he revised the play '*Ka Tyrut Kynsha*' of Reginald Nongkynrih to be produced by this troupe.

Nongrum, T.P.

Shri T.P. Nongrum's play '*U Khun Sarong Awria*' was premired by the Rympei Theatrical Centre beating all previous records by giving over 26 performances at various times and places.

Nongrum, Rash Mohan Roy

Rash Mohan Roy Nongrum wrote the drama '*Ka Damayanti bad u Nol*', based on a story from Sanskrit literature. He also penned 'U Saimuka Ka Duitara', which is no more extant. The playwright died in 1962.

[U] Nongtem Duitara

U Nongtem Duitara or 'The Harpist' is a dramatic monologue written by the eminent Khasi poet Bronath Thangkhiew and appeared in print in 1936 in his anthology of poems called 'Ka' Tienrwai Khasi' (Khasi Poetry). Comprising of 504 lines, this piece is perhaps the longest monologue in Khasi language. H.W. Sten gives a detailed account of the theme of this monologue. In his words:-

"The speaker in this poem is the harpist and the auditors are people of different walks of life. The theme of the poem is the changes in the Khasi society. The aim of the speaker is to draw the attention of the auditors to the various evils which have cropped up in the society, to warn the people of the danger of neglecting their own traditional values, and to tender sound advices to the younger generations. By proposing to give force to his thought from the point of view of the harpist, Thangkhiew could speak freely on all the aspects of life he has chosen to focus. The poet makes his speaker touch on several topics, a critic would find that the poem lack thematic unity. The speaker directs his attention now to himself, now to a young girl, to a boy, to a family, and finally to the Khasi society as a whole. He does not stick to one single action. In the first stanza the speaker announces his presence and his intention to sing of whatever comes to his mind. He states too that being a man he would not hesitate visiting as many houses as he could and singing to the accompaniment of his harp; but he apologizes in advance that just in case his song hurts anyone, the bad elements in it may be forgotten and the good ones treasured. The first character which attracts his attention is a girl whose beauty he admires. he compares her to a gragrant flower which he likes to smell upto "fifty times". He finds no defect in her dress or in her conduct. What he does here is simply admiring the girls against whom he had nothing to say. She should be an example to be emulated. In the third stanza the speaker addresses an unattractive man who, not knowing that he is so, ventures to frequent his visits to young girls. The speaker criticizes the long nose and the ugly forehead of his auditor and finally asks him to leave the place, cover himself with a blanket and sleep in the corner of the house lest beautiful girls get frightened of him. The speaker is unkind to his auditor because he seems to be firmly holding the view that man should first know himself before he ventures to offer his love to any girl. What is the harm if such a one is blessed with a wealthy and beautiful wife? The poem has no answer to this question. From the fourth stanza down to the last, the speaker takes the various unfavourable social changes in the Khasi society as his topics. The first which comes to his mind is the power of money which he says, can buy everything, including right. He who has money has power and honour; but he who has not is honourless. The speaker decries such a change in the moral standard of the people and warns that in the end, whatever a moneyed man thinks of himself today, right will be right and wrong, wrong. As he lashes at the evil of wealth, the speaker's memory flashes quickly to remind him of the scene of a Khasi dance. He praises the virgins who participate in the dance. The changes in the people's outlook is so great that even men have learnt to point themselves. An example of this is a character who paints his moustache to be acceptable, perhaps, to young girls. The speaker warns all young girls to be careful in their dealing with such men especially so at night... In the seventh stanza the speaker addresses another girl. This address is similar in tone to the one directed to the first girls, but he refrains himself from fixing a date with her because he is no sure whether or not she is a virgin. Here the speaker reflects the moral corruption in the life of a few modern girls. He next turns himself to a much matured, black and fat maid who has of late been aping foreign culture. He counsels her to uphold steadfastly the culture, tradition and religion of the ancestors. he repeats this counsel in the 15th and the 17th stanzas also. In the next movement the speaker turns himself to a minor girl. He chides and warns her that if she continues to push herself too much to men of any character, the chance is that she is going to have children without a father and caretaker. On the other hand in the depth of this address one sees the danger of too much liberty enjoyed by girls in the Khasi society. The monologue has an appeal to both children and parents. In the tenth stanza the speaker draws the attention of a Khasi young man to a well-dressed and well-behaved girl whose beauty might have engaged the auditor's attention. He tells the auditor that there are girls who pretend to be virgins and innocent; but the fact is that they have given their first love to some others who have left them. The speaker feels relief that he has done his duty of telling his auditor of what he knows and leaves him to judge things for himself. Breach of marriage contracts is not a new phenomenon in the Khasi society. It was there in the past and may continue to happen in future too; but the speaker has not ignored the awkwardness of such an event. This time he directs his weapon against a husband who has just broken his marriage contract with his wife. That apart, the husband is in search of a new one now. The speaker wants to know the reason for the breach. There is no scope for a reply in the dramatic monologue, so here too, we do not have to demand for a reply from the auditor. But as usual, the speaker warns the husband that time may come when he will return to his first love, but by then she may not have any love to return to him. Later in the thirteenth stanza, the speaker seems to return to the same man only to find that his prediction has happened already. The speaker makes a scathing remarks on the private life of one illiterate lady of whom he has heard from many people. He says that he finds the fact now himself and that she looks high and dry with the cheek bones standing high on her face. The reason for such a condition is physical exhaustion. The reference to her dirty frock suggests that the lady is a whore! He does not condemn her for good because he advises her to think also of a life hereinafter. The social evils reach the climax in the degeneration of the family life. In as many as eightyeight lines the speaker whips modern daughters who do not respect and honour their own parents. In the relationship between the mother and the daughter, the speaker finds that the society has reached the edge of the cliff when the daughter does no longer consider it a taboo to sue her mother in the court of law or to speak irreverently to her. Such ingrateful daughters will not prosper in life. A brief summary of the poem shows that it is in itself a series of monologues most of which aim at reviving the traditional values."

P

Pariat, Peace Roy

Pariat, a celebrated actor, playwright and director who later founded his own group, 'Shillong Panora Club'. Peace Roy Pariat is believed to be born in 1918, the year Germany surrended and the Allied signed an armistice on 11 November that year. Some says his parents named him Peace reportedly to commemorate the Peace Conference of Paris of 1919. Whatsoever, his birth coincided with the return of peace at the end of the first great war. He was born at Jaiaw Laitdom of Desi Pariat and a certain Leng. Bah Peace Roy could not persue much of formal education, but he proved himself to be a master playwright, theatrical artist, a practical theoretician and a promoter of dramatics. He revealed his histrionic talent at a very early age and studied hardly upto standard VIII and joined the Khasi Native Club.

Peace Roy made his debut in acting in the Khasi Native Club and gave some immemorable roles in the plays like *Ka Romily* and *Ka Maryngod*. He later broke away from this group to form his 'Shillong Panora Club' that made it debut in 1943 with the play '*Ka Romily*' staged at Quinton Hall.

Other noteworthy productions which he had written, directed and played the lead role himself are 'Ieit, ieit, ym, dei Jingieid Shet Khiew Jaikai' (1944), Ka Bor Ksuid Pyrshah Bor Blei (1945), Ka Kyrsan, Ka Rhah, Na Nongkyndong sha Sor (1947), Ka Maryngod.

A prolific author, U Peace Roy wrote a sizeable number of dramas, but many have been lost, only their names are remembered. His best known dramas are Ka Jingrhah (Malice, spite), Ka Bor Ksuid Pyrshah Bor Blei (Devilish power against diving power), Na Kyndong Sha Sor (From village to town), and Ka Shang Khawiah Ki Rang (A Snare for men). These dealt with social problems, the last being a ruthless exposure of the moral decay during the war years. A scholar writes "Bah Peace wrote plays for the stage, and not for literary vivisection, nor for scholarly criticism." He earned tremendous appreciations from the public. He would weave and produce his plays in such patterns so as to make his play apprear almost a chunk of real life played on the stage, making the audience feel as if a part of their own life story was being acted on for them.

U. Peace Roy Pariat's dramas were mostly enacted by the Khasi Native Club and later by the Panora Club. His Shillong Panora Club lost its hold by the early 1950s.

Some of his contemporaries and club members say Peace Roy Pariat died in 1970, while Prof Lyngdoh dates the death of this great artiste as 1971.

Studies

U. Peace Roy Pariat. U *Kritik*, 1982, 11 (43).

Peace Roy Pariat *see* Pariat, Peace Roy and Introduction

Phankon, Remy

A modern writer and playwright in Khasi, Remy Phankon's bestknown drama is '*U Koidi*' which was published in 1988. The play is in two acts, containing eleven scenes in all. The play is set at the backdrop of the most dreaded Nazi Concentration Camp of Auschwitz, a saga of horror and of man's inhumanity to man. The drama revolves around the story of the heroic deed of Fr. Maximillian Kolbe, an Augustinian priest, who, for pure and Christian love of neighbour, went to the extent of offering himself to take the place of another man who had been condemned to die along with nine other prisoners and Nazi vengeance for the escape of some prisoners on 12th July 1941.

Bah Remy Phankon's play '*U Kiang Nangbah*' written for the *Rympei Theatrical Centre*' in 1982 bagged the best English one-act play in 1985 at the XVIII National Short Play Competition in Allahabad.

The short play '*Sngi Khatduh U Tirot Sing*', written and revised by Kenny Shympa and produced by the Rympei Theatrical Centre in 1980. After Bah Kenny, it was rendered into English by Bah Remy Phankon and represented at the 19th National Short Play Competition in 1986.

Pugh, F.M.

A contemporary of V.G. Bareh, Frank M. Pugh made a mark for himself as an astute translator and playwright. He looked up to the masters of drama like Sophocles, Euripides, Kalidasa, and Shakespeare. But his major contribution lies in his rendition of Shakespeares dramatic verses into Khasi. F.M. Pugh has to his credit '*Ka Dialok* (not drama-proper, written in the form of dialogue; 1960), '*Ka Drama Katha Phi Mon* (translation of '*As Yon Like It*' of Shakespeare; 1960), '*U Romeo bad Ka Juliet* (translation of Shakespeare's '*Romeo and Juliet*, 1968), *Ka Temding ia ka Shla Briew* (translation of '*Taming of the Shrew* by William Shakespeare; 1964), *Ka Shemlanot* (translation of '*Macbeth*'; 1965). The author also broughtout two tragedies on Khasi traditional belief on Incest Tabboo in his dramas *Ka Sawangka ia ki Sawngut* and *Ka Sawangka ia ki Sanngut kiba iap*; both appeared in 1967.

After a series of adopted works, Frank M. Pugh broughtout his original composition in 1967 entitled '*Ka Sawangka ia ki Saw Ngut Ba iap Mynsaw*' and another drama of a similar plot which can be compared to Plato's Republic called Ka sawangka in ki saw ngut ba iap mynsaw and Ka sawangka ki san-ngut ba iap (1967). The former is a traditional drama while the latter a powerful social drama that leaves moral lessons.

Pugh, F.M. *see also* 'Introduction'; 'Ka sawangka ia ki saw ngut ba iap mynsaw' and 'Ka sawangka ki san-ngut ba iap'

Pyrbot, Bah Shaimon *see* Introduction (Jaintia Club)

R

Rapthap, B

Khasi scholar whose unpublished Master's dissertation entitled '*U.D.S. Khongdup Kum u Dramatist*' was presented to the North-Eastern Hill University Shillong, in 1984.

Reade Syiem, E.M.

Modern scholar E.M. Reade Syiem who contributed a significant essay on Khasi drama entitled '*Inadequacy of drama*' to a Symposium on Khasi literature held on May 26-27, 1975. It appeared in print in the volume 'Improved Instruction in Khasi = Ka jingpynroi bad jingpynriewspah ia ka jinghikai ia ka Khasi', broughtout by the North-Eastern Hill University.

Roberts, John

Born on 16th February 1842 at Corris, Meirionethshire, North Wales, John Roberts is reckoned as one of the founders of Khasi literature. Professor R.S. Lyngdoh hails him as the '*Father of Khasi literature*' John lost his father in his teens and penury compelled him to takeup a job in a marble mine, but being a meritorious child, he continued his studies at home. His hard work and intelligence was noticed by the Church leaders and in 1866 he was sent to Bala to study theology which he finished in 1870. In 1871 he was deputed to pursue a condensed course of one year in the Liverpool University. This course was equivalent to Master degree. In September 1871, he came to Sohra and started learning Khasi language. Soon he was posted at Shala in the foothill of the district. In 1876 he tookover as the Headmaster of the English Normal School at Sohra where he taught theology, English and Khasi literature.

Apart from theology, he took keen interest in Khasi literature and experimented with every branch of it be it poetry, fiction, drama, essay or translation. He stands as a great poet and translator in Khasi literature. His poetic out put comprises of translations of seventyseven hymns. He rendered few books of the Bible, when didactic literature was no longer appreciated by the reader, Roberts resorted to translate English poems, besides his own original compositions.

Author of Khasi Second Reader, Khasi Third Reader and Khasi fourth Reader. The last text book was designed for the higher classes which contained his Kasi version of one of the Acts of Shakespeare's '*Julius Caesar*' which set an example for the natives to produce more plays. Sten writes 'The choice of Shakespeare's and not those of any other playwrights was evidence of the esteem in which Roberts held that great English dramatist of the Elizebethan age.

In 1896 this renowned Khasi litterateur went to study at the Ripon University, Wisconsin, USA and was awarded the degree of the Doctor of Divinity. He died on the 23rd July 1908 in the midst of an epidemic cholera which broke out in 1907 while actively helping to save life in and around the Sohra area.

Roy, Dino Nath *see* Introduction

Roy, Hari Charan *see* Introduction

Royal Theatrical Society *see* Synnah, Bah Gilbert

Rympei Theatrical Centre

A leading drama society, it has all the theatre accessories. The Rympei Theatrical Centre has a team of musicians and artists, their performance being well acclaimed. Most of the plays are adaptations to suit the modern situations, the artists being well trained. It has also presented several plays consistently with acting potentiality on themes which have moral significance.

[*see* 'Introduction]

S

Sha Ka Khlemrain *see* Malngiang, Pascal

Shakespeare in Khasi *see under* Jyrwa, B.C.; Jyrwa, Webster Davies; Pugh, F.M.; Roy, Dino Nath etc. and Introduction.

Shangkhawiah Ki Rang

This is the title of the drama in Khasi composed by Bah Peace Roy Pariat. This was staged by the Shillong Panora Club, printed and published by R.J. Khongwir from Shillong in 1979. The play was later revised and rearranged by Prof. Antony Jala and broughtout as second edition by R. J. Khongwir in 1987.

Shangpliang, Syntar John

Renowned Khasi dramatist and academician whose play '*Ka Pop Jongno?*' was played by the St. Anthony's High School in 1982.

Shangpliang's two other wellknown dramas in Khasi are '*Ka Ri Umsnam*' (historical drama; 1971) and '*Ka Khet ne Phalok*' (tragic drama; 1974).

Shaw, George Bernard—Khasi Translations *see* Duncan, S.J.

Shi-har Ki Drama *see* Laloo, D.T., Bah

Shilliang Raid Club *see* Introduction (Jaintia Club)

Shullai Lakhon, Bah *see* Introduction (Jaintia Club)

Shyampa Kenny, Bah

Director, actor, playwright and the founder of the Rympei Theatrical Centre, Bah Kenny Shyampa was born on 24 September 1939 at Laitumkhrah, Arbuthnot Road, Shillong. He was the youngest of the surviving children born to late Bah Willybrodus Shyampa and Kong Moly Diengdoh. kenny lost his mother in his childhood and eventually broughtup by his devoted father.

He made his debut in acting at the age of 5 to 6 years and had received much training in histrionics from Catholic missionaries. Infact he was given training especially in script-writing chiefly by the late Bro. Santino Mantarro SDB, Frs. G. Costa, C. Bili, J. Dieste etc. He received training in stage make-up from Fr. G. Vanni and Bro. V.S. Mathew.

About his acting potentiality, Rolong Kharkong SDB writes : Kenny Shympa was himself an adaptable and agile actor who could play any role. As a comedian he could make the spectators split their sides with laughter. It is reported that on a certain occasion the audience were so convulsed with laughter that some of them inadvertently slipped out of their seats down on to the floor. He was equally effective in serious plays and tragedies; he made people quake with fear, as in *Ka Ngiew*; or shed copious tears, as in *Laingut Shipara*, and in the play *Ka Pla I Nah* he kept them laughing from the beginning to the end. Such were his exceptional histrionic talents."

Apart from his interest in theatre, Bah Kenny was actively involved in politics. He became a member of the '*Swantantra Party*', formed by Raja Gopalachari and was infact, the only one to represent the North-Eastern India for the leadership training camp at Secundrabad in the early 1960s. In the years of struggle for autonomy, Kenny was chosen a volunteer in the non-violent Direct Action sponsored by the APHLC Party in the then composite state of Assam. He even contested the multi-cornered MDC election in 1972 from the Laitumkhrah constituency which he lost by a narrow margin to Shri K.R. Deb.

A great teacher, actor, producer, director and playwright Kenny Shympa died very early at the age of forty-four, on 29th December 1983 at Mookyndeng, Jaintia Hills.

Studies

Kenny Shympa 45th Birth Anniversary Celebration. — Shillong : [s.n.], 1984.

Rympei Theatrical Centre, 1973-82: Souvenir (Shillong); 1982.

[U] Sib

'U Sib' or 'Sib' is a dramatic monologue composed by the eminent Khasi poet Soso Tham. It appeared in 1936 in the volume 'Ka Duitara Ksiar I'. In this monologue the speaker is Sib, a blind man, and the auditors are the people he meets.

In "*U Sib*" Tham makes his speaker reveal himself twice by his own name. Sib sings abut his own lot, profession, health and life. In this poem we see the dramatic effect at each stage of development. Sib, the blind man, wears rags, and moves about from place to place sing and beg. he acknowledges the reward he gets for his songs. We really feel for Sib. He might have tumbled at anything several times while moving from one place to another. He cannot see and enjoy the beauty of nature as we can; he cannot see his own dress though through senses he knows that he wears rags. We pity him that he has to beg when we recall that the Khasis of old never encouraged their relatives to go a-begging. He might not have relatives even to take care of him. The sense of solitude pervades the atmosphere because we hear that he roams about alone. He is no Teiresia to be led by a boy. He is no blinded Gloucester to be led by an old man and a beggar-noble. Sib treads the dreary paths of this world alone!

[U] Sib *see also* Tham, Soso and Introduction (Dramatic monologue)

Sten, H.W.

Prof. H.W. Sten is a reputed academician, playwright and author in Khasi. His coming on the dramatic scene is significant because of the fact that he has solid theoretical know-how of playwrighting and of writing for the stage. Sten's tragic drama '*Ka Mahadevi*' appeared in 1983.

Synnah Gilbert, Bah

Bah Gilbert Synnah was the brain behind the formation of the Royal Theatrical Society that tookup both traditional and non-traditional plays in Khasi.

T

Tham, Soso

One of the most influential poets in Khasi, Soso Tham was born at Sohra in 1873. He had his early education at Nongsawlia, an important station of the Welsh Presbyterian Mission in the Khasi Hills. He came to Shillong about 1889 and 1890 and read upto the seventh class only. Since then he had to move from place to place as school teacher till 1893 when he was appointed head masters of the erstwhile upper primary school at Shangpung in the Jaintia Hills. About 1903 he left the job and began practice as a petty lawyer in the court of the sub-divisional officer at Jowai, then a sub-division of the Khasi and Jaintia Hills disrict. He was appointed teacher in the Shillong Government High School in 1905 by the Chief Commissioner of Assam and joined the post on the 15th October that year He retired from service on the 30th June 1931. A Christian by birth, Soso Tham belonged to the Presbyterian Church and contributed to its glory in various ways. He was an active member of the Church, and of the erstwhile Christian Volunteer Movement which sought to project Christian virtues through its organ : *U Lurshai*. Though a presbyter for the best part of his life, he became a member of the Anglican Church in his last days.

In his academic career he felt the dearth of reading materials in the Khasi language. Later he contributed immensely to the Khasi language and literature through his translations and poetic creations. A modern Khasi poet of the early twentieth century, Soso tham is accepted as a poet who is very polished and poetic. A cultural revivalist through his writings, he made Khasi people self-aware. In one of his poems, he has devoted to the Khasi way of life. He was well aware of the genius of Khasi race and often sounded a clarion call to the people to be true to themselves and their distinct cultural heritage.

A poetic genius and an astute translator, his early poems appeared in 1925. He understood human life and reflected on those through his poetry. The socio-political life of the ancient Khasi was his central concern in many poems. He touched on the problems of human sufferings also. Even he is happened to be the first Khasi poet to sing of erotic love with deep understanding Soso Tham has laid down the basis of modern poetry in Khasi language. Soso Tham's literary corpus comprises of fifty three poems which he published in two volumes. In his poem 'Ki Sngi U Hynniew Trep' (The Days of the Seven Huts) narrates a story in the Bardic tradition. From the years 1913-1940, imagination was allowed free play in poetic creation and Romantic melancholy found expression in the poetry of Soso Tham.

This eminent Khasi poet wrote a dramatic monologues entitled '*U Sib*' appeared in print in 1936 and U Dieng Bilat High School, published in the same year.

His son Primrose Gatphoh is also acknowledged as a poet of great merit. Tham died on 18th December 1940.

Tham, Soso *see also* Dieng Bilat High School and 'Sib'

Thangkhiew, Bronath

Bronath Thangkhiew, who made a mark as a poet first started writing in the Khasi monthy 'U Lurshai'. In 1936 he broughtout his collection of fifty seven poems entitled 'Ka' Tienrwai Khasi (Khasi Poetry). Here we find a dramatic monologue '*U Nongtem Duitara*' or '*The Harpist*' which contains 504 lines and this is probably the longest monologue published so far which is itself a series of monologues most of which aim at reviving the traditional values. The speaker in the poem is the mouthpiece of the poet. Viewed the monologue this way, Sten comes to the conclusion that Bronath Thangkhiew is a rivivalist, a patriot, and a social critic who longs to see that people of all walks of life live circumspectly upholding all what they claim to be their own. Thankhiew's *Tienrwai* (1936) contains lyric verses and nature songs. His poems are an appreciation of beauty of nature in its diverse images adored as the animate beings. Thangkiew ranks as a satirist; his satires against drunkenress, the loose society and other vices which have crept in are parabolical themes set in verbose and redundant expressions.

Thangkhiew, Bronath *see also* U Nongtem Duitara

Theatre: art and life

This book by Roland Kharkang SDB that appeared in print in 1994 from Omsons Publications, New Delhi is a significant book that explores the beginning and growth of the Khasi theatre to its present day. The cultural experience, the Indian context of colonial rule and struggle for freedom, and the local factors and talents conspired to give a specific face to this universal and vital medium of human expression. It attempts at tracing Khasi theatre to its origin, the development of Khasi Theatre, classification of Khasi dramas, Jaintia Clubs, latest trends and bringing forth the cause of its tardy growth.

[U] Tirot Singh

This play of Victor G. Bareh depicts the Anglo-Khasi war which started in 1829 and lasted till 1833. Victor's '*U Tirot Singh*' is based on the life of the Khasi hero who made a desperate bid to drive out the British from the Khasi Hills but was captured and sent to Dacca as an exile there to die. In those days, it was impossible for a people, divided as they were, to offer any serious opposition to British troops, and in January 1833 the last of the important syiem (syiem of the Nongkhlaw state) tendered his submission. In this play, the playwright use his imagination so much that he present Tirot Singh as a symbol of patriotism rather than a concrete historial personality.

Noted dramatist and translator, F.M. Pugh while reviewing the play 'U Tirot Singh' said "the plot construction is unified, the background is characteristic of the Khasi atmosphere more particularly of the war-like people in Khadsawphra area... Though the heroic character of U Tirot Singh dominates... The drama, the minor characters of Ka Phan Nonglait and U Kohlehnoh will not be easily forgotten as life-like portraits of rural Khasi life- the tone of the drama is patriotic."

V

Vanni, George

George Vanni was a renowned theatre actor, director, manager, make-up man, singer, painter, cartoonist, who was one of the Salesians of Don Bosco (SDB) who made substantial contributions to Khasi dramatic activities. A contemporary of Fr. Giulius Costa, another missionary and gifted theatre director, Fr. G. Vanni came to India in 1950 and associated himself actively with Catholic theatrical activities in Shillong. Kenny Shympa the founder of the Rympei Theatrical Centre received his training from Fr. Vanni, who was amply gifted with histrionics. Fr. Vanni took over from where Fr. Costa left.

W

Wahlang, O.M.

A modern scholar and writer in Khasi, O.M. Wahlang has written a book entitled '*Ka Sur Pangnud Ka Kmie*' which is not a drama-proper. This border-line work written in the form of dialogue, a tragedy on the folklore of *U Sier Lapalang* was published in 1968.

Winkler, Herribert, Fr. *see* Introduction

Reference

Bareh, Hamlet. A short history of Khasi literature 3rd rev. ed. — Shillong : [Khasi Press], 1979, 179p.

First published in 1962.

2nd ed. published in 1969.

Kharkang, Roland. Theatre: art and life. — New Delhi: Omsons Publications, 1994.

Sten, H.W. Khasi poetry: critic and development. — New Delhi: Mittal Publications, 1990.

IV

KHORTHA

Khortha — Modern Dramas

Khortha is one of the major tribal languages, mainly spoken in the state of Jharkhand by the Kortha community. Kortha have a favourable attitude towards creative activities. They strive to cultivate creative literature. There is a literary achievements not only to the extent of discussing novels novellas and stories, though not enough, there is something to talk about the genre like drama. It is true that not as much is being done in this field. But towards the close of the twentieth century drama has shown considerable growth. One of the leading playwrights of Khortha is Srinivas Panuri whose chief work is '*Udbhāsal Karna*', put on boards several times in Dhanbad region. Since 1980-85, the manuscript of this drama is preserved in Ranchi University. Panuri's another praiseworthy work is '*Chabi kāṭhi*', an unpublished drama being chosen for academic study.

Many one-act plays have been published in several Khortha journals like 'Matribhasa, Titakī', 'Luāṭhī', 'Injor' etc. Very few dramas have so far been appeared as independent volume, namely, A.K. Jha's '*Mekameki ne metmat*'; Sukumar's 'Dāh' (1992) and Viswanath Dasaundhi 'Raj's '*Ajgar*'.

The play '*Mekameki ne metmāt*' (by A.K. Jha) comprises of four acts. In all it has 17 small scenes which highlight the exploitations and suppression of peasantry during the British Raj.

Sukumar's '*Dāh*' is a social drama in three acts with twelve scenes, set in the rural milieu, it depicts family relations, hatred crookedness, jealousy etc. of the village folks that results in the conflict between brothers and at the close of the drama, end the revelation of the causes of confliction.

A revolutionary social drama written in recent times is '*Ajgar*', penned by Viswanath Dasaundhi. The play is in three acts with sixteen scenes. '*Ajgar*' deals with a number of social issues like women's emancipation, casteism, superstition, sufferings and suppression of the poor people by the antagonistic characters like village moneylenders, police officer, temple priest etc. The play was broughtout in 2004 by the Balidih Khortha Samiti, Bokaro, Jharkhand.

'*Parāsachit*' (Penance) is a highly acclaimed drama of Manpuran Goswami, appeared in print in 2006 from Balidih Khortha Samiti, Bokaro, Jharkhand.

This thought provoking play that revolves around the prevalent Brahminical penitentiary run or by the upper caste Hindus. Presented in nine scenes, this is a path breaking play vividly shows the exploitations of the poor masses by the religious leaders in the name of penace and at the same time challenges the norms set forth by the Brahminical orthodoxy.

समीक्षा अखड़ा

ब्राह्मणवादी विचारधारा को चुनौती देता - परासचित

▸▸ अर्चना कुमारी

परासचित
(खोरठा नाटक)
लेखक:
मनपूरन गोस्वामी
प्रकाशक:
बालीडीह खोरठा समिति
बोकारो (झारखण्ड)
मूल्य - 25/- रुपये

खोरठा में नाटक की लम्बी परम्परा रही है। श्री निवास पानुरी की 'उद्बासल कर्न', 'चाभी काठी', एके झा की 'मेकामेकी ना भेट भट', श्री विश्वनाथ दसौंधी 'राज' का 'अजगर' और सुकुमार की 'डाह' का खोरठा नाट्य साहित्य में विशिष्ट स्थान है।

इसी परंपरा को और सुदृढ़ व समृद्ध करता है मनपूरन गोस्वामी का खोरठा नाटक 'परासचित'। नौ दृश्यों वाले इस नाटक में धर्मगुरुओं के शोषण को कथ्य बनाया गया है। 'परासचित' अर्थात् प्रायश्चित का मतलब दण्ड, वैसा दण्ड जिसका निर्धारण पंडित ही करते हैं और उसका समाधान भी पंडित ही बताता है। इसमें और किसी का भला होता हो या नहीं पंडित का हित जरूर सधता है। साथ ही पंडित के दोष का कोई प्रायश्चित नहीं होता है। इस नाटक में अंधविश्वास से लोगों को सजग करते हुए पंडितों के दोष का किस प्रकार प्रायश्चित किया जाए इसका भी संकेत किया गया है।

इस विज्ञान के युग में जहां मीडिया सत्ता और पूंजीपतियों के पक्ष में धर्मगुरुओं को महिमामंडित कर लोगों को भ्रमित कर रहा है, वैसे समय में 'परासचित' जैसे नाटक का प्रकाशन महत्वपूर्ण तो है ही, इसे गांव-गांव दिखाने की आवश्यकता भी है।

संपर्क: जनजातीय एवं क्षेत्रीय भाषा विभाग, रांची कॉलेज, मोरहाबादी, रांची (झारखण्ड)

Review of a Khortha play composed by a contemporary writer

V

KOKBOROK

The modern state of Tripura lies to the south-west of Assam, and to the east of Bangladesh. In this land-locked state, four-fifth of its land frontiers are enclosed by the Bangladesh district of Sylhet in the north, Comilla in the west, Noakhali and Chittagong in the south and the hill tracts of Chittagong in the south-east. It is only in its north-eastern border them Tripura meets the states of Assam and Mizoram. Here Bengali Hindus constitute the major group and out of the 18 tribal communities the Tipras constitute the largest tribe. Others are Riang, Jamatia, Chakma, Halam, Noatia, Mag, Kuki, Garo, Lushai, Uchai, Khasia etc. Rest are insignificant, socialy isolated six alocithonous tribes namely Munda, Oraon, Santal, Bhil, Lepcha and Bhutia.

Linguistic diversity is the foundation of the cultural edifica of India. Approximately 200 languages are enumerated in the Census and over 1,600 mother tongues being reported. The languages of India historically belong to four major languages families viz, Indo-European, Dravidian, Munda (Austro-Asiatic) and Sino-Tibetan has Tibeto-Burman. The largest number of languages (98) are in Tibeto-Burman category.

To this class belongs the not so well projected Kokborok language. Of the total tribal population of Tripura, the Kok-borok speaking tribal communities occupy majority. Out of nineteen tribal communities eight communities vic. Tripuri, Reang, Noatia, Jamatia, Rupini, Kolai, Uchai and Murasing speak in Kok-Borok, a population presumed to be more and less seven lakhs.

Besides, about one and half lakh of Kok-Borok speaking people are inhabiting in Chandpur, Kumilla, Chitgong etc., areas of Bangladesh.

It is a known to all of us the tribal culture of Tripura in general is very rich in a variety of folk literature, tales, folk music, songs and dances of the tribes which are of composite nature form great part of human culture. The Jhum song and Jhum dance find an important place among the largest Tripuri tribe. G.K. Ghosh observes 'Since the Tipperah tribe believed to have migrated from Chin hills or Arakan forests, it is but natural they have certain affinity with Lushi-Chin-Thadou group of tribes. Inspite of several changes, certain influences remains. This is particularly true in case of musical instruments. Their gongs resembling those of Burma are similar to those of Thadous or Lushais. They also use a single reed fiddle like Bengal's ektara while dancing, and many the group use such fiddle having different notations. The main musical instrument however is a very special one. In sound it gives a sound somewhere between an organ and a bagpipe. It is made from a gourd, into which long reed pipes of different lengths are inserted which have one hole stop." This author further adds 'Tipperah dances are really wonderful. Men only take part in the dance, the women being shy before a stranger. The dancers stand in a circle, Iurring alternately to right and to left in unison and at certain periods in the rhythm of the music. The music is punctuated by the dancers by bending their knees, and at the end of the movement take a sharp jerky pause".

Folk culture, the genres of literaure, music, dance would give us many dazzles. But when we venture to study the state of literary and performing arts in modern phases, nurtured by the inhabiting tribes, we find that there are several dialects spoken by the tribals of this region. Among them, however, '*Kok-Borok*' should deserve special mention which is an admixture of mainly the original Thipuri dialect with some usage of Assamese and Bengalee vocabulary. As said earlier, it is Tibeto-Burman in origin with a mixture of some non-Mongoloid elements.

Here Bengalee is the most frequently used by the urban people, but Kok-Borok runs also as a medium of instruction among a few tribal people and has also been recognized as one of the official languages of Tripura. But for this, Kok-Borok speakings people had to make a long journey. This language remain in spoken form for thousands years and came into written from only 100 years ago in 1900 A.D. Thakur Radha Mohan Dev Barman wrote the first Grammar of Kok-Borok named 'Kok-Borokma' appeared in print from Chaitanya Press in Commilla (Now in Bangladesh) in the year 1310 T.E. ie, 1900 A.D. It was later re-published by the Education Directorate in 1959. He wrote two other books entitled 'Traipur Kothamala' and 'Traipur Bhasabidhan' published in 1906 and 1907 respectively.

A contemporary of Radhamohan was Daulot Ahmed, a pioneer in writing of Kok-Borok Grammar. His writings comprise of about 25 books.

After the works of these two stalwarts, there had been stoppage for about 40 years. In the year 1942-43, a compilation of 33 spiritual songs by saint Khusi Krishna, a disciple of Saint Ratanmani was broughtout under the title 'Tripura Kha- Khachangma Khumbar Boi.' The Kok-Borok literary work was restarted with this publication.

At this juncture some newly educated Tripuri boys formed an organisation called '*Jana Siksha Samiti*' to spread education amongst the illiterate tribal population. It came into being in On 27th December 1945 (11th paus of 1352 B.E.) at Durga Choudhury Para, under Jiranih Block.

The movement of the *Janasiksha Samiti* was speedily transformed into a mass movement. It succeeded in establishing 488 primary schools, which created a tremendous enthusiasm among the tribal people.

At this time people like Sudhanva Deb Barma, Dasarath Deb, Mahendra Deb Barma, Jogendra Deb Barma and many more started writing in Kokborok.

The first Kok-Borok Magazine 'Kwtal Kothoma' was first edited and published in 1954 by Sudanva Deb Barma.

In fact, scheme of spreading education in the tribal society was taken up in fifties, and as a result, some educated tribal youths emerged from this society in the later part of sixties. those educated tribal youths started nationalist movement. They were gradually becoming conscious not only about their political rights, but also about their socio-cultural affairs, and rich heritage. In consequence of their awareness for social obligation, there had been speedy flow in Kokborok literary movement and since eightees, the Kokborok was on the way to be recognised as a developing language and literature. A well organised political party came up and fought in the fifth election of the state in 1972 'Tripura Upajati Juva Samiti' (TUJS) did not want to remain under the flag of either Communist or the Congress, both being parties of the Bengalis. Their second slogan clearly asserted the promotion of 'Kokborok language'. The party wanted to strengthen the inter-tribal communications in consolidating the different tribes into a single cohesive nationality, in the establishment of Kokborok schools, in the growing identification of the people with the Kokborok language. The cultural sub-nationalism in one way contributed to the political intergration and creation of a new elite, attempting to unify the tribals politically and culturally.

The tendencies were at work to erect the community as an entity distinct from the plain people. Though mass education and promotion of its own languages, arts, crafts and literature. The rich literary and cultural heritage which are gradually eroding due to influence of Bengali culture. The people speaking 'Kokborok' are doing splendid job. They have started making efforts to stop this erosion. Contemporary writers, poets, playwright, and performers are engaged in their creative exercises in Kok-borok.

It would not be out of context here to add that Kokborok, a unknown language from a unknown region is gradually gaining national attention today. Sahitya Akademi, India's National Academy of Letters, the central institute for literature has been giving annual awards to books of outstanding merit and annual prizes for outstanding translations in the 22 languages recognised by it. However, the Akademi soon realised that in a multilingual country like India that has hundred of languages and dialects, Akademi's activities should be 'extended beyond the recognized one by acknowledging and promoting literary creativity as well as academic research in non-recognised languages. The Sahitya Akademi, eventually, instituted 'Bhasa Samman' in the year 1996 to be conferred on writers, scholars, editors, collectors, performers or translators who have done considerable works in the languages like Kokborok, Garo, Mizo, etc.

This language could survive as a common language of the tribal communities of Tripura. But it had suffered neglect for centuries. However, it is now on the march of development to attain a language of literature. Therefore, it deserves a language of lively amplitude and distinctive originality. Here emerged Sudan Deb Burma, the harbinger of a definite modern sensibility in Kokborok literature and performing arts.

Sudhanva Deb Barman

Sudhanva Deb Burman made a pioneering contribution to the development of Kokborok language and literature, though his writings Kokborok became a perfect vehicle of creative expression. Sudhanva Dev Barman the Recipient of the much coveted 'Rabindra Puraskar, his novel 'Hachuk khurio' (Paharer Koley in Bengali) is the first novel in the Kokborok language that opened the path for modern literature in Kokborok to flourish.

Sudhanva Debbarma's 'Hachuk Kharia' in four parts was translated into Bengali in a cumulative volume under the title 'Pāhārer Koley', rendered by Kumud Kundu Chaudhuri, Nareshchandra Debbarma, and Manoj Debbarma, appeared from Akshar Publications, Tripura.

He was the pioneer of modern Kokborok literature, a multifaceted personality, a novelist, playwright, poet and journalist. In the domain of drama his first work '*Himdida*' — Egiyey chalo (Move ahead) a bilingual play written both in Kokborok and Bengali. The play is based on the Golaghati peasant uprising composed in 1948, when the playwright was leading an underground life, a founder member of 'Tripura Sana Shakti Siksha Samiti' (1945). The play led to the formation of 'Ganamukti Parishad (GMP) (1948) which fought against royal forces and the evil designs of the Congress Party which later fused into the Communist Party of India. The play was widely staged in the rural areas of Tripura.

His second play is the full length '*Parikshit Vidroha*' comprising of five acts which he composed in Hazaribag Prison cell. The play depicts the Jamātia tribes fight against the monarchic rule of Tripura led by Parikshit Jamatia set against the background of the mid-nineteenth century revolt. The play is available today in manuscript form and kept in the custody of Sri Sudhirranjan Majumdar the Principal of the Agartala Sakhicharan High School. Written in the Jatrastyle, the play was produced several nights by the Jamatias.

During the Tagore centenary in 1961, a committee was set up for Kokborok comprising of Sri Jiten Tagore, Jitendra Deb Barman (Advisor), Ajitbandhu Deb Barman and the playwright himself. On the occasion, he rendered the play '*Visarjan*' of Tagore into Kokborok in blank verse, a highly praised renderation.

Alindralal Tripura

Founder of the 'Kok-Borok Sahity Sabha', Sri Alindralal Tripura, a renowned scholar and creative writer in Kok-borok devoted his whole life for the cause of Kokborok development and creation of Kokborok literature. He started experiments at different angles on this language. He even invented separate scripts claimed to be fit for the Kokborok. But, usage of this invented scripts, was considered unsuitable under the present condition and circumstances. He contributed cepiously in various literary magazines and newspapers.

Alindralal's drama in Kokborok '*Lamani Homchang*' (Path finding torch) was performed in the Rabindra Satabarshiki Bhavan in 1972.

Shymalal Deb Barma

A wellknown writer in Kokborok, Sri Shymalal Deb Barma broughtout an one-act play in book form entitled '*Sitwtwi Siatwtwi*' in January 1984 by Yakhili Publications, Tripura.

Chandra Kanta Murasingh

Chandra Kanta Murasingh was born on 1 April 1957 in Taibanda, Tripara District (West). He is a poet of high order, he was nominated 'Best Poet—1996' by the Tripura Tribal Area Autonomous District Council. The Sahitya Akademi, New Delhi's first Bhasa Samman were awarded in 1996. One of its recpients was Sri Chandra Kanta Mura Singh for Kokborok. He has also been bestowed with 'Mahendra Debbarma Smriti Puraskar' in 1996. His two well known volumes of poetry are Haping Garingo Chibuksa Ringo (1987) and Holong Kok Sao Bolong Bisingo (1995). Chandra Kanta Murasingh has also composed a number of dramatic pieces in Kokborok. His collection of one-act plays entitled '*Risum Khikrok*' was published in 1995. He is actively associated with various cultural organisations like Tripura State Kala Akademy, Agartala, a member of the Cultural Advisory Committee, Government of Tripura and also Executive Board Member of the Eastern Zone Cultural Centre, Kolkata. Presently he is the Secretary of the Kokborok Sahitya Akademi, which is located at New Model Village, Abhoynagar-799005, Tripura.

Kokborok Sahitya Sansad

After the demise of Kokborok Sahitya Sanskriti Sansad, its members formed another forum '*Kokborok Sahitya Sansad*' published few wellknown works in Kokborok such as 'Hachuk Khuria (3rd Volume) by Sudhanva Debbarma, Chittaranjan Jamatia's drama' Khelang Bubās *Kherengbār*', Sudhanya Tripura's '*Kamikautāl*' etc.

Tripura Rajya Kokborok Sahitya Sabha

This is a literary and cultural forum for the Kokborok intellectuals to share their experiences in the various genre of literature and allied arts. On occasions it has sponsored Kokborok plays and dance-dramas which were staged in Agartala and other hilly areas successfully.

Radio Drama

Akashvani considered the dramatic presentations an important components of radio entertainment programmes and eventually Kokborok playwrights realizing its potential, started writing radio dramas which made a significant impact on Kokborok people. On every Sunday, All India Radio, Agartala telecast one play in Kokborok and so far it has produced over 25 plays in the language. Radio has thus, played a pivotal role in the furthernance of Kokborok theatre.

Reference

Choudhury, Kamal Narayan. Tribal Culture of the North East. — Kolkata : Punthi Pustak, 2003.

Ghosh, G.K. Tribals and their culture (Vol. 2). New Delhi: Ashish Publishing House, 1992.

Kunduchandhuri, Kumud. Kokborok bhasa o sahitya. — Krishna Nagar: Akshar Publications, 1999.

In Bengali.

Yakpai: seminar on 'In search of relationship among the Borok (Bodo) people held at Sukanta Academy, Agartala, Tripura, India, 2nd & 3rd Taltuk, 1410 T.E., 24th & 25th July, 2000.

VI

LEPCHA

Sikkim lies in the heart of the towering Eastern Himalayas and is bounded by Nepal in the west, Bhutan in the South east Tibet in the north and northeast and the district of Darjeeling, West Bengal in the South. Sikkim is comprised of three principal ethnic communities of the Bhutias, the Lepcha's and the Nepalese.

Lepcha belong to the Himalayan group of Tibeto-Burman subfamily. It occupies a place in the non-pronominalised sub-group of its speeches. Later, however, attempts were made to classify Lepcha with Tengsa of the Naga group of languages. This position, however, needs further confirmation after a suitable study of Naga classification. Not withstanding the strong surrounding influences of either the Indo-Aryan Nepali or the Tibeto-Chinese, Sikkim Bhutia, the Lepcha have preserved their speech surprisingly intact. Various investigations have shown that almost every Lepcha as a bilingual, he has preserved his language without much interference from foreign tongues.

Lepcha speakers are mainly concentrated in Sikkim Lepcha language is recognised as one of the ten official languages of the State of Sikkim. At present, they are recognised as Scheduled Tribes in the States of West Bengal and Sikkim.

Thus the other state having major Lepcha population is West Bengal. At the district level in West Bengal significant number of Lepcha speakers are found in Darjeeling and Jalpaiguri.

Besides the State of Sikkim, Darjeeling District of West Bengal, the Lepchas are residing in the eastern part of Nepal (Illam), Western part of Bhutan (Chamurchi). This political spread over the three countries (India, Nepal, Bhutan) can no way be explained with the migratory characters of the community. It is mainly due to the resuffling of the political power of these three different countries over the Lepcha homeland during the last four hunderd years. Lepchas did not enter Sikkim from across the Himalayan or from Tibet, and are supposed to have come from the East along the foot hills from the direction of Assam and Upper Burma. They are the aboriginal inhabitants of Sikkim and the language they use is Lepcha. The next race to enter Sikkim were the Bhutias who are of Tibetan origin and who spread at the same time into Bhutan. The dominance of the Bhutias was so overwhelming that the Lepchas remained the poorest and the most neglected of the people, barring a few who intermarried with the Bhutia elite to reach the level of equality. The first phase of Sikkim's history is linked to the "blood treaty" signed between the Bhutias and Lepchas in 1641 recognising the leader of the invaders as the spiritual and secular head. The Lepchas were converted to the Lamaist Buddhism of the Tibetans. When the British came to Sikkim, in the late eighteenth century, their missionaries converted a few of them to Christianity.

The advant of the eighteenth century saw an aggressive Nepal encroaching on the Sikkimese territory and by 1970 it established its strong hold over the land. However, Nepal's occupation of Sikkim came to an end in 1812, when the British troops of the East India Company intervened and defeated the Nepalese forces. But, the Nepalese settlers stayed back. The entire ethnic scene changed by 1947 when the British left India and India became independent. The Nepalese constituted seventy-five percent of Sikkim's population reducing the Lepchas to fourteen percent and the Bhutia community to eleven percent.

The early history of Sikkim therefore, begins in the thirteenth century with the signing of a brotherhood treaty between the Lepcha Chief Thekong-Thek and Tibetan prince Khe-Bhumsa at Kavi in north Sikkim, and moves on to the historical visit of revered saints to Yuksam in 1641 in West Sikkim and to the beginning of the Namgyal dynasty in Sikkim in 1642. With the march of history events in Sikkim saw the former princely state in the Eastern Himalayas as a state pass democracy and became an integral part of the Indian Union with the constitutional Amendment Bill passed on April 23, 1975.

General G.B. Mainwaring a colonel in the British army, first drew the eyes of the West to these unique aborigines in the nineteenth century. The redoubtable Dr. Joseph Hooker had also mentioned about the beauty of their music and mind in his famous journal. Surprisingly, such endowments have not endeared Rongs to a succession of peoples, who have mercilessly trodden their rights and culture from age to age. Despite their gift of expression and other cultural attainment, they are still known by the disparaging term 'Lepcha' (in plain English, stupid) first used about them by Nepalis. A tide of Nepali chauvnism had broken on the hills in the 1980s with a force as never before. Consequently, the position of Rongs and other hill tribes is now under real threat. At no point of time, they were made the part of the Bengali life and Rongs were left undisturbed to pursue their own way of life. But the situation has changed, as one of the hill races has became too predominant. A modern scholar points out that the way Reangs are under threat from Jamatias in Tripura, Rongs are from Nepalis in Sikkim and Darjeeling.

A gifted ancient race Rongs (Lepchas) are a most extra-ordinary, though little known Indian tribe. Lepcha culture is enriched with myths, legends, folklores, folktales, and folksongs. All these are nature based. Culturally Lepchas are related with the natural objects of the region, sentimentally attached with all the peaks, traces, rivers and worship them as God, Goddess. They consider Kanchenjunga as the divine peak from where they originated.

One of the major festivals of Lepchas is 'Sakyoo Rum Faat' in which prayers are offered to the eight immortal Lepcha couples of legendary '*Mayel Kyong*', a hidden paradise, Sangrila. It normally takes place during the Lepcha month of '*Maar Lavo*', before the commencement of Lepcha New Year, '*Naam Bun*' or '*Naam Aal*' in Lepcha. The Lepchas believe that there eight Lepcha immortal couples give them cereals, fruits seed to plant and it is also predicted that these eight immortal couples will come to the Lepchas rescue and save them from the major natural or man-made catastrophic disaster in the world. *Sakyoo Rum Faat* is also a thanks giving ceremony and offering to Mother Nature and God for fertility, good health, fortune and prosperity. '*Chu Rum Faat*' is another celebration in the form of offering and prayers to the Himalayas, their Creator which takes place when fresh snow fall in the Himalayan mountains, peaks is being experienced. They appeal to the deity to protect the Lepchas from evil, trouble, sickness, illness, misfortune etc.

There two festivals are traditional, customary, long-established, time-honowred cultural heritage, if they are to survive as the indigenous Lepchas in this world.

A documentary film was made by Sri Bappa Ray for the Anthropological Survey of India, Department of Culture, Government of India. It was filmed at Lyang Sa, a remote village in Kalimpong, on 7 December 2004, arranged by the Indigenous Lepcha Tribal Association. The film looks at the Lepcha life alongwith their relations to the supernatural and myth around their environment in '*Mayel Lyang*'. It depicts Lepcha life in a typical traditional Lepcha village environment with old and young couples and children. Lepcha songs and dances in ovation to the '*Mayel Kyong*', Himalayas, and their deity, Kingtshoomjaongboo, ie, Mt. Kanchenjanga were also filmed.

For this Tibeto-Burman language, Roman as well as Lepcha scripts are used for writing. The Lepchas have their own Rong or Lepcha language (Rong Ke or Rongring) and the script is different from that of Tibetan, though it is a branch of the Tibetan, language. 'Rong' means Lepcha and their language is known as 'ring' or 'aring', so the word is 'Rongring'.

The lepchas' love for music and dance is well-known. Music occupies a high place in the Lepcha social life. About the genesis of music, there is a myth prevalent in the Lepcha society. It goes like this:- "One day, Narok, their god of music, came down to *mayellyang* with his divine troupe and chances upon a group of people singing, dancing and playing musical instruments in a village. Narok was intrigued to see their rapture and total involvement in the dancing spree. The sight of the dancing Rong women must also have been too tempting for him and his companions. What they did was that they quietly joined the dancers. After the dance and the music were over, Narok introduced himself to the group of people and asked them to seek a boon. The awe-struck Rongs could ask for the most unusual: the elegant feather crowns adorning his and his companions' heads. The god of celestial music must have been taken aback by this demand, but he gave them these and also gave eleven musical instruments, and then disappeared towards the Narip hill. Before disappearance he told them that whenever he would be tired of catering to the whims of the wealthy gods in heaven, he would come and visit them and take part in their music and dance.

Rongs, since then, were feather crowns — as proudly as royal crowns — while taking part in a dance. They call them *yatpok*, i.e. crown coronated. These are so sacred that if anybody's crown falls from his head while dancing, this will be considered as very bad omen."

Vam is the Rong word from songs which are of four types: love songs (lenchyo vam), comic songs (than-ung-sa vam), Songs of mourning (as yot vam) and ceremonial songs (rumkat vam). In addition, there are songs on the theme of agriculture, war, marriage etc. They have nine sats or ragas, which they have evolved and classified from the sound produced by birds, such as humming bird, Ledge-sparrows and so on. Some vams are also sung with mouth shut and some in nasal tone. As it is evident from the names of these musical modes, the places also have a significant role in their classifications and nomenclature. Renzongsat, Ilamsat, Damasangsat and Tangsangsat belongs to this category. The remaining ragas are Hit, Pildong, Tashekayanto, Pik and Palik.

The genius of the Rong music lies more in its melody than in any combined orchestral effect. Yet they have inheritaged many musical instruments, varied and exotic. The simplest of them is palit keng (flute) which is similar to the type used in other parts of India. Joseph Hooker, a traveller and botanist who reached this land in the middle of the nineteenth century mentions about it. Another occidentalist, Gerer through it to be a solitary divension of Rongs unaccompanied by any vocal rendering. Pantong palit is a big pipe and nibrok palit a twin one, while satsang resembles a sarangi used in other parts of the country. They also make use of tangdar or a small drum and tangdarbong, a still smaller drum, from Narok. These are beaten with a pudgy, hooked handle. A tiny whistle-like instrument called nampathyut and a mouth organ, tangdyu. In a full-fledged musical, chakpanjar (bir trumpet) and banga (round drum), enjoying obviously a borrowed existence—are necessary to produce desired effects.

Shri Tapan Chattopadhy is a senior member of the IPS came to know about Rongs in 1972 in Northern Bengal. In Kalimpong, he witnessed a specially organised opera in which many of these instruments were used.

The Rong's musical practices appear to have undergone a metamorphosis. Playing the bamboo flutes is no longer a solitary direction, but it is necessary to accompany songs with other instruments during feasts and social functions and in operas and plays.

Their singing style and musical instrumentation are primeval and have generally withstood outside influences and maintained their inmate purity and 'tribal character'.

The Rong's songs and dances are the spontaneous outpourings of their emotions—sometimes sorrowful, often sombre, but mostly joyous. There is no fixed time for the expression of these emotions in dances, but occurs usually after harvests and during socio-religious festivities like marriage, the new-year's day, birth of a child, death etc.

The Rong lok or dances falls under six heads such as nature dance, agricultural dance (zonal lok), war dance (fen lok), historical dance (Pasya lyon-guru-tak), mystic Yaba dance and mythological dance. They have preserved the variety of forms and shunned the common tendency to adhere to a few accepted, almost ritualised forms of singing and dance. They dance the *Kagey* in religious festivals and for the Pang-Lhabsol as a seasonal dance. Songs sung at feasts and marriages use percussion, wind and string instruments. Both sexes sing folk songs, and join in the dance. They have their folklore and folktales. Now if we look into the present situation, what we witness today in the perpetual struggle of this ethnic group to survive. In the last fourty years or so, the modern practitioners of art and literature are making all possible efforts to uphold the culture of the Lephas.

Many literary and art societies have come up to preserve and spread their rich folk literature and other cultural heritages. Various Institution organise regular cultural activities in the region. The people are now participate in both folk and modern dance drama and musical performances.

Modern scholars, academicians, artists are making impressive contribution to Lepcha language, literature and performing arts and crafts.

For instance, in the field of literature the highest litrary organisation, ie, the Sahitya Akademi (The National Academy of Letters) at New Delhi honoured Sri Passang Tsherig Lepha, a noted poet and essayist with the Bhasa Samman' in 2000. He is considered the doyen of Lepcha language and literature. His 'national Song' on Lepcha heritage is sung through out the Lepcha world. Passang Tshering has broughtout twenty books in Lepcha, comprising of folk tales, folk history, details of rituals and songs for all occasions. He was also awarded by the Cultural Research Institte, Govt. of West Bengal with the '*Gunjal Award*'.

Sonam Tshering Lepcha was honoured in 1995 by the Sangeet Natak Akademi, New Delhi for folk music.

Rang Pratibha is one of a series of festivals devoted to modern theatre which is being organised by the Sangeet Natak Akademi (The National Academy of Music, Dance & Drama), New Delhi, since 2004.

It focuses on new directorial talent in the modern theatre. The purpose of the Rang Pratibha is, therefore, to identify new talent and to promote the work of theatre direction of a new generation. In the sixth event of this festival, Between 27 and 30 July 2005, plays were produced by young directors of Sikkim at Gangtok. The festival was organised by the Akademi in collaboration with the Cultural Affairs and Heritage Department of the Government of Sikkim, under whose charge the cultural Affairs and Heritage Department falls.

Six theatre directors were selected to present their plays in each evening. The mornings were devoted to free-ranging discussions between the participating theatre workers and the observers of the festival deputed by the Akademi. A photograph of the interaction session in the following pages.

The Delhi based playwright and critic Sri Reoti Saran Sharma and the Kannada actress and director Srimati B. Jayashree were the observers interacting with the directors and other participating theatre artists. Apart from participants in the festival, a number of local theatre artists, critics, as well as theatre enthusiasts in general took part in these interactions.

On the occasion, the plays '*Rakh Baje*', penned and directed by Ranjit Singh and '*Natural Disaster*', written and directed by Kamal Dakal were presented on the first day, ie, on 27th July 2005. On the second day, T.S. Subedi put up the drama '*Ajaka Yuva*', authored by Yadav Sunam. Laxmi Prasad Guragai produced the drama '*Balan*' on 29th July 2005. A stage adaptation of Kurosawa's film '*Rashomon*' entitled '*Adhraroma Almaliyeko Sathya*', directed by K.B. Gurung was presented. On the last day of the festival the Mahabharata drama '*Karna*' was presented by Phurba Lepcha.

Though all the plays presented in this festival were in Nepali but a special mention could be made of the play '*Karna*', undertaken by the socio-cultural organisation 'Mayal Nur Kurmum' which came into being on 27 July 1991. Under its banner Purba Lepcha, a 35 years old talented actress and theatre director whose mother tongue is Lepcha directed the play. She has already established herself on both stage and film. She acted in a film based on the tribal people of Arunachal and in many a Tele films. She has worked for the street theatre and acted in many one-acts. Her wellknown directional ventures are 'Anmol Jiban' Buddha Charitra', Mahabharat and Karna. She is presently working on a production to be produced in Lepcha.

In her Nepali production presented in the festival 'Rang Pratibha' many a Lepcha artistes worked both on and off stage. The play comprised of the following artistes:-

On Stage

Vimal Thatal, Suman Gujmer, Yadav Sunam, Purandip Sharma, Ravichandra Sharma, Banita Lagun, Naresh Sunar, Vinay Sunar, Sanjay Vishvakarma.

Off Stage

R.D. Lepcha, Uttam Pradhan, Rajen Rasaili, Sita Subba, Lalit Sunar, Vijay Rai, B.B. Singh, Pandamkit Lepcha, Yangki Lepcha, Somkurnari Subba, Toney Lepcha, S. Wangel Bhotia, Dava Lepcha, Kiran Lama, Norden Lepcha, Hildamit Lepcha and Karma Lepcha.

At Dzongu, Sikkim, a museum of Lepcha heritages was founded recently. This is presently under the custody of Namgyal Lepcha, an authority on Lepcha language and literature, history, culture, folk music and indigenous instruments. Every year, during the month of December-January, the Lepcha New Year is celebrated here with great pomp at the adjoining open ground of the museum. During the occasion, a Festival of Lepcha dance, music and theatre is being celebrated under his guardianship. In the year 2006, at the instance of young theatre director Purba Lepcha, a fifteen days long 'Theatre Workshop' was conducted and subsequently, *The First Lepcha Drama* entitled *'Chûramphàt'* was put on show. The lead role and the music was rendered by none other than Namgyal Lepcha.

Lepcha Museum

Purba Lepcha

Presented below is a moment from this modern Mahabharata play in Nepali directed by Purba Lepcha.

Below: *Karna,* directed by Phurba Lepcha

An interaction session

References

Chattopadhyay, Tapan. Lepchas and their heritage. — Delhi: B.R. Publishing Corporation, 1990.

Namgyal Lepcha

VII

MAHALI
(Sub-Group of Munda)

A month long workshop based production was undertaken by the Living Theatre (IPTA), New Delhi in a remote area 'Khari-Ka-Matani' (falling in the Midnapore district of West Bengal) with the local tribals belonging to the Mahali community, a sub-group of Munda. Living theatre a progressive theatre troupe of Delhi started by Biswajit Sinha in 1988 is presently headed by Sheikh Khairuddin who visited West-Bengal alongwith Sujata Pal and did the scene work of Tagore's symbolical drama 'Raja' Local artists and children participated enthusiastically in the workshop oriented production in the street theatre from utilizing classical Odissi, folk idiom 'Chhau' and musical instruments like Drum, Nagara, Sahnai etc. The play was directed by Sheikh Khairuddin. Music and chereography was taken care of by Sujata Pal. The workshop commenced in the first week of November 2003 and lasted till December.

Sheikh Khairuddin and Sujata Pal with the Mahali artists in Midnapur District (2003)

VIII

MANIPURI

Introduction

Dance and drama are a part of the Manipuri way of life. These traditions in Manipur are very rich and varied. Dr. M. Kirti Singh states 'It is the theatre and Jatra that have the honour of being the chief cultural and artistic forms during the past few decades, the other and perhaps more worldwide being its dance and kirtan forms of music. The Meitei people with their concept of the world as the sport of god are particularly fond of theatre and Jatra. This type of communication through characters had achieved phenomenal success through their Laiharaoba dance, operas and plays of Sri Krishna as far as the form, content and expression are concerned.

Folk Theatres

The origins of Manipuri performance are traced to native primitive fertility-cults and ancestor worship festivals, the ritual form perhaps established in the twelfth century.

In Manipur, some performances as the Lāi-hārāobā, Lāirik-theeba-hoibā, Wāri-leeba, Penā-sakpā, Khongjom-purba and Moirāng-sāi have intrinsic dramatic material although they are not drama proper. There are, of couses, some full-fledged folk-drama forms, including Shumāng-lilā which is the Manipuri equivalent of the Jatra.

Lai-Hārāobā

Lai Haraoba is an ancient Manipuri fertility rite celebriting cosmic union between male and female principles, later enlarged to incorporate cosmological and ideological categories of the Meitei nation, assuming an intense and complicated ritual theatre structure comprising of dance, music, sports, theatre and the ritual. This folk dance form could be looked upon as the fountain-head of Manipuri drama. Pure folk dramatic idiom '*Shumang lila*' (Courtyard play) has a strong tradition, a constant source of entertainment to the people of the soil. The celebratory rite of Lai Haraoba received its formal shape with the monarch's participation, thereby assuming a political-cultural significance later in the process of nation-making.

Wari Leeba

Wari Leeba, or the art of solo story telling before the king or community, became institutionalized in the seventeenth century.

Gosthalila (Sansenba)

It is believed that this religious theatrical form emerged in the mid-eighteenth century. Oral traditions, however, ascribe it to King Chingthangkhomba alias Bhagyachandra (1763-98), who introduced Ras Lila in Manipur.

Traditional Manipuri children theatre, *Sansenba* or *Gostha Lila* was developed, as said, in the mid-eighteenth century. It normally falls on Gostha Ashtami (the eight lunar day of Hiyangei or November) the genesis of this theatrical form and its creator is unknown.

The form depicts Krishna's experiences as a cowherd — his becoming ready to tend cows at the age of five. It combines fun, frolic, adventure and environmental enactment, with demons in body size masks and the ritual worship at the end in the evening.

The young Krishna's exploits are very popular, and games, theatrics, killing of the demons Bakasur and Dhenukasur by Krish and his elder brother Balaram, children's linguistic interplay, entertain. The mother's role provides real scope to actresses.

Based on the cantos eleven and fifteen in the tenth book of the *Bhagavata* Purana, it highlights Krishna's experience as a cowherd — his becoming ready to tend cows at the age of 5, Narada's advent at Gokul and Krishna beseeching his foster-father to let him look after the cows with his friends. After much argument and feasting, the children go out to a forest where Krishna and his elder brother Balaram kill the demons Bakasur and Dhenukasur respectively. They return when the cows go back to the sheds.

Analogous to Bahua of the Ankiya Nats of Assam, this forum also included *Balabasu*, a clown attached to Narada to offer bland jokes and impoverised humour, but unlike Bahua, who is usually silent, Balabasu of Gosthalila is outspoken and adamant.

Gauralila

Gaura lila an operatic form is regarded as a court-supported continuation of the older traditions of Sansenba. 'Gaura' refers to the ancient name of West-Bengal and 'Gaura Lila' denotes the 'Play from Gaur', a theatrical form that emerged in the early twentieth century using the Bengali language Linguistic nationalism soon effected a switch to the Manipuri medium. The folkform depicts the religious missions of Gaurchandra (Chaitanya), particularly, the encounter of two Muslim brothers, Jagai and Madhai, with him and his associates, culminating in their conversion to Gauriya Vaishnavism. Comic interludes of the boat journey and other incidents were included in which major emphasis was on the acting and theatrical aspects rather than the dance. It became so popular in rural Manipuri and peripheral areas that it led to its looser construction and lack of codification.

The royal chronicles mention an event in 1803, when during the outing, the wooden bridge on the Imphal rivar broke and a troupe member of the 'Sansenba' died in the accident.

The many innovative minor forms, operas, and ritual performances in the Krishna cycle include the unique children theatre of '*Sanseba*' and the twentieth-century *Gaura Lila*, which produced such major exponents as Thounaojam Kunjakishore Singh (1891-1982) the first Manipuri theatre artist to win a Sangeet Natak Akademi Award in 1978 who was trained under the eminent gurus patrionised by the Maharaja's Court in Imphal, eventually himself serving as a guru at the palace school of theatre arts. Aristrocratic ladies participated freely with the commoners to celebrate Krishna's egalitarian and liberating actions. The converted took to representing his deeds with a sensuous delight in the fact that divinities could be conceived as mischievous children. Environmental performances simulating the Vrindavan forests, Govardhana Lilla, and mighty Jamuna river surcharged the polity with a spiritual abandon.

As early as 1851, in the play '*Kaliya daman*' (Vanquishing Kaliya), Krishna's tryst with the serpent was enacted on a river, with Maharaja Chandrakirti's young son Kam Singh performing as Krishna.

Folk dances and music, collective enhancement of relations with ancestral spirits, and ritual control over class principalities through cyclic festivals with associated secular lessons for education and initiation of the young, developed into a national culture in the eighteenth century symbolizing the cosmos under the monarch as visible active principle.

Raslila

Raslila is Manipur's contribution to court theatres of the world. It is an ethnic version in song, dance, drama and ritual of Krishna's mythical divine play with the Gopis (milkmaids) of Vrindavan.

The performance of 'Ras Lila' was first organised for five days till the full moon of Kartik (November) in 1779. Govinda (Krishna) was crowned as God-King at an auspicious moment in the new capital Langthabal (Canchipur, in Imphal West district), and the Ras Lila was presented that evening and subsequently for five nights. The text is drawn from the '*Ras panchadhyaya*' (Five chapters on ras) or Cantos 29-33 in the tenth book of the Bhagavatha Purana.

Access to the Lord through the female principle was the sole motif of the entire Raslila tradition. It depicts the love, union, separation, and reunion of God with His devotees, the celebrating nature of man's relationship with the divine is experienced through performance.

The native felt the danger that the foreign religion of Hinduism might supplement their Meitei faith. Sectarian violence, conflicts on interpretations, disparate discourses in court circles continued to create an atmosphere of tension. The disturbed world of Manipur needed a healing system to dispel fears and anxieties. Native followers of traditional religion resisted the massive Hindu conversion of the eighteenth century leading to a division of beliefs. However, Manipur's devastation by the Burmese in the later half of the eighteenth century and subsequent liberation by the Vaishnava ruler Bhagyachandra (1763-98) gave him an opportunity to experiment with change Bhagyachandra effected a compromise between the dissenting faiths, manifested treatically in the harmonious assimilation of both cultures in Manipuri Raslila. The slow, soft lyrical dance patterns healed the annihilating struggle within the self, and in turn became the precursor to a feverish explosion of performatory genres conveying the new-found love, compassion and synthesis. Although personally a convert to Gauriya Vaishnavism, he did not set aside the traditional beliefs and practices which constituted the primal religious core of the majority. The indigenised Raslila embodied this grand synthesis.

Manipuri Rāsa is an unique combination of music and solo, duet and group dance, having dramatic elements. It depicts vividly Lord Krishna's sports in a series of song and dances. Throughout the performance, the *gopis* sing in glory of Krishna, his beauty and the melodious sound of his flute.

There are a wide variety of Rasa performance corresponding to the various seasons, like Basan Ras, Kunja Ras, Diva Ras, Nitya Ras and Maha Ras. The Rāsa Lila is enacted inside the mandap, a circular area with four openings. The performance begins with Raag or an invocation by the organisers followed by Krishna Abhisar, Radha Abhisar, Bhangi Pareng, Brindavan Pareng, Kurumba Pareng and Goshta Pareng.

Thok Lila

This is a satirical performing art form resembling slapstick, originated during the reign of Chandrakriti (1850-86). A seminal art form which had some semblance of protest in those days and the theatre of protest in Manipur owes its origin to this art style. In the Thok Lila, the performers cut jokes on anything, even on the autocratic impositions of the king. This slapstick performance became an indispensable part of the Durga Puja festival and it was enjoyed by King and his men as well as by general public. The tradition of Thok Lila continued till the second quarter of twentieth century.

The hierarchical hegemony of the noblemen bred subtle subversions within the value systems of the feudal society, as slaves in the retinue gave vent to criticism with fun and humour. After release from periodic services to the monarch, these jesters roamed the countryside and the *Phagi* (Clown Play) arose in the mid-nineteenth century, developing into the itinerant Shumang Lila of the early twentieth century. One specific variation,.the folkloric '*Moirang Parva*', held sway for nearly the whole century.

Sumang Lila

Shumang Lila has therefore, the longest history in Manipuri theatre, believed to have started as comic skirts by the jesters of feudal royalty in the nineteenth century, ridiculing the snobbish nobility and exposing their foibles and weaknesses. Ancient Manipur utilized slavery as a mode of production, and each noble's household had one or two slaves termed phunganai. These slaves developed a piece-de-resistance in new characterisation, and their jokes, puns, acrobatics, imitations, and equilibrium-destraying antics targated the masters themselves, who enjoyed the jests at their own expense.

Maharaja Chandrakirti (1850-86) possessed excellent wits, the more famous ones being Oina Bijando and Thongbai Mera. Other jesters like Abujamba Shaiton and Khari Laisuba were reported to have invented the comic skits. There is enough indication that by the 1870s these originally impromptu improvisations became regular exhibitory features, and large audiences were often exposed to such entertainment. Mrs. Grimwood, wife of the political agent, had witnessed a performance of three clowns in 1891 and left a vivid impression.

Manipuri jesters were adept in crosstalk, ie, rapid exchange of phrases and wit and in the early twentieth century they got rid of painted faces, and more down to earth crosstalk, distortion of limbs and facial muscles, utilisation of nonsense syllable, and narration of humorous tales came into currency. The plays were short but full of impromptu performances, and digs at the nobility social oppression, human foibles, and sexual peccadilloes. Strings of brief narratives linked together made one full presentation. Normally six to seven actors toured the countryside, and the most attractive members were the *Nupi*-shabi and *Phagi-puba*, who became the troupe leaders. The plays came to be named after the clown: Thus, Yotshubi Phagi Amuthoi Phagi, Chenga Phagi.

The Durgapuja at the palace was a great event, where many enactments, operas, dances, and Phagis were held as each day of the ten-day festival.

By 1918, the nature of performances were embellished by regular stories in a proper dramatic structure from texts outside Manipur, Raja Harishchandra was the first Hindu mythological play done in the itinerant manner. Their coexistend long narratives with improvised skits by the jesters who presented them between the two halves of a play, sometimes Phagis remaining more popular than the drama that sandwitched them.

Sumang Leela in the past were known as 'Jatrawali' and they must have came from Bengal to Manipur. The Manipuri talent in course of time modified what was adopted from Bengal to suit the local conditions and a new Manipuri folk dramatic form came up.

Moirang Parva, for e.g., which belong to the Shumang Leela genre is regarded as a true embodiment of ethinic Manipuri theatre that was in vogue in the early twentieth century and lasted some seventy years. The epic story of the love between Khamba and princess Thoibi of Murang in the twelfth century was divided into episodes; the Moirang chapters formed the last of the seven tragedies in the Langon cycle of lovers manifested by the deity Thangjing. Today, the new middle class reads the legend in publication only and there has been the transformation in audience behaviour and tastes, shifting of the public allegiance to other form of entertainment and the passing away of veteran performers, art form has more or less declined.

Sumang Lila is enacted in the Manipuri Jatra style. Repertoire consists of many local legends such as stated earlier also, the Khamba-Thoibi legend of the Moirang region of Manipur. The legend, among the finest examples of Manipur's oral tradition, has been sung as a ballad through the ages. For example *Return From Exile*, is one of the numerous episodes from the legend. Thoibi, a beautiful and talented princess, is exiled to Kabu, Burma, for her love for the pauper Khamba. Her father, the prince Chingkhuba, wishes to give her hand in marriage to Nongban, scion of the Angom clan. Chingkhuba yields and asks for the return of her daughter from the custody of the Kabu chief.

A. Shyamsunder Simha gives us broadly three stages in the growth and development of Manipur Sumang Lila. To quote I.R. Babu Simha:

The first stage ends up to 1891 when Manipur's independence was lost to the British; the second period begins with the conquer of Manipur by the British and continues up to World War II, and the third phase extends from World War II to the present time. Though performances resembling 'Sumang lila' in essence could be seen earlier in several folk performances, a definite turn came during the reign of Chandrakriti Maharaj (1834-1844). During the days of Durga Puja in October in his time several operatic performances were given in front of the idol of Durga, and they included some from talented performers and humorist also. The humorous performances of these artistes were very popular, and they were the precursors of the Manipuri 'Sumang lila.' In the beginning mythological themes from the puranas and the epics of India provided the plot for the Sumang lila, but in course of time other historical and legendary local themes were also taken up. Manipuri 'Sumang lila' had a hey-day during the reign of Maharaj Churachand Singh (1891-1941) during which period it extended in scope and appeal. What made the 'Sumang lila' popular among the people was the rich, spicy humour which the actors freely used. By the use of joke and humour they could criticise everything under the sun. This element of fun very often became so popular that certain 'Sumang lila' groups were known by the name of the predominant joker and humorist in the group. Yot-*subi Phagi* came to be known so as the leader of the group was dark in complexion. *Chengba Phagi* was called so because the leader of the group was usually thin around the armpit. The story element became less important during this period and the actors from their own resources often developed the plot to suit the mood of the audience in the course of performance. What was most wanted by the audience was spicy joke from the actors. In most cases in Manipuri 'Sumang lila' the female role is played by male actors.

After World War II there came a major shift in the theme and contents of the 'Sumang lila'. Along with the legendary, mythological and historical themes, social themes and current topics have become very popular. The socio-political changes have given new thrust to 'Sumang lila'. In a sense, in modern days these plays have become a potent and powerful means of criticising the evils of society. The impact of the cinema and the theatre could also be seen on the 'Sumang lila' nowadays. The performance has become more theatrical, even more violent, following the style of the formula-ridden cinema. The emergence of female performers is a new addition, and the women can easily compete with their male counterparts in performance. A very popular and once famous 'Sumang lila' group, devoted entirely to the performance of the story of Khamba Thoibi theme, is known by the name of 'Moirang Parya'. They perform the story of Khamba-Thoibi in a highly stylised acting peculiar to this group. Most of the dialogues are in folk-songs sung by the actors in stylized folk-tunes, and their costumes also are highly gorgeous. Here importance is given to the performer's skill, wit and common sense. The actor keeps the audience spellbound by his performance for hours together. There is no need of a stage; an open space is enough for this performance. The dialogues, the songs and the jokes used in such performances are impromptu expressions of the artists, and are in keeping with the mood and atmosphere of the audience and the situation. The 'Sumang lila' may thus provide the stuff demanded by the audience in a good measure, and remains still a powerful folk-theatre which can keep the audience spell-bound for hours.

The cultural transmission that took place under colonial aegis after 1891 led to a change in its nomenclature, as being derived from the Jatra of Bengal and the itinerant groups came to be known as Jatrawalis.

The Manipur State Kala Akademi, an antonomous cultural body sponsored by the government, organizes Annual Festivals with prizes for the top three plays judged by scholars and literatures. The theatre Centre when organised their first festival in 1967, They named it the '*All Manipur Jatra Festival*'.

The scripted plays a phenomenon of 1950s, the clown has been assimilated with the narrative, and situational and character interactions were given prominence, instead of having an independent presence for the sake of humour alone. Although the modern dramatists tried to retain the elements of fun and laughter, but there was obviously a gradual decline in the art of the traditional clown. It is only in 1976 that the elite coined Manipur's 'Courtyard Theatre' as 'Shumang Lila'.

Manipuri theatre possesses this traditional popular from 'Sumang Lila', originating in the nineteenth century—which can accomodate a focus on contemporary issues. Professional troupes (some all male, some all female) play up to three shows a day and plays have 'the courrage to challenge the morbrd and corrupt system and the potential to be converted into educative, creative productions aimed at changing attitudes without losing the high entertainment value. A critic writes that 'Manipuri theatre from the 1950s onwards passes through phases which to some extent reflect the situation in other Indian regions where both rural and urban forms exists, and also mirrors aspects of European theatre history in the period between 1880 and 1950. The increasingly improbable moral centainties of melodrama almost inevitably give way to more searching naturalistic examination of social and domestic life; political insecurity fuels existential anguish which emerges as formal experimentation. This however may itself begin to appear sterile or introverted, and in spite of the 'seriousness, commitment and pursuit of excellence of directors who in recent years have attempted to develop their own modes in acute awareness of political realities, Lokendra Aramban suggests that current work has not fully formed ways to link art and life. The mythical stories of Manipur, the legends connected with various personalities and incidents the history of Manipur and the folk-tales of the people have been the source-materials of the drama of Manipur from the beginning of the twentieth century till this day. The theatre-houses in Imphal and elsewhere in the mofussil would put up plays with folk themes and content, and the audience would show great interest in content, and the audience would show great interest in and enthusiasm for these plays.

Manipur is a rich storehouse of culture, most of which still remains unexplored. Today Shumang Lila has started gaining appreciation outside the state. For example, *Nungthelleima* is a Shumang Lila based on mythology in which the performers enacts a war scene involving the mythological chief of Gods, warriors, wild animals and youth. Presented below is a sequence from this Lila, staged at the Bharatiyam Cultural Centre, Salt Lake, Kolkata in 2004 in an open-air theatre, organised by the Eastern Zonal Cultural Centre at its North-east Featival.

Influence of Folk Theatre in Twentieth Century Professional Drama

There is the tradition of using folk themes on the stage and theatre houses. The main thrust of Manipuri theatre has been the use of folk themes and folk style. Rupmahal Theatre, Manipur Dramatic Union, Aryan Theatre, etc., to name a few theatre houses at Imphal of the prosecenium style, would invariably put up shows of folk origin. Haorang Leishang Saphabi, Moirang Thoibi, Henjunaha, Shanthalembi, Khongjomba, etc are some of the folk dramas which have been successfully staged for several nights. In these plays, folk idiom, language, style, costume and mannerisms were utilised successfully. For e.g. Naharol Khongthan Artistes Association produced the plays 'Refugee' in Shumang Lila idiom. The play

written by Ranjit Ningthouja and directed by Naba Wareppa was staged in 2002.

Modern Phase

The colonial influence undermined the folk theatre forms. A new social order was introduced, based on British perceptions, with support from the existing aristocracy English entered, alongwith modern literature and journals, and the semi-agrarian society was transformed with the incorporation of laissez-faire capital.

The Royal palace, at one time in Manipur, played a significant role towards the promotion of arts, culture and letters. Interestingly the entire Manipuri literature from its beginning to the middle of the eighteenth century is anonymous in nature, because no writers would ever put his name in a piece he composed during this period, as he considered himself completely under the control of the king to whom he owed unlimited allegiance and whatever he did was part of the duty he derived from the king. He may be said literally to-exist for the king.

If the claim of the copper plate of Khongtakcha who was the king of Manipur during 763-733 is accepted as the first and earliest specimen of Manipur language, Manipuri literature could reasonably claim to have existed from the 12th century with the practive of singing 'Gugri', a hymn to the king sung by royal musicians. The anonymous character of the literature continued for yet another five centuries more though a few scholars here and there used to put their names in their compositions the bulk of literature in Manipuri during the periods upto the middle of the nineteenth century is mythological, legendary, sometimes histurist, often these may be termed as Puya' literature. Creative literature was rather scanty during the period. The British conquest of Manipur in 1891 brought about several changes-social, political, educational and cultural. The period from 1891 to 1944 during which Maharaja Churachand Simha was king of Manipur maybe broadly taken as the period of remaissance in Manipur. In 1885 Johnstone Middle English School was established in Imphal which was the first such school in the state. Manipuri was allowed for the first time in 1926 as a vernacular paper in the Matriculation examination of Calcutta University which encouraged many writers to write in their mother tongue from now onwards, bringing radical change in

Manipuri literature. Several literary journal published in thirties and forties of the last century.

During this period there was a tremendous progress in cultural activity also. Manipuri culture, particularly the Manipuri dance, martial arts and folk theatrical forms etc became famous and wellknown. Gradualy the realm of Manipuri drama and stage widened.

Since time immemorial, the Manipuri language has been the court language of Manipur. It has also a separate script of its own which is found in old manuscripts. However under the influence of Bengal Vaishinavism and the British rule, the people accepted the Bengali script for their language. The modern Manipuri literature starts from the beginning of the 19th century after English pattern of administration had found a share among the people. For the purpose of promoting Manipuri language and literature, the Manipur Sahitya Parishad was formed in 1935 which helped the coming of some talents in creative writing. Though poetry has ever been the favourite form of literary expression in Manipur, but in the post-independence, Manipuri drama is no negligible.

Here the playwrights cameout as drama writers first and actors, producers etc. afterwards. Some early modern dramas which need particular mention are :-

(1) *Nar Singh* of L. Ibungohal

(2) *Sati Khonghang and Areppa Marup* of S. Lalit.

(3) *Mairang Thoibi* of A. Dorendrajit

(4) *Mainu Premcha* of A. Shyam Sundar

(5) *Kege Laimtia* of S. Bormani Singh.

(6) *Bir Tikendrajit* of M. Bira Singh

(7) *Kabai Keioiba* by A. Jai Singh.

Proscenium Arch Theatre

Manipur was defeated by the colonial British in 1891 and the Babus from Bengal started arriving in the wake of the British. Ethnic Manipuris performed in the Bengali dramas, on equal footing with Bengali actors.

The first modern drama in the land in true sense is was a Bengali play called 'Pravas Milan' played in the courtyard of Sri Govindaji, adjacent to the royal palace of Maharaj Sir Churachand Singh, a great patron of Manipuri art, literature and culture. Interestingly the actors were all Manipuris and it was directed by two persons named Gophal Singh Selungna and other was a Bengali Saratchandra Ghose. This was the year 1902.

In the semi-agrarian social environment in 1902 the proscenium arch was first introduced in the land which marked the emergence of the British educated gentleman class (bhadralok) from the landed gentry. The court elite, steeped in traditional religious values, alongwith the new class of educated gentry, created the atmosphere of the proscenium era. Proscenium arch theatre became the new performance aesthetic, imitating the latest happenings in cosmopolitan Calcutta. While Calcuttans looked toward Victorian Lonon for artistic leadership, Imphal looked to the nearest imperial metropolis. It was the Bengali community living in Imphal that gave an impetus to the theatre culture. In the year 1903, they started the '*Bamacharan Mukhopadhyay Bandhav Natya Shala*' for purpose of staging Bengali dramas especially on festive occasions.

Friends Dramatic Union

The new leisured class took to models of historical and mythological drama imported through the Bengali language, and the Friends Dramatic Union established in 1905 found Bengalis and Meiteis equally sharing responsibility for popularisation of the new theatre.

'*Friends Dramatic Union*' had a permanent stage at Babupara under the guidance of a committee. There was, however, no permanent auditorium.

In the year 1905, the first play with a regular plot, divided into acts and scenes entitled '*Pagalini*', written in Manipuri language by Bihari Singh was enacted at the playwright's residence without stage. Author of this comedy was the Head Master of Pettigrew L.P. School. The text was in Manipuri, but songs were sung in Bengali

Pagalini was followed by another social drama 'Bijoy Malati' of A.K. Amubi Singh.

In the year 1910, a cultural organisation named 'Victoria Club' was formed Regular performances were made possible in the permament hall of this club. Both communities, ie, the Manipuris and Bengalees took part in the theatrical performances. Some of the wellknown Bengali plays were rendered into Manipuri and staged during this early phase of the twentieth century. Mention can be made of Bilwamangal, Pratapaditya, Kedar Roy, Bange Bargee, Chandragupta, Savitri Satyavan, Tipu Sultan, Sita, Devala Devi, etc. Both the form and the concept of dramas were imported to Manipuri from Bengal. Again in 1918, a renderation of the Bengali play '*Parthaparajary*' was enacted thus.

Regarding the proscenium Arch Theatre Lokendra Arambam aptly summarises "The open mandap-style religious theatre of the nineteenth and early twentieth centuries, based on the Hindu epics, gradually changed into a closeted, fourth-wall representation of events, with wooden boxes in the front rows to welcome the colonial middle class.

The royal presence in a collective theatre as life-giver, protector, and protagonist of rituals now shifted into the role of non-participating patron or individual witness.

In the first decade of the twentieth century there came up new prosceniums which were simple *length-dominated* structures with openings into the national environment of a pond or moonlit meadow. Their function was not distinguished from the traditional breadth-dominated *Sanggoi* (a restructured annex) used by the community for ballads, operas and readings, over and above its multiple functions for the economic activities of the family. The audience could sit in the courtyard below, the crowd sometimes spilling across neighbours' fences or gardens. The charming proscenium aprons, the multifaceted painted wings and screens, and the petromax lanterns were cohesive stage pros."

Proscenium theatre thus came into existence at the dawn of twentieth century under the patronage of the colonial administration.

A critic records "During the period 1902-1924, Manipuri drama was a product of translation and adaptation. Female roles were played by males. As there was no proper theatre halls, most of the plays were staged at public places. In those days, theatre was mostly meant for amusement."

Before the arrival of the first original Manipuri play, the translated play were mostly related with the epics Ramayana or Mahabharata. Theatre was upto this time confined to Imphal town. Play-houses wentup in the palace, the main temples and the out-houses of well-to-do persons and even in the private buildings. Maharaj Churachand, true to the Manipur tradition of patronising the art forms, helped with men and money. It went ahead with the work of giving medals to the talented artists for their roles and performances. At his command it became a practice with school boys to perform a play under the able director-teacher in the annual Saraswati Puja celebrations. Then artists with new spirit came and introduced new experiments and techniques more congenial to the Manipur stage. What we find is that upto 1924, the trend was to adapt plays from the Bengali originals. It was only in the year 1925 that Lairenmayum Ibungohal Simha's Manipuri original drama was staged for the first time. The play '*Narasimha*' was, however written much earlier in 1922. Lairenmayum Ibungohal Simha's play '*Nara Simha*' being the first historical play written in Manipuri language exhibiting the magnanimity, sacrifice noble-mindedness and accomplishments of the king of Manipur, Nara Simha, the defeater of Burmmese. This play is a landmark in the development of Manipuri dramatic literature. Apart from L. Ibumgohal's *Nara Simha*, Angahal's *Gouranga*, Lalit's *Satikhongnang* (tragedy showing the Satidah of a women) and *Arappa Marup* (a social tragedy full of human, lust and morality) met with ground success most of the playwrights were writer - producer - actor - dramatist. A purely Manipuri stage came out of its infancy.

From 1925 to 1942 is acknowledged as the most flourishing phase of Manipuri stage. In those days, theatre was the most popular entertainment next to 'Sumanglila' and cinema still did not make its entry. In the early thirties many a number of theatre units were formed and well equipped theatre halls like Manipur Dramatic Union (1931), Aryan Theatre (1935), Society Theatre (1937) and Rup-Mahal (1942) came up which helped to boost the theatre movement in the region.

Proscenium stages on makes shift outhouses in residential localities increased in number, and the new materialism came into effect with ticketed shows introduced at the Manipur Dramatic Union in 1931, the first proscenium arch theatre in Imphal for the native Meitei people, followed by Aryan Theatre and Rupmahal Theatre.

The Meitei Dramatic Union

It was in the 1920s with the development of linguistic nationalism, the modern Manipuri drama started flourising. At the residence of Ngangbam Shyam Kishore, the brother-in-law of the Maharaja, situated in the strategic cultural area of Yaiskul Pana (whose inhabitants comprised ancient families of kings, nobles, and hereditary landowners); the first Manipuri proscenium stage was erected due to his initiative alongwith the writers and court official Sorokhaibam Lalit (1892-1955), the actor Nengmaithem Thanil Singh, a socialite Chingakham Mayurdhwaja, and the famous social activist Hijam Irawat. Later the great theatre artist Khomdram Dhanachandra who did the lead role in the patriotic play 'Nara Singh' of L. Ibungohal was invited to join the troupe and an important development took place in 1930. The troup named itself 'The Meitei Dramatic Union' and put on boards the social drama '*Sati Khongnang*' by Lalit, biding farewell to the imitative, heightened rhetoric of the Bengali group. With the story of forcible burning of a Meitei widow on her husband's funeral pyre started a naturalistic trend in Manipuri Theatre.

Lokendra Arambam informs that in 1931, the first experiment in ticketing was made by the Meitei Dramatic Union, for Lalit's play 'Areppa marup' (Abiding Friend). Irabot as the impoverished misfit became a household name. However, Maharani Dhanamanjuri of the Ngangbam household expressed unhappiness about extracting money from the public in her home, and the playhouse was shifted to Mayurdhwaja's nearby residence. The stage was built on top of a pond with bamboo and mud flooring, contiguous to the *sangoi* (traditional outhouse), the major designing work done by Irawat.

Until 1936, their repertoire comprised of plays rendered from Bengali with occasional native writings on this makeshift stage.

Chitrangada Natya Mandir

During the late thirtees of the last century, Hijam Angahal (1892-1943) left the *Meitei Dramatic Union* to form the '*Chitrangada Natya Mandir*', which returned to the Ngangbam family and renovated the former stage. Their production of Angahal's 'Ibemma' (Maiden, 1939), was refreshing production.

Both these two groups, the *Meitei Dramatic Union* and the *Chitrangada Natya Mandali*, within 1 km of each other made an intriguing phenomenon later to became a trend. But *Chitrangada Natya Mandali* died out in the post-war period, its playwrights and actors having switched loyalties to the newly established Rupmahal Theatre.

The Manipur Dramatic Union

It was in the year 1937 that the Meitei Dramatic Union shifted from Mayurdhwajas nearby residence to a permanent site and renamed itself the Manipur Dramatic Union. Started in Yaiskul area, a pioneer theatrical society which led the proscenium theatre movement and continued to flourish till the late sixties, where the old generation continued to dominate. Its character was succulent melodrama, material expansion of the stage, enlarged casts (most productions had more than forty artistes on stage) and maximum display of painted decor, sets and exotic scenes. Wheeled platforms with characters and props framed outside were pushed onto the stage, effect projectors and commercial lighting presented multiple exhibition of flashy, dazzling patterns in consonance with the advent of colour in films. The dramatic unfoldments were in the grand old manner with slow, almost turtle-paced development of scenes — most sequences embellished sentiment with old values pertaining to separation of good from evil. Large audiences grew with the massive productions of the Manipur Dramatic Union with which started a new phase of drama in Manipur. S. Lalit was the pioneer of Manipuri theatre. Many talented actors, playwrights and able singers came forward from the institution. Lalit Singh is called the father of Manipuri modern drama, who was endearingly called by all as '*Pabung*' which means father.

Hijam Irawat was deeply associated himself with the theatre movement and *created the symbol of two ploughs being crossed for the first theatrical group 'Manipur Dramatic Union' in 1931 signifying ploughing the cultural soil of Manipur.*

Shri Sorensangbam Nabakanta Singh, a dramatist of renown in Manipur, in a speech delivered on the occasion of the 9th Birth Aniversary of the Jananeta Hijam Irawat, dealing with '*Irawat as an artist and dramatist*' gave among others, a vivid description of the dramatist Irawat in the role of Chandrs Singh, a way-ward young man of a wealthy family, having relationship with a beautiful '*Mou*' (woman) called '*Rajani*', who, either from a sense of rescuing Chandra Singh from going worse or from sheer greed for money asked Chandra Singh not to show up his face again unless he came with rupees two hundred. Chandra Singh could not manage the money and he appeared shabbily dressed with half his 'dhoti' wrapped around the upper part of the body like a gambler who had lost everything he had, walked slowly across the stage muttering "*Chani*", "*Lupa Chani*" (Two hundred, rupees two hundred).

Hijam Irawat

The dramatic effect that emanated from the excellent acting of Irawat as Chandra Singh was so impressive and perfect that the audience remained spellbound. Even Maharaja Sir Churachand Singh was so impressed with his acting deeply identifying himself with the character in the Stanislavskean sense that the Maharajah, forgetting that it was only a play with suspension of disbelief threw rupees two hundred on the stage to help him, to extricate himself from the predicament in which he would be failing to pay the amount demanded by Rajani, the married woman, in whose trap he was caught inextricably from hand to foot. Such was the perfection of the Jananeta Irawat as an artist.

Persons younger to Irawat bear testimony to the fact that he was the prime worker who devoted to constructing the stage of the Manipur Dramatic Union, above the pond adjacent to the out-house of late Chingakham Mayurdhwaja Singh, a nobleman of the time who had his residence at Moirangkhom Chingakham Leirak, Imphal.

The troupe suffered its share of dissentions, internal differences and crises. Some died, many departed at different times such as Elangbam Joychandra who became a powerful purveyor of popular drama in rural areas and Huirem Motilal took up the role of a theatre teacher and director of polished social drama for the youth.

Irawat left for a political career in 1939, a setback for the group. But under the able stewardship of Lalit, some plays were produced by the Manipur Dramatic Union that rejuvenated Manipuri theatre. Sorokhaibam Lalit accented greater representation of Manipur's cultural resources and attention to folk stories as a medium of dramatic literature. The rise of linguistic consciousness, the spread of Moirang Parva enacted by itinerant troupes in courtyards, the advent of folk-drama writers and changing tastes among theatre goers perhaps accounted for the sudden emphasis on romantic subjects of the past. Lalit became the leader of the traditional form, utilizing the services of the Pena Singer Chungkham Manik in developing archaic diction and stylized falsetto speech trends of folk theatre. 'He added arrays of bright colours along with bold lines on the background scenery. Heavy wheeled platforms with actors, properties, and gorgeous decor were pushed on to the stage during dark interludes.

In the year 1954, the Song and Drama Division of the Govt. of India sponsored on All India-Drama Festival in Delhi and under the folk category, the Manipur Dramatic Union's play '*Haorang Leishang Saphabi*' was adjudged best. This boosted the national image of Manipur theatre, establishing its later typecast appeal of artistic, but somewhat exotic, costumes and design.

The Manipur Dramatic Union's plays, howeve, were contructed melodramatically, with sentimental heroism upgraded as viva rasa (Heroic sentiment) and projected as the acting system. One of the group's great performer was Ningthoujam Tombi Singh. Wellknown women artists of this group were Sairem Kanya, Chirom Gouramani, Ningthemcha Ongbi Nungshitombi, Aribam Ningol Manbi, Kshetrimayum Randhoni and these who left for Rupmahal, S. Tondon and Thambal Angoubi.

In the fifties, Manipur Dramatic Union, apart from enacting dramas based on meitie folktales, took up some Manipuri version of Bengali originals, borrowing themes from mythology and religion. In the 1960s and 1970s, it produced some social plays by S. Birendra and M. Ramcharan. But its production since then are marked by peculiarly slow, deliberate staging, large casts and schematic overacting, arroganthy brushing away the changing production styles of younger generations in other theatres, but with an identity and passion inherited from the palace culture.

The play 'Areppa Marup; of Sorokhaibam Lalit Singh, mentioned earlier also was a prescribed text book for the Matriculation Examination of the Calcutta University in the Pre-Second-World-War period. S. Lalit Singh's contribution to modern Manipuri theatre is indeed immense'.

Manipur Dramatic Union is the oldest drama unit whose aims and objectives of this theatre troupe are to produce dramas of social significance with an eye to social reform; and to increase the number of dramas for the advancement of Manipuri literature, to promote the development of theatre, dramatic literature, dance and music in Manipuri; to organise, sponsor and undertake dramatic, dance and musical presentations, study courses, publications, films and tours consistent with the objects of the Union, etc. So far, Manipur Dramatic Union has produced different categories of plays and different scripts numbering over 150 to its credit. Union is participating regularly in the state level and national level theatre and drama competitions. Its address of communition is 'Police Line, Imphal 795001, Manipur.

The Aryan Theatre

The residence of Atombapu Sharma (1899-1963), a great scholar of Hinduism, Sangeet Natak Akademi laurate had a thatch-roof wooden pavilion, which was a hub of religious activities. Sri Sharma was the first patron of Aryan Theatre, one of the longest lived Manipuri theatre groups. At his instance, a makeshift wood and bamboo stage was erected there and In September 1935 'Aryan theatre' which was named after Atombapu's faith in Aryan culture, staged the Manipuri version of Monmohan Roy's Bengali drama '*Reziya*', rendered by Arambam Dorendrajit Chirom. The role of 'Reziya' was enacted by Chiram Gouramani (1914-1982). The personnel of the theatre were educated and had aristocratic lineage or official employment under the colonial dispensation. The group was located west of the main market in Imphal, in Sagolband.

In the year 1935, the Aryan Theatre was formed by some theatre enthusiasts and newly educated youths. Its main objective is theatre-culture and it activated itself producing different plays.

From 1935 to 1939, Aryan Theatre took up plays of mythological, historical or patriotic nature, all translated from Bengali such as D.L. Roy's 'Shah Jahan', Nisikanta Basu Roy's 'Debala Devi', Aparesh Mukhopadhyay's 'Sri Krishna' and from 1939 onwards it started production of plays of native writers. In 1939, the play 'Bhagyachandra', penned by Dorendrajit was produced by Aryan Theatre. This was the first original play taken up by this group.

The Aryan Theatre which was set up in Sagolband in 1935 won huge popularity as a front ranking professional theatre troupe which later refined the Manipuri drama. This theatre witnessed the dynamics of change, conservatism and conflict played out in its architecturally seductive, graceful proscenium builtup in 1945. With this newly built theatre house at Sagolband Road, Imphal-795001, the activities of the Aryan theatre geared up. Salam Nilamani Singh associated himself as President and Arambam Somorendra as Secretary of the organisation. This stage and auditorium pressed by a dwingling economy into a municipally eroded facility, produced the largest number of native playwrights, with over 110 volumes of plays between 1935 and 1977. Here in the late sixties, the old mixed with the young generation of teachers and students in a poorer milieu of Aryan theatre. More precisely the students of the fifties, but teachers by the late sixties, the young band of theatre workers spearheaded by men like A. Somorendra, A. Shyam Sharma and G. Ravindra Sharma worked under the leadership of the theatre icon M. Biramangol and produced innovative constructs which became a springboard for a new movement.

Aryan theatre has a medium theatre house of 400 capacity and facilities of production by other groups. One of its memorable production is a translated work '*Neta ki ek sham*' (1968) a play with vital energy and realism. Another significant presentation was Sri Biren's *Khongchat* (1970) which was to begin the intellectual movement in modern Manipuri theatre, and his feverish dramatic poetry of the loss of identity began the cerebral quest of the alternative theatre.

Aryan theatre's other notable productions are Thoibi (1946). Mother (1950), Mahabharat (1958) and its sequel (1959), Sri Sri Krisha Chaitanya (1958), Macbeth (1965), Pidonnu (1966), Sijalaioibi (1967), Sanamahi Kolu Yeikhaiba (1965), Hallakpa (1971), Langoinai (1973), 1891 (1975), Irabot (1976), Yotpak Yotlei ama (1979), Khuman Chakha Moirang Ngamba (1982), Numit Kappa (1984), Phou-oibi langon (1984), Ningthou (1987).

Some gifted women artistes of this group like Chirom Gouramani, S. Tondon, Pishak Devi and Bimola Achoubi later migrated to the richer and more stable 'Manipur Dramatic Union' and 'Rupmahal Theatre'.

At present Aryan Theatre is actively engaged in cultivating contemprary theatre-trends with an intimate search for indigenous peoples culture. It presents its plays in the '*All Manipur Drama Festival*' organised by the Manipur State Kala Akademi.

1931-1943

The theatre houses of the Meiteis were Manipur Dramatic Union setup in the Yaiskul area in 1931. Ticketed shows had also begun on early as 1931. Aryan theatre in Sagolband was set up in 1935 and Rupmahal theatre appeared at Imphal Bazar in the year 1943. In Manipur theatrical life was shaken by the second world war. On account of Japanese bombing the Manipuri people fled to quieter places for life. All big towns were filled up with military people. In these turmoils starvation came upon the theatre group. The organisation ceased functioning for the time being. But the passionate love of the people for theatre could not be destroyed by the brief spell of war. Within a few years new organisations like Rup Mahal Theatre Society theatre etc. came forth. New talents and plays were produced through these bodies and later a host of other theatre groups emerged in the suburbs of the town as well as in smaller rural areas state officials and school masters alike were their founding members for survival of Manipuri theatre. The credit for all this activity in between 1930 and 1940 not merely goes to urban dramatic societies like Aryan Theatre, Chitrangada Natya Mandir, Imphal Theatre and Naba Natya Mandir but also to rural organisations in Nambol and Kakching Lila Samiti (later Nambol Dramatic Union). It was only in the post-war period in the late forties of the twentieth century, the Manipuri theatre witnessed a resaissance. Straight drama and their performance in the modern sense comparatively appeared much later.

The plays comprised of historical romances, patriotic melodramas and religious outpourings on saintly characters. There also existed folk productions with vibrant characters from medieval legends and love of chivalry, suffering and violence that filled the stage of post-independence integration-excited environment of the Nehruvian era. In the lower realms of theatre art we had the proletarian, suburban, rural groups of semi professional itinerant performers of the Shumang Leela.

In Manipur, the Post-war drama reflected a series of changes which occurred in the mind of the people after the war and Indian Independence. The playwrights before the war had a fine command over Bengali and Sanskrit. Devotion of music and dance were considered essential for the plays. The themes were mostly drawn from Hindu religious texts. The court life of the king was vividly broughtout in the dramas. The important roles required gaudy costumes, necklaces of pearls, make-up etc. The administration of the Maharajas was sound; the artists and writers had a traditional loyalty for the kings in all respects.

Rup Mahal Theatre, for eg. had produced a series of folk plays that met with hearty appreciation of the people, such as Yaithingkonu, Moirang Thoibi (wellknown epics of Moirang), all genuine folk plays the best works about romantic stories of this region. But such type of performances were seriously affected when the Congress Government took over the administration of the kingdom. The Congress movement under Gandhiji had the effect of changing costly costumes into local made cloth and simple ornaments. The playwrights of this period started reading modern western literature and the effect was seen almost in manifold ways. Rupmahal, now, came up with a varieties of new plays.

Rupmahal Theatre

The society was formed in 1943 in Imphal Bazar which dominated the commercial mainsream of Manipur drama till the late sixties.

A milestone in the growth and development of modern Manipuri theatre is Rupmahal Theatre, nurtured by intellectuals, social workers and artistes. Wayback in November 1943, six Brahmans and five Meiteis gathered at the residence of Laishram Netrajit. The Brahmans decided to look after the administrative side, while the Meitei artistes got the freedom to produce drama. The host Netrajit, himself the actor and diretor alongwith the Gandhian Hawaibam Nilamani Singh, artistic leader, Meitram Bira Singh, an actor and writer; and the playwright Ayekpam Shyamsunder, opened a new chapter in the history of Manipuri stage. A troupe which in a span of few years became one of the most successfully managed and stable Manipuri proscenium troupes.

Rupmahal did not have a permanent home at that time and so, at the out house of a royal priest Tonsana Sharma, they made their first appearance with the Netrajit's self composed social drama '*Ningamdaba*' (Repentance). Their other productions that follow won people's hearts because of the superb lyrics and music by Paonam Nabin Singh.

When the Second World War broke out, the military occupied its temporary stage. This was in May 1944 and Rupmahal was forced to use other halls. Interestingly its utilization of venues near the palace enabled it to secure direct patronage of the reigning prince Bodhchandra who later had an affair with its stunning heroine S. Tondon. Besides, his decision to put up shows at different places also benefited the group by rapidly expanding its audience and developing its organisational experience. From a British political agent, they acquired a piece of land in the heart of the Imphal town, the most strategic area for a theatre group. In July 1948, its building was inaugurated, modelled on the Calcutta's Star Theatre.

Rupmahal Theatre owned a large stage 17m wide, freshly painted naturalistic scenery, an array of thespian like M. Bira, S. Nabakanta Singh, Nilamani, Netrajit, Dhiren, R.K. Bijoysana etc. and the most beautiful damsels like S. Tondon, actress and singer, Thambal Angonbi, dancer-actress.

Its early praideworthy productions were Yaithing Konu, Sita, Ibemma (Maiden), Mainu Premcha and Moirang Thoibi. The last mention play was written by Arambam Dorendrajit was published long ago in 1939 and proved very successful on the Manipuri stage. It was enacted several times by Roopmahal Theatre.

Such productions established Rupmahal as the centre of Manipuri Theatre. The troupe developed its own distinct style of slow, meticulous, near-classical form of acting, elaborate stage properties and emphasis on speech and voice projection where volume, accent, and range became distinctive, giving Rupmahal an indelible stamp.

In 1947, when the Manipur was given back its independence status, the states's poor economic conditions forced its Council of Ministers to levy '*Entertainment Tax*' from various theatres. It was Nilamani Singh, the artistic leaders of the professional group 'Rupmahal theatre' alongwith others went on the first hunger strike by artistes for a cause, the police arrested and deported them, Rupmahal's other artistes followed them and brought them home; and eventually the state had to exempt theatre from 'Entertainment Tax' and the whole credit goes to the artistes of Rupmahal.

Bira Singh, M.

M. Bira Singh who was the director of Rupmahal Theate looked out for heroes, who fought against the British and penned a historical drama called '*Tikendrajit*' based on a Manipuri martyr who was hanged in 1891 for his war with the British. In the year 1951, Rupmahal Theatre came out with epoch-making production of '*Tikendrajit*'. Premiered on August 13, the day of the hanging of its native heroes, it surpassed all existing records for popularity. Tikendrajit's pride, arrogance, and aristocratic sensibility were portrayed by the powerful S. Nabakanta Singh, with a deep echoing voice, and his movement, phlegmatic temper, concentration of energy, and explosion of vitality perfectly conveyed the psyche of a patriot. The guile of the elder statesman Thangal was depicted by M. Bira, the director of the play. The anti-hero characters were played with cunning and skill by Netrajit and Nilamani.

In Rupmahal the old generation continued to cast its spell like Manipur Dramatic Union but here with a slight difference in its production style and acting techniques, though the genre remained melodrama. The pattern of near-classical acting set by veteran actors like Nabakanta featured slow tones and movements, dialogue pungent with the arrogance and pride of Manipur's traditional nobility—not much of intellectually probing dialogue, but exaggerating tensions and attitudes, not establishing thought structures, but caressing already existing and cherished behaviour, finally exploding into passion and violence on the stage. The nuances of social feeling, the ethnic love for patriotic sentiments were reflected by Rupmahal's best production 'Bir Tikendrajit', discussed above, put up on boards in 1951 and had its hundredth show in 1966, witnesed by the audience mostly from rural areas filling every saturday afternoon shows and still had three shows every August 13, the day of the hanging of the martyrs. The very popularity of the play got Rupmahal entangled with the establishment. The families of the Indian officials objected to the 'misrepresentation' of their forebears and the police seized the text. All subsequent performances relied on scripts rewritten from memory by the cast. Public support helped continue the production.

In the 1950s and 1960s, Rupmahal Theatre was instrumental in presenting commercially viable plays. Contemporary social drama, satire on women's materialistic attitudes, plays on the agitation for statehood, and iconoclastic comedies of G.C. Tongbra were put on boards. In 1960, Tongbra's '*Leibak houba andolan*' (Earth-shaking Agitation) was premiered at the venue where curfew was enforced. So its playwright was later summoned by the Police. *Leibak houba andolan* was directed by M. Bira. Lokendra Arambam stated 'the rest of century saw Rupmahal's material expansion, different from the modern winds blowing in younger troupes. It became the factory of popular theatre and paid well for scripts from mainstream dramatists. Its own playwrights had an intuitive understanding of escapist public values. Thus it created an ambience divorced from the aesthetic realities of the past and unattached to the deep anxieties of the present. It need not work for change, since its capital accumulation, largesse to artists, assured stability of a captive clientele, and commercial profit from extra-theatrical businesses do not provide the staff to stir the members imagination.

Khwairakpam Chaoba Simha

The poet Khwairakpam Choaba Simha (1896-1950) tried his hand in playwriting also. He composed Labanga-Lata, Madhu-Malati, Naba-Malika and an untitled one act play. All of them had been produced in his life time. His drama 'Labanga-Lata' had been adapted from a novel of the same titled by the author. The manuscript available consists of 41 pages only. The play was performed in Uripok during the pre-war days. (The Second World War or rather popularly known as the Japanese War in Manipur). His '*Madhu-Malati*' comprises of only 16 pages and was produced in Roxy Theatre, Uripok after the war. *Naba-Malika* in incomplete and comprises of 30 pages. The date is given as 28th September

1945. It was staged by the Manipur Dramatic Union (M.D.U) after the war. Later, the title was renamed '*Japan Lan*' and the play was enacted at the same venue. The title of his one-act is not available, but it dealt with the arrest of Bir Tikendrajit as well as the Battle of Khongjom. During 1946-47, this one-act was staged by the students of D.M. College in the Johnstone School Hall.

Before the war, there had already been a few theatre houses in the Uripok area and they continued to exist for a few years after war too. One such theatre used to be Shri *Tomchou Sharma's Mandap* where Chaoba's play '*Labanga-Lata*' was premiered. Shri Achom Maipak Simha (Uripok Achom Leikai), Shri Khoirom Mangol Simha *Uripok Khumanthem Leikai), Shri Wahengbam Ibomcha Simha (Uripok Yambem Leikai) were associated with the production. They confirm that the play was presented for the first time in *Agya Tomchou Sharma's Mandap*.

Wahengbam Ibomcha Simha also known as Bilaiti Ibomcha himself did the role of Labanga. He reminicised: "I was already a fully grown youth and my age at that time must be 20 or 21— I took the part of Labanga. There was one Oja Ningthemjao. He taught us play; he arranged for everything. We were lined up and he selected who would play whom. He brought the volume (manuscript of the play) also. We were given copies of our dialogues. My own was with me for a long time but it had disappeared in the confusion of shifting house... most probably it had been staged before the Nupi-Lal (Women's War)... I think Lata was played by one Amumacha, or it could have been one Radha who took the role... It was told Khwairakpam Chaoba had written it."

Roxy Theatre was established around 1945. Actors who were associated with Roxy Theatre and staged *Madhu-Malati* of Chaoba include late Thiyam Narendra Simha, Shri Khongbantabam Tolhan Simha, the late Shyamkishor and Smt. Leimaton Devi. The play was shown atleast twice or thrice. The role of Malati was played by Leimaton Devi and that of Madhu, by her husband, Shyamkishor. Smt. Leimaton Devi recalls : 'I was a youngster then; I must be about 12 or 13 years old. Manimacha from Kwakeithel was also there. She used to sing for the play."

Presently Dhanamanjuri College, the D.M. College began as a night college in 1946 in Johnstone School (not the present building) which was then located in the present Luxmi Bazaar. One of the first principals of this college was R.R. Thomas, a Khasi gentleman (Ex-principal of Cotton College, Guwahati). The college boasted of 52 or 53 students. In 1947, a one-act play written by Khwairakpam Chaoba was staged by the college students during the college annual freshers meet. The venue was Johnstone School Hall where a stage had been set up for the purpose. The late Moirangthem Gajendra was incharge of the play and Oja Nando was in charge of the lights.

Some of the students of the first ever batch of D.M. College are still alive. The dramatic personae were:-

Sahib	: B.I. Sharma
Mrs. Grimwood	: Smt. Meinam Sakhi Devi
Saheb	: Wahengbam Naran & Amar
Krishna & Saheb (both)	: E. Sonamani Simha
Maharajah Kulachandra & Saheb (both)	: Nathasana
Thangal or Paona	: Hijam Romani
Market woman	: R.K. Surendrajit
Others	: Nadiya, Sanjabihari and Smt. Nongmaithem Bimola Devi.

Smt. Nongmaithem Bimola Devi (Nongmaijing Vaishnavi, the elder sister of Dr. N. Tombi Simha) was not a student of the college. She was invited for the purpose of singing. Shri R.K. Jhalajit Simha tells us that he himself witnessed the one-act play of Kh. Chaoba, being presented in Johnstone School Hall confirmed that the late R.K. Surendrajit had taken the role of a market woman.

Most of the literary pioneers of the first half of the twentieth century Manipur invariably took part in the development of Manipuri theatre. During the pre- and post-war periods, many authors joined the movement for its development. Mahakavi Anghal and Jananeta Irawat dedicated their souls to it. Even the poet Chaoba could not escape the forceful swirls of the movement for developing the Manipuri theatre. The literary environs as well as conditions in those days made great poet like Chaoba a playwright and consequently, a few plays by him had been presented.

Joychandra

Joychandra left the Manipur Dramatic Union to form his professional troupe 'National Touring Dramatic Party' in 1949 when Manipur got unified with India, began spreading the proscenium theatre movement in rural Manipur and Meitei-inhabited areas of neighbouring Assam. His dramas exhibited the prevailing violence upon simple folk, their oppression and suffering. He became very popular among the rural folks. '*Joy Drama*' became the popular name for his group '*The Manipur Artistes Touring Drama Party*'

During this golden age, many gifted writers directors and actors came forward with definite interest in theatre Committed writers like G.C. Tongbra and A. Shyamsunder Simha started writing dramas with social cause. There were several theatrical performances which led to the formation of a number of touring companies enriched with original social, mythological, historical dramas and also lots of translation from Sanskrit classics.

Tongbra and his Society Theatre

The Society Theatre has a distinctive identity and a special place in the making of modern Manipuri Theatre. Formed in 1937-38, the centre is the innovator of realistic social play in Manipur. Gitchandra Tongbram Simha and H. Birbahu Singh associated themselves with the 'Society Theatre' as its President and Secretary respectively.

Tongbra wrote about 35 full-length plays, 36 one-act play and more than 40 plays for the radio. Manipuri stage became fertile through G.C. Tongbra's problem plays, social plays and satirical dramas. His full length plays are mostly performed by Society Theatre.

The Society Theatre is Situated at Sega Lambi, Konjeng Hazari Leikai, Imphal-795 001, the Society Theatre is also engaged in the publication of plays. It has been touring villages giving cultural performances.

Post-Independence Phase

In the early forties, in the wake of the World War II and also Indian freedom movement, Manipuri stage suffered a setback. It was only after the independence that there was a renewed interest in theatrical activities, but this time Manipuri theatre changed its course, greatly influenced by the western playwrights and movements. However, during the World War II, when the population temporarily abandoned their homes as Allied forces fighting the advancing Japanese occupied Imphal, the senior members of the Aryan Theatre secured a space on the western outskirts of the Imphal's main market. A small proscenium-arch theatre was constructed with wood, mud plaster and zinc-sheet roof. The stage was 8m by 10m and the auditorium held 400 people. Wooden box seats in the first four rows catered to the elite audience, and the balcony held women and children.

World War II had its impact on Manipuri society and literature, many age-old values fell apart. The younger generation of writers strove to establish a distinct identity of these people. These young writers, steeped in modern ideas, were no longer moved by the idealism of love of the beauty of nature. They felt called upon to expose the ailments of modern society and the moral disintegration of its members. Between 1945 and 1965, Aryan Theatre produced the largest number of original playwrights in Manipuri language.

The state of Manipur became a constituent part of the Indian Union in 1949. Although still administered by the feudalistic, aristoratic gentry, the Aryan Theatre opened its membership to all classes, including cadres of the Communist Party, which tentatively attempted to propel its activities towards the left, ideology. M. Biramangol, a Communist, who as a young worker had helped in the theatre's founding, produced Gorky's '*Mother*' in the 1950s.

In the late fifties, Aryan Theatre moved away from the mythological and indigenous folk narratives. So far, its audience was fed with entertainment and gaity, and till then the founder's Vaishnava values remained intact. But a significant change occur with the presentation of social melodramas, attacking the Hindu orthodoxy. A critic reports 'Bold depictions of drunk Brahmans, desperate amorous maidens accosting their lovers, songs lifted from popular Hindi films, and all sorts of anarchic, vehement attacks on old values without a corresponding alternative ushered in the new scheme of things. During this phase S. Ibomcha Simha's two highly successful stage parodies 'Mahabharata' 58' and its sequel 'Mahabharata' 59' were put up by this group. A major departure, thus, came in the late 1950's, when Aryan Theatre began to put up plays with arrogant social melodramas and parodies ridiculed Hindu orthodoxy.

On 27th June 1951, at Roopmahal Theatre, Khumanthem Madhumangal Singh, a celebrated comic playwright's drama '*Bokachaoba*' was staged. It was an instant hit as popular comedy in the strict sense of fun and laughter.

Theatre Centre (Manipur)

Theatre Centre Manipur is housed in Paona Bazar Imphal, Ng. Mani and Son's Building, Opposite Polo Ground, Imphal - 795 004. It deals with theatre and allied arts. Theatre Centre Manipur was formed in 1954 with S. Bhuban Singh as its President and Wareppa Naba as Secretary. Its Solo Objective is to promote and preserve the cultural heritage in Manipur. It is the only institute in Manipur where all the theatre groups are affiliated and perform artistic activities unitedly. A Board of Executive Committee from amongst the different organisations is constituted to carry out smooth administration and activities.

One of the prominent activities of this organisations is that of conducting, All Manipur Short Play Competition every year along with observation of Manipur Theatre Day, Asian Theatre Day and World Theatre Day.

Shyamsunder, A.

A highly successful venture on the Manipuri stage during this period was the play '*Mainu Pemcha*', written by *A. Shyamsunder*. Maharaja Bodhachandra was so pleased with the composition that he suggested the playwright to incorporate some elements in the character of Thakur Borachaoba's betrayal and to the suicide of Mainu Pemcha.

Distinguished delegates like Dr. Rajendra Prasad, Jawaharlal Nehru, U. Nu, Premier of Burma, diplomats, central ministers, artists and many visitors enjoyed the performances of its play during their stay in Imphal.

Langmeidong Dramatic Union

Elangbam Birkumar is a rural activist. He was born in 1938 and became blind at the age of 31. In the year 1955 he formed the '*Langmeidong Dramatic Union*', located in Langmeidong village of Thoubal district, where he directs and acts.

Prahlad Sharma, Gurumayum

The late Gurumayum Prahlad Sharma published a play in 1957 bearing the title 'Madhu-Malati' (based on a story by the poet Chaoba). This play should not be confused with the dramatic adaptation by Chaoba himself bearing the same name. It is said that Chaoba's 'Madhu-Malati was staged in Roxy Theatre after the war. While Prahlad Sharma's play had been presented not only by Paradise in Wangkhei but also by Aryan and Roopmahal Theatres.

'Nityaipa-gi Shorat' and Madhumangal Simha

Some scholars opine that the play '*Nityaipa-gi Shorat*' was composed by eminent poet Khwairakpam Chaoba. While artists like Shri S. Bhuban Simha, Shri Khaidem Bihari Simha and Shri Chandam Gopal Simha expressed the possibility that the play might have been written by late Oja Khumanthem Madhumangal Simha (1887-1962).

Actors who took part in the production of the play confirmed that 'Nityaipa-gi Shorat' was staged in the M.D.U.

Shri Chandam Gopal Simha tells us that the author of this play was none other than Oja Khumanthem Madhumangal. He informs that Oja himself came during the rehearsal of the play as Gopal Simha himself took a minor role in that play. In all probability it had been staged before 1954, for he first joined Roopmahal Theatre in Imphal in that year. And the play had been presented before he joined Roopmahal, that is to say, when he was still in the M.D.U. The play is comic in nature and the writer Khumanthem Madhumangal Simha was a known comic playwright. Those actors who took part in the play said : Lairenbam Ibohal Simha played the character of Nityaipa, Khaidem Bihari Simha played a singer and Kh. Manglem was the maiba".

Following the success of Rupmahal's folk dramas, Manipuri Natya Sangh produced the play 'Santha Lembi' and Manipuri Dramatic Union took up the productions like Haorang Leisnag Saphabi, Thambalnu, etc. Haorang Leisnag Saphabi, penned by Sarangthem Boramani Singh won the '*the Best Play Award*' in the folk category at the National Drama Festival held in 1954 at New Delhi. Sorokhaibom Lalit directed this play that took Manipuri theatre into Jawaharlal Nehru's Indian mainstream of 'Unity in diversity'.

Of the older generations the notable theatre personalities till this phase are Kh. Munal Singh, N. Thanil Singh, S. Lalit, Kh. Nabakishore Singh, Kh. Nongyai Kh. Madhumangal, Ph. Iboton Singh, K. Amuba, Gokulchandra Singh, Kh. Dhanachandra, Ng. Jugolchandra, H. Nilamani Singh, H. Nutanchandra Sarma, M. Bira Singh, Ng. Tilak Singh, M. Biramangol Singh, L. Notrajit Singh.

Women artists who made a name for themselves are Gouramani Devi, Tambal Angoubi Devi Tondon Devi, Bimola Devi, etc.

It is in the realm of drama that post-war Manipur literature attained a maturity of theme and form. Boramani, Tomba, Biramangol, G.C. Tongbra, Ramachandran, Tomchou are some of the dramatists who enriched the Manipuri stage with new productions and catered to the public with savoury literature.

Sarangthem Boramani Singh takes great interest in folk and legendary themes. An outstanding playwright, his folk play '*Haorang leisang saphabi*' as discussed above, written in 1950, bagged him the Best play award in the folk category at the National & Drama Festival held in New Delhi in the year 1954. In 1957, he penned another folk play entitled '*Tonu Laijing Lembi*', based on the folk story of Moirang. His *Kege Lamja* (The Ȯrphan of Kege), written in 1958, is also based on the folk story of Moirang. In the next decade, he composed '*Shanulembi*', also a folk play. He wrote it in the year 1966.

Manipuri theatre till the mid-fifties was full of mythical, religious and romantic plays.

In the late 50s, a new student theatre group called '*Amateur Aristes Association*', graduates from D.M. College, Manipur, comprising of leftist theatre workers like Aribam Syam Sharma (b. 1939), Dorendrajit's son Arambam

Somorendra etc. got admission into the Aryan Theatre that broughtback a dramatic changes in the production styles and modernisation became the trend. Some wellknown productions of Aryan Theatre featuring sombre realism and imagery during this phase are Sri Sri Krishna Chaitanya (1958) of K. Phulendra, Syam Sharma's revision of T. Tomba's Pidonnu (1966), Biramangol's Sijalaioibi (Princess-Deity, 1967). The group also took up Phulendra's Manipuri translation of Shakespeare's Macbeth (1965).

Sixties

In 1960, Jamini Sundar Guha Memorial Gold Medal— a three-yearly award for any original outstanding creative writing published in Manipuri was instituted by the Manipuri Sahitya Parishad from a trust fund donated by the family of Jaminisundar Guha, a noted educationist of Manipur. Books published within three years of the award presentation year are considered for this award which carries a gold medal and a citation. The first recipient was the eminent dramatist G.C. Tongbra. A critic has aptly stated that the secular modern drama of the Imphal urbanite became predominant in the late sixties, though the father figure of G.C. Tongbra still used the multiple scene structure of the earlier proscenium. Since his emergence as a master of humour and satire in 1937 under his banner of the Society Theatre, Tongbra dealt with basic human behaviour, and his productions followed the old pattern of a variety of scenes and spaces, where the relationships of his characters were strung out with a continuous outpouring of his witty pharases, so that the inner action of the plays hardly moved before the virtuosity of his language and folkish humour. The Society Theatre staged most of his plays and of which he was the playwright, director and planner. G.C. Tongbra's play '*Leibak houba andolan*' (Earth-Shaking Agitation), was published in 1960. It was Tongbra's satire on politics and morals that created a furore. The play was produced during the statehood agitation, eventually leading to a police summons.

Gitchandra Tongbram Simha was a force to reckon with in the realm of modern Manipuri theatre and drama. In the 1960s Radio drama made a significant impact on Indian popular culture. Despite the popularity of and critical acclaim for many regional plays produced by AIR, the genre had not yet gained scholarly or serious attention. Manipuri radio drama owes much to G.C. Tongbra who took this form very seriously, gave it respectability, and made it a powerful medium to express complex experiences.

A prolific playwright whose dramatic output crosses over eighty play, many of which got into clashes with the establishment, Tongbra almost singled handedly builtup his own genre and became an institution unto himself in the sixties and seventies. From the 1970s G.C. Tongbra composed major experimental plays. Most of his later scripts grew unmindful of textual logic, or of behavioural subtleties among the characters.

In the year 1961, both Kanhailal and Sabitri worked together in the former's maiden venture 'Layeng Ahanba' (First treatment), a social satire which showed the direct influence of the veteran theatre personality, G.C. Tongbra, in whose 'Society Theatre', Kanhailal had acted in his college days. Though *Layeng Ahanba* could not break new ground in theatre, but it brought Kanhailal and Sabitri together.

Theatre Mirror, Manipur

Theatre Mirror is one of the most prominent, energetic and reputed theatre organisation which was born on 1 May 1965 by a group of talented enthusiast theatre workers with a sole objective to preserve and promote the Manipuri theatre with a high sense of contemporary social milieu. The group under the direction of Wareppa Naba, a prominent theatre—director of Manipur, has produced many a successful plays inside and outside Manipur successfully with high acclamations and awards. It has so far produced around hundred 80 plays since its birth. It purticipated in many National level theatre festivals held at Allahabad, Kolkata and East Zone Festival at Orissa and many festivals organised by the Manipur State Kala Akademi and others; ie, Sangeet Natak Akademi, New Delhi, etc. Theatre Mirror has established a training school for dramatic arts-Institute of indigenous performing arts. 'IIPA' which imparts training in the field of theatre and its other allied art.

In the post-independence phase, the theatre movement had a vigorous development with the writing of modern plays on national integration, prohibition, family planning and Gandhiji's ideas. Many places of Imphal valley began to build their clubs and drama halls. New drama scripts started putting in print.

Gandhian Plays in Manipuri

E. Nilakanta Singh informs "The Gandhi Centenary in 1969 produced Manipuri dramas focussing on Gandhi and his ideologies. Few notable plays based on Gandhian themes are *Mangal Ado* (That light by G.C. Tongbra, *Meitei Khungang* (Manipuri village, by H. Motilal), *Chingda Satpa* (Flowered in the hills, by S. Krishnamohan [1968]), *Manipur Kadomda* (Whither Manipur?) and *Jadouang* (a valiant tribal Satyagrahi launching non-cooperative movement in the hills. For the first time Gandhi's relevance to the time was seriously examined by the playwrights and theatre goers of Manipur".

The revolution in the intellectual realm enables the Manipuris to grasp the momentous changes taking place in society also. They became politically very conscious and revolted against the dictatorial regime and many social evils perpetuated by a decadent society.

Manipur, the troubled state has since the 1960s atleast lived in constant political and social unrest, frequently under martial law. The Armed Forces (Assam and Manipur) Special Powers Act, inforce since 1958, confers powers to shoot and kill on the armed forces whilst also providing them with virtual immunity from prosecution. The state has been riven by internal conflicts for decades. The troubled political history of Manipur has been perpetuated by a multitude of factors including anger at economic under-development, drug smuggling and corruption. Armed opposition groups have emerged organised on the basis of community affiliations and conflicting demands for greater autonomy and self-determination. Abuses of human rights by government forces and by armed opposition groups have became a feature of daily life. In this anarchic milieu of violence, terror and lawlessness, not single organisation remains that has not been corrupted. The militancy in Manipur again raised its head. It was the educated youths who advocated the ressurection of the once powerful nation in the Indo-Burma region. They mastered Marxism and its revolunationary practices and began a liberation movement. Soon the forms of protest got reflected in the arts and literature later in the seventies which witnessed a political movement with pan-Manipuri aspirations, especially with the formation of the Pan Manipuri Youth League in 1968. To quote M.C. Arun 'The League was the driving force of the youths looking for a pan-

Manipuri identity, working against all sorts of cultural accultaration. The league also started regular observance of the historically important events and the past glories of the Manipuri nation were invoked. They also acted as a pressure group to promote regional history studies and to wipe out corruption from the stage administration. A whole new line of thinking and new ideas were brought to the fore."

Eventually the new ideas and aspirations cast a story spell on the theatre people. New directors and playwrights followed the line of Badal Sircar in creating new imageries and play structures. The change in theme and performance was tremendous. It was the beginning of '*Experimental theatre*'.

Truly in Manipur were three standing groups led by the proscenium theatre movement—MDU, Rupmahal and Aryan reigned till the alternative theatre sprang up. In the late sixties there arose the amateur theatre workers, distinct from proscenium culture, in the upper realms of theatre art with the young educated classes which became fond of rigid, spatially controlled enactments for outpourings of conflict and emotion amidst the middle class. By the late 1960s, discontent against Indian rule and commercial exploitation by traders and outside agents led to the rise of youth power, search for identity, and resurgence of the indigenous spirit in the work of dramatist's like M. Biramangol.

From the late 1960's Aryan Theatre became the spring board for conflict, innovation, and experimentation. It became the only group that stood for the original culture of the Meiteis. In 1965, it presented Biramangol's '*Sanamahi Kolu Yeikhaiba*' with great sentimental flavour, magical production values and intense acting. Aryan became the only group that stood for the original culture by the Meiteis. It was in the late sixties that Mayanglambam Biramangol of Aryan theatre discarded the use of wings from the conventional proscenium in favour of the box set revolutionized Manipuri theatre.

For years, popular dramas and Shumang Lila scripts, composed by authors like Maibam Ramcharan, capitalized on sentiment, romance, suffering and family crises gained prominence among the masses. But with the rapid urbanisation, new economic structures, and decline in moral and community values ushered in modernist, critical social drama from G.C. Tongbra and Arambam Somorendra.

Cosmopolitan Dramatic Union (Imphal)

Founded in 1968, Cosmopolitan Dramatic Union or Cosmo Drama, is an ensemble of young theatre workers engaged on full time basis. It is one of the leading theatre troupes in Manipur. Cosmopolitan Dramatic Union came into being during the beginning of renaissance mvement of Manipuri Theatre. Its areas of interest are therefore both traditional performing arts and modern theatre. The Union is an ensemble of young theatre workers engaged in a full-time manner with a serious approach towards the composite art specialising in experimenting the application of the various exuberant art forms of Manipur such as:

(1) Manipuri martial Arts,

(2) Dances of Meitei and various Naga Tribes,

(3) Khunung and Khutlangs Isehi folk songs including tribal songs and music,

(4) Narrative performing art form.

Cosmo Drama has been striving towards evolving a new performance culture, drawing strength from the rich storehouse of traditional performing art forms of the region. Major plays produced recently by the Group are, *Devil & Mask* and *Draupadi*. Apart from play production and performance, the Group frequently engages in theatre promotion by conducting theatre workshops and annual play competitions for students. Cosmopolitan Dramatic Union Conducts workshops on Manipuri martial arts. Every year the Union organises Festival of Traditional Arts. As a part of activities, regularly conducts study tours in tribal villages and participates in cultural festival. The centre is situated at Wangkhei, Thangjam Leikai, Imphal - 795 001.

During 1960 and after, a number of young playwrights and directors started experimenting with the scripts and their production styles. They started exploring untouched fields and use new form, techniques and devices. Some started taking interest in physical theatre. Some tried to produce plays without scripts.

Amongst the experimentalists the name of Biren Singh comes to the mind first for their wider acclamations. Some of his plays have also been rendered into English.

Other modern dramatists who have made significant contributions to the Manipuri drama are A. Somorendra for his social criticism, A. Tomchau for his grasp on changing human nature. L. Kanhailal for his universal human appeal and N. Sri Biren for the modern dilemma.

One of the influential playwrights in Manipuri, Mayanglambam Biramangol's play '*Sija-laioibi*' (Princess-Deity) was taken to the capital at New Delhi by Aryan Theatre for enactment in 1967. Another leading playwright of the sixties was Pacha Meitei. They all set new standards for playwrighting: subtler treatment of realistic characters expressing the futility of the middle-class rush for advancement and the insipid degeneration of their own values in the process. Lokendra pointsout for quite sometime a new image of Manipuri youth, as depicted in Mohan of *Judge Saheb ki Imung* or Ruhikanta in *Dasa* (1968), focussed on a searching, probing generation unable to place its distinctive identity amid the rush for so-called progress. It filled the socio-political scene of the early seventies. This basic image was sadly lost in the next twenty years of Manipur's dramatic characters. While Somorendra, Timchou and Pacha Meitei had set the pattern of a new character, unable to adjust to the unfolding lifestyle and changing values of the petit-bourgeois society, the youth himself lost this identity, becoming a fearsome, violent setter of public standards and morals in the late eighties. This picture of youth was also missing in later dramas.

From the late Sixties Manipuri artists came up with regular technical training in direction acting, lighting, costume designing etc. from the apex theatre school at New Delhi. Today many of the alumni of the National School of Drama have occupied places of eminence in theatrical world. They started experimenting in psychological play, abstruct play, modern techniques and styles.

Competitive Drama Festivals were conducted by the Publicity Department of the Government of Manipur from 1965 to 1972. The drama festival organised by the Publicity Department has been instrumental in encouraging folk and modern plays. It published abstracts of the scripts to be performed in the competition. Today the task of conducting such festival is entrusted to the Manipur State Kala Akademi.

Radio dramas/One-act Plays

The opening of Manipuri programme in A.I.R. programmes of Gauhati (Assam) station and subsequent establishment of a full Radio station in Imphal are responsible for the rapid growth and popularity of radio dramas. All India Radio's drama section or radio adaptations of the old Manipur dramas and has encouraged new creations.

During this decade, one act plays received a considerable significance. Various schools, colleges and state Department have from time to time encouraged dramas among the students through one act plays and holding Prize Distribution Competition in the genre. Many such works were broadcast by A.I.R.

G.C. Tongbra is a writer of popular one-act plays and Sri H. Kanhailal, a director of repute enacted many a short plays. Some of them are available today in print format.

Seventies

It was in the seventies that the cry of the existentialist despair and loneliness came from the poet N.Sri Biren, who with his short plays like *Khongchat* (Journey) *Hallakpa* (Return, 1972), and Ani (Two), is engaged at the moment in a quest for identity, and diverse images of T.S. Eliot, Becket and Ionesco struggle for clarity, giving almost a collage effect in painting. It would be unfair to call this cheap imitation. It is more of a feeling of fragmentation awaiting the way to a new integraty and an irresistible compulsion dictated by the stark reality of times.

N. Sri Biren's play '*Khongchat*' (Journey) depicts an anti-heroic, modern-verse-reciting protagonist, thereby starting a five year absurdist interregnum in Manipuri drama. This play was presented in 1970 by Aribam Syam Sharma under the banner of Aryan Theatre.

The next year, ie, in 1971, Biren's '*Hallakpa*' (Return) directed by another celebrated director Lokendra Arambam skillfully portrayed the existential anguish of youth seeking some viable identity and meaning in a ruthlessly exploitative society.

In 1971, a memorable play was put on boards by Lokendra Arambam. This was Sri Biren's *Hallakpa* (Return), presented by Aryan Theatre that depicted the existential anguish of youth seeking some viable identity and meaning in a ruthlessly exploitative society. In the words of Lokendra Arambam "As in the social and demographic firmament, restlessness and anxiety provoked the entire mood of Manipur in the late sixties. There were agitations for statehood, and youth unrest due to famine and neglect in 1965 led to the death of a girl student in folice firing. The Pan Manipuri Youth League (1968) headed the resourgence of youth and underground revolutionaries surfaced in 1972. The anguish of the young generation was reflected onto the stage in the seventh decade. It was Absurdist drama which dominated and led the experimental Manipuri drama in the 1970s.

In the seventies, Arambam Somorendra Simha wrote a number of plays beginning with his short piece '*Judge Sahebki Imung*' and established himself as a powerful young playwrights of Manipur who look at human and social problems critically and rationally. Somorendra's plays like *Mirang* (Cobweb), *Hingnanaba Hingba* (To live for the Sake of Living) and *Eigidi Cabinet Oina* (Me as Cabinet Minister) have been produced for several nights at different theatre houses of Imphal. In the late 1960s and early 1970s, Arambam Somorendra's work dealt with social tension with romantic undertones where the individual's quest for self and identity became issues. A critic writes that the most serious attempt at breakthrough was made by a group of theatre-workers who struggled to impart a contemporary touch by taking up a few themes of social protest. The playwright, A Somorendra Singh, with his plays as mentioned in the foregoing pages like *Judge Sahebki Imung* (Jugde Sahib's Family 1967) and *Tirtha Jatra* and *Dasha* (Misfortune, 1968) deals with the conflict between the old and new values in the changing social context, exposing the hollowness of the middle class virtues from the humanistic point of view and putting question marks which kept the audience wondering. His drama '*Karbar* (Business) exposes the modern fallacy that money and business is everything in life. It was Arambam Somorendra, the path breaker who ushered in a new trend who disasociated himself from the earlier romanticized style and design. M.C. Arun documents "In his plays written between 1957 and 1978, Arambam Somorendra tried to probe the prevalent social system, thus starting a process of self-introspection among the youth. The 'Society' in his plays was controlled by a few rich persons. He openly questioned the system and started a debate. But an opinion for change was lacking in his plays. Many of them were descriptive pictures of contemporary society and the different faces of exploitation. In most of his plays, the young 'hero', like Mohan in *Judge Sahebki Imung* (The Judge Sahib's Family), is depicted as an alienated youth and not as an agent of change. In spite of his writings on exploitation he is not a marxist playwright. His later plays written in the late 1970s and 80s lost the vigourous intellectual exercise. He received the Sahitya Akademi Award for his romantic play '*Leipaklei*' in 1995.

Aribam Shyam Sharma had mostly directed the plays of Arambam Somorendra. While directing the early plays, Shyam Sharma relied on realism. The stage design, dialogue rendering and other theatrical devices were totally changed from those of earlier ones. His treatment, too, contributed to the provocation of the young minds. Lokendra Arambam informs : When the social drama *Judge Saheb ki Imung* (1967) was enacted in about two choice spaces of the rich drawing room of the retired judge and the kitchen, it reflected the theatrical vision of the new generation. By 1967, the fixed space of drawing rooms, destruction of wings for creation of such areas, embellishment of design patterns in the decor, and focus on realism or suggestive space, made the proscenium the ultimate in theatre design. No one could now think of destroying or negating the proscenium and creating a mobile, physical organisation of theatre space through bodily movements. This was to became a trend after the seventies.

In the year 1972, the Manipur State Kala Akademi was formed as a composite version of the three national academies, nurturing literature, performing and visual arts. This state govt. run Akademi started conscious patronage of Manipuri theatre. Manipur State Kala Akademi is situated at Khuman Dampak, Imphal - 795 001. It was established by the Manipur State Government as its agency for preservation and promotion of arts and culture in Manipur and cultural unity of the country, Akademi deals with music, dance and dramas, literature and fine arts. It is fully funded by the State Government apart from getting funds off and on from other agencies for specific schemes. It is one of the most active academies in Eastern India. Manipur State Kala Akademi publishes books on drama, literature, dance, music, fine arts etc. and a quarterly journal in English. It confers awards fellowships and scholarships, annually, gives grants-in-aid to organisations. It organises programmes, festivals, conferences, seminars on drama, dance, music, literature and also organises exhibits and workships of fine arts; maintains a museum, archives and library which have preserved precious manuscripts, costumes, artefacts etc.

During this decade, various cultural organisations and literary centres started taking active role in the overall yearning for change. The Cultural Forum, a literary group urban Imphalities, organised short play competitions as an annual academic activity from 1971 to 1975, the venue being mostly the Aryan Theatre. Even though, the state witnessed some annual theatre festivals, but such events were chiefly pleasurable coming-together of groups with existing productions, whereas in this short play competitions, the most striking feature was the quest for form and innovative exercise of individual creations. Some wellknown productions of the early seventies were Aryan theatre's *Hallakpa* (1971), Society Theatre's *Taj Mahal* (1972) P. Shamu's Theatre Mirror Dramatic Society's *Saknaidraba Wari* (1972) and Kantailal's Kalakshetra's *Kabui Keioiba* (1973) These were freshness of approach, open outlook and generation of new aesthetics. There were fresh winds of change in the shape of the new theatre which now thirsted for freedom.

In the year 1975, Lokendra Aramban in collaboration with H. Kanhailal produced the play '*1891*' dealing with the Meitei freedom struggle against the British and the next year '*Irabot*', a play on Irawat's proletarian revolution and *Yotpak yotlei ama* in 1979 highlighting insurgency and army appression all under the aegis of Aryan theatre.

In 1976, the Manipur State Kala Akademi Award was instituted by the State Kala Akademi, Manipur and is meant for outstanding original Manipuri creative writing published within three years of the presentation year. The first award was bagged by G.C. Tongbra for his drama '*Kekulopti*'.

Besides the hosting of theatre festival, giving away prizes and awards and the inception of apex institution, ie, the State Akademi, another significant occurance was the visit of Badal Sircar's troupe 'Satabdi' that marked a new development. It is only in the seventies that new ideas started coming in to find expression in a few experimental theatres, demnding a new style of writing, mostly under the influence of Badal Sircar's '*Evam Indrajit*', who presented three of his plays in the theatre Festival in 1972.

A major trend which cast a strong spell on the theatre groups like *Kalakshetra, Roop-Raag and Theatre Mirror* is the '*Intimate Theatre*' inspired by Richard Schechner, Grotowsky and Badal Sircar, dictating a new style of writing and the discovery of a theatric world.

Kanhailal and his 'Kalakshetra Manipur'

An experimental theatre group emerged in Imphal in July 1969, with H. Kanhailal as the Founder-Director. Since 1972 the group started regular stage productions with *Tamnalai* (the Haunting Spirit) as the first production for an alternative theatre with the basis on native-culture, which is still admired as one of the masterpieces of the group. In the wake of a separatist ideology, experimental theatre thus grew in the 1970s under director like H. Kanhailal. Initially, Kanhailal, an alumni of the National School of Drama, New Delhi, with his group, Kalakshetra, produced some short plays like *Wahang Ama* (A question), *Ikhou-Lngbi* (Thirsty Lady), *Tamnalai* (Mocking Spirits) *Kabu, Kayoiba* (a folk theme) dealing with the rootlessness and restlessness of the times and staging a return to folk roots with relevance to the contemporary situation. His theatre is very localized. Very much rooted within the milieu—his own people. That's why he prefer to work in theatre. He states "If my theatre is alienated from my milieu there is no meaning for me. So my experience is this : when these insurgent or militant or terrorist people — they are call by different terms — but for him they begin to express the agony of the people. It is form of expression. He don't take them as what they are. But originally he used to look at as a form of expression. That violence is an expression of their agony, frustration, of their disillusionment with the present government. Dissillusionment with India". In the beginning he used to create theatre in that milieu. He used to look at his own people history, tradition.

It was in 1972 that Badal Sircar staged four of his plays in Imphal for a Festival organised by the Manipur State Akademi. Here Sircar introduced the concept of non-verbal physical idiom of the third theatre. In 1973, Kanhailal spent three weeks in Calcutta and studied Sircar's psycho-physical exercises which were borrowed from the Euro-American avant-garde theatre of the 60s. He came under his strong spell and began to create theatre with a sharper sense of image and movement.

Kalakshetra was the first pioneering group which introduced Manipur theatre of modern expression in the Indian mainstream as early as 1974 at Calcutta and 1975 at New Delhi. Since then it toured throughout the country with its shows. It made waves in modern, poetic, and ethnic theatre reflecting the social discontent and human anguish of Manipur's disturbed polity.

Badal Sircar's play '*Evam Indrajit*' left indelible impress on the Manipur's literary circle. But it was his workshop and production of Spartacus in 1973 which was more in tune with the spirit of change and revolt in the art and politics. It encouraged theatre workers to get rid of the inhibiting influences of the fixed proscenium and flexible open—structured idioms, physically more exact and demanding, became the norm. Kanhailal led the new movement in the discovery of the body and its language. Kanhailal assisted Badal Sircar on his Manipuri version of Spartacus which was produced in a *mandap*. The predominantly *non-verbal idiom of Third theatre had a deep impact on Manipuri theatre workers.* Bharucha observes" "One could even say that this idiom has developed much more creatively in Manipur than in West Bengal, where it has lost both its efficacy and resilience."

With the earlier experiments, *Devjani* (1969) and *Ikhoulangbi* (1971) and more particularly Tamnalai (1972), to his credit Kanhailal's association with Badal Sircar led to his own evolution of an artiste of the new body medium. It was Kanhailal who started dramatising the poems and the theatrical inferno 'Imphal 1973' which was staged in 1974 was a poem by Sri Biren steeped in the angst of the early 70s. Lokendra Arambam while reviewing the production commented : Sri Biren gave a visual, poetic commentary describing the ordeal of a native mother from a popular folk myth. The mother was boiled alive by her oppressors. Here Sri Biren visualized the gradual process of her slow death, how death reached her ankles, her knees, her waist, breast, neck— and the final passing out of the agonized soul in one prolonged Shriek. This was all theatrically projected in a phantasmagoria of movement and violence. In an interview taken by H.S. Shivaprakash, H. Kanhailal said *"You know theatre cannot start from a vacuum. Theatre needs to start from an environment-according to time, the environment changes. So do tensions of the people. Therefore, I feel the need for a kind of theatre which can respond to the dominant sense of the time. In this context, I look back at the conventional theatre-that kind of proscenium theatre which was practiced everywhere in India after independence. We know that kind of theatre is the standard public theatre. When I look back at that, I don't find anything which could be fitted into my idea or philosophy or whatever you may call it. Because that kind of theatre cannot respond to the time, to tensions of the time, that theatre creates illusions in the audiences, tells a story and bring out some characters though these characters are also very much individual characters. However, the environment I am facing needs a kind of the character which is very collective, which is group oriented, that cannot be identified with one single individual. So in the context, I began to experiment with a new kind of theatre and specifically because I needed to avoid illusion in theatre. Then what is the thing which needs to replace it? So I felt that he need of awakening the audience. Awakening. How can theatre awaken them? Then the encounter—theatre is an encounter between the performer/actor and the spectator on the sensory level. Then we could provide very authentic and original theatre that can impinge on the senses of the audience. Then once their senses are awakened then they are able to perceive whatever they experience in the theatre. Because theatre is an experience for them. But between the experience and the reflection whatever the theatre give, they have to create a new perception. So with that perception people will be able to make themselves aware of social, political, economic happenings in that environment. And I don't believe that theatre can change society. Theatre can create consciousness or awareness of the happenings, of the reality of the situation. If they are very much aware, that awareness of the educated people—for they are very conscious of the whole society politically—that awareness work in the brain only, not in the body so we need to awaken their spirit, the spirit of being a man, the instincts of the people. I don't go around talking about ideology when I need to attack the instincts of the people which is deeply hidden, deeply rooted in the people. So from this point of view, from this philosophical background, I felt the need of creating an alternative theatre. So in 1972, I began to provide a concrete new theatre for Manipuri".*

Manipur's cultural history is dominated by the imposition of Vaishnavism on the local people and its post-independence political history, by its marginatization on account of its remote geographical position and its people's racial difference from the national mainstream. Kanhailal's expressed the feelings of anger and despair of a neglected people through his work. His strong sense of ethnicity first drove him to steep himself in tradition. Then, under the influence of Badal Sircar, he moved out of the ethnic enclosure into a wider perspective. Finally, he arrived at what he terms the "*theatre of transcendence*", which goes beyond verbal language and expresses itself through movement, song and dance. Kanhailal started with reinterpretion and radicalization of the folk narratives in his productions such as, stated earlier also, in Tamnalai (Haunting Spirits), in 1972, Kabui-Keioba (Half Man Half Tiger) in 1973 and Khomden (Meiroubi) (The Last Girl).

One of the most outstanding productions of Kalakshetra was 'Tamnalai' (Haunting Spirits), produced in 1972 Rustom Bharucha writes: Here, Kanhailal reversed the norms of a popular folk tale in which Chandra Kangnal, the lazy son of a widow, prospers by marrying a princess. In Kanhailal's play, which focused on the menace of goondaism, the lazy son became at once good, industrious, and poor, his hopes for a bright future dashed by manipulative forces in his society Humiliated by a group of goondas or thugs, the boy retaliates by killing them. Using the power of melodrama to full effect, enhanced by the presence of three old men who functioned as a chorus (the first use of its kind in the Manipur theatre), Kanhailal was able to inject a new urgency in the contemporization of the folk tale. The despair of unemployment (and the violence resulting from it) provided the base, as it were, for the elemental passions of the play.

The story of '*Kabui-Keioba*' centres on an archetypical figure in Manipuri folklore, created around the tribal necessity for protection, the predatory protagonist (an 'alien' by our standards todays) abducts a virtuous girl called Thaba. He does this through the instigation, if not the actual connivance, of an old woman, who convinces *Kabui-Keoiba* that the young girl will be tastier to eat, Ultimately through a clever ruse, Thaba escapes from her abductor after burning his house. There are several variations on this tale, including gory ones in which Thaba gets a child from Kabui-Keioba. Before she escapes, she tears the child apart from the legs and hangs her remains on a clothesline. Kanhailal's explanation for this lurid act of violence is very simple. The child was not pure, so she had to be destroyed. Otherwise she would have been dangerous to the clan. In Kanhailal's production, there was no representation of Thaba at all. The statement of the play was made through the old woman (played by Sabitri), who emerged as a shamam in touch with the future. In Kanhailal's interpretation, the old woman justified her seemingly selfish action of handing over Thaba to her abductor on communal grounds. Thaba's sacrifice was necessary for the survival of the clan.

'*Khomdon Meiroubi*' is another interesting modern play in Manipuri, composed by W. Kamini. The theme is borrowed from folk material and directed by Kanhailal. The play focuses on the economic corruption practised by traders from outside Manipur, the play skillfully employed a fold game called 'Kwak Kwak', in which occurs a mock fight between a crow (another 'alien') and a group of children led by the mother. The fight is conveyed through a series of questions and answers that counterpoint the crow's attempts to snatch the last child in the line. It is said that the game was introduced by one Khongnan Thaba during the reign of Garib Niwaz as a reaction to the imposition of new ideologies. Bharucha writes "In Kanhailal's production, the images of the mayang (foreigner) were clearly localized : the merchant (with an unmistakable association of a Marwari) wore a shirt and trousers, while the politician wore a kurta and pyjama. Perhaps the most arresting image in the production was the animation of a rice bag (played by one of the actors [inspired by the physical idiom of the Third Theatre]), who blindly follows the orders of the merchant, oblivious to the cries of the people.

It is pertinent to mention here that Kanhailal's training process was very much different from Badal Sircar's approach. Their differences in techniques is vividly discussed by Rustom Bharucha in his book '*The Theatre of Kanhailal : Pebet and Memoirs of Africa*'. To quote him "his awareness of indigenous resources began only after he had been introduced by Badal Sircar to the psycho-physical exercises of the Euro-American theatre of the late 60s. For a time, in the early 70s, Kanhailal repeated these exercises with his actors, but then he realized their futility. The most positive feature of these exercises had been their capacity to 'free' the actors from social inhibitions. While this certainly proved valuable in Sircar's theatre (in the absence of a strong physical culture in the predominantly verbal Bengali theatre), Kanhailal realized that his actors did not need to be 'freed' in quite the same way. Indeed, it shoud be pointed out that Manipuri actors are considerably more athletic and flexible that their counterparts in the rest of India. Also, the male-female interaction in Manipur is refreshingly free of the inhibitions and social taboos that permeate the Indian theatre, even in metropolitan centres. Another reason why Kanhailal moved away from Sircar's psycho-physical exercises concerned their cultural values which clashed with his own ethos. For example, eye-contact is very strongly upheld in Sircar's theatre, not just among the actors but between the actors and spectators as well. It is assumed that a direct confrontion of someone's eyes signifies 'sincerity' and 'honesty'. But it is almost taboo to look someone in the eye according to the laws of physical culture in Manipur. Indeed, even in ordinary social interaction, facial confrontation in Manipur is associated, in Kanhailal's words, with 'notoriety and evil'. Besides one does not need to stare someone in the eye in order to 'communicate' with him. As discussed earlier, 'eye-power' has the capacity to distribute energy to different parts of the body. [*'Try to see with your ears. Try to hear with your eyes" This central principle of Thang-ta has inspired Kanhailal's actors to develop a simultaneity of perceptions*.]

So also the face in Manipuri physical cultural can be viewed as a reservoir of energies. For most non-Manipuris, the face of the average Manipuri is like a mask. But for Kanhailal, the seemingly impassive faces of his actors are full of expression. Like the eye, the face also has the power to distribute energy. *'If I had to force my actors to make facial expressions,'* Kanhailal explained, *'I would be imposing masks on them'."*

Lei Paklei

This is a sentimental drama which tries to highlight those women who have the 'resilience of flowers that emerge through hard soil', presented in a lyrical mode. The play was put up by Kanhailal in 1977 during the inauguration of a friend's club, that proved to be too 'serious' a play for its members.

Thambalnu

This modern Manipuri drama is composed by B.K. Whengba. Thambalnu (Lotus-girl) revolves around a village girl named Thambalnu who rejects a nobleman's sexual advances. In retaliation, he bribe's a *maibi* (priestess) to malign the girl. Through a stratagem, this maibi predicts that the flood in the village can be controlled if a girl named after a flower, with her name ending in 'nu' can be sacrificed. Though the flood is caused by the collapse of a river bank, but the ignorant villagers, after believing the devious prediction, drag Thambalnu to the river into which she throws herself. The play closes with her lover taking revenge by killing the nobleman.

Thanghon

In his next venture Thanghon where he worked with non-actors, with some young men and women of the Paite tribe, a predominantly Christian community with whom he worked on an old Meithei story 'Thanghon *Leh Liandon* (Thanghon and Liandon). Rustom Bharucha writes "Through this story he was able to remind the tribal youth of their culture heritage which they were forgetting through an imposed 'Westernization'. Not surprisingly, the missionaries did not support Kanhailal's work, objecting, in particular, to the long rehearsals on Sundays. But the young actors and actresses responded warmly to Kanhailal's creative 'proselytizing' through theatre they learned how to shape a text through collaboration, focussing on problems like the editing of action and the juxtaposition of time sequences. Not only was the play successful in the community and in Imphal (where it was performed), it even led to the formation of a regular theatre group focussing on tribal themes and history.

Huranbagee Ishei

Huranbagee Ishei (Song of the Thieves) is a satirical play in Manipuri that centres on corruption structured like a *jatra* with improvised dialogue and catchy song sung in the Kirtaniya style. The play was very popular, the lyrics of which were composed by the poet L. Samarendra Simha, a close associate and collaborator of Sri H. Kanhailal.

Pebet

It was his production of 'Pebet' in 1976 that brought him the national recognition. An oft-repeated production since the 70s, the play is a part of the repertoire of *phunga wari* (Five side stories, which are told to Manipuri children by their grandmothers). The original story runs as follows : Pebet, a bird, smaller than a sparrow, which has not been seen in many years. It could be an extinct species. This minuscule representation of life in the protagonist of the tale who is represented as a mother of seven children who nest at the foot of a tree. Guarding

A Scene from 'Pebet'

her brood, Mother Pebet circumvents the predatory attention of a Cat by flattering him. She keeps boosting his ego till her children are ablo to protect themselves. As soon as they grow up, she starts resisting the Cat, who captures the youngest in her brood, but eventually through a clever stratagem she manages to trick the Cat into freeing her child. The Pebets are finally united as the Cat disappers from their lives, somewhat dejected.

Kanhailal makes some changes in the original story. However, the first and last parts of the story are left more or less intact. He breaks with the tradition in the middle of his production after the youngest child has been captured. Here, he shows all the Pebet Children being captured, indoctrinated, tortured and then set against one another. It is in this part that the politics of the play is most keenly felt before the play closes with the happy note.

In his production, Kanhailal retained some exchanges of dialogue between the Pebet and the Cat from the oral tradition, but the rest was entirely mimed. In the first production, the 'Cat' was played by Sri Shyamkishore who was depicted as something of a sadist, who enjoys playing with his prey before killing it. The Pebet children are shown licking the Cat's arse with mute obedience. This 'Cat' of Kanhailal is clearly Vaishnavite in his rhetoric and tactics who through his Sanskrit sloka 'Janani Janmabhumischa Svargadapi gariyasi' brainwashes the Pebet children.

Using these words as weapons, they turn on their mother and stone her pitilessly. The real fear of Mother Pebet was not that to her children will be eaten by the Cat, but rather than they will be converted to 'Cat-culture'. The process of indoctrination ends when one of the Pebet sons bites the Cat's arse instead of licking it.

Indeed, both Kanhailal and Sabitri continued to work in a predominantly verbal, socially responsive theatre till the mid-70s. But it was only in 1975, when the play 'Pebet' was first staged, marked Kanhailal's gradual transition from a poetically charged social realism to a more distilled form of dramaturgy, incorporating non-verbalism and a heightened use of gesture and movement. The training of Kanhailal's actors emerged to a large degree from the physical culture of Manipur itself such as Thang-ta, one of the richest discipliness of Manipur and what attracted him are the principles of movement underlying this tradition. Kanhailal used this folkstory to comment on the political and cultural indoctrination of his time must be regarded as a shrewd dramaturgical strategy.

First 'Pebet' was performed at the famous Polo Ground in Imphal in February 1975 as part of a Jatra festival. Its second production was held at the Manipur Dramatic Union in 1976. In 1980, at the Studio Theatre of the National School of Drama, New Delhi, the play was presented for the third time. In 1982, he was invited by the Sangeet Natak Akademi for a workshop demonstration of his directional method for which he was allowed to bring only four actors with him. This compelled him to totally restructure the play with Kanhailal himself playing the role of Cat, Sabitri the Mother while the other three actors played the children. One of the spectators of this workship was the director, Prasanna who invited Kanhailal to tour his home state of Karnataka. Between October and November 1982, fifteen shows of Pebet were sponsored by Samudaya, the leading street theatre organisation of Karnataka. This tour of Kalakshetra was followed by a single show of 'Pebet' in Chennai, sponsored by the Koothu-p-pattarai. On its return to Imphal, Kanhailal's troupe stopped over in Kolkata to put up another show of Pebet, organised by Seagull Books.

His plays Khomdon Meiroubi (1974), Imphal 73 (1974) and Pebet (1975) led the theatrical arena with fluid, playful movements and striking, stark images of the spirit of revolt and anger.

Since mid-seventies, ie, after the successful presentation of '*Pebet*', Kanhailal produced a good number of plays, a sort of exploratory productions, sometimes performed only once with upcoming Manipuri playwrights. Such as *Panjal* (Scoring), written by Kshetri Sanajaoba, put up shortly after the Emergency. In 1976, B.K. Wahengba's '*Thambalnu*' (literally Lotus-girl) was staged and Leiba Ama Khunai Ama (one Country one people) based on a poem by Samarendra. His other productions of this phase is a sentimental drama called 'Lei Paklei', staged in 1977, Huranbagee Ishei (Song of the Thieves) a satirical play.

Kanhailal reached the national scene in 1978 with his *Laigi Machasinga*. From 1978-80, there were 15 shows of his play 'Laigi Machasinga which dealt with the life of the Mau tribe in Manipur.

In February 1980, Kanhailal revived his play '*Laigi Machasinga* and was presented at a Festival conducted by the Shri Ram Centre for Performing Arts, New Delhi. The play revealed more about tribal life than could be conveyed by any social anthropologist. There was the deft interweaving of song, dance, and music and the most flagrant sequence was the flashback specially created in order to lengthen the play, in which the tribal chief made love to his wife by subtle rotations of the hip. This sexual dalliance was interrupted by the rather dramatic entrance of a tiger, who promptly injured the tribal chief's wife.

In a special performance organised by the Sangeet Natak Akademi, New Delhi, Kamaladevi Chattopadhyay after witnessing the play praised this experimentation which later won him the much coveted Best Director's Award from the Akademi in 1985.

Nupilal

Kanhailal have been associated with the women's issues in Manipur. In 1978, he did 'Nupilal'. Nupi Lal (Women's War) was one of the major theatrical events in the history of Manipuri Theatre. This play was produced on 12 December 1978 by Kanhailal in an open-air involving about 70 working women from the Women's Bazaar in Imphal. What was so striking about this period was his work with non-actors from working-class and rural communities. Some of these women were attached to troupes performing the traditional Moirang Parba plays. The play was performed in Janasthana Higher Secondary School compound, closer to 17 Assam Rifles camp. It was the celebration of the feelings. They memorized the whole of 'Nupilal' women's war episode. He admits, those women know more that what he knows about it. This is non-actor theatre. We also learn very much from the non-actor. At one place he wrote "I initiated and I worked with them till late in the night. I worked with them in such a way that they created their own theatre. If I go and ask them to do like this or do like that they are waiting for that. But try to avoid that we just discussed with them sufferings, pains and everything and we found out a story from them. My purpose was to get them to make theatre themselves. That way they did very well."

The story of Nupilal was structured in three parts. Rustom Bharucha informs:

> "The first part focused on Women in the Lai Haraoba, one of the most important ritual celebrations in the Meithei people, where the ancestors are honoured through an interweaving of rites, songs, dances, processions, and theatrical sketches. This representation of women in an ancient festival was juxtaposed with scenes depicting Women in the Bazaar. Here the focus was on haggling and surviving, women fighting with their husbands on returning home late at night. Such was the enthusiasm of the enactment that many spectators participated in the bargaining. It was, at one level, riotous, but as the poet Samarendra remembers with great warmth: 'The actors were *one* with the audience. We were together. Of course, the critics didn't like it, but the people enjoyed themselves.'

The sheer effervescence of the second part of the show was, once again, juxtaposed with militant images and episodes representing Women in War. Here there were direct allusions to the historic *Nupi Lal* of 1904 and 1939-40, particularly the latter, in which Manipuri women had participated actively in political resistance. Both of these 'Women's Wars' were popular uprisings led and fought by women against the British manipulation of their economy and ethos. The upheaval of 1904 had been provoked by the insulting order of the British Resident Maxwell, who had insisted on Manipuri workers rebuilding the house of his colleague, which had been burned down by unknown persons. The second *Nupi Lal* was an even more violent reaction to the government when it arbitrarily lifted the ban on the export of rice at a time when supplies were limited in Manipur itself. Though the 'war' lasted only for a day, involving a gherao of the President of the State Durbar, it has left a deep impression on the memory of Manipuri people."

Approximately 70 working women alongwith 30 male actors recreated significant aspects of Manipuri culture and history in an open forum where the distinction between the actors and the spectators was almost obliterated.

After Nupilal, he started working with a very different community, the rural inhabitants of a village called Umatheili (or the Valley of Durga). Here he took up the cause of villagers who were out casts from a relatively prosperous village called Kakching Khunou, dominated by a group of familities who ruled on them like kings. Here was a different kind of oppression of villagers, ie, by the rural elite. After listening to villager's stories, he took up a folklore 'Sonjennaha' (Cowherd) for production. In this acute political fable, an unemployed cowherd seeks support for a job during the ploughing season. He gets the jobs but only after he has been black mailed, cheated, and threatened by various villagers. At the close of the play, he accumulates an enormous amount of grain through payments for his work, by little by little all the grain disappears as people come forth to demand their share on one pretext or the other. At the end, the cowherd is as hungry and poor as he was before getting the job.

In Februaty 1984, Sabitri gave a solo performances in New Delhi entitled '*Loi*', (outcast). An improvised piece, highlighting the plight of a slave through song and movement. When this loose performance piece was put together, the essence was '*freedom*'. A number of elements in her performance were retained later to be used in his major venture '*Memoirs of Africa*' which was staged in December 1985.

Memoirs of Africa

The play '*Memoirs of Africa*' is based on Samarendra's poem '*Africagee Wakhanda Gee*, (meaning 'Thinking of Africa), but the production is known by its English title '*Memoirs of Africa*'. Kanhailal's experiences of oppression on a more human, universal level led him to reach out to the audience almost as a distant haunting music (Memoirs of Africa, 1986).

The word 'Memoir' denotes a form of literature, but it is also rooted etymologically in the Latin word *memoria* or '*memory*'. That, in essence, is what the play is about, the almost primordial memory of oppression that activates the present and may continue to haunt the future. The plot of the play runs as follows:-

> Mi is the central character, a person who could be either male or female, an epic figure of humanity. The play deals with his eternal persecution and survival. The play has not story as such, it unfolds through repetitions of violence inflicted on Mi by Mimanu, ie three men (to be regarded as personifications of evil), which are interspersed with repetitions of lyrical interludes provided by the two women, ie, Nupi, young women who are half spirit, half-human. They also serve as 'choric figure who laments the destruction of life.

In Kanhaial's production, 'Mi' was enacted by Sabitri, who used the dual images of a tree and a slave to evoke the sheer magnitude of struggle.

Bharucha comments:-

> Kanhailal wanted to show through these three men, the psychology of the colonizes, the 'internal animality' of men who can smile and murder at the same time. If the image seems melodramatic, it is only appropriate to the poetics of melodrama used in the production, which is, otherwise, steadily debased in our performance culture. For the west, one could argue, melodrama has become a dated genre; for as it is part of our sensibility, a tradition larger then life, yet real.

The poet Samarendra said: *People, whether they are Naga or Meithei or African, cannot ultimately be suppressed. Somehow they will spring up again from the root, like plants. Neither power nor money can destroy them forever. For a time they may be lured, but slowly silently, some force will be working in them from underground. You cannot suppress Africa so easily."*

Though not a line of the poem was used in the production, but its philosophy permeated the spirit of the play. At one place, regarding the relationship between theatre and environment Kanhailal spoke about the creation of his production '*Memoirs of Africa*'. To quote him "How did we create *Memoirs of Africa*? We learnt a few songs. That makes us haunted and our body becomes amplified, augmented. Then we allowed ourselves to go further in that journey. Repeating, repeating, repeating. After the repetition of songs, we could see images. How the bird flies, scared... the images of the scare, the torture - all kinds of things. These haunting images - a spirit haunts me - its effect on my body, my senses is quite different from what we are now. The effect is essential. If we don't have that effect, the actor cannot express very originally and authentically. This kind of going back to the past and exploring the thing, in a dreamlike situation, we remain childlike. We didn't have an objective. Keeping open and remaining childlike, sometimes the person is possessed in that situation. In this way we go back to the past, the ancestral past and again come back and that makes all the images - my body becomes a field of images. We used to play with images, that is why we could disturb the audience. We can make them sensorially aware. The memory of the past is through a continuos journey of sensation, sensitization and intricate play of the images within myself and then again we try to externalize it. We have to achieve this. When I look it objecively - it is also objective - not subjective - it is a personal mythology. The actor needs a personal mythology. Myths descend upon his body, upon his senses. This is the power of a life giving force. We ultimately realized that a myth is a life giving force. If I talk such things to our academicians they can't understand. They can't find it satisfactory." He further adds "The repetition of the song, invades or descends upon our body, but that time, we face a certain kind of environment of the consciousness I am trying to explain as a dreamlike state of consciousness. When we reach that dreamlike state of consciousness, then we could see everything including dramaturgy."

Kalakshetra has travelled extensively within the country and abroad with their widely acclaimed theatre productions. It toured Japan in 1987 in connection with the International Theatre Festival. In Kalakshetra, it has aptly been stated that Kanhailal produced the vision and H. Sabitri, his actress-wife, the expression. In the year 1987 H. Kanhailal adapted and directed the play '*Rashomon*' with Heisnam Sabitri in the Key role.

Two scenes from 'Memoirs of Africa'

In 2000, Heisnam Kanhailal put on board the play '*Draupadi*' once again dealing with women issue in which he focused on the need of the emergence of female leadership. We are talking about 33% percent reservation for women in parliament and assemblies. Are they leading themselves or are they following the male track? It is questionable. He however, feels the need for the emergence of female leadership and that is what he wanted to show in his production of 'Draupadi'. In that way his theatre is completely rooted in his social, cultural, political milieu. This is what he call to *respond to the dominant sense of the time.*

Some of the prominent actors of Kalakshetra, both past and present, include Sabitri, Shyamkishore, Nandita, A. Phirojit, H. Tomba, Sanjukta, Gope etc.

Ratan Thiyam and his 'Chorus Repertory Theatre'

Ratan Thiyam got an admission in the National School of Drama in 1971 and passed out successfully in 1974. Thereafter he took up a series of exercises based on classroom productions not in tune with his native environment culminating in the '*Chorus Repertory Theatre*', which he established in 1976 with his young colleagues. Ratan's father Tarunkumar Thiyam was a Manipuri dance teacher. Before his passonate interaction with Manipuri theatre, Ratan took keen interest in literature, particularly in poetry and painting. He actively involved himself in the literary movement in the 1970s when creative expression was at a peak and the search for Manipuri identity the subject of the young generation.

It was in 1976 with his production '*Sanarembi Chaisra*' that Ratan Thiyam and his '*Chorus Repertory Theatre*' ushered in the new folk medium, a blend of pungent humour, pageantry and spectacle. This play *Sanarembị-Chaisra* (Sanarembi and Chaisra) through which he sought meaningful exploitation of traditional culture and folk theme launched him on a brilliant career. His commitment to discipline, seriousness of training, and execution of a strong visual sense made Ratan's work a tour-de-force in national theatre with a powerful presence on the international scene.

Ratan's development as a stalwart of "*Total Theatre*" was nartured by his exposure to the National School of Drama Festival through '*Uchek Langmeidong*' in 1977) at Shri Ram Centre for Performing Arts, New Delhi.

The departure from the internal dynamics that gave it life and character was led by Thiyam who, compelled by circumstances of his reputation, started working on genres understood by his adopted audience, the new urban Indian middle class. Theatre based on Sanskritic texts, like the Mahabharata triology, became his concern. His efforts with Indian classics led him to fresh new pastures of international recognition with a corresponding isolation from Manipuri audiences. Very few of his plays were seen by the people of his home soil.

In the eighties, Ratan was legendary fame through his plays '*Urubhanga*' of Bhasa in 1981, Dharamvir Bharati's '*Andha yug*' in 1984 and his own *Chakravyuha*, in 1984.

In Sangeet Natak Akademi's National Theatre Festival entitled 'Natya Samaroh', Ratan Thiyam's much acclaimed drama '*Chakravyuh*' was presented at Kamani Auditorium, Corpernian Marg, New Delhi on 18th December 1984. Designed, scripted and directed by Ratan Thiyam under the banner of his Chorus Repertory Theatre, Imphal. He used old ritualistic and dance tradition of the region contributing to Indian contemporary theatre a very distinctive idiom. The play evolved in workshop and had been scripted under a daily work-process which involved the actor's confrontation with different aspects of the science of theatre. This was his first phase of work done under the project, "*Actor's Methodology*" in which the 'actor' had been made observer, participant and performer. The cast and credit of this memorable production is given below:-

> Doran: *Sutradhar;* Sanatomba: *Pariparshwik 1;* Angoutombi: *Pariparshwik 2*; Ibomcha Sorok: *Abhimanyu*; Tomba: *Sumitra*; Makhonmani: *Yudhishthira*; Ibomcha Wang: *Bhima*; R.K. Bhogen: *Dronacharya*; Ibochouba Meetei: *Karna*; Premananda Ningthouja: *Ashwatthama*; Iboyaima: *Kripacharya*; Damayanti: *Subhadra*; *Chrous*: Angoutombi, Premananda, Jillasana, Iboyaima, Sanatomba, Doren, Ibomcha, Makhonmani;

In the year 1987, Ratan Thiyam, one of the finest directors in modern times became the Director of the National School of Drama. A man who staged his major productions for an audience outside his home state, exploring mainstream Hindu epics through Manipuri traditions of theatre, dance, music and martial arts

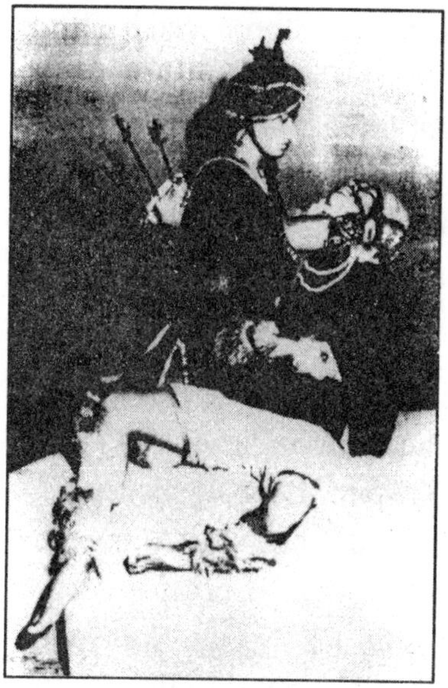

A moment from *Chakravyuha*, presented by the Chorus Repertory Theatre, Imphal 1984.

which carried him far. In the nineties Ratan took up two brilliant productions *Hirosima* (1994), based on Badal Sircar's work and Ajñeya's '*Uttara Priyadarshi*' (1996), on Emperor Asoka, both focussing on the horrors of war.

In the year 1974, '*the Avant Garde*' theatre troupe was formed in Imphal. This became a registered society which, today, stands for promotion, education and popularisation of Manipuri Theatre and theatre activities. The Avant Garde sponsors theatre training schools, theatre workshops, seminars, conferences and theatre productions. At present it concentrates on theatre training school, promotion of tribal language theatre, in the tribal zones of Manipur and theatre productions. It has also broughtout significant books on Manipuri theatre. This modern theatre centre has a small library of about 1000 books and a Mini theatre having 100 seats capacity. S. Ebotombi Haorokcham and Kh. Tuleshwar Singh associted themselves as the President and Secretary of the troupe. The group's address of communication is Keisampat Thokchom Leikai, Imphal - 795 001, Manipur.

Sanakhya Ibotombi

Another celebrated theatre personality who emerged in the seventies was Sanakhya Ibotombi. In the year 1973, Sanakhya Ebotombi directed the play '*Langoinai*' (Captive) written by Pacha Meitei. This was a creative contribution, by Ebotombi who presented the play under Aryan Theatre. Lokendra Aranbam has rightly commented that the chief oeuvre of Ibotombi was the institutional structure of serious drama, without much of an attempt to relate to his immediate ethnic realities. This gifted director applied Manipuri dance and scenography with unforgettable lyricism when he directed Kalidasa's Sakuntala for Rangamandal, Bhopal in 1990. Lokendra informs: At home and also as part of the institutional culture of the National School of Drama, New Delhi, this man produced striking gems of the realistic genre in Cage (1974), Caucasian Chalk Circle, Pacha Meitei's Na Tathiba Ahal Ama (1975) and a host of subsequent productions ranging from Beckett to Tendulkar. Ibotombi's penchant for an establishmentarian outlook in aesthetic enhancement and his universality of ideological background did not allow him at first into folk forms. Later, his experimentation with Indian dramas in native Vaishnavite forms bore results.

By the late seventies those talented Manipuri directors who were working feverishly to secure national recognition also at the international level. Two such great theatre personalities were Kanhailal and Ratan Thiyam. Leading pioneers of 'Experimental theatre' are Ratan Thiyam, Kanhailal and Lokendra Arambam. However these expotents differed in their areas of experiment. A critic observes "Ratan Thiyam experimented on visual designs and the formal aspects of the play. Many of his visual forms were imitated from the forms of Nat Sanskritana. On the other hand, playmakers like Kanhailal and Lokendra Arambam indulged not only in what they called 'Physical Theatre', but also in thematic experiments."

Lokendra Arambam, an inheritor of the Aryan Theatre legacy did some meaningful works. His political plays like *Men Without Shadow* (1972), 1891 (1975) and the Irabot [Irawat] (1976), a docu-drama on the proletarian revolutionary were remarkable. Lokendra's experiences of the individual in torment, as alienated from a demanding collective, emerged in ritual form which was difficult to read (Phouoibi Langon, 1985).

By the end of the seventies, the theatre in Manipur was at its peak. Many meaningful activities with workshops, symposium and experimentation continued. A critic reports 'The National School of Drama' drew attention to the theatre potential of Manipur, and came to organise workshops and encourage productions plays like 'Andha Yug' (1975) were brought down by Ratan Thiyam. Aryan Theatre organised a Festival of Experimental plays from 1977 to 1979, and Chorus Repertory Theatre and Kalakshetra were encouraged to secure a platform and an enthusiastic audience, from which they emerged on the national scene. The rural peasant prosecnium groups too found amble energy to activate themselves, and the '*Regional Theatre Festival* organised by the Sangeet Natak Mandir in 1978 drew as many as ten such troupes. Intercollege drama competitions of the '*Theatre Centre*' created the atmosphere for immense vitality and effort in the transformation of the theatre.

Eighties

Three major productions of this decade are Ratan Thiyam's Mahabharata trilogy, Lokendra Arambam's Phouoibi Langen (1985) and Kanhailal's Memoirs of Africa (1986).

Productions that earned Aryan Theatre both popularity and critical acclaim in the eightees are '*Khuman Chakha Moirang ngamba* (Moirang Tribal Rituals) focussing on revenge and honour. In 1982, Lokendra's balladic style production '*Khuman Chakha Moireng Ngamba*' too reached the national scene. *Numit Kappa* (Shooting the Sun), an extensively mounted play on ancient myth, a ritual play '*Phou-oibi-langon*'. (Cycle of the Rice Mother) focussing on the seething revolt of the individual against oppressive collectivity and *Ningthou* (King) an adaptation of Tagore's symbolical play '*Raja*', all produced by the Aryan Theatre in the eighties.

Manipur Ensemble

Manipur Ensemble was formed in 1986 with Kshetri Jugindro as its director. This is a centre for drama, Manipuri martial art, dance, drama and documentation, etc. The centre has made a commendable contribution for developments of Manipuri culture. Manipuri Ensemble is a centre for creative activities where eminent people work jointly for the promotion and dissemination of Manipuri culture.

The Centre has organised theatre workshops every year at the State level including tribal theatre and children's theatre workshops in Manipur since 1987 and produced many commendable plays including tribal plays like: Oedipus Rex, Antigone, Caucasian Chalk Circle, Hamlet, Naag Mandala, Ghar Sasur in Manipuri; Good Woman of Setzuan, Numit Kappa, Henjunaha, Changyen Manja, Mathanggi Yeningthada, Katinii Kajinni in Mao dialect, Hundung Khullakpagi Machanupi in Tangkhul dialect, Hringthem in Anal dialect, and Laklo Aikhoi Sannaminnashi, Aikhoibu Hinghallu, Hanubi Hentak. It has produced many plays with children's plays also. It is situated at Singjamei Wangma, Kshetri Leikai, Imphal - 795 001, Manipur. Theatre-in-Education or TIE, a field programme taken up by the group, has involved numerous children from different primary schools and different social, cultural and economic backgrounds, who are engaged in the creative process of theatre. The Manipuri Ensemble stands for a strong theatre movement in this region and for the establishment of a creative awareness of the local traditions in the milieu. Kshetri Jugindro is the founder and artistic director of this troupe.

Among the modern playwrights who came up with different socio-political issues are Athokpam Tomchou, Pukhrambarn Shamu, N. SriBiren, Pacha Meitei, W. Kamini, B.K. Wahengba and Kshetri Sanajaoba. Except Kanhailal, Lokendra Arambam, Pacha Meitei and N. Sri Biren, the others were more concerned with the selflessness and inner identity of the individual.

Encouraged by the scheme to unearth young directors as envisaged by the Sangeet Natak Akademi, New Delhi, and also by the Manipuri State Kala Akademi's policy of grants to theatres and participation in festivals, a number of new theatre groups run by some young generation of directors and some young artistes associated with established troups emerged in the eighties.

Mangang, S.K.

Belonging to the school of Ratan Thiyam, theatre director S.K. Mangang's forte is loud speech and action, a variety of judiciously mixed dance, music and martial arts, a rapid development, quick, light movements interspersed with silences, a vigorous crescendo of drums and a desire to reachout with the vibrancy of ethinic nuances.

Dorendra Singh

A Science Graduate from the Guwahati University Loitongbam Dorendra was born in Imphal, Manipur, in 1953. He took an active interest in theatre right from his schooldays and over the years he has been associated with eminent theatre personalities like Sue Weston, John Martin, Prabir Guha, Ratan Thiyam and H. Kanhailal. As an actor he has been associated with Chorus Repertory Theatre and performed major roles in plays, viz, Urubhangam, Chakravyuha and Uttarpridarshi. Apart from performing widely inside the country, he has performed in foreign countries, such as Greece, Italy, U.S.S.R., U.K., Ireland, Mexico, Peru, Colomba, Cuba, Ecuador, Japan, France, Thailand and Bangladesh.

One of the founder members of the Cosmopolitan Dramatic Union, Shri Loitengbam Dorendra Singh started directing plays of Cosmo Drama from 1989 and wom him many awards and titles in competitions organised by North-East Theatre Organisation, Manipur in the productions of *Meehat (1989), Kao Amasung Kei (1990), Chaoba Nongthon Senjaba (1991)*, all under his direction.

His play '*Draupadi*' was featured at many Theatre Festivals including National Theatre Festival of Sangeet Natak Akademi in Allahabad in 1990 and in the NSDS National Theatre Festival in 2000. Another new play '*Taj Mahal*' was also featured in the National Theatre Festival 2001 organised by South Zone Cultural Centre at Nagpur and Surat. The play '*Bhoot Amasung Maikhum*' (Devil & the Mask) was featured in the India Theatre Olympiad organised by the Utkal Yuva Sangskrutic Sangh at Cuttak in 1998.

He is presently a member of the standing committee for Theatre and Shumang Leela of Manipur State Kala Akademi, Imphal.

L. Dorendra Singh also belongs to Thiyam school who has thrown up deeply motivating pieces and has not gone in for theatric visuals as does his mentors. His speciality is the use of the actor for words, for enactment of conflict, with rare use of much-vaunted chorus. Rigour in his style.

Premchand, N.

Associated with the Aryan theatre, N. Premchand is a young director who became wellknown nationwide with his production *Ima Keithel* (1987) and later produced some memorable plays, all of them with a consistent level of productive ingenuity. He has been in the forefront with rich contemporary artistic endeavours. In the 1990s the Aryan Theatre produced a number of politically oriented drama, mostly under the direction of Nongthombam Premchand, some in collaboration with Aramban Somorendra or N. Mohendra.

Two Sequences from Aryan Theatre's 'Antigone'; directed by Nongthombam Premchand.

Rajendra, Y.

Y. Rajendra is a talented multifaceted theatre personality, a playwright, a director of immense possibilities and an artiste of poetential, raw energy pulsating his speech action and movements, who dominated the student theatre of the eighties. Regional idioms, vigour, physicality and dynamism are his strong points, and his association with Probir Guha of Living Theatre (Bengal) was fruitful, so that he became the darling of the college drama groups.

His dramatic writing comprises of over thirty plays ranging from symbolic to the melodramatic kind. Apart from Y. Rajendra, two other most promising budding directors of the nineties trying to conceptualise their own contributions to the alternative theatre are L. Kishworjit and Y. Khogendra. L. Kishworjit is an NSD alumni who has made a niche for himself. The young directors from Kanhailal's tradition — the aspects of body language, use of body movements and their expresive potential, and the curvilinear pattern in which the Meitei physically excels are — Y. Khogendra and Y. Rajendra.

Conclusion

In its obsession with form and identity, the Manipuri theatre of the eighties lost its soul. Lokendra Arambam rightly observed that theatre was no longer immediate to the changed audiences who were struggling to find their own balance and rhythm in a society increasingly becoming brutal and violent, and an establishment becoming more and more oppressive. The entire sociopolitical and cultural world of Manipur in the eighties needed more direct confrontation by the theatres—but the alternative theatre had outlived its earlier role. Direct issues of life were taken up by the Shumang Lila in the courtyards, but with a different value system. It was in such a period of anguish, violence and uncertainty that the theatre of Manipur internalised its experiences, leading to subtlety of nuances in expression but lacking open confrontations with life.

As stated before, since 1970s, theatre in Manipur has included a powerful strand of 'Alternative theatre of various kinds, dating particularly from the work of innovative directors Ratan Thiyam, Heisnam Kanhailal, Harok Cham 'Sanakhya' Ebotombi and Lokendra Arambam: This emphasised the exploration of tradition forms as well as engaging with the urgent social issues and problems the young directors saw around them. The work of these director benefited from interaction with other strands of innovation subsequent to the establishment of the 'Manipur State Kala Akademi' in 1972. Badal Sircar held workshops following a production of '*Evam Indrajit*' in 1973, leading to further production, *Spartacus*. Kanhailal spent some time both in Kolkata with Sircar and at Rangayana. Thiyam was appointed Director of NSD, their work received national and international recognition, playing in Delhi, Mumbai and London—where Arambam's '*Macbeth: Stage of blood*' was performed on the Thames in 1997. But Ratan Thiyam describes the recent situation for theatre as comparable to that of Poland under curfew: very active inspite of little scope for cultural exchange."

An outstanding dramatist of the new generation Khundrakpam Brajachand, is reckoned as a protest dramatist who passed stinging comments on the decaying values of Manipuri society in plays combining humour with symbolism and existential anguish.

In the nineties, A Somorendra's plays *Sakhangkhidraba Lanmi* (1990), *Chingungi Thawai* (1991) and *Nong Tarakle* (1992), made seductive pieces of theatrical metaphor.

Way back in 1995, Lokendra Arambam wrote: The distinctive identity of the regional theatre of Manipur was perhaps shaped by the changes that took place in the last twenty five years of the state's history. The transformation that was effected in the character and physical shape of the alternative theatre was a fallout of the overall change with the advent of a Manipuri middle class, growth of social and political aspirations leading to regional and ethnic identification movements, and development of an urban elite supposedly freed from traditional moves. Yet the regional theatre as developed during this quarters of a century revealed flashes of brilliance in form and structure, idiom and expression, without a corresponding confrontation with the dynamics of life which gave it birth. The evolution of contemporary theatre of Manipur therefore reflects contradictions in itself, contradictions posed by the ontological transformation in the creative life of its stalwarts, and unable to grapple with the problems of a traditional society coming to terms with processes of change and modernization. Manipuri theatre is on the threshold of an abiding change, yet the directions of change seem uncertain and unsure, which lends the processes of its evolution a certain poignang and pathos". Many creative young director appeared in the nineties. A critic comments. One can be sure of their seriousness, commitment and pursuit of excellence on the alternative, amateurs platform, but they lack the desire for personal development and consciousness in their relation with history and society.

Lokendra further adds 'Despite economic deprivation and socio political marginalization, struggle and turmoil vitalize Manipuri theatre. Its exceptionally talented actors like H. Sabitri and R. Bhogen, strong in traditional training, have won international acclaim in recent decades'. Sabitri Meisnam was honoured with the Sangeet Natak Akademi Award for Acting in 1991. Sri R.K. Bhogen also bagged the prestigious Sangeet Natak Akademi Award for Acting in 1997.

THEATRE HAPPENINGS (1995-2006)

Leipaklei (Earth Flower) written in 1992 by Arambam Somorendra was adjudged the best book in the language by the National Academi of Letters (Sahitya Akademi), New Delhi in the year 1995.

This year when the Aryan theatre was celebrating its sixty years, its auditorium accidentally burnt down.

Social and political fluctuations influenced the status of contemporary theatre. Creative individuals like Ratan Thiyam initially transcended local and regional frontiers to seek greener pastures, while conventional commercial theatre posing as reformist continued to pander to non-cerebral tastes. At this juncture, Lokendra Arambam of Aryan Theatre developed his '*Theatre for Resistance*' to counter both modes, but the establishment appropriated him by featuring his '*Macbeth : Stage of blood*' in 1997, an environmental production on a lake, in the celebration of fifty years of Indian Independence in London.

In the year 1998, the Public Theatre, Phoijing staged a wellknown drama of Sudhir Naoroibam (b. 1969) entitled '*Shunugi Mahao*' (The Taste of Lime). This drama was later put on boards by the leading theatre troupe the Manipur Dramatic Union, Imphal in 2000.

The '*Forum for Laboratory Theatre*' of Manipur was invited to present its production '*Awang Nong Poklamgee Nawaa*', written and directed by Lokendra Arambam, in the Natya Samaroh (National Festival of Plays) organised of the

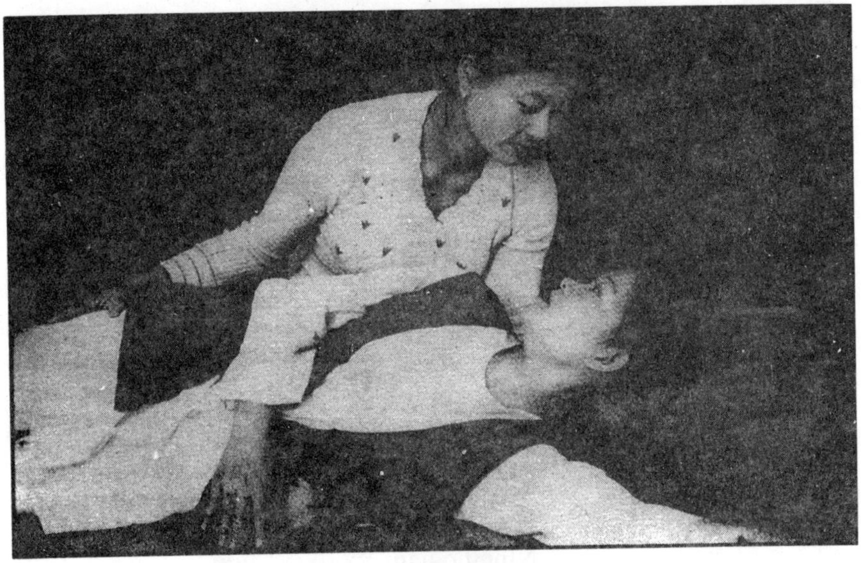

A Scene from 'Awang Nong Poklamgee Nawaa'

Sangeet Natak Akademi New Delhi and Directorate of Kannada and Culture, Govt. of Karnataka. The play was presented on 21st January 1999 at Ravindra Kalakshetra, J.C. Road, Bangalore. The play was an attempt to draw attention to the problems of violence in contemporary Manipur, brought forth by the present day dynamics of exploitation, corruption and oppression. Traditional societies are now ruthlessly exposed to contending forces of manoeuvres for power, dominance and advantage brought forth by the so-called rich for progres and modernization. Ethnic societies are now bursting at the seams, unable to contend with the character of the conflicts of growth. Death, decadence and disease of a unique character prevails at present. These issues are hardly projected on to the realm of the stage, however. Manipur theatre's radical engagement to probe the nature of its identity through a meaningful relationship with the movement for the theatre of the fourth world are being asserted by this effort. The play is an imaginative metaphor on the issues of post colonial tragedies of highly cultured traditional societies subverted by the agonized path of forced underdevelopment of modern times. The play is a surrealistic projection, part fantasy and part ritual, unusual exploration of reality, seen through the uncorrupt mind of the young. The cast and credits of this production is provided below:-

Cast

Boy/Girl	: (Miss) Usham Memtombi Chanu
Cranky Old Man	: Meghachandra Chingsuba
The Master	: R.K. Tombisana
Officer	: Firoz Angom
Chorus	: Gopi Kokngang, Rajen Sarangthem, Shyam Ayekpam, Sadananda Hanjabam, Khogendrajit, Chanambam, Mitrachand Wahengbam, Bishe Moirangthem, Miss Phajaton Chanu Kshetrimayum, Miss Thaballei Angom, Miss Ajanti Aribam
Singer	: Bhagat Helshnam, Ibohanbi Yambem, Pritamkumar Ningthoujam

Credits

Music	: N. Tiken, Ng. Prop ishak
Production	: R.K. Sanatomba
Light Y Stage Design	: Ch. Sarat
Costume	: Gope Kokngang
Management	: Kangambam Kaminikumar
Production Design	: Lokendra Arambam R.K. TM Isam, Firoz, Gope Kokngang, H.B.
Asst Director	: Firoz Angom, Gope Kokngang.

Arambam Somorendra was one of Manipur's finest playwrights. Somorendra was a revolutionary ideologue in the 1960s, but renounced militancy decade ago. This quiet, sensitive, dignified man who embodied the best of Manipuri culture was shot in cold blood as he attended a cultural function in Imphal in June 2000. This shocked the theatre community across India, reminding them once again of other outspoken fellow workers martyred for their political views. Theatre critic Ananda Lal sadly comments 'Truly, Manipur has fallen into anarchy if she cannot provide respect and safety to her finest senior representatives".

On 1st March 2001 at Abhimanch Theatre, New Delhi, Ratan Thiyam's much acclaimed production 'Chakravyuh' was staged under the banner of his Chorus Repertory, Imphal. It was on the occasion of National School of Drama's Third National Theatre Festival.

In the '*Natyotsav*' organised by the Sangeet Natak Akademi, New Delhi, Manipur Dramatic Union's play '*Paobiral Nongarol*' under the direction of Lamaban Gojendra was performed on 23rd March 2001 at Abhinav Theatre, Jammu.

In the year 2001, playwright and director H. Kanhailal's Kalakshetra produced the play '*Izzat*' on 20th March at Kamani Auditorium, New Delhi, on the occasion of National School of Drama's Third National Theatre Festival.

Under National School of Drama's Extension Programme Scheme, M.K. Raina directed a Manipuri play '*Kanglei Pagta Sunugi Paphal*'. This was the translation of Bertolt Brecht's 'Caucassian Chalk Circle', staged on 20th March and 31st March 2001 at Shri Ram Centre, New Delhi on the occasion of National School of Drama's Third National Theatre Festival 'Rangamahot sava'.

Distinguished theatre personality Naba Wareppa directed Ranjit Ningthouja's play '*Refugee*' in 2002 which was produced by the Nahard Khongthang Artistes Association.

Kalakshetra's '*Border*' was presented at the '*Bharat Rang Mahotsav*', a major theatre festival organised by the National School of Drama, New Delhi. The script and direction was by H. Kanhailal in 2002 which was rather a physical

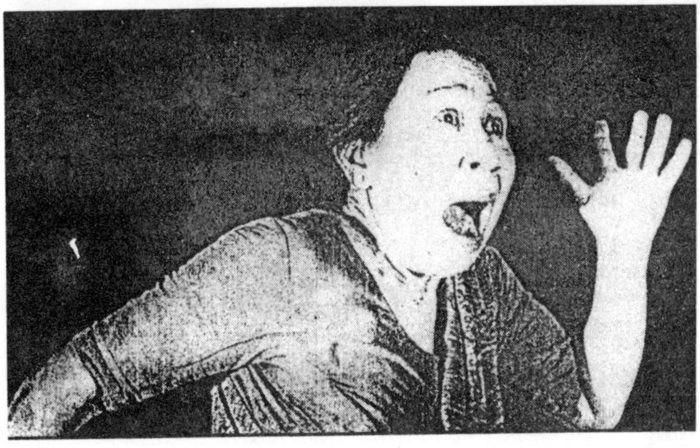

poem which celebrates the feeling of terror at the communal level of a people's life in the artistic sence. The images of two opposing tensions are terrible to each other communities, even threatening the humanity, because the root of opposition is hatred which is so politicised by history. Isn't it possible to find the 'Border' of the conflicting tensions rooted in love and politicised in acknowledgement of each other by negating the historical lesson of terror, but by creating a new mythical reality of the time.

Heisnam Kanhailal in his directorial note mentioned: "Theatre is a paradoxical and ambiguous in its nature. I have just learnt this truth when I observed recently the highly artificial ritual of the aggressive drill performed daily by the Indo-Pak Guards at the border gate at Amritsar (Punjab). Childlike foolishness of the political concept and design of the drill but 'the real' encounter between the two guards are the impressions created in me, the spectator by the way the communications takes place. Eliciting the essence of the theatrical presence in this ritual, I have conceived the performance of Border in one single force of integrated communication level. The communication which our practice demands is to create an organic dialogue between the performers and the spectators at the sensory and spiritual levels in order to make the spectator 'alert'. This is what we could experience of the artistic process of Ritual-Effect is justifying the efficiency of art while creating perception in the spectator." Here the major performer was Sabitri Heisnam who was supported by the young artistes of the Kalakshetra, Imphal. Music and Set was designed by Tomba Heisnam. Lighting was done by Ibochouba Laisran.

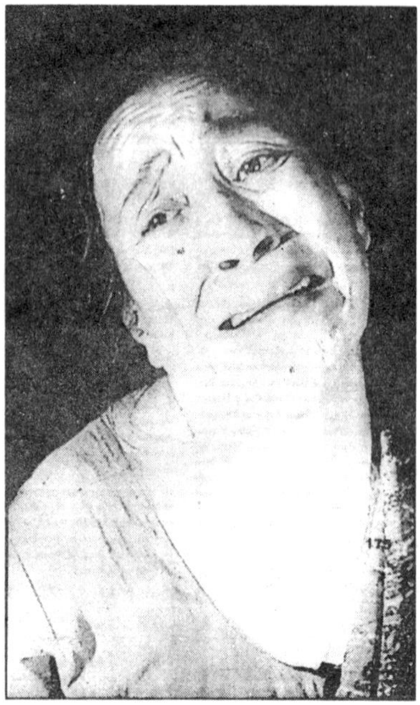

Oflate, Manipuri Ensemble, Imphal produced the play '*Numit Kappa*' under the direction of its young and energetic Kshetrimayum Jugindro Singh (Kshetri Jugindro). The play was chosen to represent at the '*Bharat Rangmahatsav*' of the National School of Drama, New Delhi. Kshetri Jugindro in his directorial note stated:- "When oppressed mercilessly by a tyrant ruler, the inherent spirit of the people as a whole had to rise up against the tyranny in the form of rebellion or revolution at the right time. The long name of the protagonist Khuwai Nungjeng Piba Yekma

Haotangla means the giver of people's latent or inherent spirit for destroying the enemy or the oppressor by rising up in civil war or rebellion or revolution. In fact, the event of Khuwai Nungjeng Pibas's adventurous expedition against two suns, oppressing day and night alternately, for the liberation of victimised people from the clutches of their enemy, form the central part of the story. The story proceeds from the enactment of the scenes where the people suffer under the iron hands of the tyrant ruler and it concludes with the preparation and shooting of Tao Huireng, the sun of nights, by Khuwai Nungjeng". Presented below is the cast and credits of this play.

Cast

Maiba (Narrator)	: S. Shanta Meetei
Maibi (Narrator)	: L. Sumita Chanu
Taoroinai Ahanba	: S. Nepoleon Singh
Sana Khomdon	: L. Tolenkhomba Meetei
Khawai Nungjeng Piba	: M. Ahendra Singh/ L. Ibochouba Singh
Tilum	: N. Ojit Singh
Laimu	: M. Joychandra Singh
Nupa & Taoroinai	: L. Nabakumar Singh
Khongballai Tinkhak Yenakha Paodaba	: H. Shamu Singh
Saijin Poliba	: M. Joy Singh
Lairen No. 1	: I Dinesh Singh
Lairen No. 2	: S. Robi Singh
Lairen No. 3	: K. Bobychand Singh
Hanonu Changkhanu	: B. Geetanjali Devi
Nupi	: B. Sobita Chanu
Chorus	: K. Bobychand, S. Robi, I. Dinesh, M. Joy, H. Shamu, L. Nabakumar B. Sobti Devi

Kserti Mayum Jugindro

Credits

Set	: M. Joychandra Singh
Props	: S. Robi; K. Bobychand
Costume	: L. Tolenkhomba; L. Sumita
Light	: L. Ibochouba Singh
Music	: M. Ahendra with Kokil Tomba, Kumar
Make-up	: L. Nabakumar Singh
Stage manager	: S. Nepoleon Singh
Script	: B.K. Wahengba
Assistant Director	: B. Sobita Devi
Design & Direction	: Kshetri Jugindro

Another wellknown Manipuri drama which was represented at the '*Bharat Rang Mahotsav*' of the National School of Drama was '*Bhoot Amasung Maikhum*'. This play was directed by Loitongbam Dorendra and script was by Thangjam Ibopishak.

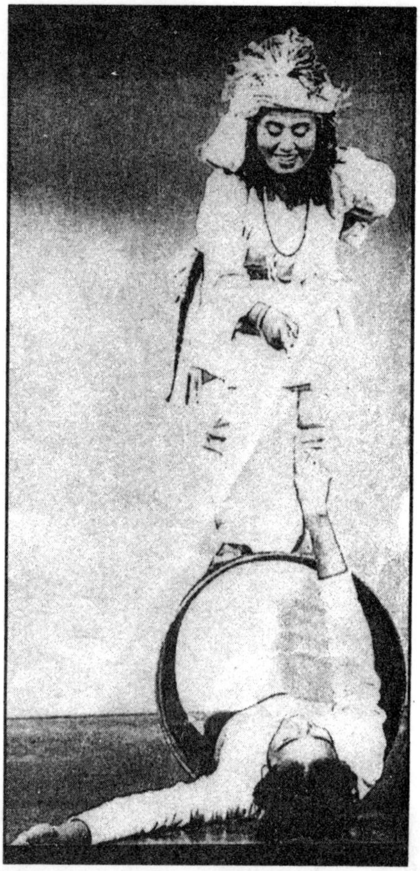

The play was based on the three poems of Thangjam Ibopishak Singh, Sahitya Akademi Awardee of 1997, the poems are (1) Story of a Dustbin, (2) Devil & the Mask and (3) Newly Arrived Creature. In these three poems, the poet depicts how the changed circumstances of the Social Environment affect the man's moral and the spiritual values. Linking the thematic thread of the three poems as a trilogy, his endeavour had been to visualise the lines of the poems. His life is like a "Dustbin" wherein people throw dust and dirty things. In the form of a half cut coal tar drum, he carried the whole world with loads of rubbish the dirty cotton, vomits of drunkards, rubbish of shadowy characters. His life of innocence and love of the world is now lost. Now he is laden with heaps of dust and rubbish. He want to worship and maintain the good qualities of love, mankind and truth. But the 'Devil' around him strangles him. He is not allowed to be a man. The weak power of 'Good' has been overpowered by the strength of 'Evil'. The more he speaks of truth and goodness, the harder the grip of the Devil around his neck. In search of his own self he finds that the devil is no one but he himself is the devil. Man with all the knowledge of Seven Seas, making King of himself now dies by hanging. Man becomes a hollow object deprived of truth, beauty and love. Man becomes a new creature being greedy,

jealous and overwanting. Man has ceased to be called as Man. Not a new name has been given yet.

The cast and credits of the 'Bhoot Amasung Maikham' are given below:

Cast

Ei	:	Khamnam Bijoy
Kaboklei	:	Kshetri Sobita
Spade	:	Angouba, Kunjabihari, Biren
Devil	:	Churachand Sharma
Chorus	:	Biren, Kunjabihari, Angouba, Imotomba, Loken, Delphirani, Nandira, Anuradha, Jillia, Sheibyasachi, Ibecha, Romala
Child	:	Master Hiyaikhomba

Credits

Stage Manager	:	Biren
Costume	:	Jayanta
Set	:	Hemchandra
Lights	:	Imotomba
Music	:	Sotananda Ranjit
Make-up	:	Jiten
Production Manager	:	Nandakumar; Moirangthem
Script	:	Thangjam Ibopishak
Director	:	Loitongbam Dorendra

Produced by the Cosmopolitan Dramatic Union or Cosmo Drama, this play was earlier featured in the India Theatre Olympiad organised by the Utkal Yuva Sangskrutie Sangh at Cuttuck in 1998.

Sangeet Natak Akademi, New Delhi in association with National Centre for the Performing Arts, Prithvi Theatre, Y.B. Chavan Centre and Ekjute, Mumbai organised 'Natya Parva 2002', Akademi's theatre festival from 1-16 December, a full two weeks of exciting theatre in Mumbai. On 1 December 2002, at Tata Theatre, National Centre for the Performing Arts, Nariman Point, Mumbai, Ratan Thiyam's production '*Ritusamhararm*' based on Mahakavi Kalidasa's Sanskrit epic was produced successfully. Performance text, music, design and direction was by Thiyam himself.

A moment from '*Ritusamharam*' presented in Natya Parva 2002

The cast and credits of the '*Chorus Repertory Company*' comprised of the following members:-

Cast

Sutradhara	:	R.K. Bhogen
Pariparshik-I	:	Nimai
Pariparshik-II	:	Angoutombi
Lamlanba Nupa	:	Modhusudon

Nupi	:	Chigkheinganbi
Nayak I	:	Modhusudon
Nayak-II	:	Somo
Nayak-III	:	Rolbindro
Nayika-I	:	Sushma
Nayika-II	:	Rasheshori
Nayika-III	:	Leimatombi
Chorus (Male)	:	Ibomcha Sorok, N. Tomba, Jilasana, Somo, Premjit, Lupachandra, Ratankumar, Santikumar, Angoutombi, Kumarjit, Nimai, Premananda, Ibomcha
Chorus (Female)	:	Sushma, Nganbi, Rasheshori, Leimatombi, Sanjuria, Dhakeshwori, Sujata, Anandi

Credits

Stage Manager	:	Premananda
Assistant Stage Manager	:	Ratankumar
Set & Props	:	Premananda, Nimai, Ratankumar
Costume Assistants	:	Somo, Chingkheinganbi, Sushma
Music Assistants	:	Basanta, L. Ratan, Manisana, L. Tomba, Premjit, Rasheshori
Light Assistant	:	Ibochouba Meetei
Consultants	:	Ojha Lakpati, Ojha Shyamchand, Ojha Chaobhal, Ojha Ibochaoba, Ojha Ibohal, Ojha P. Gandha, Ojha Khomei, Amusana Devi
Administration	:	Dolendro
Production Manager	:	Ibomcha Sorok

The group Kalakshetra expressed most crucial realities of oppression and resistance in Manipur through its plays especially Pebet and Memoirs of Africa. Presently it is embarking on a new experimental project on the Ritual of Suffering which is described as a turning point in both its art and ideology. The performances created a part of its new project were Karma and Laija (1997), Draupadi (January 2000), Izzat (October 2000), Nupi (2002).

Nupi

On 12 December 2002 at Prithvi Theatre, Juhu, Kalakshetra Manipur presented '*Nupi*', directed by Kanhai Lal Singh. This is a Manipuri play written by H. Kanhailal Singh which is about the politics of sex, the subjugation and exploitation of women through history, and how society views the need for the emergence of female leadership, *Nupi* weaves together two separate plays, *Draupadi* and *Izzat*. Although the law of nature conditioned the man-woman relationship during the primitive period, things changed as humankind enters the 'civilized' and literate age. Woman is described as being shaped after the "rotundity of the moon, the curves of the creepers, the vanity of the crane." Her beauty is extolled and denigrated at the same time. In this manner, she is subordinated to man in patriarchal society.

Ram subjects Sita to a test by fire to prove her chastity. Sita emerges triumphant in the test, but the wagging tongues prick Ram's male vanity and exiles her to the forest.

Hollywood's symbol of female beauty, Marilyn Monroe, was a prisoner of the make-believe world of the dream merchants. Her beautiful body and face were splashed in the media. Marilyn longed for a life of her own, and motherhood, which drove her into a series of failed marriages, and finally to suicide.

Comrade Dopdi (Draupadi) leads the tribal folk of Jharkhand when her husband, Comrade Dulna, is eliminated by the security forces in a fake encounter. Like the Draupadi of mythology, Dopdi is stripped and humiliated by security forces, but her spirit remains defiant.

This is a re-worked performance which contains the first, second and third episodes of *Izzat* produced in October 2000, and the fourth episode of *Draupadi* produced in January 2000. The logic behind this was to consolidate and strengthen the theme. The first three episodes were originally conceived by Kanhailal and the fourth is based on the story *Draupadi* by Mahasweta Devi.

A moment from 'Nupi' directed by Kanhailal, produced during Natya Parva 2000 at New Delhi

Heisnam Sabitri took up the key characters Sita, Marylin Monroe and Draupadi.

Other cast included H. Tomba, H. Amoubi, A. Upendra, G. Koken, S. Brojendra and Mangangsana. Music and Set was designed by H. Tomba. Light was given by L. Ibochouba and Sound was looked after by A. Birbal.

On 25th March 2003, the play '*Kunti*', written and directed by Soibamcha Indrakumar was produced at the National School of Drama's 5th National Theatre Festival. It was presented at Kamani Auditorium, Copernicus Marg, New Delhi, under the banner of Elite Group of Performing Artists, Manipur.

Turel Wangmagi Ahal Ama is a play in Manipuri, written by Brajachand Khundrukpam and directed by Wareppa Naba was enacted on 27th March 2003 at Shri Ram Centre for Performing Arts, New Delhi on the occasion of the National School of Drama's 5th National theatre Festival entitled '*Bharat Rang Mahotsav*'.

Deai Repertory Theatre, Chajing, Manipur was invited to present its production '*Ei*', penned by L. Dhananjay Singh and directed by P. Khogendra Singh in the National School of Drama's 5th National Theatre Festival entitled '*Bharat Rang Mahotsav*'. It was produced at his Abhimanch Theatre on 31st March 2003.

On the occasion of its fifty years of existence, the Sangeet Natak Akademi, New Delhi organised a programme entitled '*Rang Svarna*' — Golden Jubilee Theatre Festival from 9- 22 October 2003 at New Delhi. On the last day, The Chorus Theatre Repertory produced the play '*Uttar Priyadrashi*', a mixed play in Manipuri and Pali, under the direction of Ratan Thiyam. The play was based on a famous work by noted Hindi author Ajneya and translated by A. Krishnamohan Sharma. About the play, Thiyam in his Director's Note said:-

The world is in constant flux. And we often question its very being and our presence here. How can humankind evolve in the best possible way? The more we are developed in science and technology, the more we seem to regress, to lose our mental and spiritual equilibrium. Despite the presence of such powerful bodies as the United Nations and human rights organizations, violence and war continue to accelerate. Increasingly, it seems as though the good in man is overwhelmed by the evil. As a result, man has lost control of his innate qualities, the facility to find peace and equanimity within his very soul. Priyadarshi (Ashoka), the protagonist in this play, is one such man — confused, misguided, beset by evil compulsions. We may not choose Priyadarshi's path to overcome destructive instincts, but we can choose to be constructive and compassionate in our journey through life.

A Scene from 'Uttar Priyadarsh' produced by the Chorus Repertory Theatre, Imphal in October 2003 at the Golden Jubilee Theatre Festival organised by the Sangeet Natak Akademi, New Delhi

Thiyam's team comprised of the following artistes

On Stage

Ashoka/Priyadarshi : R.K. Bhogen

Ghor : Ibomcha Sorok

Bhikshu	:	Robindro
Samadaki	:	Somor
Samvadak II	:	Premananda
Samvadak III	:	Nimai
Samvadak IV	:	Shantikumar
Male Chorus Leader	:	Robindro
Chorus (Male)	:	Jilasana, N. Tomba, Kumarjit, Modhusudon, L. Tomba, T. Ibomcha, L. Premjit, Santikumar, M. Tomba
Chorus (Female)	:	Shushma, Chmgkhemganbi, Eimatombi, Rasheshori, Nganbi, Dhakeshwori, Sujata.

Off Stage

Music & Design	:	Ratan Thiyam
Set & Props	:	Nimai, Lupachandra, T. Ibomcha
Costume Assistants	:	Somor, Chmgkhemganbi, Sushma, Leimatombi, Dhakeshwori
Music Assistants	:	G. Manisana, L. Tomba, Basanta, L. Ratan
Lighting Design	:	Ratan Thiyam & Kanishka Sen
Lighting Assistant	:	Ibochouba Meetei
Stage Manager	:	Premananda
Production Manager	:	Ibomcha Sorok
Consultants	:	Ojha Chaotombi, Ojha Ibchouba, Ojha Samarendra, Ojha S. Thanil
Administration	:	Dolendro

In the year 2004, Dorendra Singh of 'Cosmo Drama' bagged the Best Director Award in Rupmahal Artistes Memorial Drama Festival for the production '*Mangal Yaodraba Numit*', composed by Kshetri Sanajaoba.

From 9-10 February 2005, a seminar on '*Contemporary Women Writings in Manipuri*' was organised by the Sahitya Akademi, New Delhi in collaboration with J.N. Manipuri Dance Academy, Leikol and Manipuri Literary Society at Imphal. In its second session K. Shantibala read her paper on '*Drama by Manipuri playwrights*'. It was whole-heartedly devoted to the rare plays of *Binodini, Premodini, Binapani* and *Leingaklembi*, in which much women centric issues were obviously demonstrated.

Sarungbam Beeren is a young theatre director who is best known for his political play *Eikhoi kanano* ? (Who are we?) His play was first premired on 12 June 2005 in Imphal in front of a select audience that created ripples and later produced in Delhi under the aegis of the National Institute of Performing Arts. The 75 minute play was based on the every day struggle of the residents of Molcham, which has a population of just about 500. Molcham is one of the many villages that dot a long stretch of the Indo-Myanmar border in Chandel district of Manipur. Molcham is far from Imphal and farther from the minds of policy-makers in New Delhi which explains its obscurity. But Molcham's is no ordinary story which this dynamic theatre director took up to tell it like it is. It narrates how troops from across the border routinely enter Indian territory to plunder, torture and molest. There is no Indian or state force at Molcham or any of the nearby areas. Not a single VIP from either Delhi or Imphal has ever visited this border village, writes Khelen Thokcham. India is spending crores of rupees and sacrificing lives in defending Kashmir, but out there at Molcham, unarmed and simple villagers are left to defend themselves against brutish Myarmarese forces. The director of the play, Sri Beenen primarily tries to trace the roots of the all-pervasive sense of alienation among youths across the northeastern states. Interestingly, despite not being provided protection from Myanmarese forces, residents of Molcham are still 'proud Indian citizens'. Beeren's thought provoting saga '*Eikhoi Kanano*?' is the result of his extensive study of the state of affairs in the frontier villages of Manipur,

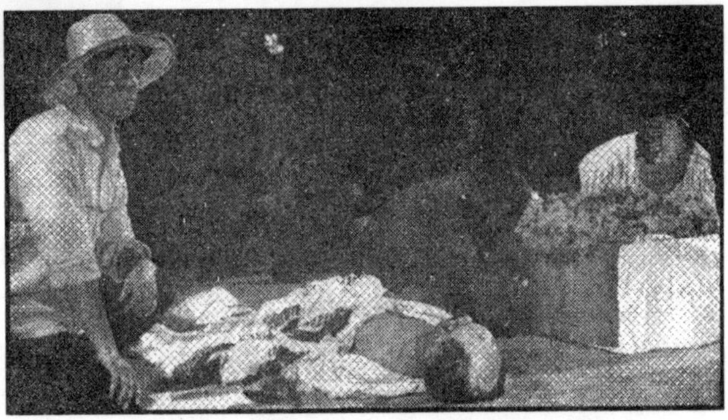

A Scene from the play premiered in Imphal.

Nagaland, Mizoram and Arunachal Pradesh and Myanmarese settlements along the international border.

In the First folk Drama Competition organised by the Manipur Dramatic Union in 2005, Loitongbam Dorendra Singh was given the Best Director Prize for play '*Tamna*', written by Haobam Tomba.

Folk theatre has a distinct character of its own Usually based on mythology or rural themes, it carries a strong social message with an undeniable national significance. Besides being the most favoured from the folk entertainment in Manipur, this folk form '*Shumang Leela*' is today, a powerful medium of mass education, discussing serious issues like communal harmony, insurgency, drug abuse and global terrorism.

A scene from Ratan Thiyam's *Nine Hills, One Valley*

On 23rd February 2005, Peace Maker, Manipur produced the drama '*Restaphen*' at Bharatiyam Cultural Multiplex, IB 201 Salt Lake, Kolkata. The play was directed by Birjit Nagangomba on the occasion of '*National Folk Theatre Festival*', organised by the Eastern Zonal Cultural Centre, alongwith others zonal cultural centres.

Restaphen is a Manipuri folk play in *Shumang Leela* (Courtyard Theatre) style. This play tells the tragic tale of its eponymous protagonist — a boy who loses his parents during USA's anti-terrorism war in Afghanistan, post 9/11, a socio-political comment on global terrorism and its devastating impact on the lives of ordinary people.

A NGO '*Panchali*' organised a multi-lingual theatre festival at Kolkata in December 2005. As usual, the play '*Nine Hills, One Valley*' of Thiyam attracted attention for his unique form, ethnic choreography, music and props. This play gave a new perspective on recent events in Manipur. On the occasion of the National School of Drama's '*Bharat Rang Mahotsav*', Ratan Thiyam again presented this drama '*Nine Hills One Valley*' at Kamani Auditorium, Copernicus Marg, New Delhi on 4th January 2006. On 8th January Sarungbam Beeren presented '*Who are we?*' at Sri Ram Centre Auditorium at Safdar Hashmi Road, New Delhi. On 14th January, the play '*Medea*' directed by Kshetri Jugindro was produced at the Kamani Auditorium, New Delhi.

"The north eastern states are sitting close to one another for centuries, sharing and revelling in the cultural distinctiveness. But sadly we are all fighting on a political platform" says Heisnam Kanhailal. Kanhailal believes in experimentation in his theatre. According to him 'theatre should be able to respond to the dominant tensions of the time and this is my attempt to address the underlying tension of ethnicity in the north-east. In his latest venture, 'Dakghar' of Tagore the text was disconnected from the play. This is his perception of Dakghar. And all we need to do today, opines Kanhailal, is to acknowledge our own perceptions, rather than go by the "method" or the "doctrine". He picked up the nuances of Tagore's play and gave it a form that was never been attempted before — by making Tagore play a multilingual production that comprises Manipuri, Bengali, Assamese, Rabha, Tripuri and Bodo, where one language flew into the cauldron of another through minimal dialogues, folksongs in Tripuri, Bodo and Manipuri, and rippleless dance movements. Under Kanhailal's direction, Dakghar became not just a play dealing with the awakening of the senses after a prolonged and dictated explanation of the universe, he tried to bring about the mutual bonding that binds everyone, including the seven northeast states. That is why his cast and crew had been living together in a remote village in Imphal for four months, practising the play which was finally produced in the Prithvi Theatre Festival, as a part of their programme of *Tagore Festival* in 2006. Rabindranath Tagore's 'Dakghar' revolves around a frail boy, Amal, who is condemnd to seclusion and inactivity because of ill health. He makes a new world for himself, by his imagination and insatiable curiosity, and the passers - by bring the outside world to him. When a new post office opens in a village, Amal believes the King will send him a letter. In this symbolical play, "Amal represents the man whose soul has received the call of the open road. he seeks from the enclosure of habits sanctioned by the prudent, and from the walls of rigid opinion built for him by the respectable".

The rythm of the play 'Dakghar' came from one fact that the core group of Kalakshetra believes in learning about and exploring the senses. "The remnants of a material life are such that the senses of the body are ignored. All actions of humankind today are concentrated just abore the head. Through their plays, Kanhailal and his crew constantly try to understand the rhythm of the body and how it responds. In this multilingual work, Kanhailal and his actors have done is to disturb the audience, stimulate their senses and make them think about notions of the universe as is taught and as it needs to be experienced and lived."

Kanhailal poured in the essences of the eastern States into this very lyrical and poetical play. A drama critic aptly commented 'The conversation between the actors and the audience that doesn't necessarily understand even a single language in the play has been successful, because of the poetry in each actor's role".

A Scene from 'Dakghar', a multilingual play produced during the Tagore Festival in MumBai in 2006

Interestingly the central character of the play is the little boy 'Amal' has been depicted by the 60-year-old-actress Sabitri, who exellently managed to defy the idea of age and its bearing through her performance.

In November 2006, Kavita Joshi and Malati Rao's 52-minute film '*Some Roots Grow Upwards*' was screened which captures the theatrical process of Thiyam and his Manipuri theatre group 'Chorus' in Imphal. It was an effort of Mumbai's Prithvi Theatre and its director Sanjna Kapoor. It was in collaboration with the Delhi Film Archives, the event titled '*Kalaa: Desh Ki Sewa Mein*' showcased nine films. This film festival gave a new dimension to theatre artists.

A–Z

A

Aburd drama *see* 'Aryan Theatre', Introduction, Sri Biren, N. etc.

Achoubi, Bimola *see* Aryan Theatre

Ador Simha, Khundrakpam

Khundrakpam Ador Simha was born in 1892. This Manipuri author's best-known drama is '*Sri Gauranga avatara*' which he himself published from Imphal. Author of this mythological drama died in 1969.

Amuba Simha, Kaisam

Kaisam Amuba Simha was born in 1902. He composed a drama in Manipuri entitled '*Chitrangada*', broughtout by K. Biren Simha from Imphal in 1951. Kaisam Amuba Simha died in 1951.

Anandamohan Simha, Mayengbam

Mayengbam Anandamohan Simha was born in 1914. Author's chief dramatic publications are *Doctor* and *Graduate*. The former was published by Shyam Kumar from Imphal in 1968 and the latter also appeared from Imphal in 1969, broughtout by Hera Simha.

Ananda Simha, Moirangthem

Moirangthem Ananda Simha's book *'Lilanacom'* is a collection of one-act plays in Manipuri, appeared in print from C.K. Store, Imphal in 1958.

Angahal Simha, H.

Author's drama 'Poktabi' in Manipuri appeared from 'Naharol Sahitya Premi Samiti', Imphal in 1984.

Anganghal Simha, Hijam

Anganghal Simha was born in 1892. A poet and dramatist of repute, he studied upto the six standard only and started his career as petition-writer at the then Cheirap Court at Imphal. Anganghal began composing lyrics and songs in his early days of youth some of which got published in the Lalitmanjari Patrika in 1933. In 1938 appeared his epic poem 'Singel Indu' (Sweet Indu). Anganghal Simha also tired his hand in the genres of novel and essays.

In the domain of drama his debut play was *'Nimai Sanyas'* written in 1927, followed by *'Thambal Chongbi'* in 1928. His social drama *'Ibemma'*, written in 1936 was widely staged.

His 'Ibemma' appeared from State Library, Imphal in 1944 and the 'Yaithing Konu' got published by K. Ibobi Simha also from Imphal in 1965.

Hijam Angahal was a renowned playwright and founder of the *Chitrangada Natya Mandir*. The group made its debut with his play 'Ibemma' (Maiden) in 1939 which unleashed fresh energy into the Manipuri stage. His group alongwith the then reigning Meitei Dramatic Union played a key role in the development of the motive theatre during the pre-war phase. Anganglal's play such as Yaithing Konu (1965) and Moirang Thoibi (based on the immortal epic love between a princess and a commoner) made the readers as well as spectators wild with excitement and joy.

Hijam Anganghal Simha was closely associated with my literary, dramatic and cultural forums of Manipur. He was an important member of the Manipuri Sahitya Parishad, Imphal, in its initial stages and took active part in the formation of many theatre houses in Imphal. He was awarded the title '*Kaviratna*' posthumously by the Manipuri Sahitya Parishad in 1948 in recognition of his literary achievements. This great Manipuri literateur died in 1943. Hijam Angahal died in 1943.

Anganghal Simha, Hijam *see also* Yaithing Konu

Angauton Maitai

This modern writer composed a play in Manipuri: *Kangla phambalda Thambal*', published from Kakcing, Imphal in 1973.

Angoubi, Thambal

Thambal Angoubi was a gifted female artist of the Manipur Dramatic Union, a professional theatre group which once occupied the core position in Manipuri theatre. She later left for a ambitious career in Rupmahal, also one of the pioneer professional theatre groups of Manipuri. Thambal Angoubi was an excellent dancer who successfully tried her hand in acting also. She achieved major success with plays like Sita, Ibemma (Maiden) and Mainu and lend a strong support to the Rupmahal in accelerating its fortune.

Angoubi, Thambal *see* Introduction (Rupmahal)

Apang Thounā

Apang Thounā (The Foolhardy) is a radio play, composed by G.C. Simha Tongbram (b. 1913), the celebrated dramatist of Manipur. In this play, the dramatist exposed the disparity between urbanites and the rural folk and the enjoyment of the former at the cost of the latter. He ridicules the sophisticated society, in which sincere and earnest people are viewed as nothing better than fools.

Aribam Kumar Sharma

Born in 1943 at Wangkhei, Ningthempakhri, Napal, Imphal, Sri Aribam Kumar has done Master's in Hindi from Calcutta University and has B.T. Knows

English, Sanskrit and Bengali too. He started his teaching career in Government College, Imphal in 1967. After his stints of deputation to different departments, resumed teaching again and elevated to the rank of Additional Director of Higher Education, Govt. of Manipur in 2000 and retired in 2001. Sri Sharma served as President of the Cultural Forum, Manipur.

An astute translation and social worker, he has been translating Radio plays since 1967 and won Sahitya Akademi Translation Prize of 2003 for his Manipuri version of Dharamvir Bharati's Hindi novel 'Suraj ka Satwa Ghoda' as 'Numiki Taretsuba Sagol.

Aribam Kumar Sharma's literary essays in Manipuri such as *Mrchhakatikam: dā samajgi punsi, Hindi theare gi khonghau and Hindi opera*' are included in his volume 'Sahityada rasa amasung atei neina wareng khara', published by Writers Forum, Imphal in 2002.

Aryan Theatre *see* Introduction

Ashangba Nongjabi

Ashangba Nongjabi (Aśambā Nomjābi, Azure Clouds of Crimson Evening) is a modern Manipuri play, composed by M.K. Binodini Devi (b. 1922). The play deals with the life of an artist named Gautam who leaves his sweetheart, Indu, and goesaway finally with Keina, a petty woman of an arecanut vendor. With sensitive overtones, the playwright portrays the romantic longings and agony of Gautam as a seeker, an explorer and aspiner after the infinite. The inner call in the artist and the psychological conflict with outside reality is excellently unveiled in a romantic manner. The play was published by the dramatist in 1967.

Atombapu Sharma *see* Introduction (Aryan Theatre)

Awang Nong Poklamgee Nawaa

This modern drama in Manipur is written by Lokendra Arambam. This play was directed by the playwright himself for his group '*Forum for Laboratory Theatre of Manipur*'. The theme of the play runs as follows:- A group of adolescents in contemporary Manipur probe the nature of violent death in the state through a series of games. The play in various ways depicts how the human body in death assumes different forms, from early human conflicts and tragedies which result in death through unrequited love, through separation and despair in folklore and legend to death in contemporary times. The contemporary picture of the nature of death, in its uniqueness, ferocity and awesomeness surpass the capacities of children to contain the event in the realm of fantasy. It assumes a character too real to be true; the play transforms itself from fantasy to reality and finally to ritual. The contemporary picture of how death becomes an object of social conflict, of hidden dynamics of oppression, corruption and manoeuver for power are violently brought into the limelight, without its protagonists being aware of the transformation of the event or their play. Bodies are now strewn into human memory's space, where trade, oppression, revenge, vendetta and mutual killings predominate, when the boys' attempt to exorcise them through ritual becomes a metaphor of the contemporary tragedy of violence. The effect of violence on the innocent mind of the young of Northeast India is thus probed by this seeming. This play was staged on 21st January 1999 at Ravindra Kalakshetra, J.C. Road, Bangalore on the occasion of '*Natya Samaroh*' (National Festival of Plays), organised by the Sangeet Natak Akademi, New Delhi and Directorate of Kannada and Culture, Govt. of Karnataka.

Ayekpa Lai (Ayekpā Lāi)

Ayekpa Lai (The Painted Picture) was published in the Souvenir of the Theatre Centre in 1977. The play, authored by P. Shamu Singh (1942-80) is a symbolic one which depicts the failure of an artist to paint a picture of his own wife. The two converse non-stop and the artist husband could not catch the real self of his wife, and he could not therefore paint her real picture.

B

Babu Simha, Irom

Irom Babu Simha translated Sophocles's Greek play '*Antigone*' from English version which appeared from Manipuri Sahitya Parishad, Imphal in 1975. Babu Simha also translated and published the Manipuri version of Shakespeare's English drama '*Julius Caesar*' from Imphal in 1980.

Babu Simha, Laisram

Laiśram Babu Siṃha was born in 1911. This Manipuri author wrote a play '*Māthur*' based on a Bengali drama, which he himself broughtout from Imphal in 1953.

Baladeve Sharma

Born in 1918, this Manipuri scholar wrote '*Prachalita Manipurinatya kala*', a treatise on Manipuri theatre comprising of approximately three hundred nine pages. The book was published by Smt. Sanahanbi from Imphal in 1975.

Bamacharan Mukhopadhyay Bandhab Natya Shala *see* Introduction

Basanta Simha, Kshetrimayum

Shri Kshetrimayum Basanta Simha was an artist of Imphal Theatre. On 27.1.1995, he was being interviewed by Dr. N. Tombi Simha. At that time, the artist was 86 years and his address of communication was Uripok Chanambam Leikai, Imphal.

Basudev Sharma, Phurailatpam

Phurailatpam Basudev Sharma translated and published the Manipuri version of Kalidasa's *Sakuntala* which appeared from Imphal in 1948.

Beeren, Sarungbam *see* Introduction

Bhagyachandra

This is a semi-historical drama, written by Arambam Dorendrajit. Based on the eighteenth century king who liberated Manipur from the Burmese and introduced Vaishnavism. In this drama, the political intrigues of eighteenth-century Manipur were highlighted, with traces of Shakespeare in a Lady Macbeth-like character who instigated her husband, Bhagyachandra's uncle, to fight for the throne. This play was produced by Aryan Theatre, its first original production in 1939. The play was revived by this troupe again in honour of Dorendrajit who had died in 1944.

Bhagyachandra *see* Dorendrajit Simha, Arambam

Bhim Maitai, Yumnam

Yumnam Bhim Maitai, a modern writer wrote a play in Manipuri '*Pānthuṅg-Vāṅgmā*', published by Budha Candra from Imphal in 1976.

Bhogen Singh, Rajkumar

Born in 1958, Rajkumar Bhogen Singh involved in theatre with Chorus Repertry Theatre of Ratan Thiyam. Under his able tutelage, Bhogen acquired substantial knowledge of indigenous narrative forms like Wari Liba and utilized them as an actor's resource in over thirty productions directed by Thiyam.

At the age of 39, he received the much coveted '*Sangeet Natak Akademi Award*' for acting, one of the youngest to win so.

As lead actor and administrator of Thiyam's troupe, he gained international recognition and touring extensively to the countries like Greece, Italy, France, Japan, Thailand etc.

Bidhu Simha, Ayam

Born in 1932, this author's chief work in Manipuri is a drama entitled '*Lamjā anī*' which he himself published from Imphal in 1969.

Bihari Simha, Khaidem

Shri Khaidem Bihari Simha was the Senior Director of Manipur Dramatic Union (M.D.U.) On 1.5.1995, he was being interview by Dr. N. Tombi Simha in connection with the Khwairakpam Chaoba's contributions to dramatic literature.

Bijoysana, R.K. *see* Introduction

Bimola Achoubi Devi

Smt. Nongmaithem Ningol Bimola (Bimola Achoubi) Devi, a Manipuri actress and singer of the past, played character role in the play '*Awa Lan Kainaba*' presented at Agya Krishnachandra's Mandop, Uripok. On 3.5.1995 the actress was interview by Dr.N. Tombi Simha in connection with Khwairakpam Chaoba's contributions as a playwright. She narrated a funny incident about the slandering of a petro-max lamp during a play in Roxy Theatre. She sang in the one-act play of Chaoba.

Binod Sharma, Gurumayun

Gurumayun Binod Sharma was born in 1947. This contemporary author wrote and published the Manipuri play '*Asīrāmī-Oibagī punsi*' in 1977.

Binodini Devi

A prominent story writer, novelist and translator. Maharaj-kumari Binodini Devi the youngest daughter of Sir Churachand Simha, former king of Manipur was born in 1922. Binodini Devi obtained her Bachelor's degree from Calcutta University and joined the Kalabhavan at Santiniketan in 1947.

Well versed in Bengali, English and Hindi besides her own language, Binodini Devi rendered some works from Bengali which include Badal Sircar's plays '*Evam Indrajit*' and '*Spartacus*'. She has also composed the ballet scripts 'Thoibi', based on the folk story of Khamba-Thoibi and Kom Hangoi and took part in promoting Manipuri dance. M. K. Binodini Devi wrote the play 'Aśaṅgbā noṅgjābī' which she herself published from Imphal in 1967. In 1980, appeared her play '*Olāṅgthāgī vaṅgmadansu*' which was broughtout by Devabrata Memi form Imphal in 1980. She also translated a few Bengali plays into Manipuri and wrote the screenplay for the Manipuri film '*Olangthobi Wangmadasoo*'.

Binodini Devi, a founder-member of Roop-Rang, a cultural organisation of Manipur, She was the Secretary of the Jawaharlal Nehru Manipur Dance Academy and a member of the Sahitya Akademi Advisory Board for Manipuri.

For her collection of shortstories '*Nungairakta Chandramukhi*' she was given the '*Yamini Sundar Guha Gold Medal*' in 1967. In 1979, she was honoured with the much coveted Sahitya Akademi Award for her novel '*Borosaheb Ongbi Sanatombi*', an outstanding contribution to Manipuri literature for its narrative power, graceful language, deep sympathy and understanding of human nature. Boro Saheb Ongbi Sanatombi is the first and the only historical novel of M.K. Binodini Devi dealing with the love relationship between a daughter of Maharaja Surchandra Simha of Manipur (1886-1890) and Major Maxwell, Political Agent of Manipur after the British annexation following the battle of Khongjim in 1891. Binodini Devi received the Padmashri in 1976 for her contribution to Manipuri literature.

Select Works

Ashangba nongjabi. — Calcutta : The author, 1967.

84 p.; 22 cm.

Play

Birachand, Thaṅgjam

Thaṅgjam Birachand was born in 1922. His drama in Manipur '*Anaubā imuṅg*', published by Sunita, appeared in print from Imphal in 1980.

Birahari, P.

P. Bīrahārī was born in 1952. Author penned and broughtout a play from Puranagram, Lakshipur, Cachar in 1978 entitled '*Inthoklambī*'.

Birahari Simha, Sarungbam

Saruṅgbam Birahari Simha was born in 1900. His biographical drama in Manipuri '*Chandidas*', appeared from Imphal Book House, Imphal in 1966.

Biramaṅgol, H.

Born in 1928, this Manipuri author penned a play '*Kege noṅgbān*', published by Abir Simha from Imphal in 1969.

Biramangol Singh, Mayanglambam

M. Biramangol Singh, a veteran Manipuri personality, in his drama searched for national identity and tried to discover lost values in the historical and even legendary past of Manipur. The integration of old faiths with the new ones, accompanied by a basic pride in one's race provides a common theme for Biramangol.

A trendsetting playwright, scholar, promoter and manager of theatre, Mayanglambam Biramangol was born in 1908. It is aptly stated that he was a unique product of the dichotomy between Sanskritic acculturation and indigenous Meitei religion. With his profound knowledge of ancient Manipuri texts, he developed the issue of the contention or struggle between Hinduism and Meitei faith.

M. Biramangol Singh wrote over 30 plays of which *Sija Laioibi* (The story of a Manipuri counterpart of Mirabai, a princess wedded to Lord Krishna, 1961, '*Sanamahi Kolu yei khaiba*' (1965) *Nara Singh* (1966), *Chingn Khonghang Thaba* (a great Manipuri King, 1966) and *Baona* (the military hero of the 1891 struggle against the British, 1968) are notable.

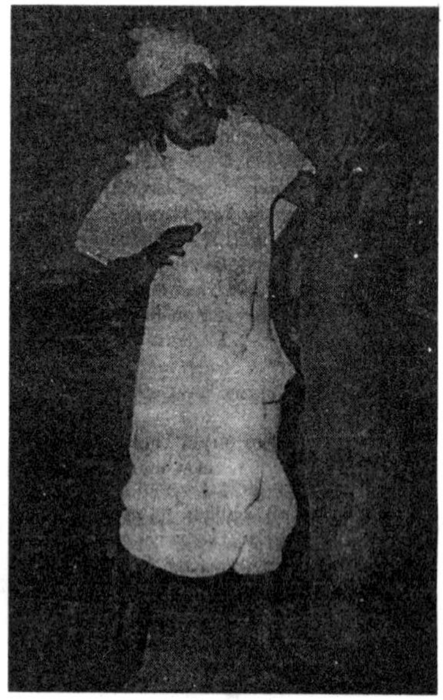

M. Biramangol's Sanamahi kolu yeikhaiba (Aryan Theatre, Imphal, 1965)

Mayāṅglambam Bīramaṅgol Siṃha's other praiseworthy dramas are *Abhimanyu, Charāiroṅgba, Chingda satpi, Chingu Khong-nang thaba, Dharma-gi jay, Garibnevaj, Henju Naha, Ima, Khamnu, Khvai Kekru, Kunjamala, Laba-Kusa, maitai athauba ahum, Manipur leishemba, Nara Simha, Pamhaiba, Panthoibi, Pauna, Pidonnu, Radiogi drama pareng Sayon alum, Sija lai-oibi, Tankak amagi lila pareng Tikendrajit and Yaithing Konu'.*

Mayanglambam Biramangol authored the play '*Sanamahi Kolu yeikhaiba*' (Breaking Sanamahi's Iran Idol), published in 1965. It symbolizes the anti-colonial, anti-Hindu sentiment of the times. The believers of the native Sanamahi religion, long suffering the hegemony of Hindu converts, resisted integration with Indian culture, and the movement gained momentum in the 1960s alongside the formation of the All Manipur Student's Union and generation of pan-Manipuri, anti-Indian feelings. This play was staged by the Aryan Theatre with O. Biramangol in the role of native sage Khongnangthaba and Syam Sarma as the Hindu missionary Shantidas. The play had a hundred shows in a year and a half.

A philanthropist, he spent all his earnings from contract work during the World War II in the cause of theatre, without financial returns to his family. He became a staunch supporter of the Communist Party after the War.

M. Biramangol, a Communist, who as a young theatre worker had helped in the Aryan Theatre's founding. He produced Maxim Gorky's 'Mother' in Manipuri, under the banner of this group in the 1950s. He modernised and the stage and acting techniques of this leading theatre group. His removal of wings from the conventional proscenium in favour of the box set revolutionized Manipur theatre in the late 1960s. Even the Absurdist drama which was in vogue in the 1970s, received his support. Biramangol was also responsible with other personalities for the formation of the 'Theatre Centre', Imphal in 1955.

He also proved his potentiality as an actor. He created innovative constructs of mythical and legendary personalities through sheer strength of will, with economy in movement and speech. M. Biramangol Singh, combined in himself the qualities of a playwright, a director and actor. Mayanglambam Biramangol died in the year 1979.

Selected Works

Abhimanyu. — Imphal: M. Tharośaṅgbī Devī, 1969.

83 p. 18 cm.

Mythological drama

Carāiroṅgbā. — Imphal: Piśak Devī; 1964.

84 p. 18 cm.

Cīṅgdā Śātpī. — Imphal : M. Naba Kumār, 1977.

85 p. 18 cm.

Cīṅgu khoṅg-nāṅg thābā. — Imphal: Kaugabam Maṅihār Siṃha, 1966.

91 p. 18 cm.

Dharma-gī jay. — Imphal: M. Kumārjit, 1977.

103 p. 18 cm.

Garībnevāj. — Imphal: Tharośaṅgbī Devī, 1967.

126 p. 18 cm.

Historical drama

Heñju Nāhā. — Imphal: M. Bābā Kumār, 1969.

ii, 80 p. 18 cm.

Imā. — Imphal: Th. Piśak Devī, 1969.

100 p. 18 m.

Drama based on Maxim Gorky's *Mother*

Khamnu. — Imphal: K. Motilāl Siṃha, 1970.

163 p. 18 cm.

Folk play

Khvāi Kekru. — Imphal: K. Motīlāl Siṃha, 1970.

165 p. 18 cm.

Kuñjamālā. — Imphal: the author.

Historical drama

Laba-Kuśa. — Imphal: Ombī Devī, 1968.

84 p. 18 cm.

Mythological drama

Maitai athaubā ahum. — Imphal: M. Naba Kumār, 1972.

171 p. 18 cm.

Maṇipur leiśembā. — Imphal: K. Prabhāvatī Devī, 1967.

ii, 86 p. 18 cm.

Mythological drama

Nara Siṃha. — Imphal: Kaṅgabam Maṇihār Siṃha, 1966.

86 p. 18 cm.

Pāmhaibā. — Imphal : Kaṅgabam Maṇihār Siṃha, 1967.

iv, 144 p. 18 cm.

Pānthoibī. — Imphal: the author.

Paunā. — Imphal : Piśak Devī, 1968.

81 p. 18 cm.

Historical drama

Pidonnu. — Imphal: the author.

Drama in old Manipuri

Radiogī drma pareṅg. — Imphal: M. Naba Kumār, 1976.

77 p. 18 cm.

Radio plays

Sāyon ahum. — Imphal: M. Naba Kumār 1972.

171 p. 18 cm.

Śija lāi-oibī. — Imphal: K. Prabhāvatī Devī, 1966.

vi, 102 p. 18 cm.

Historical play

Tāṅkak amagī līlā pāreṅg. — Imphal: Piśak Devī, 1970.

280 p. 18 cm.

Tikendrajit. — Imphal: Kāṅgabam Maṇihār Siṃha, 1966.

viii, 110 p. 18 cm.

Historical play

Yāithiṅg konu. — Imphal: Binodinī 1970.

162 p. 18 cm.

Biramangol, M. *see* Introduction (Aryan Theatre)

Biramangol, O.

Thespian O. Biramangol was closely associated with Aryan Theatre, one of the longest-lived Manipuri theatre groups. He was the epitome of sheer melodramatic power, a great performer who will be remembered for his portrayal of Macbeth. He did the role of the native sage 'Khongnangthaba' in M. Biramangol's trend-setting play '*Sanamahi Kolu Yeikhaiba*' (Breaking Sanamahi's Iron Idol, 1965).

Biramangol, O *see also* Aryan Theatre

Biramani Simha, Vaheṇgbam

Vaheṇgbam Biramani Simha rendered into Manipuri, the original Bengali work of Manmohan Goswami. The play '*Saṁsār*' appeared from Imphal in 1971 and published by Biramani himself.

Bira Simha, Meitram

Meitram Bira Simha (M. Bira Singh) is an established playwright, actor and director in Manipur who was born in 1916. In 1943 when the Rupmahal Artistes Association came into being, Sri Bira Simha took an active part in it.

Meitram Bira Simha has written several plays and his better known are *Yaithing Konu, Nangshi Laman* and *Bir Tikendrajit*. He has also translated some plays from Bengali. His historical drama '*Bira Tikendrajit*' appeared in 1965 from Rasbehari, Imphal in 1965. His other known drama is '*Nuṅgśi Lamman*', published by A. Ibobi from Imphal.

M. Bira Simha won the Gold medal for the best actor from the Manipur State Kala Akademi and was posthumously awarded the '*Natya Bhushan*' of the Manipur Sahitya Parishad. He died in the year 1978.

Translations

The Valiant Tikendrajit/ by M. Bira Simha; tr. an excerpt of the play 'Bir Tikendrajit' into English by R.K. Birendra Simha. *In* Modern Indian literature: an anthology (Vol. 3)/ ed. by K.M. George. New Delhi : Sahitya Akademi, 1994. pp. 417-425.

M. Bira's Manipuri drama 'Vir Tikendrajit's deals with the last prince who fought against the British and was ultimately hanged in 1891. This drama added a new dimension of nationalistic fervour and aspiration for freedom.

Bira Simha, Meitram *see also* Introduction (Rupmahal).

Biren Simha, A.

A. Biren Simha's drama '*Padmini*' was published by Sarojini Devi from Imphal in 1981.

Biren Simha, Nongthonbam

Nongthonbam Biren Simha was born in 1946. His Manipuri drama 'Hallakapā' was published by Raj Store, Imphal in 1973.

Sri Nongthombam Biren Simha, who writes under the nom de plum 'Nongthombam Sribiren' was born in Imphal. He obtained his Bachelor's degree in Arts in 1965 and started his career as a teacher. A tutor in Manipuri at the D.M. College of Arts and Commerce, Imphal, Sribiren has been on the Editorial Board of Wakhal, Parishadki, Sheireng Lairik and Atoppa Khonjel. He has been associated with many cultural and literary bodies of Manipur.

Besides, Sri Biren Simha has published a collection of short stories, few volumes of poems. For his book 'Tollaba Shadugi Wakhal' he received the Manipur State Kala Akademi Award. In 1990, he bagged the prestigious 'Sahitya Akademi Award' (New Delhi) in the language for his collection of 38 poems entitled 'Mapal naidabasida Ei' which stands as an invaluable addition to Indian literature in Manipur.

See also 'Introduction'

Biren, Sougaijam *see* Introduction (Rupmahal Theatre)

Birkumar, Elangbam *see* Introduction (Langmeidong Dramatic Union)

Bir Simha, M.

M. Bir Simha and H. Romni Simha jointly wrote the drama '*Yaithing konu*', published by the Manipuri Sahitya Parishad, Imphal in 1972.

Bir Tikendrajit

This Manipuri drama was initially developed by Sougaijam Biren M. Bira Simha (1916-1978) and later turned into a successful melodramatic script by the late M. Bira. The play deals with the tragic war of 1891 when the patriots Tikendrajit and Thangal were hanged. It was highly successful on the stage and is infact the magnum opus of the Rupmahal Theatre which staged it in 1951 and had effected its hundreth show by 1966.

This chronicle play recreates the tragedy and heroism of a moving episode in Manipuri history. The synopsis of the play runs as follows:- "The British, who were trying to bring the princely state of Manipur under their subjugation in the later part of the nineteenth century, took advantage of a palace feud between Maharaja Surchandra Singh and his brothers. In September 1890, Maharaja Surchandra Singh was driven out of his palace by the intrigues of his younger bothers. He left Manipur for Cachar with a few followers and on arrival in British India sought the assistance of the Government of India to regain his kingdom. Meanwhile, Yubaraj Kulachandra Singh ascended the throne of Manipur.

The Government of India decided that Yubaraj Kulachandra Singh, who had already proclaimed his accession, should be confirmed as maharaja and that Bir Tikendrajit, the crown prince, who was known to be hostile to the British, should be removed from the state. In order to carry out this decision, Mr Quinton, Chief Commissioner of Assam, arrived at Imphal with an escort of 400 sepoys under the command of Lieutenant Colonel Skene and a *darbar* was announced. Quinton's intention was to arrest the crown prince in the durbar itself. Tikendrajit got prior information about the strong contingent of guarts posted at the Residency and was suspicious of Quinton's intentions. He refused to attend the durbar on a plea of ill health, and declined to surrender himself when asked to do so. Thereupon Quinton decided to arrest Tikendrajit by force.

The troops sent by Quinton to the house of the crown prince were fiercely repulsed and a serious engagement followed; an armistice was, however, agreed to on both sides, and firing temporarily ceased. Quinton thought it expedient to negotiate with Tikendrajit and, accompanied by four British officers, entered the palace, never to come out of it. Grimwood, the political agent, was fatally speared by a Manipuri sepoy. Quinton and the other offcers who were surrounded by an excited crowd, were eventually beheaded by the public executioner.

The British who were then at the height of their power could not tolerate the existence of strong men who hurled defiance at their authority. Tikendrajit and

Thangal General, whom they arrested and hanged after the war that ensued, are regarded by the people of Manipur as peerless patriots. In the last scene of the famous play, the arrest of Tikendrajit, the courage he displays even in his sick-bed, his magnanimity and the agony of the helpless people of Manipur over the execution of the two heroes are vividly presented."

Bir Tikendrajit *see also* Introduction (Rupmahal Theatre)

Boramani Simha, Sarangthem

An authority on Manipuri folkliterature and also an accomplished playwright, Sri Sarangthem Boramani Simha was born at Chinga Makha Chanam Pukhri Mapal, Imphal in 1928.

Boramani did his Intermediate in Arts from Gauhati University in 1951 and joined government service from which he took voluntary retirement.

His wellknown dramas in Manipuri are *Haorang laisang saphabi* (1949; wnd edn. 1964), *Tonu-laijing lembi* (1949), *Kege-lamja* (1958) and *Nura-Sanulembi* (1966), all published from Imphal by the playwright himself. Most of the plays of Boramani Simha are based on folk and legendary themes. In the year 1950 he wrote '*Haorang Leisang saphabi*' which brought him the Best Play Award in the Folk category at the National Drama Festival held in 1950. His dramas '*Tonu Laijing Lembi*' and *Kege Lamja* (The Orphan of Kege), both based on the folk stories of Moirang. In 1966, he authored another folk play 'Shanulembi'.

Sarangthem Boramani Simha's non-dramatic works include *Lamitlon* (Tales on place names) a book on the naming of places and the cultural and historical ancedotes connected with them (written in 1954); Angangi paotak wari (Useful tales for children written 1964), a collection of legends and folk-tales for children), Mani pareng (Garland of Jewels written in 1964), a collection of the folk-tales of Manipur, Ching tamgi phunga wari (Folk-tales of hills and plains), a collection of folktales of the different groups of people of Manipur in 1975; Moirang sayon (Incarnations in Moirang), a collection of the legends of the different incarnations supposed to have taken place at Moirang), published in 1977.

Boramani is also credited with a book of poem entitled 'Melei Leisana Nungjumpan Kadamba Leinungshi, published in 1964.

Brajabehari Sharma, Aribam

A modern writer and translator, Aribam Brajabehari Sharma rendered Kalidasa's play '*Malavikagnimitra*' into Manipuri and himself published it from Imphal in 1964. Brajabehari Sharma is also the translator of Kalidasa's another great Sanskrit classic '*Abhijnana-śakuntalam*' into Manipuri which appeared in print from O.K. Store, Imphal in 1965. He rendered the great dramatic work '*Mrcchhakatikam*' of Ṣudraka into Manipuri which appeared in print in 1972 from Raj Store, Imphal.

Brajachand, Khundrakpam

Born in 1952, this modern playwright in Manipuri, whose forte is protest drama passes stinging comments on the decaying values of contemporary Manipuri society, skillfully mixing humour with symbolism and existential anguish. The dramatist died in 1997 at the age of 49.

C

Chengni Khujai

This is a socio-political play in Manipuri written by G.C. Tongbra. The play published in 1969 attempts to revalue the present democratic system of the government in Manipur in a humorous manner. The plot runs as follows:- The entire fund of Mayapur, an imaginary state, comes from the central headquarter. The fund is given to a council consisting of representatives elected properly by different groups of people for whom the fund has been provided. But the representatives, the so called well-wishers of the people misuse the fund allotted. They try to make their present and future out of the money sanctioned. As the fund does not reach the proper place, citizens of the state go from bad to worse. They demand food, cloth and shelter which they never get. At first they suffer with patience and wait for some new development, which never comes. At last some energetic young fellows try to revolt against the authority. Old generation tries to prevent the young from waging a war. The advice to settle the problem in a peaceful manner is not acceptable to those young citizens. They take up arms and revolt. But all the revolting groups are killed in the end.

Chakravyuh

This is a modern Mahabharata play in Manipuri, penned by Ratan Thiyam which became an instant hit production when put on boards in 1984 by the Chorus Repertory Theatre in 1984. It deals with the death of Abhimanyu, son of Arjun. The synopsis of the play is given below:-

Dhritarashtra asks Sanjay how Abhimanyu knows the art of entering the Chakravyuh. There is only one source of vulnerability, and that is Arjuna, who knows this military formation. For the rest, its invincibility has been assured by that master-trainer in military strategy. Dronacharya. The play begins. Sanjay relates the story of Abhimanyu's mystifying initiation into the technique in question. In the presence of the pregnant Subhadra, Arjuna, her husband, explains to Lord Krishna, her brother, the tactics of breaking into the Chakravyuh. Unfortunately, however, though the lifeforde in Subhadra's being—Abhimanyu in his embryonic stage—imbibes the first part of the code, it misses out on the second part: namely the principle of coming out of the Vyuh, unscathed. For she, in the meantime, has fallen asleep. During the war at Kurukshetra Dronacharya prepares the Chakravyuh at a point of time when Arjuna is engaged in a battle elsewhere. He has, however, not bargained for the fearless Abhimanuyu, who enters the formation and defeats the Kauravas several times. He is eventually subjugated by foul military tactics and killed. The play ends but the episode leaves unresolved the question of the sacrificial scape-goat and the rejection of truth.

This is one of the most widely travelled, admired and written about production of Ratan Thiyam. It was first premiered in 1984. Like other writers-directors working in post-colonial times, Thiyam too used theatre to straddle the divide between indigenous theatre traditions and contemporary issues. On the one hand, Thiyam sees the play as a symbol of the conflict between two generations — called youth pitted against experienced warriors; on the other hand it symbolizes the conflict between the individual and society—Abhimanyu against the seven charioteers. Ultimately he sees it as a protest against violence and the threat of Word War III which the younger generation faces.

Chandra Sharma, K.S.

Born in 1942, this Manipuri writer's chief publication is '*Sahar gi ical*', a play published by Radhamani Devi from Imphal in 1973.

Chaoba, Khwairakpam

One of the makers of Modern Manipuri Literature, Khwairakpam Chaoba was born on 23 January 1896 at Sorbon Thingen, Imphal. He was the eighth and the last child of his parents. He had six elder brothers and one elder sister. His father was Mukta Singh—a Nata Sankirtan singer and his mother Thaballeima. According to the Administrative Report of Manipur State, 1916-17, six students were sent to Shillong o read there to appear at the Matriculation Examination of the Calcutta University in 1918. Khwairakpam Chaoba was one of them. In 1919 he joined the Bengali School as a teacher. It was here that he started writing and contributed in almost all genres of literature. He was a poet, novelist, critic, essayist and dramatist.

His forte lies in poetry and in his life time he produced nine books - none of them was a play. Among his unpublished manuscripts we came across a title '*Naba-Mallika*', but the genre was not indicated in that. Consequently, nobody had given cognizance of the fact that Chaoba was a pioneering playwright in Manipuri literature.

After a renewed research and a close study of the extant but incomplete manuscripts; and personal interviews with those actors still alive who took part in the production of Chaoba's plays, it has now become apparent that he wrote four plays and all of them staged successfully in his lifetime. These are:-

(1) Labanga-Lata (Dramatisation of his own novel bearing the same title)

(2) Madhu-Malati

(3) Naba-Mallika

(4) One-act play dealing with the arrest of Bir Tikendrajit.

Chaoba

Manuscripts of his two plays namely, Nityaipagi shorat and Birendra-Kumari sometimes ascribed to Chaoba cannot be traced. His '*Naba Mallika*' appeared in print in 1947.

Educationist and writer Khwairakpam Chaoba died on 9th November 1950.

Chingu Khongnangthaba *see* Sanamahi Kolu yeikhaiba

Chirom Gouramani *see* Gouramani and Aryan Theatre

Chitrangada Natya Mandir *see* Introduction

D

Damodar Simha, L.

Modern Manipuri author whose dramatic work '*Manipuri Lilamacha*'. appeared from the Cultural Forum, Imphal in 1975.

Dhakeshwar, Yumnam

Yumnam Dhakeshwar's best known Manipuri Drama is '*Chandra Sakhī*', which was published by Pishak Devi from Imphal in 1978.

Dhana Chandra Simha, K.

K. Dhana Chandra Simha broughtout the Manipuri version of a Bengali drama by Prabodh Chandra Sen. The translated text '*Sadā Shivagī maṅg*' was published by the National Press, Imphal in 1973. Dhana Chandra also rendered a Bengali play of Nisikanta Basu Ray. The Manipuri version '*Debala Devi*' was published by the translator from Imphal in 1974.

Dhanachandra, Khomdram *see* Introduction (Meitei Dramatic Union)

Dhananjay

Born in 1931, this Manipuri dramatist wrote the play '*Punsi lānpham*' which he published from Imphal in 1972. His another play '*Nungśi mūrti*', was broughtout by T. Gonrton from Imphal in 1980.

Dhananjay Singh

Author penned the play 'Itaima' in Manipuri broughtout by L.M. Simha from Imphal in 1981.

Dhiren *see* Introduction (Rupmahal)

Dhiren, Koijam

Koijam Dhiren Simha was born in 1947. He has written a number of plays in Manipuri His 'Chitrakar' was published by the playwright in 1970. '*Suranya*' was broughout by Māgha Puthem in 1972. 'Phau-oi-bi' was published by him in 1978 and '*Kanādano hūkkadabā*' from P.P. Store in 1979, all from Imphal.

Koijam Dhiren is a contemporary Manipuri writer whose other wellknown dramas are: 1980 *Kumbaba* (1982), *Hingchabi Chakatha* (1982), *Ani* (1983), *Saragam Chandraba shur* (1983), all published by the dramatist from Imphal.

Select Works

Ani. — Imphal: the author, 1983.

71 p.; 18.5 cm.

Hingchabi chakatha. — Imphal : the author, 1982.

23 p.; 17.5 cm.

Saragam Chandraba shur. — Imphal : the author, 1983.

79 p.; 18 cm.

Dhiren Lauremba

Dhiren Lauremba, a contemporary Manipuri author whose chief work 'Śaśībālā', a play was published in 1979 from Imphal, broughtout by the dramatist himself.

Dinamani Simha, Wlangbam

Dr. E. Dinamani Simha was born in Elang Khangpokpi, in Manipur in 1940.

Dinamani Singh is the son of Kullachandra and Nandamukhi Devi. He obtained his Master's degree and D. Phil from Allahabad University, later pursued 'Hindi Shikshan Parangat' degree in Hindi. He started his career as a school teacher and after a short stint, joined the Centre of Post-Graduate Studies of Jawaharlal Nehru University, Imphal. Thereafter, he served as an Associate Professor of Manipur University in Manipuri language and Literature Department.

He was editor of the Ritu, a quarterly journal of the Cultural Forum of Manipur. A prolific short story writer, Sri Dinamani Singh was awarded the Sahitya Akademi Award for Manipuri in 1982 for his 'Pistuk ama Kundalei ama'. He also won the Manipur Kala Akademi Award.

A short story writer, critic, poet, his other interests include writing for films and theatre. In the year 1994, he was Awarded the much coveted Sahitya Akademi Translation Prize for his Manipuri rendering of Girish Karnad's Kannada play '*Hayavadana*'. The translated text eminently succeeds in skilfully bridging the gap between the two distinct languages and cultures. Marked by felicity of dramatic art and craft and laudable structural strength, the work is indeed a notable contribution to Indian drama in Manipuri translation.

In the branch of dramatic literature, his contributions also lie in his Manipuri rendering of Mohan Pakesh's Hindi play '*Asar ka ek din*' as 'Nongma ingada'.

Dorendra, L. ***see*** **Introduction and Dorengra Singh, Loitongbam**

Dorendrajit Singh, Arambam

Arambam Dorendrajit Singh a pioneer poet and dramatist of modern Manipuri literature was born in 1907. He obtained Bachelor's degree in Sanskrit from Calcutta University and then started his teaching career as a school teacher and remained so till his death.

In the year 1939 appeared his '*Moirang Thoibi*' a play dealing with the immortal love of Khamba and Thoibi of Moirang. In his characterisation of 'Thoibi' the influence of William Shakespeare's 'Merchant of Venice' of Kalidasa's 'Abhijnana-sakumtalam' is clearly evident.

Moirang Thoibi was a very successful play shown on the stage of Rupmahal several times.

Dorendrajit wrote his second dramatic composition 'Bhagya chandra' in 1945, based on the theme of regaining of the throne of Manipur by Bhagyachandra, a saint king of Manipur in the eighteenth century and the subsequent installation of the image of Shri Govindaji shows also an influence of Shakespeare's Macbeth. '*Bhagyachandra*' was published from Imphal in 1945 and the latter appeared from Book-land, Imphal in 1957.

His third original drama in Manipuri is *Kaurav Parajay* (Defeat of Kaurav). The former is acknowledged as one of the masterpieces of Indian literature. *Moirang Thoibi* is an idealised version of the Khamba and Thoibi Story. The character of Thoibi is made to look like a *Sati* of the Hindus. The story has been made modern by use of modern outlook and beliefs and Dorendrajit romanticised the whole atmosphere successfully.

Dorendrajit translated the Bengali drama '*Reziya*' of Monmohan Roy into Manipuri which was staged by the 'Aryan Theatre', also its debut production in September 1935. Dorendrajit also translated a few more plays from Bengali but these have been lost.

Dorendrajit Singh's other works include two epic poems, viz Kansa Badha (slaying of Kansa) and Subhadra Haran (The Theft of Subhadra). The latter remained unfinished, few poems and songs. He also wrote 'An Account of the Time of Maharaja Churachand Singh' in English and English renderation of 'Hare Maye' of Panditraj Atombapu Sharma.

The playwright died in 1944 and in 1945 appeared his epic poem 'Kamsabadha' in which he made new experiments in the language by an admixture of Manipuri and Sanskrit. He was honoured in 1948 with the title '*Kavya Ratna*' posthumously by the Manipuri Sahitya Parishad for his immence contribution to the growth of Manipuri literature.

Dorendra Singh, Loitongbam

Born in 1953 to Shri Loitongbam Tombimacha Singh and Loitongbam Ongbi Smt. Tombi Devi, Sri Dorendra Singh was drawn to theatre right from his school days in the plays written by G.C. Tongbra and performed by Cosmopolitan Youth Club, Wangkhei. He received training in the field of acting from the pioneer theatre Gurus of Manipur such as N. Tombi Singh, H. Nilamani Singh and L. Netrajt Singh. He won best supporting actor prize in the State Level Drama Festival-1971 organised by Manipur Publicity Department. He participated in three months' intensive theatre workshop 1981 conducted by National School of Drama at Nambol. Joining the Chorus Repertory Theatre in 1982 for more than ten years under the guidance of Ratan Thiyam, he participated the workshops conducted by John Martin (1985), Pravir Guha (1986), Sue Weston (1996) and H. Kanhailal (1997). He visited many countries of the world as an actor of Chorus Repertory Theatre with many plays Urubhangam, Chakraviyu and Uttarpriyadarshi i.e. U.S.S.R., U.K., Greece & Italy (1984), Holland, Ireland (1987), Mexico, Cuba, Colombia, Equador, Peru (1991), France & Japan (1997), Thailand (1998).

He was one of the founder member of Cosmopolitan Dramatic Union. He started directing plays of *Cosmo Drama* from 1989. He won many prizes in the competition organised by North East Theatre Organisation, Manipur in the productions of *Meehat* (1989)), *Kao Amasung Kei* (1990), *Chaoba Nongthon Senjaba* (1991) under his direction. The production of *Tajmahal, Draupadi, Bhoot Amasung Maikhum, Meghdoot* under his direction was participated in the National Level Festivals organised by the Sangeet Natak Akademi, National School of Drama and Zonal Cultural Centres. He directed at least 15th plays of the group productions in the State and National Level Festival and compititions. He won best Director prizes in the competitions held at Allahabad, Cuttuck, Patna, Guwahati. Utkal Yuba Sanskrutik Samittee awarded him *Natya Bhushan* in 1998. He conducted North East Regional Theatre Workshop at Aizwal (Mizoram) in 1996. He was a member of expert committee (Theatre & Shumangleela) of Manipur State Kala Akademi (1998-2000). As a playwright he has six plays to his credit. He wrote articles in the newspapers and cultural magazines and read seminar papers in the

State level seminars and symposia. At present he serves as a member of the Manipur University Cultural Committee. He obtained Best Director Prize in Rupmahal Artistes Memorial Drama Festival-2004 for the play *Mangal Yaodraba Numit* written by Kshetri Sanajaoba, presented by COSMO Drama. He got best Director prize in the First Folk Drama Competition organised by M.D.U. in 2005 for the play *TAMNA* written by Haobam Tomba.

For his immense contributions to the Manipuri drama and theatre, this eminent dramatist was awarded by the '*Huyen Lallong Manipur Thang-Ta Cultural Association, Irilbung*, during in 47th Anniversary of its Foundation Day on 25th October, 2005.

Apart from theatre he has also acted in few Manipuri feature films and has directed over six tele plays and two digital films.

F

Friends Dramatic Union *see* **Introduction**

G

G.C. Tongbra *see* Tongbra, G.C. and 'Introduction' (Society Theatre)

Ghose, Saratchandra *see* Introduction

Gitchandra Tongbram Simha *see* Tongbra, G.C. and 'Introduction'

Gokul Chandra Sharma

Sri Gokul Chandra was born in 1924. This twentieth century Manipuri writer composed two mythological dramas entitled '*Bhakta Dhruva*' and '*Ramgīabhisek*'. The former appeared from Raj Store, Imphal in 1964 and the latter, by the playwright himself in 1965 also from Imphal.

Gokul Sharma, Aribam

Aribam Gokul Sharma translated and broughtout the Sanskrit work of Bharavi '*Kiratarjuniyam*' in Manipuri from Imphal in 1964.

Aribam Gokul Sharma also rendered and broughtout the Sanskrit tragic drama of Bhavabhuti into Manipuri entitled '*Uttararam Carit*' from Imphal in 1968. Gokul Sharma also translated and published the Sanskrit classical drama '*Ratnavali*' of Sriharshadeva from Imphal in 1972.

Gokul Shastri *see* Gokul Sharma, Aribam

Gopal Singh, Chandam

Sri Chandam Gopal Singh served as the Director of Roopmahal Theatre, Imphal, who made immense contributions to the growth of Manipuri theatre.

Gopal Singh Selungna *see* Introduction

Gorky, Maxim [In Manipuri Translation] *see 'Biramangol Simha'*, Mayanglambam and '*Priya Kumar*'.

Gourchandra Singh, Vahengbam

Vāhengbam Gaurchandra Singh was born in 1915. His best known historical drama '*Māinu pemcā*', was published by the playwright himself from Sagolband, Imphal in 1951.

Gourahari Singh, S.

A celebrated musician, S. Gourahari Singh served in Manipuri Dance College, Imphal and worked with A.I.R. as an approved artist. He was a pioneer exponent of modern light songs who made classical music modern by his compositions. He received his music training at Chittagong and continued his friendship with Gyan Ghosh of Bengal, a music composer.

In the beginning he remained pre-occupied with choreography and orchestral music in Manipuri Ras, folk plays etc. for his newly founded, institute 'Lalit Kala Bhavan'. The writing and staging of dramas brought about a slight change in the style, spirit, mood of the times and content of Manipuri songs. It had attracted his attention for experimentation. He had to his credit more than hundred light lyrics and did musical direction in many plays of Rupmahal Theatre and M.D.U. Imphal. This gifted artist died in 1965.

Gouramani, Chirom

Associated with Aryan Theatre, Chiram Gouramani was born in 1914. Gouramani became a household name as Reziya, when acted in the Aryan Theatre's first production 'Reziya', a Manipuri version of Monmohan Roy's Bengali drama

'*Reziya*', translated by Arambam Dorendrajit. An influential actress, Chiram Gouramani who later worked with the Manipur Dramatic Union died in 1982.

Gouramani, Chirom *see* Introduction and Savitri

Guno Singh, Irujam

Guno Singh, a novelist, short story writer and editor in Manipuri was born in 1927 in a Hindu family. He obtained the B.A. degree from Gauhati University and the Legal Practioners Examination of the Calcutta High Court then joined the Judicial Department of Manipur State and later became the Administrative Officer of the District and Sessions Judge's Court.

Hijam Guno Singh wrote '*Hiyang athouba*' (The monster), a play based on a folk tale. His another wellknown play is '*Hare Krishna-Hare Krishna*'. Both these plays have been staged by different theatre groups and are available in manuscript forms.

Guno Simha was the co-founder of the Imarol (Mother tongue), a literary journal of the fifties now defunct, editor of the Ritu, a quarterly Manipuri journal of the Cultural Forum, Manipur, Member of the Editorial Board of Sahitya, a publication of the Manipuri Sahitya Parishad, Imphal. He was President of the Cultural Forum, Manipur, and one of its life members, General Secretary of Manipuri Sahitya Parishad and Executive Council, Member of the Manipur State Kala Academy and a Member of the Advisory Board in Manipuri, Sahitya Akademi, New Delhi.

H

Hallakpa

A modern absurd drama in Manipuri authored by Sri Biren (b. 1945). It highlights the problem of loneliness, loss of identity and search for the Self. A man returns home after some years and its greeted by his wife. They fail to recognise each other as husband and wife. The man tries to prove his identity, but fails. Confrontations followed by some revelations surprise them and ultimately end in hot exchanges, both denying recognition. Hallakpa (The Return) was published in book form from Rajstore, Imphal in 1973. An English version of the play appeared in the journal *Enact* of National School of Drama, New Delhi, in its 67th issue in July 1972.

Haobam Tamba Singh *see under* Tamba Singh, Haobam

Hijam Anganghal Singh *see under* Anganghal Singh, Hijam

Hijam Guno Singh *see* Guno Singh, Hijam

The Human Cage

This Manipuri play produced by Kalakshetra under the direction of H. Kanhailal drew its inspiration from a mythic-historic figure called 'Gomati, who emerged in his dramatic version as the incarnation of a resilient and defiant 'Womanhood'. She is pitted against Garib Niwaz, the propagator of Ramandi

Vaishnavism on a state religion in 18th century Manipur. Kanhailal was not interested in the historicity of their struggle or the romantic myths that have emerged from it. What concerned him was the evocation of an 'inner freedom' that essentializes the stage of 'womanhood'. His focus was not so much on ethnic vesistence (as in Pebits) or the survival of the human spirit (as in memoirs) but what appeared to be a triumph of the will.

Humour and Wit in Manipuri Literature

There are many distinguished authors writing in this literary genre in Manipuri Perhaps the most notable writers in this form are Elangbam Dinamani Simha in shorter fictions, B. Chitreshar Sarma in prose writings and G.C. Tongbra in the realm of drama. We can find humour and drama in almost all the plays of G.C. Tongbra, he deals with social problems and more particularly those speaks of the changes in economic, political and educational spheres. His plays are invariably based on humour.

See also 'Introduction'

I

Ibobi Singh, Ningombam

Sri N. Ibobi Singh, reputed Manipuri playwright was born in Imphal on 13th April 1921. Though formally educated upto seventh standard, he studied Bengali, Hindi and Sanskrit privately.

Ibobi Singh, N.

N. Ibobi Simha's Manipuri dramas 'Karnagi Mama Amasung Karnagi Aroiba Yahip', published by N. Heramani Simha from Imphal in 1981. N. Ibobi Singh received the Manipur State Kala Akademi Award in 1982 for Mahabharata plays 'Karnagi Mama Amasung Karmagi Aroiba Yahip'. The following year, the book was adjudged the best book in Manipuri by the Sahitya Akademi, New Delhi. Sahitya Akademi Award considered the book as an outstanding contribution to Manipuri literature for its relevant handling of an ancient theme, skilful dramatic treatment, powerful portrayals and poetic language.

Apart from this highly acclaimed book, his another play worthy of mention is Ramrajya. Ningongmbam Ibobi Simha's 'Ramrajya' was published in 1967. This play got published by Ningongmbam Munal Simha, Okram laikai from Imphal.

A noted writer of radio-plays, Ibobi Simha's other Mahabharata plays are *Nupigi michangda Gandhari* (Gandhari on the side of woman), *Nupida langjaba*

Kichak (Kichak who wronged a woman), *Ekalabya, Subhadra huba* (the abduction of Subhadra), *Gandharina Sri Krishnada shāp tuba* (Gandhari's curse on Srikrishna), *Manipurda Babhrubahan* (the defeat of Babhrubahan in Manipur) *Karnagi dan* (The gift of Karna) and *Sati Sabya* etc. Ibobi Singh's wellknown dramatic treatise is '*Natya amasung mancha*', a book on the theatre and stage, broughtout by the writer himself in 1969 from Imphal. It contains about one hundred and fortyeight pages.

Besides plays, Ibobi Simha has also broughtout collections of essays and several other books on diverse theme to his credit. A well-read in Bengali, Sanskrit and Hindi, his non-dramatic works include Ramayana Sheireng (The Ramayana in verse), Mahabharata sheireng (The Mahabharata in verse), Satimari (Four satis), a poetic composition) 'Punshi akhomba' (a collection of biographies), Meghnathbadh Kavya (a translation of Michael Madhusudan Datta's Bengali work).

Ibobi Simha was also an actor and took keen interest in painting and music also. Sri N. Ibobi Simha was associated with various literary and cultural organisations. Ibobi Simha was honoured with the state Government Award for the best teacher in 1974 and the Manipuri Sahitya Parishad conforned on him the title of 'Sahitya Bhusan' in 1981. Sri N. Ibobi Simha became blind years before he wrote the plays. Like John Milton he dictated the plays. He took active part in dramatics before he lost his eyesight in 1975. The dramatist died in 1984.

Select Works

Karnagi mama amasung Karnagi aroiba yahip. — Imphal : N. Heramani Simha, 1981.

94 p.: port.; 18 cm.

Sahitya Akademi Award of 1983.

Ramrajya. — Okram Laikai: Ningongmbam Munal Simha, 1967.

144 p.; 18 cm.

Ibohal Simha Kangjam

Kangjam Ibohal Simha was born in 1935. This Manipuri dramatist's best-known dramas are:- *Biday, Mong-yamba, Prapta-asti, Tankak amagi lila, Yu likli* etc.

Ibomcha Simha, S.

S. Ibomcha Simha wrote two parodies in Manipuri, entitled '*Mahabharata'58* and its sequel '*Mahabharata'59*'. Staged under the banner of 'Aryan Theatre', his plays were roaring successes.

Ibomcha Singh, Tokpam

Born in 1942, Tokpam Ibomcha Singh's chief dramatic composition are *Īcel, Yāthaṅg* and *Badanām*. *Īcel* was published by Thoudam Yaima Singh in 1965. *Yāthaṅg* was broughtọut by Hijam Ibobī Singh in 1967 and *Badanam*, by Youth Dramatic Union in 1969, all come out from Imphal.

Tokpam Ibomcha Simha died in 1970.

Ibomcha Simha, Wahengbam

Shri Wahengbam Ibomcha Simha did the role of 'Labanga' in '*Labanga-Lata*', written by Khwairakpam Chaoba. On 3.5.1995, the eighty years old artist when interviewed by Shri Biren was a tailor by profession, specialist in pumyat, the Meitei Kurta. His address of communication was: Uripok Yambem Leikai, Imphal.

Ibopishak Arambam

Arambam Ibopishak was born in 1933. His best known composition is '*Ashram*', broughtout by Imphal Book House, Imphal in 1966.

Ibotombi Vaikhom

Ibotombi Vaikhom was born in 1934. His chief dramatic work is '*Naṅgīsu matam lākhinī*', published by Laimayon Artist Centre, Imphal in 1979.

Iboyaima Singh

Iboyaima Singh rendered the '*Svapna Vasavadattam*' of Bhasa, a Sanskrit classic into Manipuri which he himself broughtout from Imphal in 1965.

Iboyaima Singh, Haobam

Haobam Iboyaima Singh was born in 1908. His two best-known works are '*Babhrubhan*', published by him in 1972 and '*Naladamayanti*', a mythological play broughtout by Satyabati Devi in 1973, both appeared from Imphal. Iboyaima Simha died in 1978.

Iboyaima Laṅgonjam

Modern writer, Sri Iboyaima Laṅgonjam was born in 1945. His best-known work is '*Thabak thibā*', a play in Manipuri, published by O. Kanhailal from Imphal in 1977.

Iboyaima Singh, Laurembam

Laurembam Iboyaima Simha translated into Manipuri, the Bengali plays of Michael Madhusudan Datta (1824-1873), entitled '*Krishnakumarinatak*' and '*Padmavatinatak*'. The former was published by Susila Devi and the latter by the translator himself. Both appeared from Imphal in 1968. Iboyaima Singh also broughtout the Manipuri version of Tagore's Bengali drama '*Malini*' from Imphal in 1968. Laurembam Iboyaima Singh translated and published the Sanskrit play of Bhasa entitled '*Pratimanataka*' in Manipuri, appeared from Imphal in 1974.

Select Works

Krishnakumarinataka / by Michael madhusudan Datta; tr. from Bengali into Manipuri by Lourembam Iboyaima Simha. — Imphal: Sushila Devi, 1968.

145 p.; 18.5 cm.

Malini/ by Rabindranath Tagore; tr. from Bengali into Manipuri by L. Iboyaima Singh. — Laikai : the author, 1968.

67 p.; 19 cm.

Padmavati/ by Michael Madhusadan Datta; tr. into Manipuri from Bengali by L. Iboyaima Simha. — Laikai : Sushila Devi, 1968.

111p.; 18 cm.

Svapnavasabadattam/ by Bhasa; tr. into Manipuri by L. Iboyaima L. Singh. — Laikai : the author, 1967.

85 p.; 18 cm.

Ibsen, Henrik *see* Tongbra, Gitachandra Simha

Ibuṅgo Bidhu Khuman

Ibuṅgo Bidhu Khuman was born in 1939. His Manipuri drama '*Lamja anī*' was published by Kṣh. Gandhijit from Imphal in 1969.

Ibungohal Singha, Lairenmayum

Lairenmayum Ibungohal Simha was born in 1895 Litterateur, academician playwright and parliamentarian, Sri Ibungohal Simha obtained his Bachelor's degree from Calcutta University and was the first Manipuri to have passed the B.L. examination. He worked in different capacities in various Government departments of Manipur. He was a member of the Darbar of the Maharaja of Manipur, Judge of the Chief Court and the first District and sessions Judge of Manipur. He was a member of the defunct Nikhil Manipuri Hindu Mahasubha, he ran for election to the Lok Sabha from Inner Manipuri Parliamentary Constituency after his retirement. Founder of the L.M.S. Law College, Imphal he was the President of the Manipur Sahitya Parishad, and worked for the promotion and propagation of the Manipuri language, literature and culture. He wrote two books in English entitled 'Introduction to Manipur' and 'Meaning of Mayang'. He was also the Co-editor of the Cheitharol Kumbaba, a royal chronicle of Manipur published by the Manipuri Sahitya Parishad. In 1961, Sri Ibengohal Simha was given the Sahitya Bhusan Award of the Manipur Sahitya Parishad. In the domain of drama, the author is credited with the first historical play in Manipuri entitled '*Nara Simha*', which he wrote in 1922, but published much later in 1952. One of the earliest in Manipuri, this play highlights various events from the life and deeds of Nara Simha otherwise known as Awa Ngamba, the defeater of the Burmese It shows the magnanimity, sacrifice and noble-mindedness of Nara Simha. The plot runs as follows:- Nara Simha was the king of Manipur during 1844-1850. The state of Manipur was overrun by the Burmese for seven long years (1819-1826). This period is known in the history of Manipur as the Seven Years of Devastation. Nara Simha and his elder brother, Gambhir Simha, took shelter in Cachar and with the help of the king of Assam regained the throne of Manipur. Nara Simha was modest and not very ambitious. After the death of his elder brother, Gambhir Simha, people wanted him to be the king. But he refused and made the infant Chandrakirti, son of Gambhir Simha, the king of Manipur, himself remaining his protector. But palace intigues compelled Chandrakirti to run away with his mother to Cachar and Nara Simha became the king. Ibungohal Simha's style is verbose and ornate and there is an influence of Sanskrit and Bengali plays on the style and language. Infact, the language is strewn with Bengali and Sanskrit words. In keeping with the taste of the time the playwright incorperated a good number of songs.

In 1925, Lairenmayum Ibungohal Simha composed his next play 'Babhrubahan'. His 'Jubaraj Tikendrajit' was broughtout by Hemango from Imphal in 1972. He died in the year 1966.

Imphal 1973 *see* Introduction

Imphal Theatre *see* Introduction

Indrababu Singh

Indrababu Singh's notable publication is '*Shaktam : ahānaba*', brought by Manipuri Literary Forum, Cachar in 1991. Volume one of this book contains three short plays.

Irabot, Hijam *see under* Irawat, Hijam and Introduction (Meitei Dramatic Union)

Irawat, Hijam

Hijam Irawat was one of the foremost harbringers of the renaissance in letters, culture, thought and outlook in Manipur and eastern India. He left a profound impression in the collective consciousness of men and women of old and new generation in Manipur. Irawat was born at Imphal into a humble family on 30th September 1896 about five years after the British conquered Manipur at the battle of Khongjom on 25th Aprin 1891. He lost his parents during his childhood and was brought up by relatives. He obtained his early education at Imphal. Accompanied by his cousin, he went to Dacca (now in Bangladesh) and continued his studies but inspite of being a good student, he could not finish Matriculation due to extreme hardship and poverty. He spent his youthful days in writing, theatre, music, games and sports.

Irawat was a many — splendoured personality — a poet, writer, musician, theatre artiste and worker, journalist, teacher, social worker, a god sportsman, a great leader of the masses, a visionary. Hemango Biswas rightly called him '*Simanta Prahari*' (The Sentinel of the East) A man who did so much in a span of about 55 years for his country and sacrificed his life for the cause for which he was fighting, a new dispensation where people can live with freedom, honour, justice and equality. A great social reformer and leader of the peasants and the down trodden masses, he lead the people and the women-folk of this part of the country against the British authorities and the feudal monarchy with great personal risks and dedication for ameleoration of the ills of the then society and its uplift. He threw headlong to founding and mobilising organisations of students, youths, women, peasants etc. to bring about a change in the political and social condition of Manipur.

Irawat made contacts with the communists while he was in Sylhet Jail (1942-43) and became a communist leader representing North-East Indian in various political conferences. He wrote a few poems in Sylhet Jail, full of patriotic fervour and charged with modernist rhythm. While working among the peasants in Sylhet and Cachar, his creative spirit found expression in songs and dances associated with IPTA movement and aroused artistic consciousness of the villagers.

Hijam Irawat was not only a mass leader but also a pioneer in the movement for a new literature and journalism in Manipuri language.

Irawat wrote a bunch of poetry for children, started a hand written magazine '*Meetei Chanu*', the first magazine of its kind in Manipur, in 1922. He wrote novels, townslated Bomkichandra Chatterjees novel 'Krishnakanter will' a biogrphy of Lokmanya Tilak and also a play entitled '*Gomati*', still in manuscript form. Jananeta Irawat Singh was one of the pioneers of modern Manipuri literature and involved himself in the movement to usher in proscenium theatre at the turn of twentieth century.

Irawat got intensely interested in the progressive writers and the IPTA movement which he was organising in Sylhet and Cachar. It can be discovered in him a creative artiste who could compose, sing, dance and act. Irabat Singh was a good artist equally apt, in both male and female roles. Hijam Irawat took the female role of '*Rani Durgabati*' which was much applauded by the audience. He acted in Bengali plays during the early period (1915-20) and played the role of *Kumud* in the first historical play in Manipuri '*Nara Singh*' in 1925. He took the role of Kumud, a character who was a faithful and patriotic soldier under King Gambhir Singh and prince Nara Singh and fought valiantly to free from the clutches of the Burmese who devastated the country for years, a character which was in the elements of Jananeta Hijam Irawat. Apart from his role of '*Kumud*' (in Nara Singh) '*Chandra Singh* (in Areppa Marup) *Debi Das* (in Debala Devi), he gave memorable performances in *Sati Khongnang* and *Biramangal* etc. In Debala Devi he did the role of Maratha King. He enacted the role of 'Chandra Singh' in this social play '*Areppa marup*' of S. Lalit Singh.

When Hemango Biswas, a veteran Marxist and cultural leader who helped to build up the IPTA movement came to Imphal in 1945 and met Lalit Singh of Manipur Dramatic Union was told that the first drama to be staged was written jointly by him and Hijam Irawat on a social theme. Irawat appeared in the main role the title of the play was '*Areppa marup*. Irawat was always with Lalit Singh at the head of modern drama movement in Manipur. He was a great social activist and reformer. On 21st September 1948 a big meeting was convened at Manipur Dramatic Union Hall, Imphal to protest against the formation of Purbanchal Pradesh comprising Manipur, Tipura, Lushai hills, Karbi-Anglong and Silchar with head quarters at Silchar. The Congress was in favour of the proposal and the Socialist party wanted to dovetail Manipur as a district to Assam. Irawat was much against it as he liked to maintain the territorial integrity of the State comprising the valley and the hills with all the people. Masses of people marched towards M.D.U. Hall. But the police blocked their way and made lathi-charge at Pungdongbam and in the melee a firing order was said to be given and the O.C. got hit as ill luck would have it. Irawat was preparing for the meeting at the above Hall. He then went underground since that day. The State government declared a reward of Rs.10,000 to be given to any one who could arrest Irawat. But he could not be arrested and eluded the police dexterously for the cause for which he was fighting - the right of self-determination and full responsible government in a federal structure for Manipur. It is said that when the British paramountcy was to lapse in India one Reginal Coupland, Professor of Constitutional History of India at Oxford University, had written to the Political Agent of Manipur to keep the hill regions of Manipur as British territory like Hongkong under colonial rules, and that Irawat vehemently protested against it and stood for the territorial integrity of Manipur comprising the valley and the hills as an independent state. During this period he even published his news magazine *Anouba Yug* (New Age). It is said that he started for Burma (now Myanmar) in May 1950 and stayed there for about a year doing works for the liberation of his motherland. He tried there to seek help for his cause. He expired on 26th September 1951 at a Burmese village called Tangbo on his way back to his homeland.

Studies

Birth Centenary Celebration of jananeta Hijam Irabat, 1896-1996: souvenir/ ed. by L. Damodar Singh and N. Thombi Singh. —Imphal : Deptt of Art & Culture, 1996 Joinly organised by the Eastern Zonal Cultural Centre, Calcutta and the Deptt. of Art & Culture Manipur from 29th September to 13th October 1996.

Irawat: sentinel of the east. —Imphal : Irawat Centre for Marxist Studies, 1988.

J

Jagadish Sharma, Phurailatpam

Phurailatpam Jagadish Sharma was born in 1926. Author has written a number of plays, both one-acts and full length dramas. His notable collections are:- *Drama macha mari* (One-act plays), *Karnarjun, Khamba-Thoibi, Parsuram, Ratnakar, Savitri-Satyavan, Sri Vatsa-cinta, Taruni Sen badha.*

Select Works

Drāmā macā mari. — Imphal: the author, 1970.

68 p. 18 cm.

One-act plays

Karṇārjun. — Imphal: Mukundeśvar Śarmā, 1967.

vi, 164p. 18 cm.

Khambā-thoibī. — Imphal: Mukundeśvar Śarmā, 1963.

87 p. 18 cm.

Parśurām. — Imphal: Tombī Śarmā, 1969.

72 p. 17 cm.

Mythological drama

Ratnākar. — Imphal: Tombī Śarmā, 1971.

97 p. 18 cm.

Sāvitrī-Satyabān. — Imphal: Mukundeśvar Śarmā, 1967.

94 p. 18 cm.

Mythological drama

Śrī Vatsa-cintā. — Imphal: Tombi Śarmā, 1970.

46 p. 18 cm.

Rendered from Bengali original.

Tarunī Sen badha. — Imphal: Jadumaṇi Śarmā, 1966.

ii, 73 p. 18 cm.

Jaychandra Singh *see* Joychandra, Elangbam

Jhulon Singh, Mutum

A modern writer in Manipuri, Mutum Jhulon Singh's best known dramas are :- *Chandrika* (1937), *Kyamba Chintamani* (1947), *Malati B. Sc* (1947) and *Kamesan Lanjao-Suracandra* (1948), all published by the playwright from Imphal.

Joychandra, Elangbam

Elangbam Joy Chandra contributed immensely to Manipuri theatre was born in 1927. Sri Joychandra Singh was the first modernist in Manipuri theatre. His own theatre group, 'Jaychandra's Touring Drama' was very much popular in Manipur and earned rare reputation. An actor and choreographer, Sri Singh was innovative in the use of light in theatre.

E. Joychandra Singh penned two plays-*Madhumalati* and *Sarad Purnima*.

Eminent theatre director and playwright H. Kanhailal spoke on this doyen of Manipur theatre on 12 October 2005 at Kangla Hall, Imphal in a programme entitled '*Through My Window*', sponsored by the Sahitya Akademi, New Delhi in collaboration with Manipur State Kala Akademi. He spoke on Joychandra's contribution in the growth and development of Manipuri Theatre. In this connection he also dwelt on the changes in the national and international level in the face of globalisation. Some scholars present in the audience gave their observations and raised questions which Kanhailal attended minutely. The programme was held to record the rich memories of this pioneering theatre personality in Manipuri.

After Manipur political unification with India Joychandra began spreading the proscenium theatre movement in rural Manipur and Meitei-inhabited areas of neighbouring Assam with his professional '*National Touring Dramatic Party*' in 1949 Violence upon simple folk, their oppression and suffering became the subject matters of his plays. Manipuri peasants know him well. '*Joy Drama*' became the popular name for his group, the Manipur Artistes Drama Party.

Joy Chandra, Elangbam *see also* Introduction (Manipur Dramatic Union)

Judge Sahabki Imung

This play of Arambam Somorendra (b. 1935) is an exposition of the conflict in values and ideas in the emerging middle class family. The synopsis of this drama which centres round the theme of native identity is furnished here:-

"Phulo Babu, the father, is a retired judge who cherishes the colonial culture, as he has been brought up in pre-independent Manipur. His younger son, Mohan, on the other hand, is a devout follower of the native culture and tradition, searching for the true identity of the native people. Even before he is able to discover fully that identity, the family faces problems arising from the arrival of the elder brother, a London-returned barrister. With his brash and cocksure faith in progress through western ways, he begins to dominate the pattern of life in the family. His marriage to Aruna, a modern girl, is however a disaster. For Aruna is not a shallow middle-class woman but has poise, conviction and principles associated with the old ways of life. She is a perfect foil to Mohan. From the simple differences in habits, attitudes and beliefs between the couple arises the deeper issue of the right relationship between the two in terms of their own cultural and social environment. Their different views on how to live come into conflict. The husband, proud and stubborn, refused to understand the intrinsic strength of Manipuri women and blames his younger brother who as a reactionary, he says, is responsible for the inflexibility of his own lawfully wedded wife. The entire family is entangled in a web of mistrust and division and their earlier kinship and solidarity breaks down finally with a showdown between the two brothers. Aruna is asked by her husband to leave the house. And the decision on the part of the newly married bride to leave is an agonizing one involving loss of prestige, status and goodwill in society. But Mohan intervenes, his long silence on family matters no longer under control. He exposes the shallowness of his brother's pretensions. In utter disgust he leaves the family to join the simple and innocent folk of his idyllic world."

Jugindro Singh, Kshetrimayum

A founder member and Artistic director of Manipuri Ensemble, Imphal Shri Kshetrimayum, Jugindro Singh is popularly known as 'Kshetri Jugindro'. He is a National School of Drama (New Delhi) graduate who also diploma in Manipuri Dance and Martial Arts.

[*See also* 'Introduction' (Theatre Happenings)]

K

Kabui-Keioba *see* Introduction

Kakching Lila Samiti *see* Introduction

Kalachand Shastri, Chingangbam

Teacher, scholar, transltor, poet, Chingangbam Kalachand Shastri was born in 1903 in a Hindu family. He was the son of a wellknown Nata Sanskirtana, musician of Manipur. Kalachand obtained his bachelor's degree from Calcutta University, earned B.T. from Gauhati University and 'Shastri' of Kashi Vidyapeeth. He started his career as a school teacher and retired as Head Master of Johnstone High School, Imphal. He also served as a Lecturer in Manipuri in Imphal College, Imphal. He received the National Fellowship for the best teacher from the Government of India.

Kalachand got himself involved with the theatre movement in Manipur. He could sing, act and write. He rendered many a Hindi and Bengali dramas into Manipuri.

He was the President of the Manipuri Sahitya Parishad, Manipuri Hindi parishad and Sanskrit Research Committee and many other such organisations. In 1971, the Government of India honoured him with the '*Padmasri*'.

He became the Fellow of the Manipur State Kala Akademi in 1974 and earned the title '*Sahitya Bhusan*' [in 1976?] by the Manipur Sahitya Parishad.

Kalachand Singh, Loitoṅgbam

Loitaṅgbam Kalachand Singh was born in 1922. His two notable dramas are '*Drama maca ahum*' and '*Yumjau lairenbi*' both published from O.K. Store, Imphal in 1962 and 1965 respectively.

Kamini, W. *see* Introduction (under Khomdon Meiroubi)

Kamini Vairokpam

Modern Manipuri writer whose chief dramatic work is '*Khomdon mairibi*' published from Imphal in 1980 by Vairokpam Anou.

Kangjam, I.S.

An astute translator, playwright, novelist, fiction writer, poet and linguist, Sri I.S. Kangjam was born in 1946 in Naoremthong, Imphal. An Associate Professor of Hindi in Manipur University, this writer who experimented with almost all literary genres, has published three one-act plays and five full-length plays. In 1991 he bagged the Non-Hindi speaking Hindi Writer Award of the Ministry of Human Resources Development, Govt. of Indian and Sahitya Akademi Translation Prize of 1998 for his Manipuri version of Jawahar Singh's collection of Hindi short stories entitled 'Mahakkee Waarep Amashung Atei Waareema chaashing'.

Kanhailal, Heisnam

A highly influential director-dramatist of Manipuri theatre, Heisnam Kanhailal was born in Imphal in 1941. Kanhailal started his acting career in Manipuri theatre with occasional inputs in student drama and club shows. In his college days, Kanhailal had acted in Society Theatre, a group run by the outstanding playwright-director, G.C. Tongbra, popularly called the 'Shaw of Manipuri Theatre'. Later joined the Student Artistes' Association where his efforts facilitated admission into, the 'National School of Drama' in 1968.

Kanhailal's debut play '*Layeng Ahanba*' (First Treatment) a social satire was staged in 1961 directed in which he and Sabitri worked together for the first

time. Veteran playwright-director, G.C. Tongbra cast a strong spell on this production.

In February 1962 Kanhailal married Sabitri. Though Sabitri was not allowed to do theatre, an usual joint-family problem, but Kanhailal continued to do theatre while working as a clerk in the National Building Construction Company Jobless after a year and a half, he found more interesting work in 1966 as a Primary Invstigator in the Statistical Department, which enabled him to explore tribal and rural cultures in his home land. He composed the play '*Taret laimā*' published by Adhunik Sahitya Mandir, Imphal in 1967.

Through the recommendation of Binodini Devi, a generous benefactor of the arts, he applied to the National School of Drama, New Delhi. He was the second Manipuri to receive admission. This was in the year 1963, but soon he was expelled from the school for taking leave without official permission. But the fact was that he abstained from the class owing to the languages of instructions, ie English and Hindi in the school. Unable to write home to his family, he stayed on in New Delhi and took a job in the Income Tax Journal Office and eventually at the instances of his Manipuri friends, he went back to Imphal in May 1969 and started doing theatre. In July 1969, he formed his drama group '*Kalakshetra Manipur*'.

Through Kalakshetra, he started to search an authentic expression through experimentation with Manipuri culture and traditions. He introduced his new form of theatricalization on *Tamnalai* (Haunting Deities) in 1972 that dealtwith youth unrest.

He also served in the Drama unit of the Publicity Department of Manipur State Government. He had somehow held on this job throughout the 70s while he was actively involved in theatre. This job had been his only source of income apart from many he occasionally received from various aids and awards. He left this organisation in June 1980.

Heisnam Kanhailal is an eminent theatre director from Manipur. His theatre is very deeply connected with the social, political and cultural upheavals of his State. Almost all his theatre productions are intense explorations of life in Manipur. His work in Manipuri theatre is at the forefront of contemporary Indian theatre. With his group Kalakshetra, Manipur and Sabitri, his leading actress, he has covered new ground in the use of vigorously physical, non-verbal, gestural theatre, using themes and motifs strongly rooted in Manipuri folklore and culture.

After his association with Badal Sircar in 1973, he invented a minimalists school of physical expression with lithe movements and playful form, and a distinctively lyrical style of short masterpieces followed, *namely Pebet* (1975) *Memoirs of Africa* (1985), *Migi Sharang* 1991 and *Draupadi* (2000).

Kanhailal's productions notably '*Pebet*' and '*Memoirs of Africa*' — evolve through an organic process involving improvisation, song and dance, drawing on traditional dance and martial arts traditions. He has never worked with a dramatic text for either of the above productions.

In the year 1985, he was honoured with the '*Sangeet Natak Akademi Award*' for Direction. Heisnam Kanhailal is in the vanguard of experimental theatre movement for the past few decades. He has been experimenting widely with alternate theatre forms using the rich traditions of Manipuri performing arts and culture as a springboard. He has also proved his excellence as a playwright. He has so far written 15 plays and directed 30 and has worked with various national and international theatre groups. Kanhailal has conducted acting training workshops all over the country. He has also conducted various research and laboratory schemes for the formulation of a training method for budding actors.

Of late, he undertook individual projects for the Ford Foundation, New Delhi, on acting methodology, which initiated his contact with various groups and theatre people all over the country, spreading his concept of ritualism, non-verbal energy and creativity of the self through workshops and collaborations. In the year 1997, Heisnam Kanhailal established a private school of Performance art.

Kanhailal, H. *see also* Introduction; Kalakshetra; Sabitri, Human Cage, Pebet, Memoirs of Africa, Mrituswor

Kanya, Sairem *see under* Sairem Kanya

Karnagi Mama Amasung Karnagi Aroiba Yahip

This is the title of the Sahitya Akademi and the Manipuri State Kala Akademi Award winning Manipuri book by N. Ibobi Simha which comprises of two radio dramas on the life of Karna from the Mahabharata - entitled '*Karnagi mama*' (Karna's mother) and Karnagi aroiba yahip (The last sleep of Karna). Though written separately, these two dramas could be regarded as a single play being centred round the last days in the life of Karna and the momentous revelations of many secrets of his life which ultimately acted as odds against him.

Karnagi mama depicts the incident of the Kunti's visit to Karna on the eve of his battle against the Pandavas to dissuade him from the fight by disclosing her identity to him and failing that to beg of him his right thumb. The story is built up with the touching sentiments of a mother and her apparently estranged son who longed for a reunion with her. The last part of the play where Karna is engaged in a verbal duel with Kunti each taking a rigid stand has echoes of Rabindranath Tagore's 'Karna Kunti Sambad'.

The second drama '*Karnagi aroiba yahip*' focusses on the last day of Karna who died fighting a losing battle against insurmountable odds and the grand finale of the disclosure of the relationship between Karna and the Pandavas from the mouth of Kunti to her surviving sons. The obsessive desire to known his true identity and the unexpected revelation of the real identiy of Karna by Kunti is depicted with heightened emotions.

A critic observes 'In the two plays the playwright could make his point that Karna was not killed by Arjuna but got himself killed voluntarily and that he died a heroic death fighting valiantly. Not that Karna could not keep his promise which he never pronounced. His death is a voluntarily repose he desired so intensely. In the two plays the playwright brings out the values of eternal bond between a mother and her son, brotherly affection, manly honour and above all, the compassion and humanity of Karna. The language is highly poetical and this contributes a great deal towards building up of the play's atmosphere. The play bagged the Manipurs State Kala Akademi Award in 1982 and the Sahitya Akademi Award in 1983.

Karnagi Mama Amasung Karnagi Aroiba Yahip *see also* Ibobi Simha, N.

Khogendra, Y. *see* Introduction

Khomdon Meiroubi

Khomdon Meiroubi (Khomdon the Fire Bringer) is a modern Symbolic drama in Manipuri, written by W. Kamini Singh. The drama appeared from Imphal in June 1980. It depicts how the so-called leaders ad the rich, exploit the poor villagers ruthlessly. The rich torture the villagers, cut legs, arms, etc of the helpless villagers if ever they disobeyed them. The villagers, in order to save their future generation, try to rescue the life of Khomdon Meiroubi, the last son of the last generation.

Kishwarjit, L. *see* Introduction

Krishnamohan Singh, Sinam

Freedom Fighter, Parliamentarian, educationist, litterateur and publicman of Manipur, Sinam Krishnamohan was born in 1902 at Laisom Leirak, Keisamthong of Manipur. An M.A. B.L. of Dacca University, Krishnamohan began his teaching career in High Schools. He left the job to participate in the Independence movement and associated himself with the Indian National Congress. He became a member of the Constitution making Committee for Manipur.

After independence, Sinam Krishnamohan Simha became a minister in the Manipur Government in 1948. For many years, he served as the President of the Manipur State Congress and was nominated a member of the Rajya Sabha from 1965 to 1972.

In the domain of literature, he tried his hand in its various genres, be it poetry, prose, novel or drama. His '*Wareng nachom*' is a bouquet of prose. His essays are marked by clarity of expression and ability to expand abstract concepts in simple language. *Sana leibak Manipur* (Manipur, the golden land) and Liklu pareng (A golden necklace) are books of poetry. He also rendered Tagore's Gitanjali into Manipuri. He penned a novel entitled '*Wa gangdaba Sakhi*' (The speechless witness).

His contributions to Manipuri drama and theatre is immense. Krishnamohan composed '*Manipur Govind*', a play on the installation of the image of Sri Govinda in the palace temple of Manipur. Many of his dramas were put on boards at the Rupmahal Theatre of Imphal such as *Shakkhangdabi* (The unknown) *Manipuri kadomda* (Whither Manipur), *Ngasigi Manipur* (Today's Manipur).

Krishnamohan's dramatic publication '*Chingdā, Śatpā*' got published by Gitavali Devi from Imphal in 1968.

Krishnamohan served as the President of the Manipuri Sahitya Parishad in 1963 which accoladed him with the title '*Sahitya Bhusan*' in 1976.

Kshetri Jugindro *see* Jugindro Singh, Kshetrimayum and Introduction

Kulabidhu Simha, Haobam

Haobam Kulabidhu Simha translated the medieval Sanskrit drama '*Bidagdha Madab natakam*' of Rupa Gosvamin into Manipuri. Part one of the play was published by Maibum Chandra has Simha from Imphal in 1976.

L

Laigi Machasinga

Laigi Machasinga (Children of God) is a dramatic adaptation of one of the essays of Samarendra which deals with the life of the Mau tribe in Manipur. This play was directed by H. Kanhailal for Kalakshetra in 1978 and Samarendra himself played the role of a Chaiwallah (or Tea vendor). The play exhibits contradictory relationship between a tribal chief and a Chaiwallah, a tea vendor who is a refugee from Sylhet. Though the chief is technically the landlord of the Chaiwallah, but he does all the chores like chopping wood, cutting vegetables, lighting the fire. All he wants is a little money at the end of the day, which he promptly spends. The Chaiwallah, on the other hand has a much better grasp of the basic principles of modern economy. He saves his money and, not surprisingly at the close of the play (staged in the form of a mimed code), he assumes the power of an exploiter while the tribal chief is as redundant as the heads that hang in his house, mere mementoes of the past.

When Samarendra had been appointed as the Principal of a high school in Mau, he realized how urban perspectives on this tribe with a head-hunting tradition were at once biased and ignorant. He depicted his love for the Mau people who were in his words, innocent, simple, honest brave, hospitable and not hostile or uncivilized savages. He, somewhat, idealized these people, yet what he realised is real. And it is this love for the essential humanity in tribal culture that the director Kanhailal attempted to evoke in his production.

Lalbabu Simha, S.

S. Lalbabu Simha, born in 1920, wrote a play in Manipuri entitled '*Loyrān Lamja*', broughtout by the dramatist from Imphal in 1967.

Lalit Simha, Sorokhaibam

A multifaceted theatre personality Sri Sorokhaibam Lalit Simha was born in 1893 at Imphal. An accomplished playwright, actor and director in Manipur, Lalit Simha was drawn to the theatre world at a very early age. He acted in the Manipuri version of a Bengali play '*Pagalini*', rendered by one Bihari Simha of Cachar, Assam. Lalit was the writer and court official who played a key role in establishing the 'Meitei Dramatic Union' (1930) that renamed itself the 'Manipur Dramatic Union' (MDU) which claimed the core position in Manipuri theatre. His two notable self-composed plays are '*Sāti Khongnang*' (1930) and '*Areppa marup*' (Abiding Friend) in 1931. The Meitei Dramatic Union renamed itself in 1937 as 'Manipur Dramatic Union' and one of its stalwarts, social activist Jananeta, Hijam Irawat left for a political career in 1939. But the group weathered this set back due to the increasing dominance of Sorokhaibam Lalit's aesthetics who became a powerful purveyor of folk based stories, both in dramatic literature and also onto the stage. Sorokhaibam Lalit, the father figure of Manipuri proscenium theatre, ran the Manipur dramatic Union as a strict disciplinarian. He became the leader of the traditional form, accented greater representation of Manipur's Cultural resources and attention to folk stories as a medium of dramatic literature, taking up the romantic subjects of the past in proscenium theatre presenting in ways exactly suited to contemporary tastes. Lalit Simha was actively associated with the Manipur Dramatic Union. He played a vital role in its development. As director, he directed several plays and many of them own him national and regional awards. Manipur's political integration with India in 1949 brought in the Nehruvian ethos, and melodramas on legendary folk love stories and poor-boy-rich-girl encounters attracted the national gaze after 1954, when Lalit's direction of '*Haorang Leishang Saphabi*' took Manipur theatre into Jawaharlal Nehru's Indian mainstream of 'Uniti in diversity'. The play bagged him first prize in All India Drama Competition under the Folk Category. His dramas staged at the M.D.U. several times are *Khamba shamu khongyatpa* (Khamba tied to the feet of an elephant), a folk theme taken from the story of Khamba and Thoibi of Moirang, *Sati Khongnang* (The peepal tree in the memory of a Sati), a play based on a historical incident; *Mainu Premcha*, a socio-historical play: Bhagyachandra, a historical play on the life of one of the greatest king of Manipur; *Puran meithaba* (Burning of Puran), a historical play *Areppa marup* (constant friend), a social play and *Mathur* a play on a theme from the Krishna saga.

The 'Sati Khoṅgnāṅg was published by the State Press, Imphal in 1931 and Areppā marup by the playwright himself in 1937, also from Imphal.

The dramas of Lalit Simha mark the early stage in the growth and development of modern Manipuri drama. The beginning of modern Manipuri drama shows a heavy learning on folk and historical themes written in a stylized form, and Lalit Simha played a significant part in its development. With the former, a naturalistic trend in Manipur theatre commenced. The first experiment in ticketing was made for the play 'Areppa marup'.

He had a strong belief in the Manipuri theatre tradition. He devoted his entire life to promote it and in returns, the Manipur Sahitya Parishad honoured him with the title '*Natya Visharad*' in 1960. Lalit died in the year 1955.

Lalit, S. *see also* Introduction

Leimaton Devi

Smt. Leimaton Devi, a Manipuri actress who played '*Malati*' in the play 'Madhu-malati', written by Kh wairakpam Chaoba. On 29.4.1995, she was being interviewed by Dr. N. Tombi Simha. At that time she was 65 years and her address of communication was : Vijay Govind, Imphal.

Leipkalei *see* Samarendra Simha, Arambam

Lokendra Arambam

A Manipuri cultural figure, director, and scholar, Sri Lokendra Arambam is a multi-faceted personality. He is a theatre director, film makers, critic, writer and cultural scholar, theorist of contemporary Manipuri theatre and educational film enthusiast. Arambam was born in Imphal on 27th February 1959. Son of late A. Dorendrajit Singh, a Sanskrit scholar and Manipuri poet and playwright of early twentieth century.

Lokendra Arambam is the President of the 'Forum for Laboratory Theatres' of Manipur. He headed '*Aryan Theatre*' Imphal, and the Audiovisual Research Centre of Manipur University, Canchipuri. He has done several productions for Aryan Theatre (1968-89) and Forum for Laboratory Theatres of Manipur (1990) which he founded in 1990. Lokendra first proved his calibre as a director in a number of play's, produced under the banner of Aryan Theatre. He directed the existential play '*Hallakpa* (Return) in 1971. From 1975 to 1989, his was mainly epic presentations, environmental staging with massive casts, documentary dramas on quasī-Brechtian modes, and issues of separatism, ethnic rivalries, and political rebellions alluded to in mythic lore. His well known plays are *1891* (jointly collaborated with H. Kanhailal) in 1975, *Irabot* in 1976, *Yotpak Yotlei ama* in 1979, *Moirang ngamba* in 1982, *Numit Kappa* in 1984, *Phou-oibi langon* in 1985 and *Ningthon* in 1987. The latter was an adaptation of Rabindranath Tagore Symbolical play 'Raja'.

In all he has over 30 productions to his credit. *Khuman Chakha Moirang Ngamba* was produced in Sriram Center National Drama Festival, New Delhi 1982, *Phouibi Langon* was presented in Ford Foundation Workshop 1986 and International Seminar, dance, theatre and martial arts, Calcutta 1987 and above all *Macbeth* on the occasion of 50 Years of Indian Independence, London 1997.

Arambam has toured many countries including Italy (1988, 1993), China (1994), Nottingham, UK (1994), London (1997), London and Dusseldorf, Germany (1988) as a leader of cultural delegations, and resource person for many theatre workshops and festivals.

Lokendra Arambam *see also* Aryan Theatre

M

Madhob Sharma, Laimayum

Born in 1930, Laimayum Madhob Sharma's chief work is '*Matam gī īcel*', a drama in Manipuri, broughtout by Laisram Thamil, Imphal in 1964.

Madhumalati

This is a beautiful love-story, written by Khwairakpam Chaoba, setting the events in a bygone age, possibly the reign of Bhagyachandra (1763-1798). This short story was published in 1925 as a part of *Pidam. Sri Chaoba reportedly recast it as a full-fledged drama.*

Madhumangol Singh, Kanghujam

Manipuri author and dramatist Kanghujam Madhumangol Singh was born in 1936. His play '*Headmaster*' was published by K. Biren Simha from Imphal in 1969.

Madhumangol Simha, Khumanthem

Khumanthem Madhumangol Simha was born in 1887. His chief dramatic composition '*Sri Sri Krishna*' was published by Raj Kumari Bamabati Devi from Imphal in 1966. The author died in 1962.

Madhumangal Singh, Khumanthem *see also* Introduction

Mahabharata Plays in Manipuri

In 1951, Kaisam Amubu Simha's (1902-1961) composed a Mahabhara play in Manipuri '*Chitrangada*'. *Kiratarjuniyam* of Bhāravi appeared in Manipuri version in 1964, rendered by Aribam Gokul Sharma. Phurailatpam Jagadish Sharma's Mahabharata drama '*Karnarjun*' in Manipuri was published by Mukundeshwar Sharma from Imphal in 1967.

Ningombam Ibobi Simha's magnum opus '*Karnagi Mama Amasung Karnagi Aroiba Yahip*' declared the best book in Manipuri language by the Sahitya Akademi, New Delhi in 1983. The play bagged the Manipur State Kala Akademi Award a year before. The book contains his two radio dramas on the life of Karna, could be regarded as a single play in -as-much as the theme focuses on the last days in the life of Karna and the momentous revelations of many secrets of his life which ultimately acted as odds against him. His other Mahabharata plays of note are *Nupigi michangda Gandhari* (Gandhari on the side of woman), *Nupida langjaba Kichak* (Kichak who wronged a woman), *Ekalabya*, *Subhadra huba* (the abduction of Subhadra), *Gandharina Sri Krihnada shāp tuba* (Gandhari's curse on Srikrishna), *Karnagi dan* (The gift of Karna) etc.

Manbi Devi

Smt. Aribam Ningol Manbi Devi played the role of Malika in Khwairakpam Chaoba's Manipuri drama '*Naba-Malika*'. On 4.5.1995, she was being interviewed by Dr. N. Tombi Simha. At that time the actress was 71 years and her address of communication was : Uripok Tourangbam Leikai, Imphal.

Mangang, S.K. *see* Introduction

Manglemchandra Sharma, K.

K. Manglemchandra Sharma, a Modern writer in Manipuri was born in 1944. His best known drama '*Lamjing maira*' was published from Imphal in 1973 by S. Manglemjao Simha.

Manglem Meetai, O.

O. Manglem Meetai wrote the play '*Langon mapokamada*' in Manipuri which appeared from Imphal in 1981. The play comprises of 51 pages and probebly published by Premjit Samon.

Manijao, N.

N. Manijao was born in 1931. He wrote and published the play '*Kege charyapung*' in Manipuri, appeared in print in 1980 from Imphal.

Manik, Chungkham (Pena Singer) *see* Introduction (Manipur Dramatic Union)

Marni-Mamou

This is the title of the Manipuri drma, meaning 'Mother-in-Law and Daughter-in-Law' a farcically comic play of G.C. Tongbra who in his usual style presents problems in his own individual style. Though he sets the background of the play set in a nucleus family but it has its ramifications in political and social problems. The play has six lead characters, namely-Maniratan (a judge), Manihar (his younger brother), Manmohini (his wife), Hiramani (his mother and Basant (his attendant). The plot of the play runs as follows:-

Maniratan is a judge, who has to give his verdict on several civil and criminal cases. Rasamani, his wife, always wants to idle away the time, boasting herself to be 'the wife of a judge'. Maniratan's mother Hiramani is none the better, and she is in league with her younger daugher Manmohini who could find fault with Rasamani and quarrel day in, day out. In spite of his being a judge, Maniratan cannot find any solution to the quarrels in the family and feels worried and depressed. His younger brother, Manihar, is of little use in the domestic situation and he is keenly expecting to get a wife through the generous help of his brother, the judge. Basant, the attendant of Maniratan, always tries to be with Manmohini. And his love is returned.

The demand and pressure from the opposite sides on Maniratan increases and so also the quarrels in the family. Maniratan with the help of Basant, his attendant, tries to pacify the quarrelling members in the family by resorting to the non-violent ways of fasting. This does not yield the desired result and he takes the painful decision to hang himself if the incessant quarrel between his wife and mother and sister did not stop. The warring groups request him not to resort to such a drastic step. On their request, he gives up the idea but is afflicted with depression.

Maniratan decides to visit Shillong on long leave and set to undergo a course of treatment. He reaches Shillong with Basant and gets admitted at the nursing home of Dr. Tomchou who has a daughter Ruby by name, who is a nurse by profession. He is well-treated there and under the loving care of Ruby, a divorcee, he soon regains strength and health. Dr. Tomchou understands the feelings of Ruby, and allows both of them to leave for Imphal on holiday. Maniratan owes a few thousand rupees to the nursing home and he assures Ruby that to make good the default of the payment to be made by him he would marry her.

Basant returns to Imphal in advance and tells the anguished family that Maniratan has expired. After the usual shock, the members of his family perform the *Shraddha* ceremony with borrowed money. On the very day of the *Shraddha*, Maniratan returns home with Ruby. Finding that he is not dead the ceremony for *Shraddha* is changed into one of weeding for his younger sister, Manmohini with Basant. Ruby, who learns the secrets of the family, stays away. Maniratan is deep in debt and to liquidate the debt he sells away his property to a rich man and leaves for a village to find a humble living by pursuing agriculture. His home, once the house of a judge, soon bore the sign of 'To Let' in no time. About this play, I.R. Babu Singh observes: "The plot is rather laboured and to create a comic situation, Tongbra always brings in so many extra dramatic elements. For instance, the episode of the quarrelling daughter-in-law and the mother-in-law with her daugher for a stint in musical pastime are designed to distract the attention from the main theme and arouse hilarious laughter in the gloom of the disappearance of Maniratan, the bread-winner of the family, the painful prospect of a looming doomsday and the exit of Manihar from the house when he saw no prospect of his getting married. He often delivers sharp and castigating lashes in the dialogues to drive home his message. Besides highlighting a problem in a family, the theme points to the rivalries in political parties and social institutions officially wedded to the service of the people."

The Manipur Artistes Touring Drama Party *see* Introduction (National Touring Dramatic Party)

Manipur Dramatic Union (MDU) *see* Introduction

Mani Singh, Kharibam

Kharibam Mani Singh was born in 1935. He authored the play '*Meghanạda*' in Manipuri, broughtout by Maino Das Charan Simha from Imphal in 1970.

Mani Singh, Mutum

Shri Mutum Mani Singh played minor characters in '*Nava-Yug Theatre*'. On 29.4.1995, he was being interviewed by Dr. N. Tombi Simha and at that time the actor was 86 years old and his address of communication was : Uripok, Imphal.

Mani Singh, Rajkumar

Born in Imphal in 1939, Sri Mani Singh is a renowned short story writer and translator who has to bis credit the Manipuri version of O'Neill's play '*Long days journey into night*'. Winner of Manipur State Kala Akademi Award (1990) and the Sahitya Akademi Award (New Delhi, 1994). Sri Singh's achievement is, however, in the domain of shorter fiction.

Mani Singh, Takyenjam

Takyenjam Mani Singh, a modern writer in Manipuri was born in 1944. His dramatic composition '*Hugi polang*' was published from Imphal in 1969, broughtout by the playwright himself.

Matum, K.S.

K.S. matum is the translater of the Bengali play of Kabichandra entitled '*Sri Sri Jagabandhu nirupam*', broughtout by Ks. Ibobi Simha from Imphal in 1968.

Meghachandra Heirangkhongjam

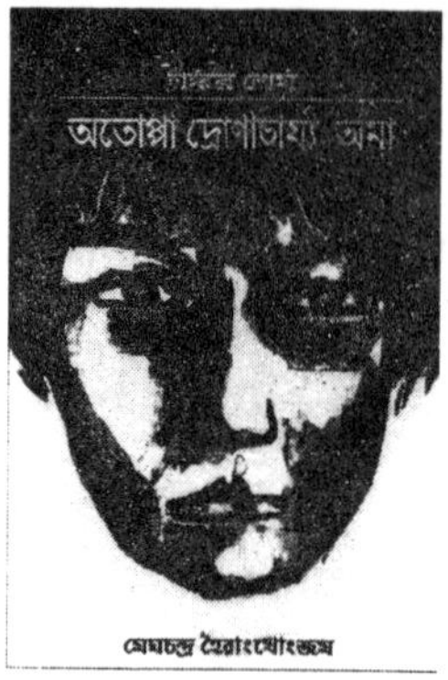

A modern writer and translator in Manipuri, Meghachandra Heirangkhongjam was awarded the prestigious Sahitya Akademi Translation Prize of 2002 for his Manipuri version of Shankar Shesh's Hindi drama 'Ek Aur Dronacharya '*Atoppa Dronacharya Ama*' is the rendered title, published by Sudhir Nauroibam from Imphal in 1999.

Memoirs of Africa

This is the title of the play produced by Kalakshetra under the direction of H. Kanhailal. This is a short theatre piece based on a poem by L. Samarendra Simha in which the history of oppression in Africa stands for appression anywhere in the world. The play focuses on the eternal persecution and survival of Mi, who could be either male or female. The play evolved through an organic creative process involving improvisation, song and dance, drawing on traditional dance and martial arts traditions.

[*See* 'Introduction']

Memot Singha

Born in 1937, Memot Singh's chief dramatic work is '*Inshanke khoj*', broughtout by O.K. Store, Imphal in 1965.

Mineketan Singh, A.

A versatile and gifted writer, Sri A. Minaketan Singh was born on 2 May 1906 at Imphal. An eminent poet, folklorish essayist, grammarian and literary critic, he also tried his hand in playwriting also.

He was a graduate of Calcutta University, he studied Sanskrit and old Manipuri language and literature. A Government officer who left his job and preferred teaching as career at a High School Minaketan later taught at the University and retired as an Associate Professor and Head, Manipuri Language and Literature Division, Centre of Post Graduate Studies (J.N.U.), Imphal. A prolific writer, Sri Singh has some twenty one books to his credit. Minaketan's literary output comprises of plays poems, short stories, historical romances, treatises on Manipuri grammar and translated works of Rabindranath Tagore and Shakespeare into Manipuri. But it is as a poet he has made his mark.

His literary achievements has brought him many titles and awards. He was a Fellow of "Manipur State Kala Academy". Received '*Sahityaratna*' from Manipur Sahitya Parishat. He has also been honoured with *Kavi Samrat* from Thangal Marup, Hailakandi, Cachar.

Minaketan was the first autobiographer in Manipuri who wrote 'Punsigi Saktam'. For his anthology of poems 'Aseibagi Nitaipod' he bagged the prestigious Sahitya Akedemi Award (New Delhi) of 1977 in the language. This collection is considered an outstanding contribution to Manipuri literature for its exquisite language and rhythmic patterns, superb command over the medium, creative use of the folktale and legend, and its faith in the immortality of love.

In the realm of drama, Minaketan's '*Sita Banabas*' was published in 1946 and staged several times in those days and appreciated by the educated reading public as well as commoners. As an idealish he aims at establishment of a humanitarian society, the Ram-rajya' on this earth.

Ashangbam Minaketan rendered the English drama '*Rape of Lucrece*' of William Shakespeare into Manipuri which he himself published from Imphal in 1965.

Minaketan Singh's play '*Tonu-laiginglembi*' appeared in 1976 from Imphal. In 1978 cameout his '*Ashaibagi Jay Bhaig*', all published by him from Imphal.

He was one of the prominent personality in the Manipuri intellectual life, who associated himself with scores of literary cultural and educational institutions of the land.

Select Works

Ashaibagi jay bhaig. — Imphal : the author, 1978.

155 p.; 18.5 cm.

Tonu-laiginglembi. — Imphal : the author, 1976.

102 p.; 18 cm.

Mohendra, N.

N. Mohendra who associated himself with the Aryan Theatre. Directed single handed and some with Nongthembam Premchand in the 1990s under the aegis of Aryan Theatre.

Mohendra Sharma

Mohendra Sharma, a modern writer in Manipuri penned and published the drama '*Nongdam*' from Imphal in 1967.

Moirang Thoibi

Acknowledge as one of the masterpieces of modern Indian literature, Moirang Thoibi is a play written by Arambam Dorendrajit Singh (Simha), a celebrated poet and dramatist. The play deals with the Khamba and Thoibi story. Set in 1945, the locale is Moirang, an erstwhile principality of the Moirangs, by the side of the Loktak Lake, on the south-western fringe of the Manipur valley. The lead characters include Khamba (a young man of the Khuman clan), Puremba (his father, a prominent noble of the Court), Nongban (a noble of the Court of Moirang), Thonglen (an old general, a friend of Puremba), Chaoba (an old, witty minister, a friend of Puremba), Puriklai (king of Moirang), Thoibi (princess, daughter of the Yubaraj), Senu (Thoibi's maid), Khamnu (Khamba's elder sister). Sri A. Samarendra Singh gives the symopsis of the play in the following lines: "Inside their poor house, Khamba consoles his elder sister Khamnu not to brood over the conditions of their poor life any further because he will be able to help her as he has grown up to be a young man. The next day Khamnu goes to Loktak lake in search of food. Meanwhile, Thoibi the princess, is fishing with her friends and Senu, her maid, happens to see Khamnu and she is brought to the princess. They make friends and Khamnu joins fishing. By this time, Khamba reaches the lakeside as he has lost his way in the water and sees Thoibi. He is charmed by her beauty and he speaks to himself in praise of her beauty. He is overheard by Senu, and the girls prepare to arrest him as he disobeyed the king's orders for men to keep indoors on that particular day. As he happens to be the younger brother of Khamnu he is released at last, but Thoibi has fallen in love with Khamba at the first sight.

Thonglen the General and Chaoba the Minister who are friends of Puremba, the deceased father of Khamba and Khamnu, once a prominent noble of the court, remember Khamba and Khamnu whom they forgot all the while and start searching for the poor Khamba and Khamnu.

Thoibi and Senu have gone to Khamnu's place and met Khamba while he was hiding behind a mat to which Thoibi bowed assuming him to be the presiding deity of the Khumans. Thoibi and Khamba exchange their love and promise to stand by each other.

Thonglen and Chaoba introduce Khamba and Khamnu to the royal court. Khamba is made a noble and he is given the charge of the area under the care of the Yubaraj. He and Nongban, his future arch-rival, are asked to make friends and they are ordered to collect flowers for offering to Lord Thangjing, the ruling deity of the Moirangs at the ensuing Lai-haraoba festival and they are asked to prepare for sports. In the festival, Khamba proves to be superior to Nongban in all respects.

Nongban feels depressed at the thought of defeat at Khamba's hands and is more disturbed at the prospect of Khamba having Thoibi as his wife, for Nongban too aspires to win over Thoibi. He plans to ruin Khamba. He pretends to be possessed, and gives the oracle that bull grazing at Ekop should be caught by a man not above 30 years of age without arms and should be offered to Lord Thangjing. The king feels depressed to learn the oracle and as suggested by the Yubaraj, Khamba is asked to catch the bull. Khamba subdues the bull and he is given promotion as well as many rewards and above all, the king bethrothes Thoibi is Khamba in the presence of all the nobles of the court except the Yubaraj who has left the court earlier.

The Yubaraj, Thoibi's father, is furious on seeing Khamba wearing his favaurite shirt on the day of shooting a target, a royal ceremony. The shirt was given away by Thoibi to Khamba as a present. He takes Khamba as his arch-enemy and decides to destroy him. He plans with Nongban to finish him off. Khamba is called out in the dark night by Keithellakpa on a pretext and Nongban and his gang who waited pounced on Khamba and beat him up severely. Khamba is tied to the leg of the royal elephant and is dragged to and fro in the market-place over hard pebbles. The goddess of the market, in the form of a woman, asked Thoibi in her dream to save Khamba. Thoibi wakes up instantaneously and runs to the market with a knife in her hand and rescues Khamba.

Chaoba takes up the matter to the court and Thonglen wages a war against the Moirangs. A trial follows at the royal court and the culprits, the Yubaraj and Nongban, are sent to prison for three years. After coming out of prison, the Yubaraj asks 'Thoibi to be Nongban's wife, but Thoibi refuses. The Yubaraj in anger banishes Thoibi to Kabaw (Manipuri name of Burma).

Thoibi returns from exile but on the way at Kumbi she finds Nongban waiting to receive her. She feels dejected but Naijahanba, her escort, conceives a strategy to hoodwink Nongban by asking Thoibi to feign illness. He informs Nongban that Thoibi is sick and the only cure is a horse. Nongban brings his horse and Thoibi gallops away. Feiroijamba, Khamba's brother-in-law, informs him of the situation and Khamba stops the horse. She is taken to his house.

Khamba and Nongban are asked by a royal order to catch a tiger at Khoirentak. The two go for the tiger and Nongban is killed by the tiger at the first encounter. Khamba kills the tiger and presents the animal to the king. At last Khamba marries Thoibi, and thus they are united."

See also Dorendrajit Simha, Arambam

Momon Singh, Haikham

Haikham Momon Singh was born in 1942. This modern writer's chief dramatic work is '*Prem gi pirang*', published by Ks. Biren Simha from Imphal in 1968.

Motilal Singh Huirem

Motilal Singh was born in 1926. He wrote the drama '*Maitai Khungang*', broughtout by the Manipur Administration and Publicity Department, Imphal in 1963.

Motilal, Huirem *see also* Introduction (Manipur Dramatic Union)

Mrituswor

This is the title of a triad of short plays which was presented by Kalakshetra Manipur and was funded by Ford Foundation as part of a larger Scheme to reinvestigate folk forms. This was Kanhailal's first directorial attempt to explore new possibilities of humour through the acting idiom of Moirang Parba. Though all three pieces offer variations on the theme of Subterfuge, it is, perhaps, the first play in the triad that is most effective where an actor playing Ravana is seen to refuse to die on stage till his director pays him his dues. In this contemporary fable one can read a comment, if not protest, on the part of Manipur theatre workers, most of whom are unemployed and act for nothing.

Muhammad Abdul Kadir

Muhammad Abdul Kadir was born in 1951. He wrote and published the drama '*Nunsinabadi kaynabani*', came out from Imphal in 1979.

N

Naba Malika

This drama is written by late Khwairakpam Chaoba which was staged by the Manipur Dramatic Union — a premier theatre in Manipur — successfully staging it many times in the fifties and the sixties. But it was put on boards under the title '*Japan Lan*' (Japanese War). A page in the manuscript of this play bears the signature of Kavi Chaoba put on 28th September 1945. Hence the date of the play is 1945.

The play Naba-malika tells us a love story at the backdrop of the War. The plot runs as follows: Naba (Nabakishor) sets up a school in his friend Nabin's house where he started teaching a large number of students. The blaring sound of a siren is heard, the students take shelter inside large trenches. Naba, Malika who had recently lost her mother and Chaoba set out for pilgrimage to Nabadwip. They met with Japanese soldiers on their way to Dimapur and battle scenes are inserted. A scene shows the railway station. There arose, then, problems regarding the taking of food commensurate with the Vaishnavite set of rules regarding the pure and the impure. Naba and Malika are shown disclosing their hearts' secrets to each another on the banks of the Ganga at Nabadwip. Malika also expressed her readiness to support Naba if he studied in Calcutta. The scene then shifted to Imphal where Chandra had betrothed his daughter Tharosana to Nabin. The smoke of war slowly subsided and life saw a gradual return to normalcy. Naba, Malika, and party returned home and the two became finally united in the last scene. Much use of Hindi and Bengali words were made in this play. Such scenes as Gora and Gorkha soldiers buying pan from Meitei women in the market were also included in the play. There is a prayer, too, for universal peace by Nabin and Naba.

About this play, Smt. Meinam Sakhi Devi who played Mrs. Grimwood says — "... We belonged to the first ever batch of D.M. College — there were only two girl students, Chandrakala and myself. On the occasiön of the Annual Freshers Meet a short-play about something like the arrest of Koireng Yuvaraj and the battle of Khongjom was shown. They decided not to hire any outside artiste; so I was given the role of Mrs. Grimwood. I looked more of a man that a woman, figure-wise, too and womanly softness was a rare thing in me. I dressed myself in trousers. I had a short line to recite and a small act to perform — the Sahebs were holding a secret meeting discussing methods to arrest Koireng Yuvaraj and I eavesdropped. The five officers left. I wanted to save Koireng Yuvaraj. So I called in an orderly and sent a letter to Koireng Yuvaraj through him. I kept on looking intently as he left with the letter..... R.K. Surendrajit played a market woman, o what resemblance! Sonamani played Krishna. He is fair in complexion you know. So, they daubed him with some green colour because Krishna was blue complexioned. As there was no student among us who could sing, we had to hire Bimola for the singing parts". It is quite true, the songs had been sung by Nongmaithem Bimola Devi and she made the following remarks in this context — "I was not a student of that college; they requested me to sing those songs as none among them could. My role in the play was that of Niyati or Pathik. Actually, it was the lamentations of the Goddess of the Market on the sufferings in *Meitei Leibak*. There were about three songs. I can't recollect the tune, but a little of the words I remember — 1. *Mangle mangle ngasi Manipur Leibak*, *Sha mamangda tare Angouba makok* (Gone are the days of Manipur, the British had been beheaded before the *Kangla Sha*), 2. *Shaklon pubi mangalgi thambal, Fugaina shatle Ita*... (The lotus of the morning light, that has many forms is in full bloom, my friend)"— Shri B.I. Sharma is of the opinion that a few songs besides these were also sung in the play. he comments — "The play was interspersed with snatches of English and Hindi songs. The lines went something like this — "*Kongba suit, Singjamei hat, Khamlang Leirak fountain pen*.... Among the spectators were M.K. Priyobrata, a few Durbar Members, Major Khating.... Gun-fire sound was imitated by drawing a rickety table over the floor.... Pleased with my performance in the role of a

Saheb, Shri M.K. Priyobrata gave me an appointment in the Police Department. I received forty-five rupees a month."

Nabachandra, V.

Born in 1934, V. Nabachandra wrote and broughtout the Manipuri play '*Nupina nipa lonba*', which appeared in print from Imphal in 1964.

Nabakanta Singh, S. *see* Introduction (Rupmahal)

Nabakumar *see* Introduction (Rupmahal)

Naba Natya Mandir *see* Introduction

Naba Wareppa *see* Introduction (under 'Theatre Mirror')

Nadiya Singh, Wahengbam

Manipuri artist who took minor roles in professional theatre. He was being interviewed on 29.4.1995 by Dr. N. Tombi Singh. At that time, Nadiya Singh was 74 years and his address of communication was : Uripok Polem Leikai, adjacent to the Roxy Theatre.

Nambol Dramatic Union *see* Introduction

Nandita

Manipuri Actress Nandita associated with the leading theatre troupe '*Kalakshetra*' of Kanhailal. She did the role of 'Cat' in Kalakshetra's famous production 'Pebet'. She was also one of the 'Nupi's' in Memoirs of Africa, playing young woman, half-spirit, half-human, embodying the deepest sources of creativity.

Nangyai, Takhellambam

Takhellambam Nangyai was born in 1938, he penned and published the Manipuri play '*Mai koyba asidadi yao hanjakhige*', from Imphal in 1964.

Nara Singh *see* Ibungohal Singh, Lairenmayum

Narayan Singh

Narayan Singh was born in 1942. He authored the play '*Madhavi*' which was published by Salam Kishorchand Simha from Nambol Bazar in 1969.

Narendra Singh, Thiyam

Thiyam Narendra Singh was born in 1937. He wrote and published the play '*Bapuji*' from Imphal in 1969.

Natya amasung mancha *see* Ibobi Simha, Ningombam

Netrajit Singh, Laisram

Laisram Netrajit Singh was born in 1916. His best-known drama is '*B.A. Thiba*' was published by Imphal Book House, Imphal in 1966.

Netrajit Singh Laisram *see also* Introduction (Rupmahal)

Nilamani Sharma, Hanjabam

Shri Hanjabam Nilamani Sharma was an artist of the Imphal Theatre group from the early times. Later he joined the Manipur Dramatic Union as a prominent actor. On 27.1.95, he was being interviewed by Dr. N. Tombi Simha. At that time, the artist was 79 years old and his address of communication was Uripok Tourangbam Leikai, Imphal.

Nilamani Singh, Hawaibam *see* Introduction (Rupmahal)

Nimai Singh, Ngangbam

An outstanding music composer, Sri Ngangbam Nimai Singh was the son of Ng. Shyamkishore Singh who was the brother-in-law of Maharaja Churachand Singh, also a pioneer of clarinet and drama.

In his childhood, Nimai Singh lost his left arm by falling from a tree and suffered fracture in his left arm. He became a keen student of both vocal and instrumental music by virtue of his devotion and effort. After receiving further training from Pankaj Mullick at Calcutta, he started composing music for plays of Manipur Dramatic Union. His noteworthy musical composition such as '*Jati Kaubi Sakhenbi*', '*Nungeibi Takhellei* (addressed to flowers), as recorded in the gramaphone were once on the lips of everybody.

Ningol Manbi, Aribam

Aribam Ningol Manbi was born in 1925. A determined and talented artist of the Manipur Dramatic Union, she died in 1996 at the age of seventyone.

Nipamcha

Arambam Nipacha is the author of the Manipuri dramas '*Moirang Nongbam*' '*Iraima*' '*Khuman Puren ba*', '*Nungthilgee mong*' which he himself published from Imphal 1982, 1983, 1984, 1985 respectively.

Select Works

Iraima . —Imphal : the author, 1983.
 47 p.; 17.5 cm.

Khuman purem ba. — Imphal : the author, 1984.
 58 p.; 18 cm.

Moirang nongbam. — Laikai : the author, 1982.
 105 p.; 18 cm.

Nungthilgee mong. — Imphal : the author, 1985.
 92 p.; 18 cm.

Niras

This Manipuri playwright's drama '*Mangkhraba lambi*' was broughtout by S.K.M. Imphal in 1973.

Nutanchandra Sharma, Hidangmayum

Hidangmayum Nutanchandra Sharma's translated Manipuri version of Utpalendu Sen's Bengali drama, entitled '*Partha sarathi*' was published by E. Nabakumar Simha from Imphal in 1964.

O

Ongbi Nungshitombi, Ningthemcha

A wellknown actress, Ningthemcha Ongbi Nungshitombi was born in 1911. She worked with the frontranking professional Manipuri theatre troupe the 'Manipur Dramatic Union'. This gifted artist passed away in 1985.

P

Pacha Meitai, Loitongbam

Novelist and playwright, Pacha Meitei was born in Imphal in 1943. He wrote his first novel at the age of fourteen. He devotes all his time in reading and writing. He was the Editor of the Manipuri weekly, *The Imphal Times*. Pacha Meitei's novel '*Imphal Amasang magi Ishing Nungshitki Phibam*' (meaning 'Imphal and its climatic condition'), his fifth novel bagged the Sahitya Akademi Award (New Delhi) of 1973.

Pacha Meitei's play 'Langoinai' (Captive) was produced successfully by the prestigious Aryan Theatre, directed by Sanakhya Ebotombi. It was published by Rajen Dresses, Imphal in 1975.

Pacha Meitei *see also* Introduction

Parratt, John

A foreign scholar who alongwith Arambam Saroj N. made an intensive study of the '*Lai Haraoba*'. The publication entitled '*The pleasing of the gods: Meitei Lai Haraoba*', broughtout by the Vikas Publishing, New Delhi in 1997.

Pashot Simha, Achom

Achom Pashot Simha translated the plays of Shakespeare namely *Hamlet, Julius Caesar, King-Lear, Macbeth, Othello, Romeo-Juliet, Tempest and Twelfth night.*

Pebet

This is the title of the play produced by Kalakshetra under the direction of H. Kanhailal. Viewers saw 'Pebet', an ant-Indian and anti-Hindu play, based on a folk story about birds outwitting a cat. Pebet is deeply entrenched in the psyche of the Manipuri people, in which a mother bird fights to protect her children from a predatory cat. Kanhailal in his production, politicizes this familiar story, turning it into a struggle against the political and cultural colonization of Manipur. The play evolved through an organic process involving improvisation, song and dance, drawing a traditional dance and martial art traditions.

The play, 'Pebet' made its debut in 1975, later travelled to Japan in 1987 and Egypt in 1991.

[*See* 'Introduction']

Phirojit, A.

A. Phirojit is a Manipuri stage actor. He is associated with the wellknown theatre group 'Kalakshetra' of Manipur. He did the role of a Pebet's son in the '*Pebet*' and Mimanu 2 in '*Memoirs of Africa*'.

Phulendra, K.

An outstanding playwright in Manipuri, K. Phalendra D. was closely associated with the Aryan Theatre. In 1958, his play '*Sri Sri Krishna Chaitanya*' was staged that featured excellent imagery and sombre realism. In 1965, he rendered Shakespeare's '*Macbeth*' which was produced by the Aryan Theatre with O. Biramangol in the lead.

Pishak Devi *see* Aryan Theatre

Pishak Singh, Chingakham

Chingakham Pishak Singh was born in 1905. He authored the play '*Tonu laijing lembi*', published by Manihar Sharma, Imphal in 1968.

Prahlad Sharma, Gurumayum

Gurumayum Prahlad Sharma was born in 1916. He wrote the play '*Madhu-Malati*' which appeared in print in 1957, published by Ph. Thombi Sharma, Imphal (2nd edn. 1963).

Prahlad Sharma, Gurumayum *see also* Introduction

Pravas Milan *see* Introduction

Premchand, N.

Nongthombam Premchand, a wellknown Manipuri director took up the artistic leadership of the Aryan Theatre since 1990s. He continued the trend of politically oriented drama, some in joint venture with Somorendra or N. Mohendra.

See also Introduction

Priyakumar Singh, Arambam

Arambam Priyakumar Singh, (b. 1957) wrote the drama '*May-day*', published by Achouba Simha, from Imphal in 1980. Arāmbam Priyakumar adapted into Manipuri, a Russian work of Maxim Gorky (1868-1938) which Priyakumar published himself from Imphal in 1976. This play of Priyakumar also appeared from Shingjamai by the Bharatiya Communist Party (CPI) in 1981.

R

Rabindranachom

This is the title of the volumes which contains select writings of Rabindranath Tagore translated by various Manipuri writers. The book in two parts was published by Sahitya Akademi, New Delhi from 1971-78.

This two volume works in Manipuri contain select writings of Rabindranath Tagore, translated by various Manipuri writers; broughtout by the Sahitya Akademi, New Delhi from 1971-1978. Volume 1 contains xiv, 326 pages while volume 2 has 464 pages. The volumes include some of the Manipuri version of Tagore's Bengali dramas.

Radhamohan Simha

Radhamohan Simha, a modern Manipuri author and translator broughtout the Manipuri version of Tagore's '*Chitrangada*'. The translated text appeared from Manipur State Kala Academy, Imphal in 1978, comprising of fifty pages.

Radhesana Devi, Rajkumari

Rajkumari Radhesana Devi was born in 1950. Playwright's chief drama '*Pithadoi*' was published by R.K. Radhesana from Imphal in 1970.

Rajanikanta Singh, Elangbam

Popularly known as R.K. Elangbam, Rajanikanta is an outstanding novelist and short fiction writer in Manipuri who was born in 1929 at Keishamthong Elangbam Leikai, Imphal. Rajanikanta Singh obtained his Master's degree in Arts from the Centre of Post Graduate Studies, Jawaharlal Nehru University, Imphal.

Rajanikanta Singh started his teaching career in Government High Schools and later joined D.M. College of Science. Sri Singh was the editor of the two literary bi-monthlies '*Ee ra*' and '*Makhal Mathel*' and associated with several literary and cultural organisations in Manipur. An executive Member of the Manipuri Sahitya Parishad, Sri E. Rajanikanta Simha bagged the Sahitya Akademi Award of 1981 for his short-stories 'Kalenthagee Leipaklei' which is considered an unparalled contribution to Manipuri literature for its rich human content, sympathetic portrayals, sensitive style and evocative language.

He published novels, plays and volumes on folk tales and songs. His two wellknown dramas are '*Aikhoigi yojana*' and '*Praja raj*', both published by the playwright himself from Imphal in 1960 and 1962 respectively. Rajanikanta's play '*Aikhoigi yojana*' (Our plan) expresses a longng for an ideal society. His interest in tradition and idealism deserves mention.

Rajendra, Y. *see* Introduction

Rama plays in Manipuri

All aspects of the Manipuri literature, specially the drama has been influenced by the theme of the Ramayana. *Sitavanavas* (Exile of Sita) is a wellknown Manipuri drama, which was written by Ashangbam Minaketan Simha in the early thirties of the last century. Mayanglambam Biramangol Singh wrote a play '*Labakusha*', based on the epic Ramayana. It may also be mentioned here that the Rupmahal Theatre, Imphal produced a play entitled '*Sita*' based on Rama story.

Gokul Chandra Sharma (b. 1924) wrote the play '*Rāmgīabhiṣek*' published by the dramatist from Imphal in 1965. G.C. Tongbra's mythological drama '*Lamja Parasuram*' was published by Gandhi Memorial Press, Imphal in 1966. Niṅgombam Ibobī Siṃha (1921-1984) penned the mythological drama '*Rām rājya*' in Manipuri, published by N. Munal Simha from Imphal in 1967. Bhavabhuti's magnum opus '*Uttararama charitam*' was translated into Manipuri by Aribam Gokul Sharma. This tragic drama was published by him from Imphal in 1968. Bhasa's Sanskrit classic '*Pratima natak*' was rendered into Manipuri by Laurembam Iboyaima Simha and published by the translator himself in 1974. Based on Ramayana themes, Phurailatpam Jagadish Sharma's two Manipuri mythological dramas are :- '*Parsuram*' and '*Ratnakar*', published by Tombi Sharma from Imphal in 1969 and 1971 respectively.

Ramayana *see* Rama plays in Manipuri

Ramcharan Simha, Maibam

A prolific playwright in Manipuri, Maibam Ramcharan was born in 1928. He has written over severty-six popular plays and over twenty Shumang Lila scrips, capitalized on sentiment, romance, suffering and family crisis.

Maibam Ramcharan Simha wellknown Manipuri dramas are:- *Anauba ayuk, Icagi imau, Laibak, Laibak chaubi, Loya Laima, Manipur andolon, Ningol (in three parts), Poktabi, Sharat purnima, Sharu macet, Thadokpa, Thambalnu, Uphullakki lairang* etc.

Select Works

Anaubā ayūk. — Imphal: C. Khombā Siṃha, 1962.

122 p. 18 cm.

Icāgī imau. — Imphal: R.K. Sanajāobā Siṃha, 1967.

x159 p. 18 cm.

Lāibak. — Imphal: the author, 1968.

72 p. 18 cm.

Lāibak cāubī. — Imphal: the author, 1961.

100 p. 18 cm.

Loyā laimā. — Imphal: Manipur Student's Emporium 1964.

79 p. 18 cm.

Manipur āndolon. — Nambol Bazar, S. Kiśor Candra Siṃha 1968.

78 p. 18 cm.

Niṅgol. — Pt. 1, Imphal: A.R. Śarmā, 1953.

110 p. 18 cm.

Niṅgol. — Pt. 2, Imphal: Students Store, 1959.

92 p. 18 cm.

Niṅgol. — Pt. 3, Imphal: Th. Nopur Siṃha. 1970.

132 p. 18 cm.

Drama

Poktabī. — Imphal: R.K. Sanajāobā Siṃha, 1966.

127 p. 18 cm.

Śarat pūrṇimā. — 2nd ed. Imphal: the author, 1966.

84 p. 18 cm.

First published in 1947.

Śarū macet. — Imphal: Manipur Admn. 1958.

68 p. 18 cm.

Thadokpā. — 2nd ed. Imphal: the author, 1968.

64 p. 18 cm.

Thambālnu. — Imphal: Students Store, 1959.

81 p. 18 cm.

Uphullakki lairāṅg. — Imphal: Tribal-Maitai Co-operative Works 1972.

104 p. 18 cm.

Uphullakki lairang. — Imphal : Ibopishak Simha, 1972.

104 p.; 18 cm.

Ramcharan Simha, S.

S. Ramcharan Simha's Manipuri drama '*Ngakpiba*' was published in 1972 from Imphal, by the dramatist, comprises of ninty five pages.

Ram Singha, Laitanthem

Born in 1927, Laitanthem Ram Singha wrote the plays '*Jat onba*' and '*Khanggani poloida*' in Manipuri. The former was published by the playwright from Thoubal in 1954 (2nd edn. 1963) and the latter from O.K. Store, Imphal in 1963.

Randhoni, Kshetrimayum

Kshetrimayum Randhoni was born in 1932. She proved herself as a fine actress in the Manipuri Dramatic Union, an apex professional theatre organisation of the state which still stands as a vital mirror of the forgotten artistic glories of the past.

Ravindra Sharma, G. *see* Introduction (Aryan Theatre)

Ritusamharam

Based on Kalidasa's work, this epic has been dramatised by Ratan Thiyam into Manipuri *Ritusamharam*, is description of the Indian cycle of seasons, portraying the close interaction of life and nature. Kalidasa writes about the six seasons — Grishma, Varsha, Sharad, Hemanta, Sheet, Vasanta — in graphic detail. He narrates in impccable manner the impact of the seasons not only on the human psyche, but also on insects, flora and fauna. His poetic images are insightful, graphic and powerful. This is a narrative poem, and not a play in the conventional sense. Kalidasa describes the six seasons in as many episodes, and they were being presented by Ratan in visual interpretation. Each episode is complete in itself. There is no tangible story line and there is no effort to create one. When put on boards, the play tried to underline the fact that all human energy is derived from nature. Now that man is isolating himself and moving away from nature, he is losing the power and energy that he derived from nature. It is a simple expression, through his own vocabulary, of a director who lives in the contemporary world. It is that simple.

R.K. Elangbam *see* Rajanikanta Simha, Elangbam

Roel, Robinson

Robinson Roel is a modern writer whose chief work is '*Mahakna Hayrammi*' a play in Manipuri, published by the playwright himself from Imphal in 1981, containing ninety two pages.

Roma, Y.

An actress of Manipuri Stage, Y. Roma matured as an artist, under Aribam Syam Sharma's tutelage in the 1950s under the bannet of Aryan Theatre.

Romani Singh, Hijam

Shri Hijam Romani Singh took part in the one-act play of Khwairakpam Chaoba and did the role of '*Paona*', but according to Smt. Meinam Sakhi Devi (an actress) he played '*Thangal*'. The play was staged at D.M. College in 1947. On 27.4. 1995, Dr. N. Tombi Simha interviewed him and his address of communication was : Yaiskul, Imphal.

M. Birasimha and H. Romani Simha jointly wrote the Manipuri drama '*Yaithing konu*', broughtout by the Manipuri Sahitya Parishad, Imphal in 1972.

Romoni, Hijam *see under* Romani Singh and Yaithing Konu

Rupmahal Theatre *see* Introduction

S

Sabitri, Heisnam

Foremost actress of contemporary Manipuri theatre who has been acknowledged at the national level. Sabitri was born in 1946 in a rural area of Mayana Imphal. Broughtup in a predominantly rural milieu without receiving much formal education. She was introduced into the world of performing arts at a very tender age by her aunt C. Gouramani, a celebrated actress and star of the yesteryears. Her mentors were her aunt, and the famous actor-manager-director, Elangbam Joychandra Simha, in whose '*National Touring Drama Company*', Sabitra received her informal training in theatre. Her father himself was a bandmaster who specialised in the clarinet. This company used to put up four to five shows a day for rural and sub-urban audiences. Sabitri herself played the role of 'Chaitanya Mahaprabhu' for atleast 100 times between the ages of ten and twelve. As a child artiste, Sabitri travelled widely in the villages doing this central role in '*Nimai Sanyas*', a play produces in 1955 by the Elangbam Joychandra's popular travelling opera troupe that had a record shows of over 1000.

Before joining the Kalakshetra, Sabitri worked in the groups like the longest-lived Aryan Theatre and Student Artistes' Association. When set met Kanhailal, her life companion, for the first time as a young woman, she was a thorough professional. It was in 1961 that they worked together in a social satire called '*Layeng Ahanba*' (First Treatment). This was Kanhailal's first venture as a director.

In February 1962, Kanhailal and Sabitri got married. But as a young bride in a Manipuri joint family, she was prevented from acting until she could prove herself to be a good wife and daughter-in-law. It was only in January 1970 that she was allowed to start her own home.

Kalakshetra has done over thirty productions, featuring predominently H. Sabitri. Sabitri first attracted public notice as mother in Kanhailal's *Tamnalai* (Haunting Deities, 1972) Her body, gestures, movements and voice became representative of the Manipuri woman, deeply pained within, full of love and generosity, but ferocious and awesome when provoked. She carried this language into her major collaborative works with Kanhailal, such as the *mother bird* in Pebet (1975), *Mi* in Memoirs of Africa (1985) and the eponymous *Draupadi* (2000). Shanta Gokhale rightly comments "Nobody who has seen her performance in Kanhailal's most celebrated production, *Pebet*, in which she plays the mother bird anxious for one of her seven babies captured by a cat who teaches it to speak and behave like itself, can ever forget her expressive body movements and her extraordinary voice. In 1991, she was bestowed with the Sangeet Natak Akademi Award, New Delhi for Acting.

Presently, this gifted actress serves as 'President of the *Theatre Women Artists Association*' of Manipur.

Sadanba Ningthon

Sadanba Ningthon [Śādānbā Nimthaw; The Hunter King) is written by Sanajaoba Khetri which appeared in the journal 'Sahitya Leichal', published by the Manipuri Literary Society, Vol.1, Nos.2, 4, 5, 6, 1989-90. The play is presented in the form of a rehearsal in which the artistes enact a scene from Kalidasa's *Shankuntalam*. The central theme is the problem of imagination and reality. The artistes re-create the characters of the text with their own artistic individuality. The artistes are dual persons: they are performers as well as the creators.

Sairem Kanya

Born in 1899, Sairem Kanya established herself as a fine actress of Manipuri theatre. This gifted artist who had a stinct with the Manipur Dramatic Union died in 1961.

Samarendra Singh, Arambam *see* Somorendra Singh, Arambam

Saroj N. Arambam

Saroj N. Arambam, a modern author who jointly wrote the book '*The pleasing of the gods, Meitei Lai Haraoba*' with John Parratt that cameout from Vikas Publishing, New Delhi in 1997.

Sakhi Devi, Meinam

Smt. Meinam Sakhi Devi played the role of Mrs. Grimwood in the one-act play of Khwairakpam Chaoba. On 2.5. 1995, she was being interviewed by Dr. N. Tombi Simha. The actress was then 74 years old and her address of communication was Kangjabi Leirak, Meinam Leikai, Imphal.

Sanajaoba Ksetri

Sanajaoba Ksetri was born in 1941. Author's '*Māytonphi*' is a drama adapted from '*Tangkhulgivari Singbul*' by Y.K. Simney. It was published by Soibam Dhani from Imphal in 1979. Another wellknown Manipuri play '*Sadanba Ningthon*' (The Hunter King) appeared in 1989-90, in the journal 'Sahitya Leichal'.

Sanakhya Ibotombi

A celebrated theatre personality who emerged in the seventies, directed '*Langoinai*' for Aryan Theatre (1973) and '*Shakuntala*' for Rangmandal, Bhopal (1990).

Sanakhya Ibotombi's significant book in Manipuri is '*Manipurda, theatre amasung drama*, broughtout from Imphal in 1987.

Sanamahi Kolu Yeikhaiba

This is a significant drama in Manipuri written in modern times. Broughtout in 1965 by Mayanglambam Biramangol, the play was renamed as '*Chingu Khongnangthaba*', focussing on the issue of the contention or struggle between Hinduism and Meitei faith. The play became a major anti-Hindu historical project that fanned the movement for the displacement of Hinduism in the 1970s, generating pan-Manipuri and anti-Indian feelings. The play highlights the historical experiences of the people during the reign of Pamheiba or Garibniwaz (1708-49), when a Hindu missionary from Sylhet in Bengal, *Shantidas Goswami*, instigated the King to introduce the Ramandi cult as state religion, and how the native sage-intellectual *Khongnang Thaba* fought for the dignity of the autochthons. It detailed the intrigues at court, the open debates on religion and ethics, the Hindus' condescending attitudes, the burning of Meitei sacred literature, the breaking of Sanamahi is statue, the afflication of the Ramandi guru, and re-establishment of the native deity's power and grace. *Sanamahi kolu yeikhaiba* (Breaking Sanamahi's Iron Idol) was staged by the Aryan theatre in the sixties with O. Biramangol as the native sage '*Khongnang thaba*' and Syam Sharma as the Hindu missionary '*Shantidas*'.

Sanjukta

Manipuri actress who associated herself with the famous theatre group 'Kalakshetra' of H. Kanhailal. In *Pebet*, she was seen as one of the Pebet Children. In another signifiant production, '*Memoirs of Africa*', she did the role of Nupi 2, a young woman, half-spirit, half-human, embodying the deepest sources of creativity.

Sati Khongnang *see* Introduction (Meitei Dramatic Union)

Sharat Chandra, Nongthomba

Nongthomba Sharat Chandra, a poet, fiction writer and playwright in Manipuri wrote the drama '*Jaat Tinnadrabi Mehru*', broughtout by the Sarat Publications, Manipur in 1981. It comprises of eightyseven pages.

Sharma, B.I.

Shri B.I. Sharma played '*Saheb*' in the one-act play of Khwairakpam Chaoba, staged at D.M. College in 1947.

On 27.4.1995, he was being interviewed by Dr. N. Tombi Simha. At that time Sri Sharma was 72 years and his address of communcation was : Keishamthong Longjam Leirak, Imphal.

Shivanand

Swami Shivanand penned the play '*Radhagee prem*' in Manipuri, broughtout by Nadiachand Simha from Kangjam Laikai in 1981.

Shyam Sharma, Aribam

Aribam Shyam Sharma was born in 1939, a product of D.M. College, Manipur, the premier education institution and was an active member of the student theatre group called Amateur Aristes Association, made up of the almunis of the college. In the late 1950's they joined the Aryan Theatre, the oldest theatre troupe in Manipur. Syam Sharma directed and acted in many a productions of Aryan theatre since th 1960s. He revised H. Tomba's *Pidonnu* (1966) and brilliantly portrayed the character of a Hindu missionary 'Shantidas' in M. Biramangol's '*Sanamahi Kolu Yeikhaiba*' (1965).

Aribam Shyam Sharma

He also took up social dramas of Somorendra with which reflected the anticolonial sentiments, presented by Syam Sharma and his younger colleages. He modernized the production idioms with altering scene changes, doing away with cut-outs and curtains, concentrating conflict in single rooms, designing simple but imaginative interiors, and withdrawing background music, though he himself was a fine musician. His actors applied underacting, sensitivity, and detachment.

Shyam Sharma's challenging production '*Khongchat*' (Journey), written by N. Sri Biren and produced by the Aryan theatre in 1970, with an anti-heroic, modern-verse-reciting protagonist, started a five-year absurdist interregnum in Manipuri theatre.

He has tried his hand in writing also. A modern scholar and writer Shyam Sundar Simha's book '*Manipurgee Shumang Lila amasung theatre*' appeared from Manipuri Sahitya Parishad Imphal in 1980.

Shyam Sarma, H.

A wellknown Manipuri painter and set designer. The Manipuri stage has the honour of having him who did the scenery painting and stage works for innumerable production.

Shyamsunder, Ayekpam *see* Introduction (Rupmahal)

Shyamsunder Singh

Shyam Sundar Singh's play in Manipuri 'Osman-Thambal' was published from Imphal by Raj Store in 1979.

Society Theatre *see* Introduction

Somorendra Singh, Arambam

Arambam Somorendra Singh was born in Sagolband Meino leirak, Manipur in 1935. Son of the erudite Sanskrit pundit and poet. A Dorendrajit, Arambam Somorendra was born in a royal family. Somorendra was the great-grandson of King Surchandra who was disposessed by the palce revolt of 1891. A playwright and translator, he took his M.A. from the University of Pune and started his career in drama with the adaptations of world classics such as *Antigone* and *Macbeth* for the Manipuri theatre. He is acknowledged as one of the finest dramatist of Manipur.

A prolific playwright, Somorendra wrote over forty plays. His plays include 8 adaptations and 6 translations besides original dramas, both one-acts and full length. He represented the new generation of democratized middle-class social workers interiting the values and heritage of the landowning nobility. His early works reflect this humanist temper. He highlights sharply the anomalies and characteristic weaknesses of the Manipuri middle class and their perpetual tendency to exploist simple and innocent folks of the lowest rungs of society. Apart from his general thought, social observation and critical comments on contemporary society, he is engaged in the search for a true native identity. His drama 'Judge Sahabki Imung deals with this theme of native identity.

Somorendra's plays were first put on boards by the amateur groups and college dramatic societies and later found a permanent forum in Aryan Theatre.

Samorendra excelled in the art of short plays. His first short play '*Judge Sahebki Imung*' (the family of Judge Saheb) broughtout in 1973 brings out the dichotomy of the members of a family of a judge who are brought up in the atmosphere of liberal education, but with little moorings in the cultural tradition of the society where they were born. Arambam Somorendra's next play was 'Karbar', published by himself in 1976, followed by *Dasa* (misfortune) in 1978 which bagged him *the Manipur State Kala Akademi Award for Literature* and Yening Thagi Ishei (Song of Vernal Time) in 1981.

Samorendra's one acts play of note are Tirtha Yatra (1975), Nong Tarakle (The Rain Comes; 1979).

Somorendra was one of the leading figures in literature who modernized the Manipuri dramatic literature and stage, while politically starting the insurgency in the state (1964-75). He did not dabble in experimental writing, rather in his drama he subtly underplayed the political. His works in the late 1960s and 1970s dealt with social tension, with romantic undertony where the individual's quest for self and identity became issues. He was at the forefront of anguishes youth searching for roots, dignity, and freedom from oppression. Aping of western values opposed to native culture, conflict in families vying ruthlessly for space in the fast-developing false environment, changing lifestyles, anti-heroic search for Meitei consciousness, degeneration of values, the profit-seaking concerns of official employees, their dehumanizing treatment of lower classes, were all sensitively handled and criticized on stage. Somorendra's plays are marked by an intense

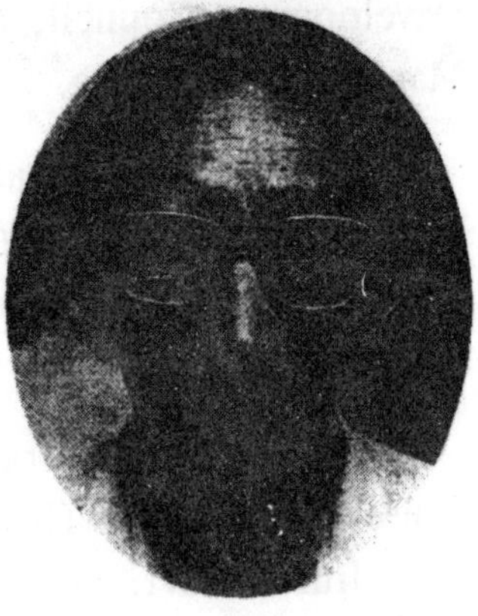

awareness of the contemporary social problems of Manipuri society which is passing through a period of upheaval in all spheres and a crisis of confidence of the people which he dramatises through rich dialogues in a mixed language of Manipuri and English. The conflict between tradition and modernity, and a quest for new values in place of the old characterise his plays. His powerful dialogues especially in the plays adwelling on social economic and political issues grip the reader and make up for the weakness in the action of the play.

Somorendra's drama '*Leipakalai*' received the prestigious Sahitya Akademi Award of New Delhi in 1995. The book appeared from Maino & Khomdon Publications, 1933. This play explicitly intended to foreground a woman protagonist's courage and grace in the hour of crisis. With its authentic depiction of consciousness, its ingenious use of the local idiom and meticulous craftsmanship, Leipkalei is a major contribution to Indian drama in Manipuri. His '*Leipaklei*' is a woman's struggle for an independent existence, for the right to live her life with dignity and self-respect. This rural tale garbs a predicament that is very contemporary and relevant.

Somorendra's '*The Unrecognised soldier*' tells a story of courage and patriotism, played out against a backdrop of foreign invasion, where resistance is weakened by internal fiction.

The playwright Somorendra was also a fine actor who could be seen in Manipuri version of Shakespeare's drama '*Macbeth*', produced by the Aryan Theatre, Imphal in 1965 and in many other memorable production of this longest-lived group. He also associated himself with radio drama, ininerant clowns of the Shumang Lila and altruistic organisation of writers and rural workers.

Somorendra was associated with various theatre houses, literary and other socio-cultural centres. He was a member of the General Council and the Executive Board of the Manipur State Kala Akademi. He became a member of the Film

Development Council, a Government of Manipur Undertaking.

In 1981, this leading dramatist in Manipuri was bestowed with the prestigious *'Manipur State Kala, Akademi Award' for literature*.

Arambam Somorendra (right) in *Macbeth* (Aryan Theatre, Imphal, 1965)

Somorendra worked on a research project on Manipuri Theatre for the Dept. of Culture, Govt. of India. He actively associated himself with several cultural institutions in the state including Kala Akademi, Manipuri Sahitya Parishad and Playwright's Association. This gifted theatre worker who received the State Kala Akademi Award, Certificate of Honour, Govt. of Manipur, Sahitya Akademy Award, New Delhi and Dr. Ambedkar Fellowship, etc. fell to assassin's ballets in 2000.

Select Works

Dasha. — Imphal: the author, 1978.

64 p.; 21.5 cm.

Karbar. — Imphal: the author, 1976.

62 p.; 21 cm.

Leipaklai. — Imphal: Maino & Khomdon Publications, 1993

62 p.; 22 cm.

Sahitya Akademi Award of 1995.

Translations

Family of the Judge/ by Arambam Somorendra Simha. *In* Modern Indian literature: an anthology (Vol. 3) ed. by K.M. George, New Delhi: Sahitya Akademi, 1994.

Tr. by the playwright himself of his play '*Judge Sahabki Imung*' (Excerpt) pp. 425-431.

Leipaklei/ by Arambam Somorendra; tr. into English. — New Delhi: Rupa, [2003] (Rupa Natika Series)

The unrecognised soldier/ by A. Somorendra; tr. into English. — New Delhi: Rupa, [2003] (Rupa Natika Series).

Somorendra, A. *see also* Introduction (Aryan Theatre)

Sonamani Singh, Elangbam

Elangbam Sonamani Singh portrayed the roles of '*Saheb*' and '*Krishna*' in Khwairakpam Chaoba's one-act play, staged at D.M. College in 1947.

Sri Biren, N.

A poet, editor, short story writer, playwright and teacher, Nongthombam Sri Biren was born in 1946. His forte is however, poetry.

He obtained his B.A. degree from the Gauhati University in 1965 and later joined the D.M. College of Arts and Commerce at Imphal where he served as a Senior Demonstrator teaching Manipuri language and literature.

N. Sri Biren wrote the play '*Khongchat*' (Journey) which depicted an anti-heroic, modern-verse-reciting protagonist, starting a five-year absurdist interregnum in Manipuri drama and theatre. His experimental play was directed by Aribam Syam Sharma in 1970 for the Aryan Theatre.

Nongthombam Biren Singha

N. Sri Biren's another acclaimed play '*Hallakpa*' (Return), 1971 was also produced by the Aryan theatre. Directed by Lokendra Arambam it depicts the existential anguish of youth seeking some viable identity and meaning in a ruthlessly exploitative society.

Nongthombam Sri Biren is the winner of the Manipur State Kala Akademi Award of 1973. His short play Hallakpa (The Return) was broughtout in 1973.

A leading poet, who, with his unconventional themes and sometimes audaciously obscene language, represents the mood of the young Manipuri poets of the late sixties and seventies. His poems are thematically, conceptually and linguistically unconventional and the style is pronouncedly modern.

Sri Biren is the founder Secretary of the Naharol Sahitya Premi Samiti, Imphal.

Sribiren *see also* Biren Simha, Nongthombam and Introduction (Aryan Theatre)

Sudhir Naoroibam

A modern short story writer editor and playwright in Manipuri, was born in 1969. He did his Master's degree in Manipuri language and literature. He began his literary career in late 1970s. He won the much coveted Sahitya Akademi Award (New Delhi) in 2003 for his book '*Leiyi Khara Punshi Khara*' (Some sketches, some lives), which is a message of universal significant. He has so far published a few volumes of short stories collections.

Sudhir Naoroibam (b. 1969)

He has also tried his hand in playwright. His drama '*Shunugi Mahao*' (The Taste of Lime) was played by the Public Theatre, Phoijing, in 1998, and by the top ranking Manipur Dramatic Union, Imphal in 2000.

Sri Sudhir has bagged many a prestigious award such as the Thoekhom Jogendrajit Memorial Gold Medal (1999) by Naharot Sahitya Premee Samiti, Imphal. Presently, Sudhir is the Features Sub-Editor of '*Pokhapham*', a Manipuri daily.

Surchandra Singh, Sanabam

Sanabam Surchandra Singha authored and published the play '*Mańgal*' from Imphal in 1967.

Surendrajit Singh, Rajkumar

Rajkumar Surendrajit Simgh's play of note is '*Panchajanya*' which was published by Krishnakumari Devi, Imphal in 1991. The play comprises of one hundred and ninety eight pages.

Syam Sharma, A. *see* Shyam Sharma, A. and Introduction (Aryan Theatre)

T

Tamana Lai

Tamana Lai (The Evil Spirit) is a Manipuri drama of H. Kanhailal Singh which was published in the volume 'Manipuri Leela Macha', broughtout by the Cultural Forum, Manipur in 1975. The drama revolues around an innocent but courageous young man who turned a murderer by circumstances. He is a good, young man and lives with his widowed mother Ngangbiton, a local girl, tries to win his love by any means. The local goondas are jealous of him and always insult him. Unable to bear the insults Chandrakangnan kills them. The drama, in an experimental way tries to bringout the problem of unrest among restless youngmen in a changing society.

Tamanalai *see also* Introduction

Tapta

This Manipuri drama entitled 'Taptā' (name of a mythical animal) is written and published by G.C. Tongbra in 1973. It shows Baba, an honest man of 65, and his son Heiton who advocates real progress and civilisatin. Baba's other children Pharangji and Indubala are corrupt persons. They think that material progress is need of the hour. The conflict of the two values and the final victory of Baba is presented with intellect debate, brilliant dialogues, humour and symbols.

Tejkumar Sharma

Born in 1946, Tejkumar Sharma, a modern writer composed '*Ingallai*', a play in Manipuri, published by Shantibala from Imphal in 1979.

Thambal Sharma, Hidangmayum

Shri Hidangmayum Thambal Sharma belonged to the Manipur Dramatic Union (M.D.U.). He played the role of 'Naba' in *Naba-malika*, written by Khwairakpam Chaoba. On 1.5.1995, the actor was interviewed by Dr. N. Tombi Simha. at that time the artist was 74 years old and his address of communication was :Chingkham Leirak, Imphal.

Thanil Simha, Nongmaithem

Nongmaithem Thanil Simha adapted the Bengali play '*Sarathi*' of Mahendranath Gupta into Manipuri which appeared in print from Vina Printing Works, Imphal in 1968.

The Theatre of Kanhailal: Pebet and Memoirs of Africa

This is the title of the English book, written by Rustom Bharucha and published by Seagull Books, Kolkata in 1992. This volume takes a close look at the world of H. Kanhailal in which his theatre is so firmly located : the political and socio-economic heritage of Manipur, its cultural politics, Kanhailal's life in theatre, the partnership with his actress-wife Sabitri, her contribution to the productions, and the influences of Manipuri cultural forms on his style, technique and subject matter. *His two major productions 'Pebet' and 'Memoirs of Africa' are reconstructed in the form of detailed performance texts* (alongwith comprehensive photographic documentation) in this absorbing book.

Thiyam, Narendra Singh *see* Narendra Singh, Thiyam

Thiyam, Ratan

Ratan Thiyam was born on 20th January 1940 at Nabadvip of Nadia district of West-Bengal. Ratan studied in USA, Japan, Philippines, Thailand, Burma,

Hongkong and Indonesia. An avant-garde Manipuri director. Ratan has been active in theatre from his early youth.

About dozen of Ratan's own dramatic compositions could not see the light of the day, even after rehearsals, because either the season was over or they had short-lived themes. Thiyam has also tried his hand in composition of poetry, novel and even shorter fiction in Manipuri. His non-dramatic literary output comprises of four novels, collection of short stories and poems. He also served as the Joint Editor of *Lasani* and *Ritu* and *Shaktam*.

The North-east from where Thiyam belongs has its own traditional dance, drama, and story-telling traditions on which he draws. Trained in Theatre at the National School of drama (1971-1974), he returned to Imphal to set up his own theatre group, the '*Chorus Repertory Theatre*' in 1976. Back in home, Ratan built a complex for his company where the artistes live in a collective, sharing all day-to-day activities. His *Chorus Repertory Theatre*, Imphal, has one of the best stages and auditoriums in the country today.

A veteran director, Ratan Thiyam has a directorial oeuvre of some fifty plays among which half are major ones, some have sustained runs abroad. Notable productions of Ratan Thiyam are the Mahabharata triology Urubhangam (1981), Chakravyuha (1984), Karnabharam (1989). Other wellknown directorial ventures are Samarembi - Chaisna (1976), Urubhanga (1981), Andhayug (1984), Hirosima (1994) and Uttara Priyadarshi (1996). His play 'Uttarpriyadarshini was premiered in Bangkok.

Thiyam also extensively designed, choreographed, and undertook artistic responsibilities for international festivals.

In 1998, appeared in print the performance text of his production '*Chakravyuha*', compiled by Kavita Nagpal and brought out by Seagull, Kolkata. Ratan Thiyam plans to come out with his latest play based on the themes of Suffering and loss of morals in a warring society. At the turn of this century, he has started experimenting with less and less plot-oriented plays like '*Uttar Priyadarshini*' and '*Ritu Samhar*', which are less structured. He prefer to dispense with readymade versions and test the strength of a performance: with skill, technique and methodology alone. But what if it fails to capture the audience ? He clarifies "My role in theatre is like that of Shabari, who used to taste a fruit's sweetness herself before offering it to Rama. I must offer my audience, what I find apt myself". He says that 'A play may be a condensed version of socio-religio-economic matrix, but to him, it is the effect of time, with history giving you a clue what to do, which is important. Suffering, over the decades, remains his *leit motif*. Our time has seen the loss of life of many scientists, teachers and common men : all suffering in diverse ways. For the last few years, he is looking at himself as an individual placed in a society, amidst the said happenings of this world. He is being surrounded by palestinians, Iraqis, Osama bin Ladens — both the terrorists and the terrorised ! To quote him "I am no longer immune; the outrage and carnage occuring in the world get close to me and become my own calamity. I learn to unlearn — to learn the process of dismantling the brand of theatre. I havebeen doing this all these years. In the process, I discover a challenge of creating an altogether new dimension of theatre, Since I know what conventional theatre is, I'm examining what I can do otherwise as my contribution to future theatre".

Vikramorvaśīyam, Act IV, directed by Ratan Thīyam (Chorus Repertory, Imphal) The picture depicts Urvaśī and Vikrama. It was staged at the kalidasa Samaroha, using the production elements in pure Manipuri dance style including music and costumes

Ratan Thiyam has been honoured with various award and titles for his creative accomplishments such as Sangeet Natak Akademi Award; First Award (Edinburgh) 1987, National Academy Award 1987; Nandikar Award 1992. He has been conferred '*Padma Shri*' by the Govt. of India in 1989.

He had once declined to accept the '*Padmashri*', as he did not agree with what he called "the official oppression of the Manipuris" in his land.

Ratan Thiyam

Thiyam had been the Director of Evkhoi Theatre and National School of Drama. Fellow of Ford Foundation, USA, Manipur State Kala Academy, Japan Foundation, Korean Foundation, Vice-Chairman of Jawaharlal Nehru Manipur Dance Academy (Imphal) and Member of the Advisory Committee of the Sangeet Natak Akademi (National Academy of Theatre, Dance and Music), New Delhi.

Thiyam has attended many a National and International events such as Asian Arts Festival, Hong Kong, Festival of India, UK, USSR, France, Germany.

Thoibi

This is the first modern Manipuri play on a folk theme, the legendary princess of Moirang, written by Khumanthem Madhumangol and staged by Aryan Theatre in 1946.

Thoibi Devi, Takhellambam

Takhellambam Thoibi Devi rendered the drama '*Vikramorbasi*' of Kalidasa into Manipuri which he himself broughtout from Imphal in 1962.

Tikendrajit

This play written by M. Bira is based on the 1891 freedom struggle when the native heroes Tikendrajit and Thangal were hanged by the British. The play was produced by Rupmahal Theatre in 1951 under the direction of the playwright himself who also played the role of the elder statesman Thangal. Tikendrajit's pride, arrogance, and aristocratic sensibility were portrayed by the powerful actor of the troupe S. Nabakanta Singh. The play focussed on the anticolonial prejudice against Indian clerks and officials like Rasiklal Kundu and Baman Charan Mukherjee, though employed by the state, were anti-Manipuri British agents, enacted skillfully by Netrajit and Nilamani. In the play a mistress of Tikendrajit was idealized as a heroine who resisted the British and wreaked revenge on the clerks — sentimental fiction with no connection to history.

The play became an instant hit and surpassed all existing records for popularity. In 1966 it celebrated its hundredth show, put up on August 13, the day of the hanging.

Tirtha Yatra

Tirtha Yatra (Pilgrimage), a Manipuri drama of A. Samarendra Singh (b. 1934) was published by the Cultural Forum, Manipur in 1975 in the volume '*Manipuri Leela macha*'. The drama centres on a religious old man named *Tonsana* who plans on a pilgrimage to Vrindavan. Knowing that he has kept some money for purpose, his delinquent children, two sons and a daughter, try to exhaust the money demanding it for various purposes. After fulfilling their demand and showing their follies, *Tonsana* sets out for Vrindavan with the balance. An interesting social drama which excellently deals with the problem of generation-gap in post-Independence Manipur.

Tolhal Simgh, Khongbantabam

Khongbantabam Tolhal Simha was born in 1921. Playwrights best-known dramas in Manipuri are Imphal kaba, Laikangda iraknaba, Thaballai, Thabaton, Tung-gi Khallu, Varep etc. He belonged to Roxy Theatre, Manipur and later became the Vice-President of the Roopmahal Theatre. On 28.4.1995, he was being interviewed by Dr. N. Tombi Simha and his address of Communication was : Takhelleikai, Imphal.

Select Works

Imphāl kābā. — Imphal: The author, 1960.

104 p. 18 cm.

Laikaṅgdā irāknabā. — Imphal: The author, 1972.

106 p. 18 cm.

Thāballai. — Imphal: The author, 1958.

98 p. 18 cm.

Thabāton. — Imphal: The author, 1968.

73 p. 18 cm.

Tuṅg-gī khallu. — Imphal: The author, 1962.

185 p. 18 cm.

Vārep. — Imphal: The author, 1970.

220 p. 18 cm.

Tomba, H.

Stage actor, Sri H. Tomba a member of Kalakshetra Manipur of H. Kanhailal did the role of a Pebet's son in '*Pebet*'. He could also be seen as 'Mimanu 3' in another production entitled '*Memoirs of Africa*'.

Tomba Simha, Haobam

Playwright, lyricist and teacher, Tomba Simha was born in 1909. He passed his Matriculation examination from the Calcutta University in 1933 and then joined the Ramlal Paul High School.

He distinguished himself in composing dramas based on folk themes, particularly on the legends and myths of Moirang. He went deeper into the folkroots in his dramatic compositions and discovered a world of jewels in the seven incarnations of Khamba and Thoibi associated with the ancient culture of Moirang, resulting in nostalgia and a yearning for a lost grace and sweetness of life. Haobam's plays are though written in a folk idiom, but his language is highly stylized. The experiment in language, poetic and idiomatic, which he made in the plays is noteworthy.

Haobam Tomba Simha's folk drama include '*Tamna and Pidonnu* (written in 1964) *Nura Shanthelembi, Thainagi Leirang* and *Sayon Saphaba* (written in 1965), *Thaja Thaba* and *Shajik Thabha* (written in 1967). etc. Besides these published works, he wrote several other plays which are in manuscript form.

Tomba Simha always preferred to work in isolation without much publicity. But his creativity brought him many awards. In 1976 he received the '*Sahitya Bhusan Award*' of the Manipuri Sahitya Parishad for his contribution to Manipuri literature. He won the best playwright awad in many competitions organised by the *Manipur State Kala Academy* and other literary institution of Manipur.

A better-known playwright of the twentieth century, Tomba Simha died in 1976.

Select Works

Nūrā śānthalembī. — Imphal: Manipurī Sāhitya Parisad, 1966.

55 p. 18 cm.

Pidonnu. — Imphal: The author, 1964.

218 p. 18 cm.

Śajīk thabā. — Imphal: Acom Ibobī Siṃha, 1967.

174 p. 18 cm.

Śāyon śāphabā. — Imphal: The author, 1965.

178 p. 18 cm.

Tam-nā. — Imphal: The author, 1964.

180 p. 18 cm.

Thāynagī lairāṅg. — Imphal: The author, 1965.

148 p. 18 cm.

Thāja thabā. — Imphal: Acom Ibobī Siṃha, 1967.

68 p. 18 cm.

Tombi Mutua

Playwright and writer, Mutua Tombi was born in 1935. His two best known dramas are '*Ithay panam-cing*' and '*Sari vasak*'. The works published by Mutum Chanu Mandakini in 1979 and 1980 respectively from Imphal.

Tombi Singh, N.

Dr. N. Tombi Simha did a painstaking research on poet Khwairakpam Chaoba and opened a new vista to us of a long neglected side of the poet Chaoba as a playwright and eventually the contributions he gave to Manipuri dramatic literature came to light with his new findings. For the purpose Tombi Simha interviewed many octogenarians and other elderly associated with theatre and took part in his plays. An English Manipuri version of his article, rendered by B.S. Rajkumar appeared under the title '*The Unpublished plays of Khwairakpam Chaoba' in Chaoba Centenary Souvenir of 1995.*

Tombi Singh, Ningthoujam *see* Introduction (Manipur Dramatic Union)

Tomcha Simha, Vahangbam

Vahangbam Tomcha Simha was born in 1916. The playwrights chief dramatic publications are : - *Kunjamala, Tha-jaba* and *Anauba Khungang*. All published by Tomcha Simha from Imphal in the years 1960, 1967 and 1969 respectively.

Tomchau Athokpam

Tomchau Athokpam was born in 1950. This modern playwright's chief dramatic compositions are:- *Promotion, Jalīmī, Nungshiba thiba* and *Shambal*, all published by the Maitai Artist Union, Imphal in the year 1974, 1975, 1978 and 1979 respectively.

Tomchau, A. *see* Introduction

Tondon, S.

Prima donna of *Rupmahal Theatre*, one of the most stable and richer professional theatre groups of Manipur; S. Tondon became the cynosure of all eyes with her beauty, doe-like riveting eyes, and the piognancy of her songs.

Earlier she had a brief stinct with the *Aryan Theatre*. With her key roles in Rupmahal's '*Yaithing Konu*' (1948) adapted by M. Bira and Hijam Romani and

S. Tondon

'*Moirang Thoibi*' (Thoibi of Moirang) by A. Dorendrajit (1948), she made a niche for herself in the hearts of Rupmahal's audience and earned the immediate attention of royalty — the reigning princes of the time Bodhachandra's affair with her became a cause celebre, specially when she insisted on the title of a queen. S. Tondon also had a stinct with the premier theatre troupe '*The Manipur Dramatic Union*'. An excellent woman performer who finally shifted to Rupmahal.

Tondon, S. *see also* Introduction (Aryan & Rupmahal Theatres) and Yaithing Konu

Tongbra, Geet Chandra

Geet Chandra Tongbram, pioneer playwright of Manipuri stage, was born in 1913 at Imphal. Better known as G.C. Tongbra, he was the only son of his parents. His character and outlook were moulded by his father and Panditraj Atombapu Sharma greatly.

Graduating in Arts and Teaching, Tongbra started his career as a clerk in the Revenue Department and then joined teaching profession as a teacher at Churachand High School, Imphal. Sri G.C. Tongbra served as High School teacher for 15 years and as College teacher for 20 years. Later on, he headed the Department of Manipuri Language and Literature of Imphal College from where he retired in 1974 as its Vice-Principal.

After World War II, he started writing plays based on numerous social and economic problems. He was the playwright, director and President of the Society Theatre, Manipur since 1946 and a number of his plays won honours and awards. In most of his plays ridicules men and their manners, especially their pre-conceived notions of civilization and progress which is reality negate the real progress of society.

The most respected modern dramatist, Tongbram Gitachandra, a Shavian by temperment and outlook, his social dramas, staged always by his Society Theatre, are marked by brilliant wit and laughter. He challenges the accepted social values and conventional norms, exposes the hypocrisy and hollowness embedded in the bourgeoise society and runs the risk of having some of his plays banned by the Government. He struggles, atleast, to breathe an air of freedom. To introduce the readers and the audience to the human situation where laughter and tears meet is the characteristic feature of his writing.

He founded '*Society Theatre*' in 1937, G.C. Tongbra was a withdrawn intellectual who remained distant, aloof and sphinx-like, yet deeply beloved, creating a niche for himself in modern Manipuri Theatre.

Tongbra's dramatic output crosses over 100 comprising of full length comedies, radio drama and scripts for touring professional opera groups. His praiseworthy dramas are *Hingminnaba* (Coexistance, 1963), Matric Pass (1964), *Anee Thokra Chingkhaire Thamoi* (Thou hast left my heart in twain, 1965), *Lamja Parasuram* (Orphan Parshuram, 1966), *Mani Mamou* ('Mother-in-law', and 'Bride', 1967), and the State Akademi Award winning title '*Keku Lotui, Kao phabi*' (Hide and seek and female matador, 1971), dealing with human situations bordering on absurdity. G.C. Tongbra established himself as an acomplished short play writer, some of his short plays which won several awards in competition being, *Rajkumar Shollibi* (Delicate Rajkumar), *Kao phabi* (Tamer of bull), *Shikari* (Humtress), *Tapta*, etc. Other significant plays of Geet Chandra are *Leibak Louba andolan* (Earth-shaking Agitation, 1960), Mister Damncare, *Imphal Thoibi* (Imphal's Thoibi), and Ngabong Khao (Flesh Trap) etc.

It was he who began a controversial genre of 'dialogue plays', severly criticizing the gradual loss of intrinsic values in Manipuri society. Intolerant of injustice, corruption, and degrading treatment of women, he wrote most of his drama in a unique mixture of wit and declamatory style, where tirades, home truths, and verbose outpourings flowed like torrents. Nursed on peasant humour rather than sophistication and finesse, he introduced a radical change in attacking social mores. As said before, Gitchandra Tongbram Simha's plays are marked by witty dialogues, powerful arguments, less of action and an atmosphere of social outlook. In the later phase of his career he was very much influenced by existentialist writers like Ionesco, Samuel Beckett, etc. and composed many short plays on their models. Often called '*G.B. Shaw of Manipuri literature*', he read Shaw and Ibsèn, his plays are distinctly problem plays which he presented humorously and sarcastically.

In the year 1959, Tongbra's satirically humorous play '*Mani-Mamou* (Mother-in-law and Daughter-in-law) appeared. *The play is hailed as one of the masterpieces of Indian literature*, set against the background of modern Manipuri Society. The play has as its theme the dilemma of a judge who could not find any solution to the incessant quarrels between his wife on the one hand and his mother and younger sister on the other. The background of the play, though set in a nuclear family, has its ramifications in political and social problems. G.C. Tongbra is inimitable in his sarcasam. Tongbra is his short play '*Chengni Khujai*' (1969) examines the practical side of democrary as practised in Manipur and depicts its possible result which in his opinion, is full of dangerous and injurious consequences, if allowed a free rein. The excellence of the play rests with the suggestion of tempering democratic practice with reason. The humour and satire of the playwright are praiseworthy. The pervading sense of irony in the play is something which cannot be lost sight of. The playwright, however condemns any kind of violence in thought and in action.

In the year 1976 came out his play '*Upu Baksi*', a significant work, concerned with the problem of man's existence and survival in life in the midst of evil and falsehoods. To bring home his point he attacks irrational human customs and institutionalized conventions in the play with a sense of humour. The language is humorous even satirical and powerful enought to be able to become an apt medium of expression.

For his play '*Ngabong Khao*', he was accoladed with the *Sahitya Akademi Awarded* (New Delhi) of 1978 in the language. The play is hailed as an outstanding contribution to Manipuri literature for its penetrating social insights, brilliant sense of the comic and the absurd, effective use of dramatic language and deep human sympathy and understanding.

Tongbra's plays *'Lamja Parsuram'* and *'Khut-thang Lamju'* were successfully made into film. The former was filmed in 1973. In almost all his plays, ideas play an important role, while the characters are more or less a comouflaged Tongbra with different labels.

Besides such excellent original plays, Gitchandra adapted and translated several plays of Shakespeare, G.B. Shaw and Ibsen. He rendered H. Ibsen's famous drama 'Doll's House' into Manipuri entitled *'Lāiphadibi āmagī yūm'*, broughtout by Gandhi Memorial Press, Imphal in 1966. Tongbra made Manipuri version of G.B. Shaw's works, Shakespeare's *Hamlet* into Manipuri and also Sophocle's work.

G.C. Tongbra was elected to the General Council of the Sahitya Akademi in 1973 and received 'Padma Sri' in 1975. He was also elected as the 'President' of the Manipur Sahitya Parishad the same year and was also a member of Manipur State Kala Akademi.

Gitchandra's Awards and prizes include Jamini Sunder Memorial Gold Medal (1960), Sahitya Ratna of the Manipuri Sahitya Parishad (1973), Padmashri (1975), Manipuri State Kala Akademi Fellowship Award (1976) and the Sahitya Akademi Award (1978).

This veteran playwright of Manipuri theatre, died in 1996 at the ripe age of eightythree.

Select Works

Akāśvānīdā takhrabā Khara. — Imphal: Gandhi Memorial Press. 1968.

70 p. 18 cm.

Anithoknā ciṅgkhāyre thammoy. — Imphal: Manipur Co-operative Publishing Society, 1963.

iv, 86 p. 18 cm.

Aṅka-amagī-līlā khara. — Imphal: Manipurī sāhitya parishad, 1965.

175 p. 18 cm.

Hamlet / tr. from the English original by Tongbram Gitchandra Simha — Imphal: The translator, 1965.

xi, 105 p.; 18 cm.

Heloyan pubā. — Imphal: Huidrom Tombā Siṃha 1960.

106 p. 18 cm.

Hiṅgminnabā. — Imphal: O.K. Store, 1963.

ii, 101 p. 18 cm.

Hingminnabā. — Imphal: Kangla Book House, 1974.

101 p.; 18.5 cm.

Imāmacā anithokna ciṅg khāyare. — Imphal: Gandhī Memorial Press, 1965.

v, 100 p. 18 cm.

Imphāl thoibī. — Imphal: Gāndhī Memorial Press, 1969.

92 p. 18 cm.

Imuṅgī ijat. — Imphal: Gāndhī Memorial Press, 1969.

112 p. 18 cm.

Julius Caesar / tr. from the English original by Tongbram Gitchandra Simha.— Imphal: Gandhi Memorial Press, 1969.

Kabā-kabi kāynabā amāsuṅg līlā macā ahum. — Imphal: Citrāṅgadā sāhitya mandir, 159.

vii, 78 p. 18 cm.

Kalidā Bhīmnā mantrī oibā. — Imphal: Gāndhī Memorial Press, 1968.

71 p. 18 cm.

Keku lotpī, kāophābī. — Imphal: Gāndhī Memorial Press, 1971.

82 p. 18 cm.

Kumari Rambhagee Mang. — Imphal : Society Theatre Manipur, 1974.

83 p.; 18 cm.

Laibāk macā. — Imphal: Gāndhī Memorial Press, 1970.

81 p. 18 cm.

Lamjā Paraśurām. — Imphal: Gāndhī Memorial Press, 1966.

140 p. 18 cm.

Based on mythological story

Lāiphadibī āmagī yūm/ by H. Ibsen; tr., of 'Doll's House' into Manipuri by G.C. Tongbra. — Imphal: Gandhi Memorial Press, 1966.

v, 140 p.; 18 cm.

Līkli nuṅgśi laumambī. — Imphal: Gāndhī Memorial Press, 1967.

128 p. 18 cm.

Līlāmacā taruk. — Imphal: H. Tombā Siṃha, 1965.

ii, 132 p. 18 cm.

One-act plays

Lūdā mī caṅgbā. — Imphal: Gāndhī Memorial Press, 1969.

102 p. 18 cm.

Macbeth/ tr. from the English original by Tongbram Gitchandra Simha. — Imphal : Gandhi Memorial Press, 1969.

104 p.; 18 cm.

Maitai canu. — Imphal: S. Bābūdhān Siṃha, 1965.

123 p. 18 cm.

Maṅgāl ado śātlammi śiṅgel amā. — Imphal: G.M. Press, 1979.

81 p. 18 cm. Rs. 6.

Maṇi mamau. — Imphal: Kṛṣṇamohan Siṃha, 1959.

85 p. 18 cm.

Matric pass. — Imphal: K. Gunendra Siṃha 1964.

129 p. 18 cm.

Memthoibī. — Imphal: Gāndhī Memorial Press, 1969.

124 p. 18 cm.

Noṅgpok Laimā. — Imphal: Gāndhī Memorial Press, 1967.

181 p. 18 cm.

Othello/ tr. from the English original by Tongbram Gitchandra Simha. — Imphal : Gandhi Memorial Press, 1966.

vii, 140 p.; 18 cm.

Sanā Yāthaṅg. — Imphal: Gāndhī Memorial Press, 1969.

108 p. 18 cm.

Śangom-miṭhāi lānmī/ by G.B. Shaw, tr. into Manipuri by Tongbram Gitachandra Simha. — Imphal : Gandhi Memorial Press, 1969.

101 p.; 18 cm.

Tr. of '*Arms and Men*'.

Tāibaṅg Jāmbā. — Pt. 1, Imphal: Umābatī Devī, 1973.

89 p. 22 cm.

Tāibaṅg jāmbā. — Pt. 2, Imphal: Kamalā Devī, 1974.

207 p. 22 cm.

Taptā. — Imphal: Society Theatre, 1973.

84 p. 18 cm.

Translation

The Foolhardy/ by Git Chandra Simha Tongram; tr. into English by A. Somorendra Singh. *In* Modern Indian literature: an anthology (Vol. 3)/ ed. by K.M. George. — New Delhi: Sahitya Akademi, 1994. Pp.404-416.

Tongbra, G.C. *see also* Introduction

U

Upu Baksi

Upu Baksi is a satirical play of G.C. Tongbra presented in his usual humourous manner, dealing with a human problem. The story is developed in the manner of a folktale focussing on a certain Senjeng who felt defeated in life. Previously a Havaldar who was discharged from active service for a petty mistake. He finds his sons, daughter and wife indifferent to him since they consider him a useless and penniless old man. He constantly kept a small wooden box with him wherein he kept whatever he thought valuable. He adopted a son and a daughter, leaving aside his own sons and daughter, in order to bring them up according to his own wishes, and took a second wife also who would spare no pains to look after his comfort. For the member of the new family he acquired, Senjeng would spend the money from his wooden box, thinking that they fulfilled his expectations. Unluckily, the newly adopted members also failed him, and Senjeng, in desperation, left home with his wooden box. After sometime he returned and died in the presence of the members of the new and the old families. His dying words were : 'Distribute equally whatever in the box'. When the box was opened, they found inside leaves and a piece of paper on which was written that to survive happily man had to tell lies but he must create them beautifully as if they were true.

In this play, Tongbra employs as novel method by introducing the characters of story-teller in the manner of a chorus. The play was broughtout in 1976.

Uttar Priyadarshi

This is the title of the play available in manuscript form, borrows it theme from a poem composed by the celebrated Hindi litterateur Ajneya. The play is translated into Manipuri by A. Krishnamohan Sharma was produced by the Chorus Repertory Theatre, Imphal, during the Golden Jubilee Theatre Festival at New Delhi in 2003. The production was presented in Manipuri/Pali and directed by the distinguished director Ratan Thiyam. The play commences with the chanting of prayers by the four Samvadaks (monks). These narrators are joined by eight members of the chorus bearing symbols of the eight-fold path of Lord Buddha. They pray to Lord Buddha and praise his benevolence. There is a flashback to a child playing with dust in a courtyard. He stops suddenly as the wandering Sakyamuni (Lord Buddha) stands before him smiling, asking for alms. The child offers a handful of dust to Lord Buddha who sprinkles it on the surface of the earth, sanctifying it, for this child will be reborn as Ashoka (also known as Priyardarshi), future king of the Mauryas.

As the Samvadaks extol Lord Buddha, who looks upon all with eyes of compassion, they form a Mandala (time wheel), and move from the past into the present. In the background, prayers are chanted. Riding an elephant at the head of his victorious army, Priyadarshi returns home, having vanquished the kingdom of Kalinga. The *Samvadaks* recount his exploits as conqueror of the vast continent. Priyadarshi commands his Bhat-charans (royal musicians) to sing Nandi, glorifying his victory and fame. But the emperor is mocked by the Samvadaks, who call him a proud and lonely king. He throws away his bloodstained sword and laments his unfulfilled dream of an empire where people can live a contented life free from fear. Once more he orders the royal musicians to sing Nandi. Instead, he is greeted by the agonized cries of war widows. He is engulfed by sorrow and grief, and feels the ghosts of his fallen foes advance and surrounded him. To drive them away, he vows to punish them by throwing them into Hell. His minister chooses Ghor, wanton destroyer, and Priyadarshi — against the will of the people — appoints the malevolent Ghor Lord of Hell.

Ghor declares himself to be Mahakal, the deity of total destruction. He performs a dance of death and devastation with his female attendants. He commands his attendants to destroy anyone entering his domain, including Priyadarshi. Crossing hills, valleys and streams, the travelling Samvadaks are lured into Hell by Ghor's female attendants, disguised as pretty girls. The Samvadaks are trapped and abused but finally escape. Ghor's means of torments are unveiled, their use illustrated as victims are tortured and killed. A Bhikshu (mendicant monk) enters with a message of hope for liberating all humanity from the wheel of suffering; he prays for the light that will wash away ignorance and bring enlightenment. Discovered by Ghor, who taunts him, the monk finds the strength to endure. The flames of Hell are extinguished as the Bhikshu sits alone on a lotus; the space around him turns calm and serene. Priyadarshi enters Hell, finding it tranquil and still: Ghor torments him, ignoring Priyadarshi's remainder that he himself made Ghor the Lord of Hell. Priyadarshi, seeing that the Bhikshu is undisturbed by Hell's misery, asks the mong how he has escaped. The Bhikshu challenges Priyadarshi to look deeply into himself; to recognize and embrace the evil within him as well as the good, for only by doing so will be be able to liberate himself. Priyadarshi, longing for release from human suffering, accepts this gift of enlightenment and feels Ghor depart from within himself.

W

Wareppa Naba *see* Introduction (under Theatre Mirror)

Y

Yaithing Konu

This is the title of the play, dramatised by M. Bira and Hijam Romani, from a work by Romoni's father Hijam Angahal (1892-1943), himself an eminent poet, playwright and director. The play is based on a romantic tale culled from the Moirang cycle of seven tragedies of lovers. The dramatic version retained the spine of the tragedy but in simple melodramatic sequences, new middle-class language, and avoiding sexually exploitable scenes and including a secular moral on needs of parents to understand the wills of their daughters. In aesthetic and structural terms it was premodern, but the theme of a beautiful girl hiding her lover in a room for months and their essentially sexual relationship projected onto the colourful proscenium of the Rupmahal enraptured the Manipuri audience in the 1948 with S. Tondon in the lead female cast.

APPENDIX

Major Theatrical Events (1902–)

1902 *Pravas Milan*

This is infact a Bengali play staged in 1902 before a royal audience in Manipur at a 'mandap' and not in a regular hall. The actual Theatre in the modern sense began in Manipur with this Bengali play.

1903 *Bamacharan Mukhopadhyay Bandhab Natyashala*

Named after Bamacharan Mukhopadhyay, this is the first theatrical hall in Manipur established in 1903 at Babupara, Imphal.

1905 *Pagalini*

This is Manipuri translation of a Bengali play first staged in 1905. Its dialogue was in Manipuri but songs were sung in Bengali.

1918 *Parthaparajay*

This is again a Manipuri renderation of a Bengali play, staged in Manipur in the year 1918.

1924 Upto 1924 drama in Manipuri comprised invariably translations from Bengali originals.

1925 *Narasimha*

This is the first Manipuri original drama written in 1922 and staged in 1925. It was composed by Lairenmayum Ibungohal Simha (1895-1966).

1931 Birth of '*Manipur Dramatic Union (Theatre Hall)*' to encourage the theatre movement in Manipur

The first experiment in ticketing was made for Sorokhaibam Lalit's play '*Areppa marup*' (Abiding Friend) enacted by the Meitei Dramatic Union

1935 '*Aryan Theatre*' a well managed theatre hall was formed

With '*Reziya*', *Aryan Theatre* made its debut with Chiram Gouramani in the lead role.

1937 The '*Meitei Dramatic Union*' shifted to a permanent site and renamed itself as '*Manipur Dramatic Union*'.

'*Society Theatre*' came into being.

1939 Aryan Theatre staged its first original Manipuri production '*Bhagyachandra*', a semi-historical play composed by Dorendrajit.

1942 'Rup-Mahal' was formed.

1943 In December, Rupmahal Theatre made their first appearance with Netrajit's social play '*Ningamdaba*' (Repentance).

1948 In July, A miniature version of Calcutta's Star Theatre was built, a permanent proscenium theatre for 'Rupmahal'.

1954 Under the folk category, the Manipur Dramatic Union's play '*Haorang Leishang Saphabi*' won the *First Prize* in All-India Drama Festival, organised in Delhi by the *Song and Drama Division* of the Govt. of India. The play was composed by Sarangthem Boramani Simha.

1955 Sorokhaibam Lalit, the playwright of eminence died.

'*Theatre Centre*', was founded in Imphal.

1960 G.C. Tongbra received the First '*Jamini Sunder Guha Memorial Gold Medal*'.

A curfew was enforced at the venue where the premiere of the play '*Leibak houba andolan*' (Earth-shaking Agitation) (by G.B. Tongbra and director by M. Bira) was held. The playwright received a police Summons after the show.

1961 Professional actress Sairem Kanya passed away.

1966 Rupmahal celebrated its hundred in show on August 13 of its magnum opus '*Tikendrajit*' written & directed by M. Bira.

1968 Arambam Somorendra won the *Manipur State Kala Akademi Award* for his drama '*Dasa*' (Misfortune).

1971 Ratan Thiyam enrolled in the National School of Drama, New Delhi.

1973 Gitchandra Tongba received '*Sahitya Ratna Title*', conferred by the Manipuri Sahitya Parishad.

1975 Playwright G.C. Tongbra was honoured with '*Padmashri*' by the Govt. of India.

1976 The play '*Kekulopti*', wrjitten by G.C. Tongbra won the Manipur State Kala Akademi Award.

The '*Chorus Refertory Theatre*' was formed by Ratan Thiyam.

G.C. Tongbra was declared '*Manipuri State Kala Akademi Fellow*'.

1978 G.C. Tongbra's play '*Ngabongkhao*' bagged the *Sahitya Akademi Award* (New Delhi)

Thounaojam Kunjakishore Singh (1891-1982) became the first Manipuri theatre artist to bag the prestigious *Sangeet Natak Akademi Award*, an exponent of Sanseba and Gaura Lila.

1979 Mayanglambam Biramangol (b. 1909), the founder-member of Aryan Theatre died.

1981 Arambam Samarendra Simha, a leading playwright of contemporary Manipuri literature was honoured with '*Manipur State Kala Akademi Award*' for literature.

1982 Chirom Gouramani, a veteran actress of Manipur stage died, who became a household name for her lead role in '*Reziya*' produced under '*Aryan Theatre*'.

'*Karnagi Mama Amasung Karnagi Aroiba Yahip*' of N. Ibobi Simha won the Manipur State Kala Akademi Award.

1983 N. Ibobi Simha's book of radio plays '*Karnagi Mama Amasung Karnagi Aroiba Yahip*' bagged the *Sahitya Akademi Award* (New Delhi)

1985 Heisnam Kanhailal was honoured with '*the Sangeet Natak Akademi Award*' for *Direction*.

1985 Ningthemcha Ongbi Nungshitombi, an actress of Manipur Dramatic Union passed away.

1987 Ratan Thiyam became the Director of the National School of Drama, New Delhi.

Thiyam bagged the *Fringe Firsts Award* at the Edinburgh Festival.

Ratan Thiyam was chosen for the *Sangeet Natak Akademi Award* for *Direction*

1991 Sabitri Heisnam bagged the *Sangeet Natak Akademi Award* for *Acting*

1992 Ratan Thiyam won the '*Nandikar Award*' (Kolkata).

1995 During '*Aryan Theatre's sixty years*' celebration, its auditorium accidentally burnt down.

Arambam Somorendra Simha's play '*Leipkalei*' received the *Sahitya Akademi Award* in the language. '*Leipaklei*' (Earth Flower) got published in 1992.

1996 Aribam Ningol Manbi, celebrated actress passed away.

Geet Chandra Tongbra passed away at the age of eighty three.

1997 Khundrakpam Brajachand, a protest dramatist died prematurely at the age of fourty-five.

La Grande Medaille (France) was bestowed on Ratan Thiyam.

R.K. Bhogen won the *Sangeet Natak Akademi Award* for *Acting*.

Lokendra Arambam's play '*Macbeth*' created a stir when presented on the occasion of 50 years of Indian Independence in London.

Heisnam Kanhailal founded a private school of performance art.

1998 Loitongbam Dorendra Singh was accoloded with the title '*Natya Bhusan*' by the Utkal Yuba Sanskrutik Samittee.

1998-99 *International Man of the Year in the Field of Theatre and Humanism* went to Shri Ratan Thiyam.

2000 Arambam Samarendra, renowned dramatist and playwright fell to assassins bullets.

Shri Ratan Thiyam won the '*B.M. Shah Award*'.

2004 Best Director Award was bestowed to Loitongbam Dorendrajit Singh in the '*Rupmahal Artistes Memorial Drama Festival*'.

Lokendra Arambam received the *Sangeet Natak Akademi Award* (New Delhi) for *Direction*.

2005 In the *MDU*, sponsored the '*First Folk Drama Competition*', Loitongbam Dorendrajit won the Best Director Prize for his production '*Tamna*', penned by Hao bam Tomba.

SHAKESPEARE'S PLAYS IN MANIPURI

Hamlet/ translated from the English original by Achom Pashot Simha. — Imphal: The translator, 1972.

ii, 27 p.; 18 cm.

In prose style.

Hamlet/ translated from the English original by Tongbram Gitacandra Simha. — Imphal: the translator, 1965.

xi, 105 p.; 18 cm.

Julius Caesar/ translated from English original by Achom Pashot Simha. — Imphal: the translator, 1972.

iv, 50 p.; 18 cm.

In prose style.

Julius Caesar/ translated from English original by Irom Babu Simha. — Imphal: the translator, 1980.

129 p.; 22 cm.

Julius Caesar/ translated from English original by Tongbram Gitchandra Simha. — Imphal: Gandhi Memorial Press, 1969.

124 p.; 18 cm.

King-Lear/ tanslated from the English original by Achom Pashot Simha. — Imphal: the translator, 1972.

ii, 28 p.; 18 cm.

Macbeth/ translated from English original by Achom Pashot Simha. — Imphal: the translator, 1973.

ii, 31 p.; 18 cm.

Macbeth/ translated from the English original by Tongbram Gitchandra Simha. — Imphal: Gandhi Memorial Press, 1969.

104 p.; 18 cm.

Othello/ translated from the English original by Achom Pashot Simha. — Imphal: the translation, 1972.

ii, 36 p.; 18 cm.

In prose style.

Othello/ translated from the English original by Tongbram Gitchandra Simha. — Imphal: Gandhi Memorial Press, 1966.

vii, 140 p.; 18 cm.

Rape of Lucrece/ translated from the English original by Ashangbam Minaketan Simha. — Imphal: the translator, 1965.

iii, 179 p.; 18 cm.

Romeo-Juliet/ translated from the English original by Achom Pashot Simha. — Imphal: the translator, 1971.

26 p.; 18 cm.

Tempest/ translated from the English original by Achom Pashot Simha. — Imphal: the translator, 1971.

26 p.; 18 cm.

Twelfth night/ translated from the English original by Achom Pashot Simha. — Imphal: the translator, 1971.

29 p.; 18 cm.

THANG-TA

Under the modernity project, experiments with the body as a source of theatrical expression formed part of the general movement in post-colonial Indian arts. The richness of gestural language in martial arts like Theng-Ta in Manipur has enamoured a host of theatre workers. Literally 'Thang-Ta' denotes '*sword-spear*', the common name of the Manipuri martial art called '*Huyen-Lallong*' (Art of War-fare). It comprises of four aspects: *Ta-khousarol* (Spear-dancing), *thang-hairol* (sword play); *sarit-sarat* (unarmed combat) and the rare *thengkouro* (touch and call) to ritual motions that marically guarantee triumph. When British annexed Manipur in 1891, they banned its practising. In the post-independence period, it grew in popular appeal not only as an art in itself but also as part of the training imparted by Manipuri theatre directors and dancers. They usurped this lifting motifs onto their productions. The coded vocabularies, choreographic patterns, and combat principles were incorporated physically in, for example, adaptations from Sanskrit classics like Ratan Thiyam's '*Chakravyuha*' in 1984, and the precision of execution, the skills of the performers, and the tension of the action created exotic images which dazzled audiences, specially those at theatre festivals outside Manipur and on the international cricuit.

One prominent centre of Martial arts of Manipur is "*Huyel Lallong Manipur Thang-To Cultural Association*" which was formed in 1958-59 to preserve this rare culture of Manipur martial arts by way of imparting training to the younger generation. It was established under the patronage of Guru G. Gourkishor Sharma, the Sangeet Natak Akademi Award winner of Kairas. it is located at Irilbung Bazar, B.P.O. Irilbung, Imphal East II - 795008, Manipur. Apart from this headquarter, it has seven district branches.

In June 1977, '*Hula Sindam Sang*', another cultural institute was formed which imparts lessons in Thang-Ta (Sword and spear). Sarit-Sarak (Unarmed combat) and Mukna (indigenous wrestling). The organisation took part in India Festival UK 1982, visited France and Spain on special invitation. France and Germany, 1985. U.S. 1986, Indian Manifestation Sweden 1987.

Hula Sindam Sang also invited to participate in the Asian Theatre Featival and 'International Seminar-cum-Workshop on Theatre', Dance and Martial Arts, and earned universal applause. In the year 1988, it attended the 'Chieri Festival', sponsored by ICCR and Festival of Indian Culture at Monopolis, August, 1988 along with performances at Rome and Messing, Sicily, 1988. Particiticated in the 'Festival of India' at Germany, 1991 and visited the Soviet Union on special invitation in September-October, 1991 sponsored by ICCR. It collaborated with Audio-visual Research Centre, Manipur University and Forum for Laboratory Theatre of Manipur, Imphal, for organisation of Workshop on affinities and differences between Kalaripayyatu of Kerala and Huyel Lalong or Thang-Ta of Manipur.

References

Arun, M.C. The Manipur experience: Theatre of protest. *Theatre India*; May 2000; No.1. Pp. 26-33.

Bagchi, Sukumar [Bengali Theatre in Manipur] A.M. Th. C (Imphal, 1968), Pp.55-68.

Baladev Sharma. Prachalita Manipurinatya Kala. — Imphal: Smt. Sanahanbi, 1975.

309 p.; 22 cm.

In Manipur.

Bira Singh, M. "*Manipuri natyakala*". Manipur Sahitya Parishad, Imphal, 1959.

Included in the speech collection.

Ibobi Simha, Ningombam. Natya amasung mancha. — Imphal: the author, 1969.

vi, 148 p.; 18 cm.

In Manipuri

Kanhailal, Heisnam. Ritual Theatre: Theatre of transition. *Theatre India*; (National School of Drama's Theatre journal); no. 10; Nov. 2004. Pp. 3-16.

Lokendra Arambam. Manipuri theatre: a new look upon tradition. *Sangeet Natak Bulletin*; 1985; Nos. 77-78; Pp. 67-77.

Lokendra Arambam 'Manipuri theatre' *In* Rasa: the Indian performing arts in the last twenty-five years (Vol.2). — Kolkata. Anamika Kala Sangam, 1995. Pp. 163-170.

Madhu Maibam (b. 1933) Thengaulon. — Imphal: the author, 1973.

25 p.; 18 cm.

Manihar Singh, Ch. History of Manipuri literature. — New Delhi: Sahitya Akademi, 1996.

The Oxford companion to Indian theatre/ ed. by Ananda Lal. — New Delhi: Oxford University Press, 2004.

Saroj N., Arambam. The pleasing of the gods: Meitei Lai Haraoba/ by Arambam Saroj N. and John Parralt. New Delhi: Vikas, 1997.

Shivaprakash, H.S. Interview [with] H. Kanhailal. *Theatre India*; No.10, Nov. 2004; Pp.17-27.

Shyamsundar, A. Mainu Premcha. — Imphal: [s.n.], 1955.

Preface to the play.

Theatre for the ritual of suffering. — Imphal: Heisnam, 1997.

"Theatre in Manipur today", *Seagull Theatre Quarterly* (Special Issue); June/ September 1997.

Traditional performing arts of north-east India/ ed. by Birendranath Datta. — Guwahati: Assam Academy, 1990.

Theatre Journal/ ed. by W. Bhagirath Singh (A quarterly journal).

IX

MIZO

Introduction

Geographically, this state of India is surrounded by Myenmar in the east, south and Bangladesh in the west and the states of Assam, Manipur and Tripura in the north, north-east and south-east, respectively. About seventy percent of its boundaries form international borders. Literally the word 'Mizo' refers to the hill people and the compound word 'Mizoram' means, the '*Land of the Mizos*'.

Until its annexation to India by the British in 1890, 'The Lushai' tribe ruled the land Mizo (or Lushai) is one of the five major tribes living here. Others are Ralte, Hmar, Paite and Pawi'. There also exist a subtribe called 'Awzia'.

Politically, even after independence 'Lushai Hills' was a hill district of Assam and then after their demand for the Right of self-Determination this was declared a Union Territory in 1972 and attaining the Statehood in the next decade.

The Mizos are justifiably wellknown as a singing tribe. Their musical tradition unlike that of some other tribes of the country is well developed in several ways. They also have the rich tradition of oral literature in the form of folk tales, traditional oral poetry, folk songs, ritual chants and so on.

We view the folk art of the north-east Indian tribes as an aspect of its various socio-religious systems. But at the present we find a deliberate and conscious search of beauty by the modern writers, poets, dramatists, musicians, singers. Art here is secular, a flight into the realm of emotion and imagination, exploring different dimentions of human existence with a wide range of concerns. We find versatile amalgamation of modern perspectives with the wealthy folk traditions.

From the time immemorial the Mizos enjoyed their yearly festivals with dance and rice-beer, and a kind of religious sacrifices were given to their gods with solemn functions. It was the customs of the Mizos of the past to organise *Rallu-lam* (Head-dance), to hold a dance in celebration of a head taken in a raid and *Sa-lu-lam* (Animal-dance), to hold a dance and a feast to celebrate success in the chase and to perform *ai* ceremony. *Ai* ceremony look forward to the blessing for another kill and to control the soul (of the killed/slain) in after-life. When killing an enemy it was obligatory to perform the *ai* ceremony. This was done not only with a view to getting the spirit of the slain into the power of the slayer after death, but also to show the slayer's overall superiority. The souls of these animals and men killed would accompany the man on his way to Paradise (or *Pialral*). The dispenser Pawla would be convinced to see the procession of the hero with so many wild beasts and raiders and would welcome the hero in the main entrance of the *Pialral*. A modern art historian has rightly said that these instances involved a series of actions and deeds, which formed the background of the Mizo Drama.

Scholar Laltluangliana Khaiangte of the Pachhung University College gives us three periods in the development of Mizo Drama as follows:-

(I) *The Root Period* (Religious or Entertainment/ From the beginning till 1924)

(II) The Budding Period (Moral or Early Plays/ From 1925-1958)

(III) The Flowering Period (Artistic or Modern plays/ From 1959 onwards).

The Root Period

The foundation of Mizo drama was directly linked with the ritual of the Church. It was customery to organize a variety show every Christmas Day. It all began with a special fest in 1903 on December 25 which later became a regular yearly event adding musical and dramatic performances along with a grand feast.

The year 1912 is a red letter day in the history of Mizo drama. In the evening of 25 December, the first ever dramatic performance was held in the small thatched roofed theatre of Thakthing Veng, Aizawl. For the first time, the Christmas Variety Entertainment programme was organised by the missionaries the event was highly successful.

A well attended function enjoyed by the theatre goers of that night which comprised of twenty six items. Apart from speeches and songs, some had humorous dialogues containign plot, acted in the land for the first time. Though not drama proper these items had some dramatic elements in it which amused the people.

(I) *Sap mi Khual Leh Tawng Let Ling tu,* denoting English Stranger and Interpreter)

The story of this first piece runs as follows:- When the foreigner arrived in Mizoram for the first time, the native Mizos were really surprised to see such a man with fair skin and brown hair, not knowing the language, but uttering something. They came around him with a puzzled look, then a close look and touching his hands and feet. One determined person stepped out and interpreted whatever he said to the people around. It was a make believe interpretation and when they really understood the language later, it was funny encounter for them. And they would repeated the same thing with certain variations in the process.

(II) *Krismas hria Leh hre lo* (One who knows the meaning of Christmas explained to his friend its significance)

(III) *Kristian leh Kristian lo in biak na* (a dialogue between Christian and non-Christian)

(IV) *Sap putar leh Mosolman putar lem in biak na* (a dialogue between an English old man and Mosolman old man).

(V) Khasi Dialoch (a dialogue between two Khasis).

Of these shows, the most important one was '*Borsap lem, Leh thu chhia nei tu 2 leh rasi lem chang* be (Superintendent's Court Scene)'. *This was the first drama proper ever staged in Mizoram*. It not only had plot and dialogues, but also action, another essential element in a drama. A short piece, the story centres on a greedy man, who had stolen his neighbour's goat. The owner reported the matter to the Borsap (Magistrate) The court summoned both of them to appear before the District Magistrate. The theif, therefore, invited the Rasi (Circle Interpreter) to defend him and gave the Rasi a good amount of money. Mean while, the Borsap was informed about the bribery. The court decided in favour of a legal owner of the goat. The disillusioned convict, helplessly asked the Rasi to return his money. Then, the embarrassed Rasi has nothing to say, but simply produced a bleating sound of goat, be... be... and he went away."

The first show of 1912 was an instant hit and eventually some sort of dramatic representation became an indispensable part of the Christmas Entertainment programmes of the following years. Such cultural event were held not only in Aizawl, but extended to different villages.

Sooner, the Church authority started encouraging a kind short play to propagate certain moral and religious lessons in the Church. Till 1924, the theatre people were those good Christians. The audience in the theatre also expected some moral lessons to learn from the drama itself. And if moral lesson is to be inculcated, the religious tone must be the dominate theme of the play. Starting from the Biblical stories, the playwrights, could not but, follow the same trend in their plays.

Khiangte informs us that in 1919, the wave of *Spiritual Revival* completely threw the dramatic performances out of the Church and was a major set-back in the development of Mizo drama. Even during the Christmas season, such stage performances and other variety entertainment programmes were banned. The emphasis was on the Cross and suffering of Christ, revealing the love of God for man and demanding the corollary of brotherly love and Christian affection. Hymn singing in praise of god were allowed ans such a great change in the lives of the Mizo people had switched the dramatic instinct off until the advent of secular drama. This occured with the emergence of Pasena, the pioneer of Mizo dramatics. His period is termed as Pasena Age or Period covering 1925 to 1933.

Pasena

An outstanding educationist and a man of theatre, Pasena was born in 1893. He obtaind his Diploma in Education from London and settled in Aizawl in 1925. It was he who was responsible for spearheading modern Mizo theatre.

Here he witnessed the absolute abstinance of theatrical. This was due to spiritual awakening, but interestingly people were very much tempted by the *Puja Variety Show of Bengali Babus at Babutlang (Officers' Complex) and the Nātak' (live dramatic performance) of 1st Assam Rifle Regiment at Drill shed in Aizawl*.

Pasena took advantage of the situation and revived the dramatic performances with his six extempore works, all staged in Sikulpui Hall (Boys' Middle English School) located at Mission Veng, Aizawl. His debut '*Heroda Chawimawima* (King Herod's Glory) based on a story from Bible was produced in 1925 at Sikulpui Hall by the artists of Mission Veng. This Biblical story preached moral lesson..

His other plays which borrowed their themes from Bible are Fapa Tlanbo (The Prodical Son) and Khualbuka mi a (A Fool at the Inn), staged in 1927 and 1933 respectively.

His original creations are Tinreng daih Khawl (Robot or a machine with brain), Ransa Khawmpui (Animals' Conference) and Rorelna (Court), performed in 1928, 1929 and 1933 respectively. All these plays were written to preach moral principle for day to day living. It is pertinent here to mention that *Pasena had also guided Chuauthuama to produce the first Shakespearean play in the land entitled 'Sailoka', adapted from the Merchant of Venice, also staged at Sikulpui Hall in 1929.*

Lalkailuia

Pasena cast a strong spell on the playwrights of his times as well as his successors. *After Pasena, the most significant dramastist to be reckoned is 'Lalkailuia'*, who was the son of Reiek village chief. He was also a good actor who played the lead role in his drama. *He is credited with the first Mizo play to be written and staged on love theme entitled 'Tualvungi and Zawlpala'*. Lalkailuia and his friends acted in this play dealing with the love story of Zawlpala and Tualvungi. His another important drama is '*Liandova te unau*'. Both these dramas are based on popular Mizo folk stories, performed at Assam Rifle Drill Shed in the year 1935.

Rev. Samuel Davies and The Zosiami Cup Drama Competition

Rev. Samuel Davies was a major presence in the Mizo dramatic scene in the late thirtees. This missionary came in the land in 1937 and stayed till 1951. He obtained a Diploma from the London School of Drama which helped him to improve the Mizo theatre. He introduced various sophisticated theatrical devices whether it is lighting, background music, scenery, stage decor or systematic presentation. A critic has rightly said that his coming was a blessing for the theatrical performers. The quality of the productions enhanced with the introduction of a theatre competition called *Zosiami Cup* in 1940. The prize was donated by Samuel Davies and his wife and named after their first daughter, Zosiami. The first festival was held on the 3rd October 1940. Zosiami Cup Drama Competition Report, appearing in Kristian Tlangau Thubelh (October, 1940), Pp. 81-82 informs "The Entry fees were collected for *War Fund of British Empire*, and the total amount reached rupees seventy. The cup was a running trophy, those who can win for the second will take the cup permanently. critic Laltluangliana Khiangte adds 'But due to Second World War, the competion was never held again in the following years.'

There are several socio-cultural organisations in Mizoram. The oldest are being the Young Mizo Association (YMA) During the time of McCall, the Superintendent, Lushai Hills district under the inspiration of Mrs. McCall, in 1936 the Young Lushai Association (Y.L.A.) was formed at Lungleh. Soon all over the Lushai Hills district (Y.L.A.) established its branches. It became popular and received the patronage of the Government, Church and the village elders. This organisation took active part in the aforesaid drama competition. After independence, Y.L.A. Changed its name and became Y.M.A. It is the most powerful socio-cultural organisation in Mizo today.

Samuel Davies inspired the playwrights like Upa Chawngzika and Lalzuithanga who sought to fame with their productions like *Princess Pocahontas* and the *Black Corner of Aijal* in 1999 respectively. The former won the first prize and the latter got the second prize in the competition acted by Mission Veng Young Lushai Association Kulikawn Y.L.A., third prize went to 'Wolf Club's presentation of '*One good turn deserves another*'.

It was because of him that the Mizo theatre improved in its various aspects. Even Davies and Chawngzika jointly authored many a plays and acted some four to six plays.

Chawngzike Age

A renowned playwright, actor an theatre director, Chawngzika made his debut with the dramatization of Krista Palai (Ambassador for Christ, translated into Mizo by Challiana). *His play ts supposed to be reckoned as the first written play with a type copy in Mizo language*. Performed in 1934 at Sikulpui (Aijal) by the Aijal Theatre Performers under his direction. For the first time entry ticket was sold particularly for this show to raise 'Pawngi's Memorial Fund'. He was the organiser of this drama society. In 1938, he alongwith Rev. Samuel Davies made the dramatic version of the rendered novel of the Kristiana Vanram kawng Zawh' the play was put on boards first in Sikulpui and later in Dawrpui Sikui. It was the first true professional production, brilliantly directed by Davies.

As said earlier also, in 1940 his play '*Princess Pocahontas*' got the first prize in 'Zosiami Cup'. The Suprintendent of Lushai Hills who witnessed the play commented "It was marvelous; the English actors were no better than them". His other wellknown plays which were successful on the stage are the *Royal Robes* (1948), *Rabboni* (1948), *Christmas Spirit* (1949, *The Star of Christmas* (1950), and *Naamana* (1950) (All based on Biblical stories).

Changzika also rendered and dramatized some stories from other literature into Mozo. He also contributed some enlightaining articles on drama in various monthly journals.

Apart from these, Samuel Davies also assisted him in dramatization of some four to six play in which both acted.

Khiangte writes that all these plays were meant to portray certain moral meaning above its amusing elements. Khiangte further comments: Mizo playwrights may be called Christian playwrights, for they always tinge their dramas with Christian concept of love and good moral. For them, therefore, theme of brotherly love come naturally from the Christian perspective. Upa Chawngzika depicted the value of true friendship or brotherly love in his three dramas, namely *Pheikhawk Siamtu* (staged in 1938); *Travelling Companion* (staged in 1950); and *Martina* (showed in 1951) A devoted Christian by nature, Chawngzika had tried to show the price of good living and the value of faith in Jesus Christ. His characters had shown brotherly love in their day to day living and inculcated religiousness in their lives.

Lalzuithanga

Another playwright of repute who emerged in the last phase of the budding period was Lalzuithanga who was born in 1916. He wrote a prophetic play entitled '*The Black Corner of Aijal in 1999*' which achieved the second place in the first 'Zosiami Cup' drama competition organised in 1940. It was produced under the banner of 'Kulikaun Y.L.A.' A fine production, the missionaries remarked that "there is no difference in the English drama" The playwright who was a gifted actor took the lead role. On October 17, 1941 he also organized a grand cultural show which he termed as 'The Cosmopolitan Variety Entertainment', held at Assam Rifle drill shed. A musician and comedian per excellence his variey items include *Lushai Fantasy* and *Hawaiian Fantasy* and also a tragedy called '*The Horrible*'. He was multifaceted theatre person who was highly appreciated. In his play 'The Black Corner of Aijal in 1999' and the novel 'Thlahrang', Lalzuithanga tries to convince that love of money is a root of evil. He skillfully reveals how the love of money ruins one's life. It is clear that a useful servant of a master may ruin the other master-Money leads man astray to extent that out of such love, man meets his sad end. The temptation of money or wealth can arise from anywhere, and if man follows that glitter with all his will, the sparkling gold will lead him to the darkest night. One of the leading figures in Mizo theatre, Lalzuithanga died in 1950.

Sixties onward: The Flowering Period

The history of modern Mizoram theatre began in 1912. But from the fortees of the last century the theatre continued to gather strength. During this period the dramatic art was acquired by a group of actors in almost every village. Khiangte inform when the Gospel Golden Jubilee was celebrated in 1944, Samuel Davies dramatised the coming of Christianity into play, Thuhriltu, 'The herald' acted in Aizawl. About this time, almost every village started organising dramatic performances. Theatre reached a turning point in 1963 when the first published play 'Sangi Inleng' by Lalthangfala Sail appeared in print. There after many new playwrights emerged and so did many new drama societies. The notable among the playwright's who became popular are:-

(1) Lalthangfala Sailo (b. 1933)

(2) Mr. Lalhmuaka (b. 1915)

(3) R.K. Dingliana

(4) Lalzamliana

(5) H. Lalsiama (1909-1983)

(6) Selthuama (1910-1971)

(7) James Dokhuama (b. 1932)

(8) Lalsangzuala

(9) K. Saibela (b. 1935)

(10) C. Sangzuala (b. 1937)

(11) Khawlkungi (b. 1927)

(12) C. Laizawna

(13) H.K.R. (Pseud)

(14) C. Lalsiamthanga

(15) Laltluangliana Khiangte (b. 1959)

(16) Lalsiama (b. 1931)

(17) R. Lalhmingmawia

(18) Lalengmawia Ralte (b. 1947)

(19) B. Lahanhranga

(20) R.F. Irish (Pseud)

(21) Liansailova (b. 1949)

Celebrated Mizo playwight Lalthangfala Sailo is credited with the first published play in the Mizo language. His tragi-comedy 'Sangi Inleng' was written and first staged in October 1959. at MZI Hla Kutpui (Music Festival) and the venue was the Mizo High School at Aizawl. His next significant work was a ccomedy '*Liandova Te Unau*', appeared in print in 1969.

After Sailo, the next dramatist who made his presence felt was Mr. *Lalhmuaka* (b. 1915). This was the second published dramatic work compiled by him. This was an anthology of dramatic pieces entitled '*Lemchan Bu*' broughtout on 28 October 1965. It comprises of six short dramas, out of which four are written by the compiler himself. Lalmuaka established himself as a prolific writer who wrote seven dramas, three of which found place in the book '*Drama Pasarih*', a collection of plays, broughtout by the Zoram Writers' Club in 1981. Lalmuaka's noteworthy dramas are enlisted here. These are '*Lo Kir Leh Mai Rawh* (1965), *Ranthleng Mak* (1965), *A ni mai thei* (1965), *Moutam tam* (1965), *Pathian thu nung – Mizoramah* (1981), *Sumdeng Zu* (1981), *Ramthanga te chhung* (1981).

In the collection '*Lemchan Bu*', appeared two more plays by two different dramatists. They were:- Mr. R.K. Dingliana and Mr. Lalzamliana. The former wrote a Christmas play called '*Lal Chibai an bak a*' and latter wrote a comedy with a good plot.

A litterateur who write in different genres of literature Sri *H. Lalsiama* penned two plays for the Text Book of Class VII and VIII in High School Mizo Vernacular. The plays '*Pa Awk Hrawl*' and '*Ukil Hilawhtling*' got published in 1970.

The playwright *Selthuama* also emerged in the seventies with the play '*Saikuti Lungzeh*' broughtout in 1975.

In the same decade the Padma Shri Award Winning writer James Dokhuma (b. 1932) wrote plays on social issues such as *Tumna chu a hlawhtling thin* (1976), *Hmasawnna* (1978), *Hausak aiin Hrisel a Hlu zawk* (1978), *Finna Hmahruai* (1980).

In the eighties appeared many dramatists *Lalsangzuala* is one of them whose work is the only Mizo play so far, published outside Mizoram. The work entitled '*Christmas drama*' appeared from Churachanpur, Manipur.

A fiction writer and dramatist Sri *K. Saibela* (b. 1935) penned two plays, namely, "*Chhura Leh naa*" and "*Thu a Tawp e Lumam*", which were included in the volume 'Drama Pasarih', published by the Zoram Writers' Club in 1981.

A renowned editor and writer *C. Sangzuala* (b. 1937) penned his drama "*Mizoram Sande Sikul intan dan leh a than zel dan*" which was completed on 26th October 1977. But the play appeared in print only in 1981, included in 'Drama Pasarih', an anthology of plays, as mentioned earlier also, published by the Zoram Writers' Club.

It can, therefore, be seen that the present day Mizo writers and dramatists have succeeded in buildingup a small modern dramatic literature in the Mizo language, a language which has not so far well projected.

Eighties: Mizo Cultural Club

The Mizo Cultural Club was formed in October, 1979 under the leadership of Sri H. Kaibuaia with the aim and objectives to promote Mizo culture amongs the younger generation and also to encourage cultural exchange through participating in cultural festivals, etc in other states of the country. Folk songs, folk dances, dramas etc. are organised by the Club and training are also conducted occasionally. It also participates in AIR and Doordarshan programmes. It has brought many Mizo folk songs. The Govt. of Mizoram pays for hiring the club within and outside the State. The club has, thus, represented the Mizoram Govt. on different occasions including the Zonal Cultural Festivals and Republic Day Celebration in New Delhi. The Cub participates in cultural programmes organised by All India Radio, Delhi, Guwahati and Shillong. The Club has also participated within North Eastern State, UP, Kerala, New Delhi under Cultural Exchange programmes. Above all, the traditional costumes, crafts, instruments etc. are kept at its own theatre. Mizo Cultural Club is situated in Aizawl, Ramhlun, Mizoram-796012. It has several branches such as :-

(1) K. Pahlira & Party Sakawrtuichhun, Aizawl, Mizoram

(2) Ramhlun Vengthar, Aizawl, Mizoram

(3) Chandmary, Aizawl Mizoram.

In this decade appeared emerged in print a play 'Zawlpala Thalan Tlangah' written by *Khawlkungi (b. 1927) the first and the only woman playwright* who however, wrote few more plays which were staged in the seventees. Her '*Pangpar bawm*', a dramatization of C. Schmith's story '*The Basket of Flower*' was an unpublished work. The play was, however put on boards in 1977 by the local Christian Youth Association (KTP). It was a highly successful drama. Her 'Zawlpala Thalan Tlangah, based on a Mizo folk-tale later appeared in the form of fiction with a minor change in the title as '*Zawlpala Thlan Tlang*' in 1983.

Her play '*Monu Sual*', written in 1982 is still in manuscript from. In the same year this family drama bagged the *First Prize in State Level Drama Competition.*

Lai Cultural Society

Lai Cultures Society is located at Saikah, P.O. Lawngtlai-796891, Mizoram. It came into being in 1981 to promote and preserve the cultures and traditional performing art legacies of the region. It organises programmes of folk songs, dance, drama music and variety shows etc. Also participates in various programmes organised by State Tribal Research Institute.

A writer of shorter fictions and novels, Sri *C. Laizawna*, however, made his debut with a play entitled '*Kan tiam tawh si*', broughtout in 1982.

Using his acronym 'H.K.R.', this dramatist whose real name is still unknown authored a detective play dealing with drug abuse entitled '*Khawchhak Lungpui*' published in 1984.

Academician, playwright and translator Sri *C. Lalsiamthanga* composed his social drama '*Dik tea Vahvaihna*' appeared in 1986. Earlier he had translated Sophocles Greek drama '*Oedipus: the King*' into Mizo. The manuscript completed in 1983 remains unpublished.

Teacher, playwright and drama historian *Laltluangliana Khiangte* is a prolific writer in the genre of drama. His debut '*Thupha ka raun chawi e*' written in 1982 was staged in the same year at Shillong. His other praiseworthy dramas to name are :- *Nu leh pa bum-mahni inbum* (1987), *Faki te chhung* (1987),

Thawmmawia (1988), *Thawmvunga* (1990), *Zorama* (a tragedy composed in 1988), *Duhawma leh lalfaki, Chharmawia and Thupha ka chawi*, (all comedies, written in 1989).

His magnum opus is, however, a treatise on drama entitled *'Mizo drama origin, development and themes'*, published by the Cosmo Publications, New Delhi in 1993. it covers the whole of Mizo drama, from the beginnig to date, that is from 1912 to 1990, discussed in the English language, giving the treatise an unique place in the history of Indian drama.

It is important to add here that Lalsiama (b. 1931) broughtout a number of short dramas in the eightees. But his first play *'Nu Mawl'*, now extinct, was staged at Lawngtlai long back in 1961. His play *'Zoluti an man'* was published in 1987 and then appeared book 'Zonun', in 1988 comprising of four plays entitled Ka ha Jaiga, (a short play written in 1962 at Tuipang), Pastor leh Zurui (written in 1986), Mene, Mene Tekel Upharsin (written in 1970) and A Setana a zam ta (written in 1970 at baktawng).

The drama *'Buannel Farm'* is a propaganda play which got published in 1987, composed by *R. Lalhmingmawia*. This is, perhaps, his only work.

Another dramatist of this period is *'Lalengmawia Ralte'* (b. 1947) whose dramatic output compises of many plays, but mostly available in manuscript form. His two wellknown published works are Nausen Vang and Khawiah nge (both published in the anthology 'Christmas Drama'.

Next play that appeared in print, ie, in 1989 was penned by B. Lhanhranga. The play entitled *'Harh Rawh: Vengtu Drama'* has a bold patriotic theme.

In the same year, a Mizo by birth proclaimed himself R.F. Irish Philosopher wrote a play *'Romeo & Juliet Part-II'* published by Arbee Publication.

Liansailova, library professional in Mizoram has proved himself as a dramatist of distinction. His play, *'Zovi te chhung'*, a prize winning drama is available in cyclostyle copies. In 1989 appeared his book 'Lawm a Kim' a collection of four interesting dramas, namely, *Lawn a Kim*, *Dunia a duai bik lo*, *Krismas Drama* and *Tlai ngailo Pathian* etc.

Art and Culture Department, Mizoram has been very active in mobilising the talent of their youths who are interested to learn the theatre. The Department organised three threatre workshops under the Extension Programme of National School of Drama, New Delhi. 28 selected students from the previous three workshops were selected to participate in the first Central Workshop organised in Delhi during February-March 2002. The hard work put in by the students culminated into the production of a play titled '*Zanriah Ei Hmain*'. This was a team work and no one was responsible or could demand a credit for the designing of this play. As a workshop production, it was a result of the interactions between teachers and students.

Imaginative historians described primitive theatre as a media of sharing experience. And theatre is performing that role still now. To touch the first experience of man, the actors decided to enact that. Through improvisation they prepared this play. It did not contain any story as such. It was a combination of various small experiences. Since they have originated from a common life, one may discover a story line in it. In their imagination alongwith sharing the experience, theatre took birth as a strong weapon against evils and production tried communicating that with sounds not through fully developed language. Those who appeared on the stage are:-

H. Chhawntluanga	R. Lathmingmawia	Lalramvanneia
Lalhariata Zadeng	K. Lalremruata	Samuel Zohmingliana
Zoremthanga	Rosangupia	Vantalhuma Khawlhring
P.C. Zothansanga	C. Lalrotluanga	F. Lalringenga
Lalhunrunata	Lalthlamuana Varte	Zoherliana
R.K. Chhunga	Lairamchhana	R. Lalhariat Chhuaha
Lalchhuankima	Lallawamawma	C. Lalrintluangi
C. Ramsangliani	G. Lalpanmawli	Jaointa Lalhmangaihi
Lawmsangkimi	Lalnipali	R. Lallianzuali
Lalzawmmawll		

Credit

Teaching Faculty	Partha Bandyopadhyay, Sandip Bhattacharya, Yogesh Pant, Satya Brata Raut
Camp Direction	Sidhartha Chakraborti.

BIBLIOGRAPHY OF MIZO DRAMA
(Includes both published and unpublished works)

Chawngzika

Christmas spirit

[written in 1949]

——. Krista Palai/ [Ambassador for Christ]

The first written play with a type copy in Mizo language; staged in 1934.

——. Kristiana Vanram Kawng Zawh

[Dramatised with the help of Samuel Danies; staged in 1938].

——. Naamana.

[Written in 1950]

——. Princess Pocahontas.

[Written and staged in 1940].

——. Rabboni

[written in 1948].

——. The Royal Robes

[Written in 1949].

——. The Star of Christmas.

[Written in 1950]

Davis, Samuel

Hausakna nun dik take. 1938.

Jointly written and staged with Chawngzika.

Dingliana, R.K.

Lal Chibai an buk a. *In* Lemchan Bu/ compiled by Lalhmuaka. — Aijawl: Modern Printing Press, 1965.

Dokhuma, James

Finna Hmahruai. — [s.l]: The State Social Education Wing, Department of Education, 1980.

——. Hausak aiin Hrisel a hlu zawk. — [s.l.] : The Community Development Department, 1978.

——. Hmasawnna. — [s.l.]: Mizo Writers Association, 1978.

——. Thla Weinga Zan. 1971.

——. Tumna chu a hlawhtling thin. — [s.l.]: The State Social Education Wing, Department of Education, 1976.

H.K.R.

Khawchhak Lungpui — Electric Veng, Aizawl: R.D. Press, 1984.

Detective drama

Playwright uses his psuedonym (Abbreviated his name) in this detective play.

Khawlkungi

Monu Sual. 1982.

——. Pangpar bawm 1970.

Adaptation of C. Schmith's '*The Basket of Flower*'.

——. Zawlpala thalan tlangah. 1981.

Khiangte Laltlungliana

Chharmawia

(Comedy)

——. Duhawma Leh Laltaki

(Comedy)

——. Faki te Chhung *In* Thungai-hnawm—Thalaite tan. [s.l.] : SCERT, 1987.

Included in the volume essays & dramas by diverse hands.

——. Nu Leh pa bum-mahni inbum. [s.l.]: SCERT, 1987.

——. Thawmmawia. *Golden Jubilee Souvenir of Lungpho YMA*. 1988.

——. Thawmvunga. *In* Hnam Lungphum: Annual magazine of Mizo Student's Union, Shillong. 1989-1990.

——. Thupha Ka Chawi. 1989

(Comedy)

——. Zorama. 1988

(A tragedy)

Laizawna, C.

Kan tiam tawh Si. 1982.

Lalhmingmawia, R.

Buannel Farm.

(Written and published in 1987).

Lalhmuaka

Lemchan Bu. — Aizawl: Modern Printing Press, 1965.

Collection of six short plays.

——. Lo kir leh mai rawh 1965.

Included in 'Lemchan Bu'.

——. Mautam tam 1965.

——. A ni mai thei. 1965.

Morality play

——. Pathian thu nung-Mizoramah.

Historical play first appeared in 1981 in Drama Pasarih. (The Zoram Writers' Club Series; 5)

——. Ramthanga te chhung. 1981.

——. Ranthleng Mak. 1965.

Biblical play.

——. Sundeng Zu. 1981.

The Lalkailuia

Liandova te unau.

Staged in 1935.

——. Tualvungi and Zawlpala.

Staged in 1935.

Lalsangzuala

Christmas drama.— Churachanpur, Manipur: The author, 1977.

Lalsiama

Ka ha Jaiga.

(Written in 1962 at Tuipang).

——. Mene, mene tekel upharsin

(written in 1970)

——. Pastor leh Zurui

(written in 1986)

——. A Setana a zam ta

(written in 1970 at Baktawng)

(Book includes his four dramatic pieces)

——. Zoluti an man. 1987.

A historical play.

Lalsiama, H.

Pak Awk Hrawl. *In* Mizo Vernacular. 1970.

——. Ukil Hlawhtling *In* Mizo Vernacular. 1970.

Lalsiamthanga, C.

Diktea Vahvaihna. 1986.

——. Oedipus/ tr. of Sophocles's Greek drama into Mizo by C. Lal Siamthanga. 1983.

Unpublished.

Lalzam liana

Isua Neih Ka Dub Zawk. *In* Lemchan Bu/compiled by Lalhmuaka. — Aizawl: Modern Printing Press, 1965.

Lalzuithanga

The Black Corner of Aijal in 1999.

[Staged in 1940].

——. The Horrible

[A tragedy staged in 1941].

Lhanhranga, B.

Harh Rawh: Vengtu drama. 1989.

Liansailova

Duaia a duai bik lo. 1989.

——. Krismas Drama. 1989.

——. Lawn a Kim. 1989.

Collection of four plays; also the title of the first play written in early 1989.

——. Tlai ngailo Pathian 1989.

——. Zovi.

Pasena

Fapa Tlanbo [=The Prodical Son]

Staged in 1927.

—— Heroda Chawimawina [=King Herod's Glory]

Staged in 1925.

——. Khualbuka mi a [=A Fool at the Inn]

Staged in 1933.

——. Ransa Khawmpui [=Animal's Conference]

Staged in 1929.

——. Rorelna [=Court]

Staged in 1933.

——. Tinreng daih Khawl [=Robot or a machine with brain]

Staged in 1928.

Ralte, Lalengmawia

Khawiah nge. *In* Christmas drama 1988.

——. Nausen Vang. *In* Christmas drama. 1988.

R.F. Irish (Pseud)

Romeo & Juliet Part II. — [s.l.]: Arbee Publications, 1989.

Saibela, K.

Chhura. leh Naa: *In*. Drama Pasarih. — [s.l.]: Zoram Writers' Club, 1981.

——. Thu a Tawp e Lumam. 1980.

Sailo, Lalthangfala

Liandova te unau. 1969.

——. 4th ed. — Kulikawn: Gilgal Press, 1988.

——. Sangi Inleng. — Aizawl : R. Vanlawna Press, Republic Veng, 1963.

First published play in Mizo

Second edition published in 1969.

Sangzuala, C.

Mizoram Sande Sikul intan dan leh a than zel dan. [Aizawl]: Drama Pasarih, 1981.

(Manuscript completed on October 26, 1977).

Selthuama

Saikuti Lungzeh. *In* Mizo Zia Rang. 1975.

Shakespeare, William

Sailoka [=the Merchant of Venice]

Staged in 1929 by Chauthnama with the help of Pasena.

A–Z

A

Aijal Theatre Performers *see* Introduction

A ni mai thei

This is a morality play of Lalhmuaka. The boss Lucifara and his colleagues discussed the best method to convert a righteous man to a sinful life. To deceive a man to hell is the puspose of their meeting.

B

The Black Corner of Aijal in 1999

The dramatist Lalzuithanga (1916-1950) made his debut with this play which bagged the second prize in the first drama competition of Zosiami Cup held in 1940. A prophetic play, it centres on an action in 1999 as George Orwell wrote 1984 a novel. This is a detective story about one youngster, who frequents an hotel with a bar, who is later sentenced to death for robbery and murder.

Borsap lem, leh Thu chhia hei tu 2 leh rasi lem chang be *see* Introduction

Buannel Farm

This is a modern drama in Mizo written by R. Lalhmingmawia: The hero Hminga was a mere student with no special qualities, but a deligent boy. He would do any work to earn his living. Whenever he was on holiday, he tried his level best to earn something. With the passage of time, he got a master's degree. He availed department loan for his own industry named *Buannel Farm*, which was quite productive after sometime. The Farm's products were popular and distributed over the whole country. A special award for successful industry had been awarded to Hminga, and the thanks giving celebration closes the play. This is a propaganda play and the playwright depicts the dignity of labour in the life and works of the hero. The play written in 1987 was broughtout in the same year.

C

Chawngzika *see also* Introduction

Chhura leh Naa

The Mizo drama is conmposed by K. Saibela, published only in 1982. Awarded a prize in 1962, this is based on a Mizo folktale with Sakhming chullo Chhura leh Naa as the subtitle. The plot runs as follows:-

The two comic characters, Chhura and Naa were said to have blood relation, may be brothers or cousins. The play highlighted some important adventures and encounters made by the two comedians. Naa was a cunning, but a lazy fellow, whereas Chhura was rather diligent and straight-forward man. The play, therefore, relates all those fortunes and misfortunes in the life of Chhura, incorporated with the zealous intervention of Naa in the affairs.

Christmas Drama

This is the only Mizo play so far, published outside Mizoram is the *Christmas Drama* (1977) by Lalsangzuala. It was printed in Churachanpur, Manipur. The play depicts the very life of modern youth, how young men and women used to spend the Christmas festival for their own sake. With fried chicken and drink some other eatable things were served in special party night. Life was easy and carefree. And the play satirized the folly of the contemporary society. And even the older generation could not understand how the young people would like to enjoy life in their own way.

Christmas Spirit

This Mizo drama was composed by Chawngzika, a wellknown theatre personality in 1949. Based on a Biblical tale, it was staged under the leadership of the playwright himself.

Chuanthuama *see under* Sailoka

D

Davies, Samuel *see* Introduction

Diktea Vahvaihna

An astute translator and author Sri C. Lalsiamthanga published this social drama in 1986. The plot developed from the greed and folly of the contemporary society into a tragic drama. The protagonist Lalnundika (Diktea) was found in the side drain of the town one evening. The church elder took him home and enquired about his adventure in that place. But he knew nothing. On further enquiry Diktea could somehow explain his mother's connection with one youngman, who has led him to an unknown destination. The founding elder looked after the boy for sometime, but transferred to his brother's house, who was the Finance Minister. From that house, Diktea was sent to goal for his discloser of the minister's confidential note. After the release, he contacted some office on behalf of his new master, the master, the first class contractor. After passing the Matriculation, he applied for the post of Lower Divisional Clerk in Public Welfare Department. Wherever he was, Diktea advocated truth. He worked honestly and deligently. He could not keep quiet but to speak truth and live righteously. He was, therefore, thrown out of the house the moment he asserts the real things. So the rejected youngman could not find reality in man's behaviour and their doings. One day he left a long letter in his rented house, and locked the door and went somewhere. After two weeks' time, the Office authority and the householder were curious about the disappearance of Diktea. The search party then, opened the locked door to find out what was going on. Two sealed letters explained the whole story. To the landowner, Diktea wrote a note, telling about his sudden vacation of the house, and the remaining balance of his rent enclosed in the envelope. In another letter addressing all the readers and hearers of his account, Diktea disclosed the very picture and temparament of the contemporary society, where truth never prevailed. For a just a righteous man, there was no place in the present society. And the tragic disappearance shows how truth is left alone in the street while the people live in the house, closing and locking their door from inside. That is why in the cover page of this Mizo drama runs the sub-title "truth is left alone in the street".

Dingliana, R.K.

This Mizo writer is credited with a Christmas play called '*Lal Chibai an buk a*' dealing with the birth of Lord Jesus in the small township of Bethlehem. The play appeared in the collection of plays '*Lemchan Bu*', compilied by Lalhmuaka; printed at the Modern Printing Press, Aizawl in 1965.

Dokhuma, James

A great man of literature, James Dokhuma in the first recipient of Padma Shri Award for Literature in 1985. A novelist, poet, short story writer, linguist, essayist, playwright and politician James Dokhuma was born on 15th June 1932, the youngest son of Hrangchina and Kapkungi of Sialsuk village, Aizawl district of Mizoram. Though he had little formal education, he acquired proficienty in English and Hindi, by his sheer zeal and determination, during his service in Assam Rifles from 1947 to 1952. Later, he served in various capacities as teacher, sanitary inspector etc. in Aizawl. Infact after retirement, he served as the Hindi Teacher in St. Paul's High School in Aizawl where he taught for four years. Hereafter he got actively involved in Politics.

As a creative writer, though Dokhuma made his presence felt as a novelist, but his four dramatic compositions are also well received. He wrote '*Tumna chu a hlawhtling thin*' which was published by the Social Education Wing of Education Department, Mizoram in 1976. Wrote this play at the instance of the State Social Education Officer, Mizoram, designed to impart non-formal education among the illiterate adult and induce them to the formal stream of education.

At the invitation of the Director, Community Development, Government of Mizoram, he composed '*Hmasawmna*', published by the Mizo Writers Association in 1978. It also requested him to author '*Hausak aiin Hrisel a hlu zawk*', a play on 'Nutrition and Development' in 1978, published by the Mizo writers Association in the same year. His fourth and last propaganda play '*Finna Hmahruai*' appeared in print in 1980 by the Social Education Wing, designed to inculcate some lesson to the community people. James Dokhuma depicted Christian brotherhood or fellowship in his drama 'Finna Hmahruai' in the characters of Lalthawma and Than zingi, Rochami and Thanzingi, Zosap and Lalthawma and so on.

Apart from plays, Dr. James Dokhuma has written a number of poems, novels, historical works, treatises and essays in the Mizo language '*Twang Un Hrilhfiahna*' is his painstaking compilation of a lexicon in Mizo for which he is called the '*Father of Mizo Lexicography*'.

James Dokhuma, author of Gabbatha, a talented writer in Mizo language is also an excellent orator. His scholarly and creative pursuits brought him many awards and titles. Mr. James Dokhuma awarded the quinquennial 'Mizo Academy Award' in 1984. He was also voted as the 'Best Writer' in Mizo literature in a popular poll conducted in 1984, 1986, 1988, 1991 and 1996. He was the winner of the 1st prize of state level poetical composing competition in 1986. And he was the first to be awarded '*Padma Shri*' 1985 in literature among the Mizos. The International University of California (USA) conferred him a Degree of Doctor of Philosophy in Literature in 1998. He was also the first Mizo to have been awarded '*Bhasa Samman*' It was in the year 1997, he was honoured with this much coveted '*Samman*' given by the apex Indian literary body 'The Sahitya Akademi', New Delhi. The same year, a honorary doctorate was conferred on him by the University of Altos Atlos, California, U.S.A.

Duaia a duai bik lo

Written by Liansailova, this Mizo play was included in his collection of four plays published in 1989, under the title 'Lawn a Kim'. A Character, an illiterate man, couldnot really understand the wordings of a song. Later, he was convinced that he had to learn reading and writing. After mastering the basic thing for reading and writing, he could read the book and knows the correct composition of words. Duaia therefore, reads one song from the song-book and he understands the content correctly. He is so surprised and happy to know that he is no longer an ignoramus.

F

Faki te chhung

Written by Mizo dramatist Laltluangliana Khiangte, Faki te chhung is a short piece, the main character Faki was a religious girl in the Christian way. Her friends enjoyed the wordly pleasures with all their boy-friends, but Faki abstained from all those meaningless entertainments. Like her friends, her family members were involved in Christmas eve joy. However, Faki becomes the consoler of her brother, who met with an accident that night, and all other family members and her endless endeavour led them to a good and religious footsteps. The play, in the end, focusses the joys share by the family and the complete changes of the family set-up. The play is included in the volume 'Thungai-hnawm-Thalaite tan, an anthology of essays and plays, broughtout by SCERT in 1987.

Fapa Tlanbo

Fapa Tlanbo (The Prodical Son) is a Mizo drama which draws its theme from Biblical tale. This play was *staged* by Pasena (1893-1961) in 1927.

Finna Hmahruai

Published in 1980 by the Social Education Wing. Finna Hmahruai is written by James Dokhuma. In this play the palpable design of inculcating certain lesson to the community people is almost absent. The play dramatised some important events in the lives of early Mizo believers. The preaching of one new convert

Lalthawma was strongly and sternly resisted by the chief Vanrikhuma. When Lalthama preached about Jesus, the chief caught hold of him and hit him with a fire wood and then ousted him from the village. In spite of al those oppositions and humiliation, Thanzingi agreed to accept Christianity and follow the footsteps of her cousin brother Lalthawma. The moment she believed, Thanzingi was thrown out of the house and was totally separated from her family. In those days, the new believers were mocked and humiliated by the villagers. Thanzingi had no other choice, but submitted herself to the Missionary at her earliest opportune moment. She received education and stability in her faith. The missionaries constantly inspired the new believers to preach the relatives. Therefore, Lalthwma and Thanzingi visited different villages and once again alighted in Vanrikhuma's village. Thanzinga earnestly prays for her parents, and she constntly asks God to bring and show them of his love. But it takes time. The stiff resistance from the conservative native could not stop and spil the enthusiasm of the preachers. Their constant work and prayer were heard by God, and even the most hateful chief became Christian. The very parents of Thanzingi also embraced Christianity and received their daugher with love and repentance. The village chief also recounted his hateful behaviour and his wrong doings for his citizens and asks God to forgive him and to lead him and his people in the right path to Godliness. It is a true play in which the artistic beauty can be seen even in the stage performance.

H

Harh Rawh

This Mizo play by B. Lhanhranga got published in 1989 with the sub-title 'Vengtu Drama'. The playwright depicts the contemporary society and seeks to inject his patriotic fervour so that his countrymen are aware of assimilation of any kind. The play shows that the native have been pushed to oblivion that if they do not wake up, all developmental and business activities would be controlled by others. However, with the exhortation and deeds of the two characters Hera and Hmufiaha the natives undertook a giant step for the production of indigenous goods, which ushered as industrial revolution.

Hausak aiin Hrisel a hlu zawk

The Community Development Department invited James Dokhuma to prepare a play on 'Nutrition and Development'. Therefore, he wrote his play in 1978 and was published by the Mizo Writers Association. In this play, Dokhuma could follow a proper plot for the story, with a better characterisation. Tlangrawta and his wife are the major characters. They lost their two sons because of their poor feeding, and their only daughter Rosiami also began to lose her strength and energy. However, the Nutrition Department arrived in the village. Tlangrawta took urgent advantage to avail free distributed nutrient food. After some time, Rosiami has shown quick improvement in her health and she secured first position in some competition in school. She became completely healthy and strong. When she finished her academic pursuit, she joined the Community Development Department to preach the same message that health is better than wealth.

Heroda Chawimawina

This is the first dramatic venture of Pasena, the renowned Mizo theatre personality and educationist. Pasena borrowed his theme from the Bible. A tragedy, it was staged in 1935 at Sikulpui Hall by the actors of Mission Veng. The story runs as follows:- The king Herod is being glorified by his countrymen with a song of praise "Great is the King, Herod; the greatest king of kings. Let everyone glorify his name". In honour of his everlasting greatness, his daughter, the best dancer of the age, danced around the king's throne, which really pleased the king to promise whatever she asked for. The dancer Salome, after consulting her mother asked for the head of John, the baptist. The grief striken king was helpless but to give order for the head, and John was beheaded. The play closes with a sad note.

H.K.R.

The real name of this Mizo dramatist is unknown. He used the acronym H.K.R. for his only social drama '*Khawchhak Lungpui*', printed from R.D. Press, Electric Veng, Aizawl in 1984. This detective play deals with drug abuse.

Hmasawnna

At the request of the Director, Community Development, Government of Mizoram, Dokhuma prepared this play in 1978 which was published by the Mizo Writers Association. Three different stories are linked to meet the purpose of preaching community development slogan. The story takes ignorance as a stumbling block to development and how knowledge spurs man to follow various developmental process one after another, and to make him wiser and wiser each day.

Horrible

This is a tragedy which was presented by Lalzuithanga, during a variety entertainment which he termed '*The Cosmopolitan Variety Items*', held on 17

October 1941 at Assam Rifle drill shed. In this drama, the protagonist of the play was hanged to death at very outset, then the ghost reappeared while the Doctor had been undergoing post-mortem. The strange transformation in the process was very horrifying.

I

Irish Philosopher, R.F. *see* R.F. Irish

Isua Neih Ka Duh Zawk

This is a comic drama of Lalzamliana comprising of eight characters. Here the heroine is Lalsangliani. The well to do family of the town Vanlalliana and his wife Zuithangi had only one daughter Lalsangliani. They loved her excessively and endowed with sufficient money and all other amenities were provided, while Lalsangliani is studying her B.A. degree in Shillong. As other do, she has got a boy friend called Ropuia, to whom she made beautiful promises. In the same way, Ropuia had been waiting for her completion of B.A., and the M.A., after which they planned to have a nice time together. The parents also eagerly waited for their fortunes which they expected to receive through the marriage of the boastful daughter to an enlightened son-in-law. Meanwhile, there was a great change in the life of Lalsangliani, after she received Christ as her personal Savior. She, therefore, wrote a long letter describing her new found joy and her life long ambition to serve the Lord in a distant country where the Gospel was never preached before. Her parents reacted to this letter and sent urgent telegram for her quick return. As soon as Lalsangliani reached home, her father scolded with all those painful words and threatened to disown her if she does not repent in that particular night. Left alone, Lalsangliani meditates and thinks over again her decision to serve the Lord. She loves her parents so much but the, she decides to follow the footsteps of Jesus. While singing one son — '*I Would Rather Have Jesus*' with all her heart, tears flow down her cheeks and Lalsangliani prepared her baggage. Early in the next morning she leaves her home and utters, '*Lord, how I enjoy my home, but I'll carry your Cross by leaving this house, for I have chosen you. Please be my Guide*'. When she starts for her unknown destination, the father realizes that his daughter means well, he seeks her advise and explanation of her new found Savior. The mother and cousin sister also reconcile themselves to Lalsangliani's faith.

K

Ka ha jaiga

Ka ha Jaiga, a short play written in 1962 at Tuipang which depicts the variation of the Mizo social life. This play by Lalsiama appeared in the volume 'Zonun', a collection of four dramatic pieces, published in 1988.

Kan tiam tawh si

A renowned fiction writer, Sri C. Laizawna has also tried his hand in dramatic composition. The plots starts as follows:-

Two lovers, sitting under the bush in a particular hillock outside the village exchange words of love. Over powered by sex urge, Zova pleades with Hmuni to yiel in there itself. The girl's philosophy of a real love goes to an opposite direction. She confesses that she really loves him but is determined to realize the love only after a proper ceremonious marriage according to the tenets of the Church. She is blessed by the play-wright with a rare wisdom. The boy was still studying and her plan for the marriage is landable she is ready to wait till Zova graduated. Zova then reached Aizawl to continue his works in the office in the day and attended college classes in the evening. The lonely lover had contemplated all the time about love and its effect on man. One of his co-worker could recognise that Zova was in love and feeling lonely. And he, along with others, tried to make Zova off his thoughts by teasing and discussing some other topics in a light mood. The play has double plot. In another village, Puia loved Zeli so much, but Zeli pressed him to obtain from drinking in order to share their mutual love. Puia, with all his might agreed to put off the idea and the habit of drinking. His parents also consistently gave good instruction not to drink and behave properly in the society and to study well. Putting all those pressures at the back of his mind, Puia decided to win the love of Zeli by abstaining from wine. The lovers in this sub-plot agree to marry after Puia completes his studies. The academic attaiment counts in this play because only a boy with good academic background is expected to shine in the Mizo society of the playwright's world. In Aizawl, the Chowkidar of Zova's department Rema invites Zova to have a dinner in his house. On that very night Zeli arrived from the village to continue her education in the same College. When Zova and Zeli had their first contact in that house, before any dialogue, both of them were very much impressed by facial and attitudinal considerations. In the soliloquy, it was all cleared that Zova loved the new girl from somewhere and he recollected all his pleadings and promises made to Hmuni. Zeli, in the same way surrendered herself for Zova and she no longer remembered her acceptance to become the wife of Puia in her village. Where love at first sight originated in the minds of the two lovers, the fate of their own respective friends become shaky. With the passage of time, Hmuni and Puia did not have any alternative but to rush into the spot of contact, where the disappointing lovers find themselves to be the right match. Zova and Zeli made convincing refusal for Hmuni and Puia respectively and they decided to get married. With a hasty development, Puia and Hmuni agreed to the same procedure to follow. Respective arrangement was made and the two pairs of lovers undergone marital services in the same place, to be solemnished by the same Pastor. The play ends with the entertainment caused by the unusual comic behaviour of Rema, and their happy friendly association and hasty preparation of party in the house of Rema, in Aizawl. This Mizo drama appeared in print in 1982.

Khasi Dialoch *see* Introduction

Khawchhak Lungpui

A modern detective play in Mizo, appeared in print in 1984 from R.D. Press, Electric Veng, Aizawl. The anonymous playwright only abbreviated his name as 'H.K.R.'. However it was a patriotic endeavour on the part of the playwright to try to maintain the lively social life of the Mizos. With the passage of time, the social life of the people underwent drastic change. Western civilisation and eastern civilisation had side-effects on the lives of the people. The play severely attacks the introduction and misuse of various drugs and all other evil practices, mainly flowing in from the east. Hmara and his friends Rawia and Faka had been deeply involved in the detection of the real trader or trafickers from the east. These drug-trafickers, however, would sacrifice their lives to become rich overnight. The anti-drug volunteers, Hmara and his friends, lost their lives for love of Mizoram and the Mizos. The end with the tragic death of the main character Hmara, an educated patriot from the Aizawl.

Khawiah nge

Written by Lalengmawia Ralte, a novelist, this Mizo play was published in 1988 together with his another drama 'Nausen Vang' in the publication entitled 'Christian Drama'. This play *Khawiah nge* traces the life and endeavour of the fourth wiseman from the east. Due to his late arrival, all his efforts were frustrated.

Khawlkungi

A renowned dramatist of Mizoram, Khawlkungi was born on 14th September 1927 at Aizawl. She is probably the first woman dramatist of this region. Her play '*Zawlpala Thalam Tlangah*' based on the Mizo folk-tale' Tualvungi leh Zawlpala' received both critical and popular acclaim. This fictional Christian love story was dramatised and published in 1981. The original script of fiction was also later appeared in print in 1983 with a slight change in the title as '*Zawlpala Thlan Tlang*'. In Khawlkungi play 'Zawlpala Thlan Tlangah', we see the love relationship which is a triangular one — Remi and P. Zaii and Hmingi. Their love had been shown as a love which sprang out of faith in Christ. Khawlkungi is a prolific writer who composed many dramas of which twenty are available in manuscript forms. Here two notable dramas are: - *Pangpar bawm and Monu Sual.*

Khiangte, Laltluangliana

Scholar, academician and playwright Sri Laltluangliana Khiangte was born in 1959. He hails from an learned family. His father Tlanghmingthanga was a

teacher and one of the elders of the Presbyterian Church. His grandfather the Rev. Liangkhaia happened to be the first Mizo historian and the winner of Mizo Academy Award, the first literary prize instituted in Mizoram. A doctorate, Khiangte teaches at the Pachhunga University College.

Author of the following non-dramatic books in Mizo language : Lehkhabu Ramtiam (Collection of Literary Essays: 1993), Thalai Chanchin (Histoory & Activities of Christian Youth Fellowship: 1993), Thuhlaril (Literary trends & History of Mizo Literature : 1995), Biakliana Rabawm (First Mizo Novelist & his works: 1996), Besides, he is the author of 6 booklets, Co-author of 5 books and Edited more than 10 books and Contributed over 300 articles in standard magazines. His English works include English Poetry - Study Aid : 1988 (Eng), Folktales of Mizoram : 1997 (Eng), Contributor of Poems & Articles in English in various journals.

Some notable plays of Khiangte are:-

Chanchintha Meichher (The Gospel Torch drama, 1993)

Chharmawia (written in 1989)

Duhawma leh lalfaki (written in 1909)

Fake te Chhung (Published in 1987)

Lemchan Khawvel-I (Collection of Plays, 1994)

Nu leh pa bum — mahni inbum (Published in 1987)

Pashaltha Khuangchera (Collection of Plays, 1997)

Thawmmawia (Published in 1988)

Thawmvunga (published in 1990)

Thupha ka chawi (written in 1989)

Thupha ka rawn Chawi e (Published in 1982)

Zorama (written in 1988)

Khiangte's play '*Thupha ka rawn chawi e*' written in 1982 was staged successfully in Shillong in the same year.

His magnum opus is however a critical work '*Mizo drama: origin, development and themes*', brought-out by the Cosmo Publications, New Delhi in 1993. His work deals with the genesis of Mizo theatre and its subsequent development ie, from 1912 till 1990.

Member of University Board of Under-Gradute Studies & Post Graduate Syllabus Committee for Mizo Subject. Member of Mizo Subject Expert Committee in various levels, Member of Mizo language Board (Govt. of Mizoram). Joint Secretary of Mizo Academy of Letters. Secretary of Mizo Lecturers's Academy. General Secretary of Council of All Mizoram Teachers' Association. President of ZOPPEN (Mizo Poet-Playwright-Essayist-Novelist Club).

Leader of Christian Youth Fellowship in Mizoram, North East and National level in India. As a President of North East Indian Christian Council Youth Assembly and as a Secretary of the Presbyterian Youth Fellowship of India, he had participated International & National Conferences, Seminar, Workshop, Consulatation, Training, Orientation, Convention etc. Also participated in Socio-Cultural & Literay Special Sessions in the State, Regional and National levels.

Winner of prizes in Drama & Essay Writing Competitions, Writer of School, College & other Academic reading materials, Fellow of United Writers Association of India, Awardee of Distinguished Leadership Award for Outstanding Contributions to Contemporary Society in the field of Christian Youth work and Literature by A.B.I. and National Academy of Letters/ Sahitya Akademi included His Bio-data in the latest edition of Who's Who of Indian Writers.

Dr. Laltluangliana Khiangte edited the volume 'Mizo songs and folktales', published by the Sahitya Akademi, New Delhi under the series 'Indian Literature in Tribal Languages' in 2002.

Khualbuka mi a

Khualbuka mi a (A Fool at the Inn) is a dramatic version in Mizo of a Bibal story, adapted and directed by Pasena, the harbringer of Modern Mizo dramatics.

Krismas Drama

Written by Liansailova, this Mizo play was included in his collection of four plays published in 1989 under the title 'Lawn a Kim'. In this play, the performance was based on the events of Bethlehem, when Christ Jesus was born. The new-born baby of Mary was greeted by the humble Shepherds and the three Wisemen of the east.

Krismas hria leh hre lo *see* Introduction

Krista Palai

Krista Palai (Ambassador for Christ) is a work that was first translated into Mizo by Challiana. Later, it was dramatized by Chawngzika, an outstanding theatre personality. The play was directed by him for the Aijal Theatre performers in 1934 at Sikulpui. This was the first written play with a type copy in Mizo language which was staged to raise Fund for Pawngi's Memorial Fund with an entry fee for the first time.

Kristian leh Kristian lo in biak na *see* Introduction

Kristiana Vanram Kawng Zawh

This title is reckoned as the first true modern drama in Mizoram, adapted version of the novel of the Kristiana Vanram by Chawngzika Kawng Zawh with the help of Rev. Samuel Davies. It was adapted and staged in Sikulpui and later in Dawrpui Sikul in 1938. Various theatrical devices were introduced for the first time like, disguise, lighting system, background music, scenary, stage decor and systematic dramatic presentation.

Kulikawn Young Lushai Association *see* Introduction

L

Laizawna, C.

Novelist, Short story writer Sri C. Laizawna has also tried his hand in dramatic composition. His play '*Kan tiam tawh si*', published in 1982 is based on love theme.

Lalhmingmawia, R.

A modern Mizo writer, Sri R. Lalhmingmawia has composed '*Buannel Farm*', a propaganda play that highlights the dignity of labour in the life and works of its hero 'Hminga'. This social dama appeared in print in 1987.

Lalhmuaka

Sri Lalhmuaka was born in 1915. Next to Sailo who made his name in the domain of Mizo drama is Lalhmuaka who is credited with the first anthology of dramas to be published in the language. Sailo's work 'Sangil Ingleng' is the first solo drama to have appeared in print, ie. in 1963. Lalhmuaka's collection entitled '*Lemchan Bu*' included six short dramatic pieces, out of which four are written by him. His dramatic output comprises of seven plays. Three of his plays appeared in *Drama Pasarih*, a selected Mizo plays broughtout by the Zoram Writers Club. The titles of his plays are *Lo Kir Leh Mai Rawh* (1965), *Ranthleng Mak* (1965), *A ni mai thei* (1965), *Mautam tam* (1965), *Pathian thu nung-Mizoramah* (1981), *Sumdeng Zu* (1981), *Ramthanga te chhung* (1981) etc. Lalhmuaka in his two plays, '*Lo Kir leh mai rawh*' and '*Ramthanga te chhung*, depicted the endless desires of men, which finds its expression with money. Critic Khiangte points out that Using his two protagonists Liana (Lo Kir leh mai rawh) and Ramthanga (Ramthanga te chhung) Lalhmuaka has shown to us that how money can spoil one's life and also one's family. There was a time when money gives contenment, but it will soon fly away. Love of money can be a real temptation for Christian, that money is the means but not the end in itself. Every Christian should be aware of the attractiveness of money or riches. The playwright believes that money is a means to achieve something. However, he tries to convince his readers that money can bring temporary joys and pleasures, but not the end of everything.

Lal Kailuia *see* Introduction

Lalsangzuala

A modern Mizo writer whose best known work is '*Christmas Drama*', a satirical play which came out from Churachanpur, Manipur in 1977. This is the only Mizo play got published outside the land. The play depicts the folly of the modern society.

Lalsiama, H.

An eminent litterateur in Mizo, H. Lalsiama has written in different genres of literature. He was born in 1909 at Thithek Village, the second son of Venga and his wife Suaki. Lalsiama pursued his I-A (Intermediate Arts) and thereafter he did diverse jobs as Rahsi, Forest Guard, Head Master in ME. School and Assistant Teacher in St. Pauls High School, Aizawl. After serving for nearly 47 years, he retired on the 12th March 1977.

Lalsiama took up two plays in Mizo entitled '*Pa Awk Hrawl*' and '*Ukil Hlawhtling*' which were broughtout in 1970 for the Text Book of Class VII and VIII in High School Mizo Vernacular. The author wrote his autobiography '*Hmasawnna Kawl*' which came out from the State Social Education Wing, Aizawl in 1979. The academician, scholar and writer Sri H. Lalsiama died in the year 1983.

Lalsiamthanga

An academician, playwright and an able translator, Sri C. Lalsiamthanga is a college teacher by profession who translated the famous Greek classical drama '*Oedipus the King*' of Sophocles into Mizo in 1983. In 1986 came out his original '*Diktea Vahvaihna*' in a forceful social drama that ends with a tragic note.

Lalzamliana

Lalzamliana penned a comic play in Mizo entitled '*Isua Neih Ka Duh Zawk*' This is a brilliantly portrayed family saga which included in the volume '*Lemchan Bu*' compiled by Lalhmuaka and printed at the Modern Printing Pres, Aizawl in 1965.

Lalzuithanga *see* Introduction

Lawn a Kim

Written by Liansailova, this play was included in his collection of four plays, published in 1989. The title of the book also bears the play's name. This is a comedy which contains a character named Rama who came to Aizawl in search of his father, after the death of his mother. With the advice of another man from a village, Rama contacted one prominent citizen, Rina, and stayed in his house. Without openly announcing his real purpose, Rama willingly tackled every work ahead of him. He developed a close intimacy with the daughter of Rina named Makhumi. Makhumi however, could not treat Rama as a mere male servant in the house. She was quite impressed by Rama and his behaviour. She therefore, began to act like a lover, speaking in a softer manner and meaningful ways. Rama was reluctant to respond as it should be, for fear of mission his main purpose. As the investigation had turned out to be in a most unexpected way, Rina realised that he was the real father of Rama, but married for the second time in Aizawl. Such a shocking news was unbearable for Makhumi, who already fallen in love with Rama. It was, nevertheless disclosed that Makhumi was the adopted daughter in the family, and the parents allowed to continue their love as usual to make themselves husband and wife. The wedding was organised and the new family lived happily.

Lhanhranga, B.

B. Lhanhranga's best known Mizo drama is '*Harh Rawh: vengtu drama*' which was broughtout in 1989. It depicts the contemporary Indian society and seeks to inject his patriotic fervour into it.

Liandova te unau

This is a well known drama which is based on a Mizo folk tale. The play was written, directed and acted by Lalkailuia, the son of Reiek village chief. It was enacted in 1935 at Assam Rifle Drill shed.

Liandova Te Unau

This well known Mizo drama of Lalthangfala Sailo goes like this:- The father of Liandova and Tuaisiala now knows that he is dying. Liandova and his mother look after the ailing father of the house, in a *Charchhawn* locality of a particular Mizo Village. Liandova constantly asks his father to keep on breathing and live with them longer still. But the father pronounces his last words to his wife, exhorting her not to lose faith but to go on courageously, and to his sons, not to worry anything about their mother. The mother, thereafter, promises loyalty to her husband not to get married again, but look after their sons properly till herself is dead. The grand old woman Pi Fangi rejoices to her such a beautiful promises made by the mother... So, the father dies. However, a short while after the death of her husband, Liandova's mother embraces Thangseia for her husband and eloped with him, while Liandova and Tuaisiala were crying knowing that they are really helpless to convince her and stay together. They do not have any social status but the villagers put them to the lowest, poorest of the poors. They do not enjoy their share and are not given any due consideration in the society. But the virtue in Liandova's character finds its way in its own part. King Lersia becomes the unexpected guest of the two brothers one day. As a result of their warm welcome and petty consideration, Lersia stretches out his helping hands for the two brothers. Hence they are prospering each day, and becoming one of the richest families in the Village. Such undiscovered wealth is secretly recognised by the princes through Pi Fangi, and then, Tuaichawngi agrees to become the wife of a disguised poor man, Liandova and crowns him in the selection ceremony. The new couples proved to be a real family and it ends with the Grand *Khuangchawi* festival. The family member-Liandova, Tuaichawngi, Tuaisiala and also Pi Fangi are all on the big drum and the people carry them in the steer with full ornamentation and honour.

Liansailova

A Mizo playwright of repute, Liansailova was born in 1949. He is son of Mr. Vana of Mission Vengthlang, now working as Librarian after obtaining his Bachelor's Degree in Arts. Liansailova dramatic output comprises of many plays of which '*Zovi te Chhung*' bagged him an award. The play is available in cyclo style forms. His book '*Lawn a Kim*'' which appeared in 1989 comprises of his four plays namely, *Lawn a Kim, Duaia a duai biklo, Krismas Drama, Tlai ngailo Pathian* etc.

Lo Kir Leh mai Rawh

This is one of the six short plays included in the volume '*Lemchan Bu*'. 'Lo Kir Lehmai Rawh' is penned by Lalhmuaka. Three leading characters of the play are Liana (the protagonist), his elder brother Hminga and their father Pa of Chawnghawih village. One day when the Father gives the day's work instruction to the two brothers, Hminga responds fairly as usual, whereas Liana murmurs for their continuous hard work with no enjoyment. From that day Liana's rebellious attitude towards his father's administration bursts. The heavy daily routine work renews his anger each day. He, therefore asked his father to give all his share of the estate. He puts forward a heavy pressure so that he can go away with his share to enjoy the world. The father tries his best effort to cool down Liana's dream of luxurious life, but the destined son collects, his share and leaves the house.... The father thereafter reaffirms his real love for him while giving his money, and asks him to live circumspectly with tears in his eyes and a broken heart, the father watches his younger son leaving his house for a distant country. Living luxuriously with a crowd of friends, Liana squanders all his wealth till he became empty handed. There was a great famine in that land and Liana began to beg for his living. He looked after pigs to earn his food for no one gave him anything. When he came to his senses, he decided to go back to his father and to work as one of the hired man in his father's house. While he was still a long way off the house, the father saw him and was filled with joy and compassion for him. He quickly ran to his son and threw his arms around him and asked him, '*Taite*, are you alright? How are you? Tired? How happy I am'! The runaway son asked forgiveness while the father commanded his servants to bring all good clothings for him, and to kill the fattened calf for the feast of celebration. This makes the older son Hminga quite angry and he refused to go home as a sign of protest. But the father pleaded by asserting him that all his belongings were his and to make himself happy for his lost brother is found and the dead brother is alive again. So, they began to live as a happy family.

M

Mautam tam

Written by Lalhmuaka, the great famine of 1960-1961 and its effect on the people is the target of this play. The playwright focusses a typical Mizo life in a famine hit areas of Mizoram. The play got published in 1965.

Mene, Mene Tekel Upharsin

This is the short dramatic piece by Lalsiama. *Mene, Mene Tekel Upharsin* was written in 1970 tells how Daniel explained, the dream of the King. This is the last drama of the volume 'Zonun' that comprises of four playlets, published in 1988.

Mission Veng Young Lushai Association *see* Introduction

Mizoram Sande Sikul intan dan leh a than zel dan

A Mizo drama authored by C. Sangzuala (b. 1937). The drama is devoid of unity of time, place and action, still an important addition to the Mizo dramatic literature which tells about the origin and growth of Sunday School in Mizoram, from 1894 to 1975. The zeal of the missionaries were clearly seen in the play. They believed that this can be the best and most effective way of preaching the Gospel among the Mizos. Such a quick and systematic progress may not be found anywhere except in Mizoram. Starting with two to three pupils in 1894, the Sunday

School enrolment reached over one lakh in 1975. The great enthusiasm shown by the people (in fact 43 characters in this drama) of Mizoram was the very foundation of Mizo Sunday School Union, as it really was in the drama. The missionaries and the early church leaders were the characters of the play, with no specific hero or heroine.

Monu Sual

Modern Mizo drama, penned by Khawlkungi in 1982. The plot starts with a rich bachelor, who had fallen in love with a poor girl of slum dweller. The rich parents were reluctant at the beginning for fear of that she would not fit into the family. But the pressure from the son resulted that the poor girl was accepted as the bride in the family. Since then, the family atmosphere had been twisted to another direction. The mother died and the rich old father was badly treated and ousted from the house. The removal of the old made the bride so happy now. But the grandson could not bear the whole idea and brought the old man back in the house. The action and argument of the grandson made his parents realise their shameful act of pushing the old man out. The plays ends with the reconciliation in the family. And the grandson plays the peace-making role which the playwrights employs as the torch bearer of justice and love. The play available in manuscript from, bagged the 1st Prize in State Level Drama Competition in 1982.

N

Naamana

Naamana is a Mizo play written in 1950 by the famous theatre person Chawngzika that is based on a Biblical story.

Nausen Vang

This play was published by the novelist Lalengmawia Ralte (b. 1947) which got published in 1988. This Mizo play highlights some events on the night when Jesus was born in Bethlehem. The Shepherds and the three Wisemen from the east sought for the new-born king in the King Herod's palace. Hence, the King Herod tried his best to find out the new-born king, so that he could ironically greet him in his own way. The tragic result was, each male-born child below two years was all killed because of that very new-born child called Jesus.

Nu leh pa bum - mahni inbum

This is one of the published plays of Laltluangliana Khiangte (b. 1959). It deals with the lives of contemporary Mizo society, in which parents were often deceived by their children. This play deals with the life of one young girl who spent her life and money luxuriously in the town, neglecting her studies. After sometimes, she found herself to be the most unfortunate girl by conceiving a child. The play ends with the moral tone of the heroine that 'to deceive parents is to deceive self'. The drama was published by SCERT in 1987.

O

Oedipus

Sophocles Greek drama Oedipus has been translated by the playwright and academician Sri C. Lalsiamthinga into Mizo, available only in manuscript form.

P

Pa Awk Hrawl

This drama was published in 1970, composed by Lalsiama for the Text Book in High School Mizo Vernacular. The gist of this Mizo drama written in modern times is given below:- The richest family in the village Neihkunga and his family used to help the needy and spent their money lavishly for the poorer section of the society. In spite of that the generous couple Neihkunga and Malsawmi had been suffering from a serious ailment and they were in their death-bed. Their two children Laltawig, a boy of six years old and Thiangkungi, a girl of four years, did not exactly know the condition of the parents. The parents, knowing that both of them were about to die, think over how their children would lead a life after death. Pensive mood and careful consideration made them realise that it would be best to leave them in the care of Thatvunga, the younger brother of Neihkunga. They therefore informed the matters to Thatvunga of the Pherzawl village. In the meantime, Neihkunga and Malsawmi died and Thatvunga took over the whole charge of looking after the household and the two children. Thatvunga, sold off whatever is possible, then he returned to his own village to support Laltawia and Riangkungi. His wife Chalchani was overjoyed to see such a huge amount of money and decided to oppress her neighbour with those wealth. However, when she came to know about the messages and testament of will put forward by the dead father, Chalchani broke out with anger and disgust. She then proposed for the dismissal of the boy and the daughter. Accepting her suggestion, Thatvunga led the two kids into the thick jungle and left them there to die. Nevertheless,

Thatvunga and Chalchani could not enjoy their wild luxurious lives for long. Before the expiry of even a year, all their domesticated animals were eaten up by a roaring tiger and they themselves died one after another.

Pangpar bawm

A dramatic adaptation of the story of the Basket of Flower by C. Schmith, the play is about the life of a faithful young maid Mari, and her problems in the process. The play closes with virtue rewarded and vice punished. Played by the local Christian Yough Association (KTP), it won wide applause, the play is available in manuscript form, penned by Khawlkungi.

Pasena *see* Introduction

Pathian thu nung-Mizoramah

This play first appeared in 1981 edition of the *Zoram Writers' Club* series-5 called *Drama Pasarih*. Three of the seven plays of this book are written by Lalhmuaka of *Zotlang* village. *Pathian thu nung-Mizoram-ah* is a historical short play, which depicts the fertility ritual for good harvest of the ancient Mizo Religion and the early life of new believers who suffer stern resistance from their chiefs. being cast out of their villages, they gathered in a Christian village called *Saitual*, there the enlightened chief Dorawta had welcomed every Christian to profess their faith freely.

Pastor Leh Zurui

Mizo drama by Lalsiama was written in 1986. *Pastor leh Zurui* deals with the life of a drunkard and the Pastor's invitation to visit at least some congregational services. The drunkard dies when the Pastor revisits him, saying that it was too late. It appeared in the volume 'Zonun', broughtout in 1988, containing three more playlets by the author.

Princess Pocahontas

This drama is ascribed to Chawngzika, an eminent Mizo playwright and dramatist. The story is adapted from the lives of some Red Indian, which the writer had heard from some missionary. A comedy, it depicts the personal life of the Princess, who systematically rescued the white captive, Sap tlangval from her fellow red Indian warriors just before the white man was sacrified to their gods and goddesses. The play bagged the first prize at the Zosiami Cup Drama Competition held on the 3rd October, 1940.

R

Rabboni

This drama is Mizo was penned by Chawngzika, a wellknown theatre personality in 1948. The play borrows its plot from a Biblical story. It was staged under the supervision of the dramatist himself.

Ralte, Lalengmawia

Novelist per excellence, Lalengmawia Ralte was born at Biate village in 1947. This modern writer has also composed many dramas in Mizo, but most of them are available in manuscript forms. However his two praiseworthy dramas published so far are:- '*Nausen Vang and Khawiah nge*', broughtout jointly in a book entitled '*Christmas Drama*' in 1988.

Ramthanga te chhung

In this Mizo drama, the playwright presented more than ten characters which revolve around the central figure *Ramthanga*. The title of the play itself suggests 'the family of Ramthanga'. The plot goes like this: Ramthanga has been employed as LDA (Lower Divisional Assistant) in the Department of Supply & Transport, Mizoram. Due to his habit of heavy drinking. Ramthanga could not carry out his routine work in the Office, but spent most of his time in a small home made wine cottage. In a particular month, he paid the loan share of his wages (Rs.300/- out of Rs.450/-) to the wine seller Mrs. Vungi, and he could hardly gave Rs.50/- to his wife Rokimi for the management of the whole family. When Rokimi argued about it, the father became more angry not to listen to her Ramthanga made no sign of improvement in his duty and after a fair warning, the Director had no other alternative but to discharge him from his service. Ramthanga as he proposed earlier, met the Minister in charge to reinstate him in the post, but the Minister who never drink anymore could not act folishly against the Department executive's fair deal. There is no alternative, the mother decided to search for a daily labout work for feeding their children. A sad note of the mother, 'Oh, you drank the whole family', hiding her face as a sign of woe. This play is written by the prolific playwright Lalhmuaka, published in 1981.

Ransa Khawmpui

Ransa Khawmpui (Animal's Conference) is an original dramatic piece in Mizo language, penned by Pasena (1893-1961). The play vehementhy protests the use and drinking of wine in the society, which is the source of all evils. This social drama was staged by the playwright in 1929.

Ranthleng Mak

Published in 1965, the play is composed by Lalhmuaka. In this play in Mizo, the story outlined about the biblical account of the wonderful manger, in which the expected new born baby who would ruled the world was born. The new baby, Jesus the son of Joseph and Mary was greeted by a distant wisemen of the east and some shepherds of the nearby field. So, also King Heroda tried to greet the new born King by killing all those make babies under two years. But the Lord protected Jesus, his own son.

R.F. Irish Philosopher

This Mizo writer uses his nom de plum 'R.F. Irish Philosopher'. His chief dramatic work is '*Romeo & Juliet Part-II*', broughtout by Arbee Publication in 1989.

Romeo and Juliet Part-II

Written by R.F. Irish Philosopher was published in 1989 from Arbee Publication. The story relates the life of Romeo's previous girl friend and the relation of Mantague and Capulet after the death of Romeo and Juliet, especially in the town of Verona.

Rorelna

Rorelna (court) is social drama in the Mizo language, authored by Pasena (1893-1961). This original piece revolves around a bad boy who was punished by the court. It further shows the reward of sin and its effect in the family. The play was staged by the dramatist in 1933.

The Royal Robes

This Mizo drama was composed by Chawngzika in 1948 which he himself directed. This drama draws its theme from a Biblical story.

S

Saibela, K.

This Mizo dramatist was born in 1935, the son of Tlangkhuma of Biate village. After pursuing his Bachelor's degree in Arts, he joined the church's ministry for full time engagement as Manager of the Bookroom, under the framework of the Presbyterian church of Mizoram. He is, today, one of the Church's elders of Republic locality of Aizawl. In the field of literature, K. Saibela carved out a path for himself as a fiction writer. He has also tried his hand in playwriting and has written many short pieces. His two well-known dramas namely '*Chhuraleh Naa*' and '*Thu a Tawp e Lumam*' appeared in the collection entitled '*Drama Pasarih*', broughtout by the Zoram Writers 'Club' in 1981.

Saikuti Lungzeh

This drama of Sethuama was broughtout in 1975, available in Mizo Zia Rang. It revolves around the Mizo poetess Saikuti who had *tucked* one small stone in a particular branching edge of tree in the gate way of *Thingsai* village. The play simply depicts how this stone is named as Saikuti lungzeh.

Sailo, Lalthangfala

A wellknown playwright, Sri Lalthangfala Sailo was born in 1933 at W. Lungdar, Mizoram. He was the son of Dohleia, the chief of the Lungdar village. L.F. Sailo obtained his Bachelor's degree from the St. Xavier's College at Kolkata in 1959. Thereafter, he took up the teaching job at the St. Paul's High School, Aizawl as Assistant Teacher in 1959. It was in this year that he tried his hand in dramatic composition and wrote a tragi-comedy entitled '*Sangi Inleng*' which was put on board in October 1959 at MZI Hla Kutpui held at Mizo High School, Aizawl. This play later came out in 1963, printed from R. Vanlawma Press, Republic Veng Aizawl. Its second edition was brought out in 1969. *His was the first play to be published in Mizo language*. His second venture a comedy in five acts was based on one of the most popular folk-stories of the land. A well written play '*Liandova Te Unau*' was published in 1969 from Gilgul Press, Kulikawn. Its fourth edition appeared in print in 1988. Sailo admits that his play '*Sangi Inleng*' is designed to be a tragedy but which has been modified to be a comedy or some calls it a tragi-comedy. He had simply modified the last scene, with the advice of his colleague, who wanted the play to be comedy being the playwright's maiden attempt. Such an unforseen changed made the play a tragi-comedy other than a pure tragedy or a pure comedy.

Sailo, Lalthangfala *see also* Introduction

Sailoka

Sailoka is the Mizo version of William Shakespeare's drama '*The Merchant of Venice*'. This is the first Shakespearean play acted in Mizoram in 1929 at Sikulpui Hall, the popular name for Boys' Middle English School at Mission Veng, Aizawl. It was Pasena, the pioneer of Mizo dramatics who had helped Chuanthuama to produce this play. Sangi Inleng

Sangi Inleng

This is the first published play in Mizo, written by Lalthangfala Sailo broughtout in 1963. This play was earlier presented at MZI Hla Kutpui held at Mizo High School Aizawl during Musical Festival. The plot of this famous Mizo drama runs as follows:- It is in Kanghmung Village, the Guest Speaker preaches in the Church and a good sound of singing is heard from Ngura's house. While Ngura and his wife Thangi are chatting by the Fire-side, two mediators Bela and Kunga enter to seek the favour of Sangi for Hranga, the only son of the well-to-do family of the Village Ngura gives a green signal and asks the mediators to come again for a final decision. Meanwhile Thangi wants to make final agreement there and there. She, therefore put forward a strong pressure to Sangi, to accept Hranga the love child of a family as husband. When Sangi hears it, she protests because Hranga as 'old by birth, funny smile, one who plays clumsy whisling with mouth'.... 'Ghost, Demon, that Evil-Spirit? If you want, marry him'. However, her mother keeps on busy to force Sangi to marry Hranga and she continues Sangi to accept him for various other considerations than love. But Sangi said she will not surrender herself for Hranga, till her death and waited for the intervention of her love Muana and asks him to do the best he can for their re-union. After a long time the fixed date arrives, but Sangi is not yet prepared. She writes her last letter for Muana disclosing her love once more and telling him that her love for him will live forever. Her friend Mawii, despatches the last letter to Muana in the last hour of the wedding day. Knowing all the circumstances, Mawii asks Muana to act as quick as possible and move down to the Cave, where the wounded Tiger chased Sangi as his easy prey. However, Muana arrives in time to the spot, to kill the tiger thereby to save her life. When Sangi regains consciousness Ngura readily offers Sangi to her real lover Muana, to live in peace for the rest of their lives.

Sangzuala, C

Journalist and writer Sri S. Sangzuala was born on 25th May 1937. He earned his Bachelor of Divinity examination and is today one of the elders of Chaltlang Presbyterian Church in Aizawl. He is known Chiefly for his editorship of the Presbyterian Church's monthly Christian magazine '*Kristian Tlangu*'.

In the field of creative writing, he authored a play that deals with the genesis and growth of Sunday School in Mizoram, that is, from 1894 to 1975. The manuscript of the play which he titled '*Mizoram Sande Sikul intan dan leh a than zel dan*' was completed on 26th October 1977 and published in the anothology '*Drama Pasarih*' broughtout, bu the Zoram Writers' Club in 1981.

Sap mi Khual leh Tawng let ling tu *see* Introduction

Sap putar leh Mosolman putar lem in biak na *see* Introduction

Selthuama

Born in 1910, Selthuama's chief dramatic composition in Mizo is '*Saikuti Lungzeh*' which appeared in print in 1975 was found in Mizo Zia Rang. The Mizo poetess Saikuti had tucked one small stone in a particular branching edge of tree in the gate way of Thingsai village. The drama shows how this stone is named as 'Saikuti lungzeh'. This playwright died in 1971.

A Setana a zam ta

Mizo drama composed by Lalsiama, *A Setana a zam ta*, written in 1970 at Baktawng, is about a rich men's son who decided to follow Jesus, leaving aside all those treasures and pleasures. When the man really dedicated his life to Jesus, his old master, Satan was immediately desperate and was defeated by the power of God. The play appeared in the volume '*Zonun*', an anthology of four playlets, broughtout in 1988.

Shakespearean Drama *see* Sailoka

Sikul pui

This refers to the Boy's Middle English School, Mission Veng in Aizawl where dramatic performances were held in earlier time.

The Star of Christmas

Written in 1950, this drama in Mizo by Chawgzika draws its theme from a Biblical story. The play was staged in the land under his own guidance. The play portrays one kind of drinking festival in a typical Mizo society. The chief and his counsellors, with the help of some more prominent citizens of the village convene such a special meet, in which the *Tlangval tlawmngai ber*, the most perfect gentleman of the village will be awarded *Nopui*, a special Wine Cup and only after that the rest of the people will drink in an ordinary Cup called *Noleng*.

T

Thawmmawia

This is the published play of Laltluangliana Khiangte, appeared in print in 1988 during the Golden Jubilee *Souvenir* of Lungpho YMA. The conflict of good angel and bad angel in the mind of Thawmmawia during the happy occasion of Winter festival was the main content of this play. A morality play, it was however written way back in 1984.

Thawmvunga

Authored by the prolific writer in Mizo, Sri Laltlungliana Khiangte, this is a short drama published in 1990. The play centres on the hero, Thawmvunga who proves himself to be an extraordinary *pasaltha*, warrior by helping the king against the assault of his enemy counterpart. The heroic intervention of Thawmvunga amidst the confrontation between the two chiefs, Vuttaia and Lalpuithanga has been unsurpassed by any bravery act in the history. The play ends with the return of the hero and his subsequent marriage with the princess. This is a historical drama which appeared in the Annual Magazine of Mizo Students' Union, Shillong entitled 'Hnam Lungphum'.

Thu a Tawp Lumam

A well received modern Mizo drama written by K. Saibela (b. 1935) in 1980 and published a year latter is an award winning work comprising of massive

twenty-six characters in the play with Zoduhawma, who latter pursued his M.Sc. degree and becomes an important Officer is the main character in the play. Zoduhawma was a poor boy, who could not afford to obtain good clothes, and meet most expenses during his School days. He worked hard in his studies though looked down upon by classmates coming from well-to-do family. After sometimes some of his friends had to discontinue their education because they fell into bad habits. By this time Zoduhawma passed M.Sc. and joined Government service. He remembered his friends, especially Rally, who came to seek for his help for survival. Zoduhawma kept up his warm friendship and alloted work to Rally and his son under his department. Rally readily accepted the offer. A short while after, Rally failed to maintain discipline and acted as carefree lazy authoritarian. Zoduhawma reprimands him for his wayward style of life and then, terminates Rally from his service. The dramatist clarifies the plot of this drama aims at depicting "Character makes fate'.

Thuhriltu *see* Introduction

Tinreng daih Khawl

Tinreng daih Khawl (Robot or a machine with brain) is a original Mizo drama composed by Pasena, the father of modern Mizo dramatics. The play was directed by the playwright in 1928. The play was designed to preach moral principle for day to day living.

Tlai ngailo Pathian

Written by Liansailova, this Mizo play was included in his collection of four plays published in 1989 under the title 'Lawn a Kim'. In this play, the two lovers Liana and Mawii were prepared to get married. Meanwhile, the whole plain was hattered by the intervention of Miss Rovi, who accused the groom to be Liana as an agent of her pregnancy. This made the parents of Mawii quite angry enough to cancel the proposal. But the confession of Bela to the effect that he was the cause of pregnancy solved the problem. Then, the parents change their mind and allow the lovers to unite.

Tualvungi and Zawlpala

This is the first romanic drama written in Mizo language by Lalkailuia, the son of Reiek village chief. This is also the first love story ever being staged in the state. Directed by Lalkailuia himself at Assam Rifle Drill Shed in 1935, the play borrows its plot from one of the popular love stories of the Mizo folk repertoire.

Tumna chu a hlawhtling thin

Published in 1976, this play is composed by James Dokhuma. The play is designed in such a way that the illiterate adult may be imparted with non-formal education and to lead them formal stream of education. One prominent character *Chhinga* made a mistake when he presumed by extempore the content of one letter, which he read for the grand old woman. But when he, after learning alphabets became accustomed with the method of reading and writing he realised his previous awkward behaviour. He himself admitted that 'will conquers' and illiterate like him becomes literate. The play was written in response to the invitation of the State Social Education Officer, Mizoram.

U

Ukil Hlawhtling

This play was first published in 1970 for the Text Book in High School Mizo Vernacular, authored by Lal Siama. The title of the play literally denotes '*A Successful Lawyer*'. The theme of this play goes like this: Zirliana, a successful lawyer finds it a tough time even to earn a daily living. His wife Lalawti has been complaining about her worn out clothes and all other old fashioned instruments and facilities. Zirliana agrees that new ways and means of acquiring something must be devised now. Thereafter, he set out to the main market and visited a rich cloth merchant. After a fair deal, Zirliana agreed to take six meters of suit piece at the rate of Rs. 24/- per meter. The merchant Sumparlawma readily cut the required cloth material and handed it over to him. Zirliana did not have ready money to pay, but suggested that he will give the money after an hour in his residence. Further, he informed Sumparlawma that he will be offered a nice lunch cake by his wife, and left for home. Soon after Sumparlawma closed his shop to proceed to Zirliana's house. Meanwhile, another debtor Lianbela interrupted. Sumparlawma refused to see him, but directed him to meet the Police and face the Court. When Sumparlawma reached Zirliana's house, he was told by the wife not to speak loudly lest the voice disturb the mental illness of her husband. Standing amazed, Sumparlawma demanded the money from them. The wife looked so surprised and claimed that her husband never go out, but sleeps all the time. The embarrassed merchant left the house. The wife, the congratualated Zirliana for his tactic of getting a valuable material. A short while after, Lianbela came to meet Zirliana for his legal help. Zirliana jumped off from his bed quickly and met Lianbela casually. Lianbela agreed to pay Rs. 500/- if he is acquitted which Zirliana accepted on the ground that Lianbela was a poor shepherd. So, they appeared together before the judge. Sumparlawma accused Lianbela for stealing his sheep. Then, Zirliana defended Lianbela maintaining that Suparlawma never paid his wages and with no other alternative but to steal a sheep. As soon as Sumparlawma saw his debtor Zirliana, he mentioned his clothes and demanded for the price. This confused the judge greatly. Besides, Sumparlawma could not express his charge in a proper way for his mixed up his anger towards Lianbela and Zirliana. He continuously outer strange and disconnected outburst before the court. On the other side, Lianbela could only utter the bleating sound of a sheep. Methodically, the lawyer called Sumparlawma as a madcap and Lianbela as a man half lived among man. The confused judge therefore dismissed the case without punishing either party. The successful lawyer then asked Lianbela to give him Rs. 500/- for his legal aid but Lianbela was wise enough to keep on producing the bleating expression as taught by Zirliana himself. Zirliana could not force him to pay the money for Lianbela knew well that the judge would not like to listen to his parrot like talking any more. With this ends the lawyers legal adventures.

W

Wolf Club *see* Introduction

Z

Zawlpala Thalan Tlangah

Written by Khawlkungi (b. 1927), this play was published in 1981, a dramatisation of the Christian love story, culled from a folk tale. Khawlkungi's heroine Vanlalremi's father was buried in the very hill where the legend suggests Zawlpala' corpse was laid. Hence the title of this play arised. The story begins with the heroine herself. Vanlalremi looked after her dying father. The father, Upa Liana, knowing that he was dying any moment instructed and consoled his only daughter. He read the Bible, and refused to eåt anything. He assured her that God will be with her throughout her life. He added that Remi should maintain her innocence and chastity and asked her not to get married to any man who used to drink wine. Vanlalremi eagerly accepted her father's last words and began to cry when the ailing father passed away. A young drunkard from the village well to do family Lalmuana stepped in, while Remi was quite busy in arranging things in the house. Lalmuana, who was attracted to Remi's beauty found the convenient time to ask Remi's favour and began to embrace and to sleep with her. The bereaved Remi hit him with the nearby Iron and escaped to tell the neighbours of the fate of her father and of the evil intention of the youngman. Vanlalremi was all alone after father's death. She was then taken to her maternal uncle Ruala, who was addicted to drinking. Remi was badly treated and life became unbearable in the house. Besides, Ruala proposed that Remi should marry Lalmuana, so that he could get hold of Lalmuana's double-barelled breach-loading gun. Remi vehemently protested, but had no other choice but to flee from her uncle. With the help of

Hmingthangi, who later became as her true friend, Remi was taken to one missionary of Aizawl called Pi Zail (Miss Katie Hughes). In the lady missionary's house Remi learned stitching, sewing, and all other domestic works including reading and writing under the guidance of the missionary. Not long after she had adjusted herself with a new life, Vanlalremi met Malsawma, a Mission School teacher and leader of the Boys Scout. With the advice of Pi Zail, Remi decided to go to Reiek village in serch of her maternal uncle Ranga. On the very same day, Malsawma sailed to Reiek but stung by a green ovoviviparous snake, while entering the old farm hut. Remi found that it was Malsawma, who slept in the corner with pain. She therefore looked after him and asked him to stay in her maternal uncle's house for the time being in Reiek. Malsawma assumed the Headmaster Office in Reiek, and he became deeply in love with Remi. Unconsciously, Remi had already developed a strong attraction to Malsawma. When the two lover exchanged their feelings and deep regards for each other, they developed pure romantic love which led to a secret engagement. In Reiek village there was another young girl Lalkhawthangi who had tried her best shamelessly to win the love of Malsawma. But Malsawma refused to show any favour. Just to vex Malsawma, she had affairs with Naik Vanthanga and unfortunately she conceived while Vanthanga availed leave in Reiek. Her brother Lalhluna blindly accused Malsawma as her partner without ascertaining from Lali. Malsawma won the case in village court, but the Mission authority had to take action against him. However, the suspension from Middle School Headmaster made him join Army as Indian Commissioned Officer. After the training days were over, he came out to Mizoram as 2nd, Lieutenant, availing leave, and married the same lover Remi who had faithfully waited for him. They were blessed with a son and lived a happy married life. The play ends with the climax of their love, when the couple made a function of memorial stone erection on the grave of Remi's father at *Zawlpala Thlan tlangah*, a particular hillock in Phulpui.

Zoluti an man

This is the title of the Mizo play, written by Lalsiama that got published in 1987. It is a historical play about a Mizo chief Bengkhuaia who attacked Alexandrapur Tea Estate, killing Winchester and capturing his daughter Mary

Winchester, *Zoluti* Mary had been kept in Sailam for a year, but the British Expeditioner took her back. From that story, the Arthington Mission reached the drama Mizoram to preach the Gospel. And his agent set their feet on January 11, 1994, at Aizawl.

Zosiami Cup Drama Competition *see under* Introduction and Chawngzika

References

Khiangte, Laltluangliana. Mizo drama : origin, development and themes. — New Delhi : Cosmo Publications, 1993.

Lianhmingthanga. 'Kum 1912 Kristmas hman dan'. *Mizo leh Vai Chan* chinbu [official Monthly journal of Superintendent, Lushai Hills, Aizawl]; January 1913; Pp.8-12.

Young Lushai Association Thubelh. *Kristiam Tlangau* [Monthly Christian Journal of the Presbyterian Church of Mizoram (Aizaw)]; October 1940; p. 81.

Zosiami Cup Drama Competition Report *Kristian Tlangau Thubelh*; October 1940; Pp. 81-82.

X

NAGAMESE

Naga Tribes live in four contiguous different administrative units of Nagaland, Manipur, Assam and Arunachal Pradesh. There are about two dozen Naga Tribes spread over these four administrative units such as Angami, Ao, Lotha, Sema, Cheksesang, Maring, Zeliangroung and Tangkhul etc.

The Angami Naga language is slowly developing into a literary language. The role of Ura Academy, Kohima, under the guidance of Surhozelia Angami in developing this language is praiseworthy. His collection of stories '*Netaya*' is the first creative literary publication in this language.

Ao is another language spoken by over 84 thousand Ao people of Nagaland. It is also the language of elite in the sense that a great number of Government servants are Aos and many of them hold top posts. Aos being the pioneer in Christianity and education, they started precaching the religion among other tribes. Not only the Ao Baptist Christian Association organised the Christian activity among others but also it was that organisation which brought out Bible in other tribal languages too.

But it is the Nagamese that has made much headway among the less educated people. It became popular, and practically the second State language after English, the official language of the State since 1964. Even the Kohima Station of All India Radio broadcast programmes in Nagamese.

Each of them has got its distinct identity of language, dress, culture and physical feature. Inspite of all the differences they are all known by the generic term 'Naga' and they all consider themselves Naga and it is more a matter of sentimental feeling of oneness than any real unity, ie, a unity in diversity. There are therefore different tribes who are nowadays known by the common name Naga, originaly they did not have any generic term for the whole of the race. Nagamese is by far the most effective *lingua franca* of this state. Nagamese is nothing but broken Assamese as spoken by the Nagas, that is Naga-Assamese, and shortened form of it is Nagamese. The term Nagamese has come into use not long ago but from the 60s of this century though the language, that is broken Assamese, was in use for long, say many centuries, probably from the earliest time of Ahom-Naga contact, that is 13th century.

Sri R. Luikham aptly said that the Nagas were hitherto known to the civilized world as naked head hunters and savages. It is admitted fact that once the obnoxious practice of head hunting was part of their life. This was the time when they were fighting among themselves for supremacy and suzerainty over one another. Although these were cases of hunting during the British regime, this practice was much more prevalent before the British fully established their rule over the Nagas in 1866. It was only through ceaseless efforts of the pioneer missionaries from 1842 onwards that Christianity was introduced in North East India and it was only Christianity that tamed the Tribals.

There are numerous legends as to why the Nagas do not have any old written history or ancient literature of their own. Naga folk-songs and folk-tales have been treasured in the memory of these tribes and are being cascaded down from generation to generation.

The present Nagaland, the then Naga Hills came under British administration in 1876, and so was opened to modern civilisation. It is said that some evangelists had gone to Ao area to preach the gospel on earlier occasions, it was only in 1876 that Rev. Clark established his headquarters at Malungyimchen and later at Impur to carry on permament evangelical work. In the case of Angami area, it was Rev. Rivenburg who came to communicate the Good News to them in 1881. Similarly, it was in 1896 that Rev. Peltigrew came to Ukhrul to spread the gospel amongs the Tangkhul Nagas. It was through this three-pronged evangelical initiatiative that Christianity gradually spread to all Naga areas of the erstwhile Naga Hills, Manipur, Assam etc. Although the Central Government and respective State Governments have taken steps towards the overall development of the Tribals, it is an established fact that none had contributed as such to the ushering in of the new era of enlightenment as the foreign pioneering missionaries had done. It is Christianity which brought them from darkness to light. The blessings of modern education has brightened their life. However the cultural locate of the Nagas have greatly been damaged by their conversion. Among many other aspects some downright casualities are their socio-cultural milieu, prominant features of their literature, songs, artistry exquisite handicrafts and performing arts.

Christian hymns have taken place of the traditional songs. Dancing feats were discouraged by the missionaries. But such traditional songs and dances have been an indispensable part of the Nagas. Dances have a place in their festivals and also on ordinary occasions forming a part of their recreation. There are a number of dances and each with a different name. All these dances are performed with the accompaniment of songs and music, using dramas and cymbals. Songs comprise of legendary songs, warsongs, dancing songs, songs about self by old zemis duct songs etc. etc. Nagaland is the home of numerous folk and cultural traditions of some of the tribal people of North-East India. Naga people enjoy distinct socio-cultural diversities and its people from time immemorial has given a distinct colour and contour to their joys and sorrows of life. Their contributions to Indian composite culture through the folkart, dance and colourful handicrafts and handloom has been immense. Through their performing and visual art traditions, it present part of the cultural heritage not only of Nagaland but of the entire nation. There are hundred of folktales prevalent among various naga tribes.

Today the Naga Society is adopting western culure, but it must be realised that Nagas have inherited, distinctive tradition, and culture art and literature of their own which should be preserved and allowed to flourish.

Directorate of Art and Culture is run by the Govt. of Nagaland, located in Kohima, Nagaland. It has seven cultural centres-one in each of the seven districts.

The Department was established in 1965 with the objective to promote and develop the cultural heritage of the people of the state inhabited by 15 tribes and sub-tribes. Considering the size of the State and its population, the various subjects are grouped together and constitute a single Directorate. The activities include promotion of music, dance, drama and development of museums, libraries, archives. Also propagating plastic and fine arts and participating in various exhibitions and bringing out books on Naga literature, arts, crafts, history and performing arts. The State Government has thus set up a separate "Department of Art and Culture" whose aim and functions are a stated earlier also to forster the continuity, promotion and preservation of Naga culture. Tapping and exploring of its myth, love and legend, usage and custom, song and dance, antiquity and abundant oral literature and thus naturally the most vital test of the Department. Side by side participation in the National festivity, organisation, sending and receiving of cultural troupe, etc. are some of the other normal activities of the department.

Under 'Research and Study' Programme, recording of folk literature has been given priority. Already hundred of folk songs and tales are collected. Recordings and collection of materials on oral tradition are also continuing side by side. Reports are being prepared on customary laws. Significant achievement in this regard are the establishment of the State Museum at Kohima. and "*North-East Zone Cultural Centre*" at Dimapur and in different parts of the state seven cultural centres.

The Promotion of performing art has taken an institutionalised shape with the establishment of an '*Academy of Music and Dance*.'

North East Zone Cultural Centre

This is an autonomous society under the Department of Culture, Govt. of India representing the seven states of the North East India, viz, Assam, Nagaland, Manipur, Meghalaya, Mizoram, Arunachal Pradesh and Tripura, Formed in 1986, it was set up with a view to preserving and promoting culture of the North East Zone comprising of the above mentioned member states. The centre was, however, formally inaugurated by the Prime Minister of Indian on 6th October 1987.

The main aims and objectives of NEZCC are

(i) to develop and promote the rich diversity and uniqueness of various arts of the zone.

(ii) to upgrade and enrich consciousness of the people about their cultural heritage.

North East Zone Cultural Centre arranges zonal cultural Festival in the Member States and other parts of the country. The Centre has succeeded in generating a great spurt in the cultural world of the North East and in the country as a whole through programmes of festivals, concerts, grassroots research and documentation camps, intensive cultural acquaintances and rapports with the rural folk, cultural events for children, etc. Collection of cultural data at the grassroot level; their vanishing art forms is an area where the Centre is doing useful work. In this genre the Centre is bringing out a series in volumes on the musical instruments of the Nort East. The first volume entitled 'Tuning in to Dimasa Folk instruments authored by Sri Tarun Goswami has appeared in print. The location of the Centre is at Dimapur in Nagaland.

Presently a number of cultural, literary, performing art centres have sprang up. Few such organisations of note are:-

Kohima Sahitya Sabha

Kohima Shitya Sabha is housed at P.R. Hill, Kohima -797 001, Nagaland. This is the oldest socio-literary cultural organisation of North East India, formed in the year 1895 by the eminent scholar and writer Padma Nath Gohain Barua. The aim and objectives of the Sabha have been to forge cultural and literary unity in diversity, in this socio-culturally and ethnically mosaic region. The Centenary Celebrations for the Sabha was organised in 1994 when important scholars, writers and artists of the region participated. Activities include socio-cultural performances such as dramas, music and dance, literary seminars, writers meet etc.

Longmisa Cultural Club

Based in Nagaland, this cultural organisation was formed in 1982 at Village Mokokchung, B.P.O. Longmisa having branches at Kohima, Dimapur etc. Its areas of interest are dance, music and drama and aims at preserving the tribal culture and to promote activities in the above mentioned fields of performing art. This society participates in North East Cultural Festivals and organises conferences, lectures, dance, drama, music performances.

Merangkong Cultural Club

This cultural forum became a registered society by the State Govt of Nagaland in January 1988, but existed in the Merangkong Village since 25 years. Basically a dance forum, it aims to promote national integration of India through cultural exchange within and outside the State of Nagaland; to promote and maintain Merangkong traditional cultural dances which are regarded as some of the best dances among the Naga tribal communities. It imports training in cultural dances and participates in cultural festivals. It also taken part in cultural programmes. It is located in Merangkong village, P.O. Changtongya-798 613, Dist. Mokokchung, Nagaland, having brance at C/o T. Penza, MLA, Sangtemla Peak Cottage, Opposite Circuit House, D.C. Hill Mokokchung - 798 601.

Mopungchukel Tazulenden Cultural Society

A performing art centre established in 1983, it aims to preserve tribal culture. The society organises a cultural show, cultural music, cultural dance and exhibition-cum-sale during 'Muatsu' and 'Jsungrim Mong' festival in the village. Folk songs and traditional dances are practised on every Friday night. It bringsout yearly bulletins. The centre has a library-cum-museum having collection of head hair, spear, horn, bill feathers, Oram sophy, aporm armlet and bone necklace. Its address of communiction is P.O. Impur Village, Mopungchuket-798 615, Nagaland.

Young Naga Club (YNC)

This performing arts centre came into being in 1974. Its President being S. Lipak Imsong and Director Sentilamzung. The centre is located at Ungma Village, P.O. Mokokchung, Nagaland. Its aim and objective is to promote traditional social structure, to teach our youth so that they may learn and understand the old literary heritages in the form of poetry, songs and also to learn dancing. It takes up publication programme and awards prizes for competitions. Conferences are also held and a grand cultural show is organised during Muatsu festival (Festival of Ao tribe). Drama, dance and music performances are taken up regularly. *The Club attends North East Drama Festival-cum-Workshop organised by the Zonal Cultural Centre.*

* * *

Started in 1999 by the National School of Drama, the premier theatre institute located at New Delhi '*Bharat Rang Mahotsav*'. National Theatre Festival has came a long way and has made significant contribution in galvanising the theatre movement in the country. The Festival bring many a creative works together in the year on a common platform. In the year 2002, the Festival focussed on theatre from North-East region and West-Bengal. Initiated as a part of Golden Jubilee Celebrations of India's Independence, the First ever National Theatre Festival of India was Christened Bharat Rang Mohotsav. From the North East Region, there was 5 plays in Assamese, 4 in Manipuri and 1 in Nagamese. The National School of Drama Extension Programme Workshop Production '*Nisheli*' in Nagamese directed by Robijita Gogoi was represented and appreciated in this festival.

However, much earlier from January 4 to 28, 1999, a Production Oriented Theatre Workshop was held at Dimapur, Nagaland organised by the National School of Drama in collaboration with North East Zone Cultural Centre held A similar production. oriented theatre workshop, was also organised at Dimapur from 1st to 30th November 2000. production Oriented Theatre Workshop was again organised by the National School of Drama, New Delhi in association with North-East Zone Cultural Centre from 15th February to 15th March 2002. It was held at Dimapur under the leadership of Rabijita Gogoi, a graduate from the school who passed out in 1997.

The Nagamese production which was presented in the Bharat Rang Mahatsav of 2002 was the outcome of all these previous workshops undertaken. The director of this Nagamese drama was Rabijita Gogoi who did her graduation from NSD with specialization in design and direction in 1997; She is also a political Science Graduate from Guwahati University Before joining NSD, she studied Acting from Assam Acting Institute and was actively associated with various theatre groups such as Seagull and Jirshong. After her graduation, she directed two Assamese play '*Kanchanjangha*' and '*Gotirodhak*' for Jirshong. '*Dhruvaswamini*' was her first major directorial venture with National School of Drama Repertory Company.

About her Nagamese play 'Nisheli' she stated in her directorial note that: "Human beings by their very nature are expressive. They have crossed through a long history of evolution of expression and communication. Painting, sculpture, dance, music, literature are the major medium. Now, theatre is a medium where we can see the presence of almost every form of expression. May be that is why this is most complex form of expression. The sound of music and the harmony of various graceful body movements can lend the theatre its unique style. They have a high potentiality for that. It could not be explored earlier because of so many justifiable reasons. The art forms also do not get generated because of frequent changes of socio-political situations. Alienated from the main land of the country, Nagaland is today more known as the land of secessionist movement that started from the golden movement of Independence. A trouble torn province of Nagaland, Dimapur is known for its age old cultural heritage and hundreds of folk tales among different ethnic Naga groups. That still influences the life and living of hundred thousands Naga people even the motif, the colour and the design Nisheli who was an excellent weaver, was supposed to prefer for her attire still popular among the Sema Nagas as Nisheli Amehmi. Lively Nisheli is here today to remind us about a few glorious pages of the history of simple, peace loving patriotic and heart warming Naga people who had settled down in this part of the world since times immemorial. We have taken up a semi Naga folk story which is very popular known amongst them. Without a written script the participants themselves improvised and developed the whole story which finally led to the performance. In terms of performance we simply tried to stick to their own narrative traditions."

The plot of the play runs as follows:- "Nisheli a sema beauty grows with the dancing spring in the refreshing green terrain of Naga hills. The lone daughter of a rich gaoanburha (head of the village), Nisheli was always appreciated by the villagers for her charming personality. Her beloved Pheo though hails from a poor economic background, is a good looking warrior. But the proud parents of Nisheli reject the marriage proposal of Pheo's family. Here comes Kutpa another young guy from a rich family in the same village. Though with a high social status and a favourable family equation between the two families. Nisheli was against Kutpa's desire. Disappointed by the social system. Nisheli and Pheo come up with a divine idea "to go away from the village, get married and live happily thereafter". Nisheli was supposed to leave with Pheo from "Eliki" (the traditional girls dormitory) on one night but, things turned out differently. It was Kutpa who could learn about the plan and took away Nisheli in the darkness of Night. Soon Nisheli discovered the fact and protested vehemently against Kutpa's designs. The desperation finally leads Kutpa to kill Nisheli. Years roll by. Pheo never married retaining memories of Nisheli in the core of his heart even on a hunting expedition with a few of his friends. Suddenly, thunderstorm sweeps the forest. The expeditors take shelter under a big tree that was garlanded by bunches of orchids. Incidentally, they observed that a bunch of orchids followed Pheo to protect him from the rain water. Out of curiosity and affection, Pheo plucked a full bloomed stick of orchid and took it home. That night Pheo had a nice dream where he could interact with Nisheli and come to know about the real story behind her sudden disappearance from the village at that fateful night. Nisheli also reminded Pheo that what he plucked from that tree was actually one of her arms. The news of the dream spread like wild fire in the village. Convinced with the facts, the villagers come out to accuse and punish Kutpa. And, Pheo deprived of his fiance in his life, goes for heavenly abode to meet Nisheli forever."

The production comprised of the following artistes

On Stage

Nisheli	Yemchachitla
Pheo	Temjen Sangba
Kutpa	Ikato Y. Tsuqu

Pheo's Mother	Imtirenia
Pheo's uncle	Hotose L. Aomi
Pheo's Friend	Imjung
Nisheli's Father	Lima
Nisheli's Mother	Amenla Pongen
Relative at Nisheli's House	A. Asenla, Lensa
Guest at Nisheli's house	Ponatiba Longhar, B. Meren
Kupta's spy	Henry, C. Among
Villagers	Tenjen Sangba (Asung), Lensa, Senti Jamir, Akok Jamir, Lipoktemsu, B. Meren, Punatiba Longchar, Henry, Imchung, Merchizuk Imchem
Old widow at dormitary	Lyvis
Nisheli's Friends	Rebeca, Arena, Imtirenaia, Hokbuli, Asenla, Achetla
Tiger	C. Among
Narrators	Hotoshe J. Aomi, Marchizuk Imchen Akok Jamir, B. Meren Lima Longchar, Punatiba Longchaar, Lipoktemsu Ponger

Credits

Set	Ikato, Iipok, Ikma, Akok, Meren
Guided by	Robijita Gogoi
Costume	Hotoshe, Ikato, Lyvis, Itokhun
Guided by	Robijita Gogoi
Music	Hyeny Lyvis, Meren Asang, Arene Hoknu
Guided by	A. Zhumlizhumo, H. Lasivi, Ahomi
Singers	A Zhurrlizhumo, H. Lavisi Amomi
Property	Ikato, Arenia, Hatoshe, Asenia, Achetla
Make-up	Amenia, Rebecca, Achetla, Arenla

Guided by	Veena Bhusnoormath
Lights	Punatiba, Senti Jamir, Lensa, Among
Guided by	Veena Bhusnoormath
Poster	Chizuk, Lipok, Aren, Imjung Walling
Choreography	Ikato Lipok Chizuk
State Manager	Tali
Direction	Robijita Gogoi

Oflate, a full fledged theatre organisation has been formed in Nagaland, named 'Nagaland Theatre Foundation' with which Robijita Gogoi associated herself for, its production 'Aham Naga'

XI

NAGPURI

The tribal people of the Chotanagpur Plateu lived in 'Primeval darknes', without schools, hospitals, roads or electricity, with their lands seized by outsiders and their forests closed to them by the State. And the oppressive was not merely economic, ie, Hindu and Christian missionaries pressed the tribals to change their faith, and give up their own traditions of art, dance, and music.

Jharkhandi people were being exploited politically, socially, economically and culturally, even in the independent India. They had a glorious past, but their language, literature, traditional arts and crafts and other tenets of cultural values were facing extinction.

Now with the formation of a State under Indian Constitution, various measures are being taken up for their emancipation and progress. Today this most disadvantaged section of Indian society, the adivasis are making all possible effort to protect their respective languages from being swallowed up by the wider world.

The Jharkhand culture is the product of historical synthesis of Austric, Dravidian and Aryan cultures — the three great cultures which have immensely contributed in coming to-days India.

In Jharkhand, three language groups, are dominant. There are:-

(I) *Austro-Asiatic Mundari Group*: It comprises of Santali, Mundari, Asur, Ho, Birhor, Kheria, Mahali, etc.

(II) *Dravidian Group*: It includes Oraon, Malpahari, Kurup, Malto etc.; and

(III) *Kurmali Group*: Consists of Kurmali, Kurukh, Khotta, Panch Pargania. Besides, a common market place language in the form of Sadri/Sadani, Nagpuria has been evolved, the most dominant languages in the Jharkhand Kurmali and Sadri, are spoken by 10 million and 5 million people respecively.

Kurmali has remained the spoken language of the Kurmis. Various cultural groups have come up to project the issues concerning identity and culture of the Kurukh and Kurmali people. Since late 1940's writings in Kurmali started by Basant Mehta with his slogan '*Save Kurmali Mother tongue*'. The first book in Kurmali, *Kapila Mangal* by Rajendra Prasad came out in 1953 followed by publication of journals like Silalipi, Sarhul, Akhra, Salpatra, Gairik Pataka, Furung, Jharkhand, Manbhumek Katha etc. Later books on Kurmali language, grammar, poems etc. came out to justify the identity of the community. The Kurmis (Mahato/ Mahto/Mohanta) of Chotanagpur have got in the religious rituals and festivals like Tusu, Akhan Jatra, Bhadu, Karma, Jama, Jita, Sarul Ind and Chata Dassai and Bandana. They have got commercial folk songs and folk dance. Apart from these songs and dance they have got marriage songs. Chau/Cho dance, Jhumur dance etc. They worship their deities at Jaher Than or Gram Than and used to dance in Akhara.

With the spread of interaction based on economic relations, and formation of market, need for a common language was felt. A mixed language came up with the traits of interacting languages, viz, Indo-Mongoloid, Austric and Dravidian. This market place language has been known as Sadri/Sadani, Nagpuria. People having Bengali, Hindi or Manbhumi as mother tongue, got used to this language in daily affairs. To some extent, it has become a some sort of lingua-franca among the Jharkhandi people. Of late, there has been an attempt to integrate, Kurmali, Sadani/Sadri, Khotta, Pargania, Nagpuria into a common Jharkhandi language, ie, to bring the other language groups closer too to form a consoliduted Jharkhand identity.

Songs and dances are life blood of this region. These are traditional in nature sucha Chhau, Dard, Karma, Jawa, Kanthi, Bhadu, Jhumur, Panta, Sohrai, Tusu, Nachni, Natua, Judur, Gonu, Jupi, Raca, Arandi, Jagaran, Hejor, Jatra, Bhajan, Citid, Labun, Large, Dhanthan, Bapla (*dang serang*) Rijha, Burigari, Matoya, Machhani, Bhogta, Bhuang, Marriage songs and dances.

Literature in its verbal form is the hidden treasure of this region. They continues primarily through songs like Tusu, Jawa, Bhadu, Bhogta, Dhua, Ahira and marriage songs etc. and secondly through stories like Jankahanis, proverbs, *dant katha*, Chhara, mantra, rumujha sakhi, jant, kavigan and so on. *Maharaya*, the great epic of this region is again there in its verbal form and is preserved through oral tradition from generation to generation.

Apart from the massive Christian literature, Sadani is very rich in the published folklore and Vaishinav poetry. The names of Gaurangia (Gaurang Singh) and Vinandia (Vinand Singh) need special mention among a large member of Vaishnav poets of the *Git Govinda* and Chaitanya tradition. Sadani has a massive Vaishinava literature and folklore.

Most of these languages are now growing into literary languages, some have a few literary dramatic pieces.

Nagbanshi are a community of Jharkhand who consider themselves to be the descendants of the Nagbanshi, the rulers of Chotanagpur. It is believed that their mythical ancestors, Phani Mukut Rai, was the son of Pundarik Nag and was broughtup by a Munda chief named Madra, of Sutiambe village. When Phani Mukut Rai grew up he was found more accomplished than Madra's own son. Hence, he succeeded Madra and established the Nagbanshi Kingdom of Chotanagpur.

His descendants call themselves Rajdariya Nagbanshi. The other group of the Nagbanshi called Lohar dagiya are concentrated in Lohardaga district. The Rajdariya Nagbanshi mainly inhabit the Ranchi and Palamau districts, while their agnates are sparsely distributed in the Kalahandi district of Orissa. The Nagbanshi use Shahdeo as their surname, and Shah as the title. They speak *Nagpuri*, an Indo-Aryan language, and use the Devanagari script; with others they speak Hindi. They are Hindu, and Durga is their chief deity. They also worship the Nag (Cobra). Education is wide spread among the Nagbanshi with a rich literary heritages.

A significant organisation to preserve and uphold its Nagpuri culture, language, literature, culture arts in all its manifestations is '*Nagpuri Sansthan*' at Pithoria. Nagpuri people has rich cultural and oral literary traditions. They have epic stories which are never-ending stories. Now the modern scholars, at the one hand desire great pleasure in collecting and publishing such folk traditions and on the other hand they have started composing original songs, poems, plays, novels, on modern lines. Biju Toppo and Meghnath have broughtout a musical. Video album titled '*Gadi, Lohardaga Mail*' comprising of seven songs in the language sung by Mukund Nayak, Madhu

Mansuri Hashmukh and Dr. Ramdayal Munda. The album was screened at 'Nagpuri Sansthan 23th April 2005 during its Annual Day Celebrations.

Modern Nagapuria writers have already started putting their hands into genre of drama.

Upendra Pal Singh '*Nahan*'

A renowned author in Napuri, Sri Upendra Pal Singh 'Nahan' was born on 15 October 1930 in Taragutu village at Gumla. In 1952, he passed his Matriculation examination. He wanted to pursue his higher education in Saint Zavier, Ranchi but owing to dometic reasons, abandoned his studies and took to farming for livelihood. He started his literary career in '*Adivasi Patrika*' and his first book to appear in print was '*Narad Moha Lila*'. He has made a name for himself in various branches of Nagpui literature, be it as poet, story writer, essayist, critic, humourist, translator, editor or as a playwright.

Shiv Avtar Choudhari

The veteran litterateur in Nagpuri language, Sri Shiv Avtar Choudhari has composed a number of plays. On 17th August 2005, his three plays in book form, namely '*Asur Kanya*' (both in Hindi and Nagpuri), '*Mahadan*' (Nagpuri) were released by Sri, Balbir Dutt, the editor of '*Ranchi Express*' at Ranchi Sri Choudhari is now eightysix years old and still active in his creative pursuits. Dr. Shravan Kumar Goswami and Dr. Siddhanath Kumar spoke at length about his dramatic writings. Others presented on the occasion were Kariya Munda, Dr. Sushil K. Ankan, Dr. B.P. Keshari, Nilkanth Munda etc.

XII

SANTALI

Santali community is living in a democratic country and one of the crucial function of democracy is that people who have not been represented are represented. Similarly, artistic and literary persuits of this developing people need to be open to all. Santalis so long unrepresented, should have a voice and be represented accordingly. Santalis have been a victim of perpetual cultural subjugation. Their claim and sentiments have always been relegated into the backwaters. But the scenerio is fast changing now. This marginalised section of the society is making steady progress in all walks of life. A rare treasure, their traditional dances and music are not unknown to us. Santali oral literature is considered as significant as any folk heritages of the world.

Since pre-historic stone age, different groups of people have migrated in different times, from different countries to this land. We have no evidence of the genesis of human being, more precisely, all the population of India. A modern scholar, however, reports that the latest Anthropological findings state that the first group of such people entered in pre-historic stone age from Africa via Arab. They are known as Negrait or Negribotu.

The second group of such people entered next to them and spread all over India and beyond India like Melanesia, Polynesia, etc. from West-Asia known as

Proto-Australoid people, ie, Kol people like Munda, Santal Goand, Khond, Sabar, Bhumij, Birhor, Kurku, Kora, Godob, Ho etc. as we see in modern days, a sub-divided different groups, a development of later days. More than 50% of these people speak in Santali languages, the main stream of Kol people's language. Santali is one of the oldest specimen of the all world languages.

The Santals are mainly concentrated in the state of Jharkhand and the adjacent district of West Bengal like Bankura, Purulia, Bardwan, Midnapur, Birbhum, etc. and have also migrated to other parts of India in search of livelihood and settled there. They are divided into exogamous clans (paris) like Soren, Hembrom, Tudu, Hansda, Kisku, Murmum, Baske, Mandi.

Santali language falls under the Munda branch of Austro-Asiatic family of languages. It has five scripts namely, Bengali, Al-Chiki, Devnagari, Oriya and Roman.

Christian Missionaries tried to use the Roman script for Santali language and their activities began in the early nineteenth century. In 1836 American Baptist Mission started in Balasore district of Orissa. In 1852 Rev. J. Philips wrote 'An Introduction to the Santali language' in which he used the Bengali alphabets for transcribing Santali words. He also rendered some gospels from the Bible into Santali language. Now the Bible in Santali is very nice to read which are polished by the educated Christian Santals. In 1868 E.L. Puxley published a 'Vocabulary of the Santali language' in which he made an attempt to adapt the Roman script to Santali and in 1873, L.O. Skrefsrud in his 'A Grammar of the Santal language', made the most able and comprehensive study of the Santali language attempted til then. But nothing much can be said about the literary accomplishments during the first half of the twentieth century.

It is true that Santals has rich store house of folklore and folk poetry in their language. But it is only after the post-independence era that the original Santali creative writing has truly found full expression in various literary genres like poetry, prose, novel, short story, biography and drama.

The dramatic compositions, in particular, have made a relatively late start. Infact the dramas as a literary genre emerged only in the seventies of the last century.

A number of factors have contributed to this untoward state the most significant of which are their poor economic conditions, illiteracy and the dilemma pertaining to their script etc to mention a few. Indian independence had very little effect on the socio-economic conditions of this tribal people. The post war years witnessed radical changes and socio-cultural and economic progress in the society but the conditions of the Santals remained unchanged. Like the British Government, the Government of India, also did not pay much attention to the growth and development of this tribe. Alienated and disillusined for a long time, few educated Santali youths realised that in order to save their cultural identity and ethos they have to be united and fight for their survival. The development of Santali language and culture occupied the agenda of government programmes in West Bengal and Bihar. Santali literary activities became more prominent in these states. The books published by Santali Literary Society, Calcutta, book on Santali grammar, West-Bengal Government's recognition of the language and its publication, of 'West Bengal' (Pachion Bangla) in Santali may be mentioned here.

In 1970, Geetanjali (or the Sereng Sepeng) of Rabindranath Tagore, with a long introduction by the National Professor Dr. Suniti Kumar Chatterjee appeared in print under the editorship of Prof. Suhrid Kumar Bhowmik, a landmark in the history of Santali literature. The society was now gradually becoming more and more conscious to save and enrich their identity.

The wave of uplifting the society and culture started with *Sadhu Ramchand* and the Ol Chiki movement.

Sadhu Ramchand was a social reformer who wanted to make the Santal conscious of their language and culture which were getting diminishing very rapidly. In his childhood days he experienced the influence of the Christian Missionaries. A section of the tribal people was being proselylized into Christianity. He wanted to check this flow. He turned into a religious prophet or Sadhu and preached Sari Dharam or Sanatan Dharma (Eternal Religion) which was based on Santal-faiths and traditions. Soon a large number of people became his followers. He composed a number of religio-patriotic songs. The tide of his compositions fleeng on to the busy hills of Purulia district with that flow Sadhu Ramchand's Sari Dharam, Sereng Puthi or Songs of Elernal Religion reached the young minds.

Sadhu Ramchand Murmu is hailed as the most significant dramatist in Santali. Infact the first modern drama and most famous drama '*Sangsar Fend*' (The Net rounds the World) goes to his credit. Based on the problem of the common people, '*Sangsar Fend*' appeared in book form in 1978. But earlier the play was put on boards for several nights with the handwritten manuscripts. The playwright himself portrayed the Central character when it was staged.

Next important personality is *Pandit Raghunath Murmu* who discovered a new script for this language.

Since 1927, Pandit Raghunath Murmu started propagating the *Ol* script in the villages of Orissa, Bihar, and Bengal. He got its printed form in 1935-36, in 1947 the first printed book in *Ol* came out from Tatanagar, Bihar. Ol-chiki denotes the scripts for writing. Ol Chiki movement from 1967 to 1975 in West Bengal became very remarkable for the Santhal Renaissance. Santals, beyond number through meeting and gathering made demand on the Govt. of West Bengal to affiliate it into the group of Indian scripts. Government accepted their demand in 1976 and assured to make it popular among the Santals.

They geered up the speed of consciousness of the Santals about their demand for saving their language, art and culture. A type of Alphabet having the phonetic characters of the Roman script but in different forms came up. They urge Santalis to use these scripts for writing Santali. The movement inspired the Santals to cultivate their own language, literature art and artistic pursuits.

During 1958-59, Ol-script became know to outside world, since 1960 the script had been popularised among the Santals in Bihar, Bengal and Orissa. The organisation as Socio-Educational and Cultural Association, journals as *Santal Barto, Jug jarpa*, *Taras*, etc. have contributed much to its propagation.

The new script said to perform the long desired aim of expressing the suppressed phonetics in pronouncing Santali words, a problem which became chronic with the use of diacritical marks in Roman script, which actually complicated the problem.

After Pandit Raghunath Murmu's movement for Ol chiki, the speed of publication of Santali books was very fast. He himself wrote plays, stories and grammer book 'Ronor'. He also collected the story of creation in his book 'Hital'.

Though *Ol-chiki Movement made Pandit Raghunath Murmu* a famous man, but he also made a permanent place for himself in the realm of drama. His two excellent drama books in Santali are '*Bidu Chandan*' (Bidu and Chandan) and '*Dave ge Dhan*' (Strength is wealth). These became very popular stage dramas. His another drama of note '*Kharwar Bir*' also made indelible impress on the Santal mind.

Other playwrights of eminence are *Rup Narayan* and *Bal Kishor Basuki*. The former authored the drama '*Ato*' (Our Village) and the latter cameout with the Drama '*Shyam*' and '*Akil arsi*' (Mirror of Knowledge).

Marshal Hembram, an outstanding dramatist has broughtout nearly six dramas of which '*Dahar*' (Road) is most significant. His popular anthology *'Akhara' contains several short dramatic pieces.*

Novelist and playwright *Badal Hembram* made his presence felt with the dramatic compositions. His wellknown drama books are '*Dharam Ayo Baba*' (Adopted Parents), *Manu Haramren More Hopon* (Five sons of Old Manu) and

'*Judasi Gayan Mala*'. The last mentioned drama appeared in print from Marangburu Press, Midnapore in 1990. The play comprises of eightyseven pages.

Lahanti is a very famous journal in Santali and its editor is *Swapan Kumar* who first proved his calibre as an actor in Santali operas. Later he took to writing dramas. He has so far broughtout over seven dramas. His two wellknown dramas are *Ulgulan* (Revolution) and *Kaireak Kurai* (Result of a Sin) is presently associated with a good number of opera parties.

Chaitanya Prasad Majhi (Tudu)

A talented young writer in Santali, Chaitanya Prasad presently stays at Kalakada, P.O. Patbil, P.S. Koranjia of Mayurbhang district of Orissa. Broughtout by Smt. Saraswati Majhi, his short drama book entitled title page lf 'Mare Hatag Tala Tungki Naonwa Tuplag' (a short drama).

'*Mare Hatag Tala Tungki Naonwa Tuplag*' in Santali language appeared from Bhubaneswar in 2004.

(Chaitanya Prasad Majhi 'Tudu')

Presented below is a select inventory of few more contemporary Santali drama writers who are trying to carve out a path for themselves. They are:-

1. Dr. Krishna Chandra Tudu, Tribal & Regional language Deptt., Ranchi University, Ranchi, Jharkhand
2. Sri Jadu Nath Tudu, Chief Producer, All India Radio, Akashvani Bhavan, Kolkata 700001, West Bengal.
3. Sri Rabilal Tudu, At Noarah, P.O. Baharkuli, Dist. Burdwan, West Bengal
4. Sri Bhogla Soren, At. Kumar Para, (Maludbom) P.O. Parsudih via Jamshedpur, Dist. East Singbhum, Jharkhand.

5. Sri Kalipada Soren, State Bank of India, P.O. Via Jhargram 721507, Dist. West Midnapur, West Bengal.
6. Sri Madan Mohan Tudu, LIC of India, Sector-19, Rourkela 769005, Dist. Sundargarh, Orissa.
7. Sri Gangadhar Hembram, At-Thakrapal, P.O. Khuntapal via. Moruda - 757020, Dist. Mayurbhanj, Orissa.
8. Sri Jamadar Kisku, At P.O. - Khanyan, Dist. Hooghly, West Bengal.
9. Sri S.K. Paramanik, At - Gorurubasa. P.O. Barkona, Dist. Bankura, West Bengal.
10. Sri Shivlal Kisku, Assembly of Jharkhand, P.O. Via Ranchi, Dist. Ranchi, Jharkhand.

It is true that modern Santali dramatic writing has yet to grow in respect of power and depth of expression, but a surge of genuine creative self-expression has come to stay in Santali language in the form of one-acts, operas and full length dramas.

From the domain of dramatic literature we now move on to dramatic performances. Here Santali operas has shown its excellence and gaining popularity among the Santals day by day.

Dr. Suhrid Kumar Bhowmik of the Department of Bengali, Uluberia College, Howrah, West Bengal in his essay '*Modern Santali Literature*' written on 14th February 1998 stated 'Today Santali opera parties are fully responsible to enrich or to change the Santali colloquial prose style and music through dramas. Only ten or fifteen years before it was impossible to imagine that Santali operas could be much popular. In the fairs and festival of the Santal-base localities, today mobile opera parties take part under a big tent where ten to fifteen thousand audience gather to enjoy the play. Santal men and women take part in acting. Most of them are reported to be professional.

Mayurbhanj in Orissa, Asansol, Durgapur and Bankura in West Bengal are the main centres for opera organising. There are some Calcutta-based opera parties.

Their dramas are mainly on social problems. Apart from operas, the social dramas written by modern writers are often staged. Though their literary value is debatable, but the Santali playwrights, are well aware of social commitments.

Through sheer creativity, trying to expose their struggle for existence, their bitternes, their resentments, their painful oppression of daily life. Dramas are inbeded with both joys and sorrows. Satircal as well as purely humorous works also find place, there by, touch upon the ligher sides of the life also. This is a known fact that traditionally these people enjoy through their rich dancing and singing traditions but now-a-days, cinema, television, radio, theatrical operas and modern stage dramas highlighting social realities have contributed to a great extent for their enjoyment and upliftment.

An established name in the field of Santali Jatra playwrighting is Dr. Hiranmay Mandi. In an interview dt. 6-10-2006 with the correspondent of *Lahanti Patrika*, published from Gorurbasa, P.O. Barkona, Bankura dirstrict of West Bengal expressed his concern over the continuous distortion of this traditional folk theatrical style in the name of modernization, particularly seen in the present day Santali Jatras produced in the tribal sectors of Orissa. Here one can witness the strong spell of unwanted western dance and music supplanting the actual styles and furthermore copious incorporation of vulgarous dialogues and text of very poor literary merit has become a permanent phenomenon.

A youth drama festival was organised in Jharkhand in 2005 to give the theate movements a new direction. The apex body 'Sangeet Natak Akademi', New Delhi chose Jamshedpur as venue for a weeklong event. With this the steel city bagged the recognition that it does not lack theatre-loving audience. Here it was organised in association with the Department of Art, Culture, Sports and Youth Affairs, Ranchi. The entire programme was arranged by the '*Kalamandir*'. The Celluloid Chapter Art Foundation, Jamshedpur. The festival was held from 31st January to 6 February 2005. On 2nd, a Santali play '*Hopon Mai*' (Little Sister) was staged at Rajendra Vidyalaya auditorium. The play was composed and directed by the young theatre director *Jitrai Hansda* under the banner of Meidiz (Maidīja) (eSnht) Artist Association of Tribal, Jamshedpur.

This was a touching play with a social message which borrowed its theme from a famous Santali folk story. The play revolves around 'Hopon Mai' a girl who has five caring brothers. Hopon Mai is fortunate enough to have such affectionate brothers who make every efforts to keep their only sister happy and satisfied. They devoted much of the time to 'Hopon Mai' which eventually infuriates their wives. Envious sister-in-laws resort to a stratagem to kill 'Hopon Mai'. Once while the five brothers leave for hunting in a deep forest. They avail of this opportunity to torchure her mercilessly. At this juncture appears the folk deity 'Marangguru' in diferent forms to help her out. At the close of the play when they finally try to kill her, they fail in their evil mission.

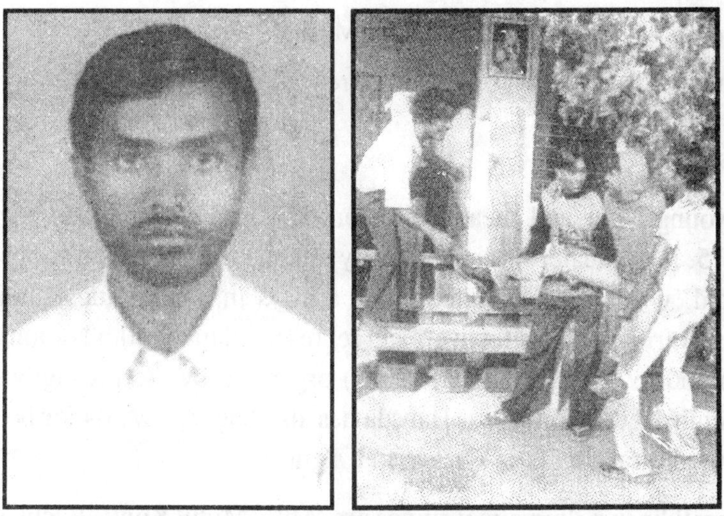

A sequence from the Santali drama
'*Hopen Mai*' & its director Shri Jitrai Hansda.

The cast comprised of the following artistes :-

On Stage

Hopon Mai	...	Reshma Mardi
Five brothers	..	Jitrai Hansda, Surendra Tudu, Ranjit Tudu, Manu Murmu, Nageshwar Murmu
Five Sister-in-laws	...	Sabita Tudu, Parvati Soren, Phulo Murmu, Phulmati Tudu
Baagraaj/Maidakraj	...	Thakura Soren
Nayake	...	Narsingh Tudu
Four fairies/birds	...	Nutan Hansda/Rukmini D. Mai Hansda
Gairani/Sigraj dancer	...	Pradip Chandra Kesari

Off Stage

Light	...	Mahendra Nath Tudu
Music	...	Madhav Chandra Sahu
Music (Assit)	...	Jitrai Murmu
Make-up	...	Kuldev Mahato
Costume	...	Mahi Soren

Jitrai Hansda

An young actor and theatre director, Sri Jitrai Hansda was born on 3rd February 1975. A gruduate, Jitrai has already established himself as an able director who has acted, written and directed many a plays in Santali and Hindi. He has participated in various theatre festivals and represented in the 10th National Theatre Competition and in 'Rang Pratibha' (2005) organised by the prestigious Sangeet Natak Akademi, New Delhi. Jitrai Hansda has also bagged awards for both writing and acting in cultural events in Orissa and Agra.

His well known dramatic writings are 'Ah!', Mutul Kunti, Bachkar', Sagun Supaḍi, Sara Segel, Saravana, Akhir Kyon (Hindi), Ekta (Hindi) etc.

His directorial ventures are Rahi rapud ena, Nichol Jharna and 'Hopon Mai' to name a few. Jitrai Hansda presently stays at Bagbera, Jata Jhopri, P.O. Bagbera, East-Birbhum (831002).

Jiten Tudu a wellknown choreographer, dance-drama director, actor intrumentalist and actor. Sri Jiten Tudu passed away on 16 October 2006. He was a resident of Phulgaria village of Mohammed Bazar Block, Birbhum district of West Bengal. He was a member of 'Paschimbanga Adibasi Lokshilpi Sangha'. This multifaceted personality died at premature age of 51.

Another wellknown theatre director of this region is *Basai Murmu*. A Santali stage person from the Jharkhand region in Jetha Marandi.

Bahamoi Baske, a renowned folk singer, actress of Santali stage was born in 5 May 1953 in the village Kushbona of Shushunia, Bankura district of West Bengal. Her father was Ganshi Ram and Mother's name was Radani. She spent her childhood in acute poverty and was forced to work as labourer in various places. When the Santali Division was established by the All India Radio, Kolkata in 1975, she became regular artist of the centre. An active Jatra actress, she served as the heroine of Chādān Opera.

Bahamoi Baske
(Veteran Santali Actress)

Kalamandir—The Celluloid Chapter Art Foundation

Based in Jamshedpur, Jharkhand 'Kalamandir came into being in 1997 with specific aims and objectives to promote art and culture with a mission to play a role in reviving and nurturing the tribal heritage, culture, artefacts and traditions most rich and vibrant in its primitive aesthetic contents and expression. The

Foundation with its well structured plan and programme seeks to create a greater interaction and undertanding of the tribal tradition. Thus the Foundation has, infact, initiated a process of emotive integration of the primitive culture into the national main cultural stream yet retaining its own distinct, grace and beauty. Kalamandir can modestly claim that it is the only organisation centre of this region to have ventured into this field with a comprehensive plan not only for the revival and regeneration of the tribal art, culture and handicrafts which is spontaneous and integral part of tribal life and society, but also to help them inclucate and pursuit various art forms in the modern light. It played a key role in organising the first Youth drama festival, discussed earlier, at Jamshedpur, sponsored by the Sangeet Natak Akademi, New Delhi and the Department of Art, Culture, Sports and Youth Affairs, Govt. of Jharkhand at Jamshedpur in January-February 2005 in which plays were presented by the local theatre directors in the languages comprising of Bengali, Hindi, Oriya and Santali.

Santali is wellknown for its rich culture and literature in folklore. It has a long history of struggle — a real struggle for expression. The oppression of Adivasi literature was there in the past and also prevails even today. We have to be sincere and should work more to protect its identity. The development of a language depends on the development of education in that language. Santali is now being in all universities in Jharkhand. Santali language is developing fast. Very recently, Sahitya Akademi (The National Academy of Letters) New Delhi has given recognition to the Santali language and to its script Olchiki. The recognition of a language in the Constitution of India is not the only criteria for the development of any language. More of creative literature contributes to recognition of any language. All India Santali Writers' Association, Jhargram, West Bengal and Sahitya Akademi, New Delhi organised a two day seminar on '*Creative prose literature of Santali*' from 11-12 February, 2006 at Monihar Reception Hall, Raghunathpur of Jhargram. *Those who presented papers on Santali plays on the occasion were Rabilal Tudu, Bhogla Soren, Madan Mohan Tudu, Gangadhar Hembram, Jamadar Kisku and Swapan Kumar Paramanik. Sri Kishna Chandra Tudu*, Head of Santali Department, Ranchi University, Chaired the session. The participants discussed the need for the professional drama units of Jharkhand, West Bengal and Orissa. Every participant pointed out the richness of Santali literature in general drama and the modern drama in particular. Many Santali plays are being staged every year. Sri

K.C. Tudu in his presidential speech suggested that the easist way to rich out to the common people is drama. Santali drama plays a vital role on the Santal society.

Anik, a well established theatre group based in Kolkata started '*Ganga Jamuna Natya Utsav*', a theatre festival since 1998, chiefly representing Bengali plays, but have started inviting troupes from other parts of the country with their non-Bengali productions. Between the months of December 2006 and January 2007, Anik undertook a Theatre workshop and training about thirty Santali boys and girls from the districts of Birbhum, Midnapore, Bankura, Purulia etc. of West Bengal with the chief aim to familiarize young theatre workers with the present trends in the productions of Bengali, Hindi and Urdu plays and broaden their visions by enabling them to witness some productions, chosen to represent in this theatre festival.

AAHLA OPERA
Hadamdih, Burrupur, Burdwan
Contact
Surajmani Soren
(Producer)
0 94341 63180
K. P. Kisku
(Manager)
0 94342 15084
S. R. Paramanik
(Writer)
0 94346 50165

১৪১৩ সালরে বাংলা বিহার উড়িষ্যা হুলাচমকাও আকাৎ

আদিম অওয়ার জারপা অপেরা

বারয়া সরেশ থন সরেশ উতাঁর গায়ান পুঁথি
অনলিয়াঁ মাষ্টার দুর্গাপ্রসাদ হেমব্রম গমকে তাকিনাঃ —
হারাতরা গাতে দুলাড় রেনাঃ মিৎ সারি জিয়ন চিতাঁর ঃ-

পান পুঁগি জিরাঁউাঁর
তাগিএও মেনাঃ কারাম ডাঁর

দশার গায়ান — অনলিয়াঁ কাশরায় সরেন গমকে
তাকিনাঃ — ঘারঞ্জ জিয়ন রেনাঃ মিৎ সারিজিয়ন চিতাঁর

সার ঔঞে মে পিয় সাগুন ঔঞেমে
ᱥᱟᱨ ᱚᱸᱧᱮ ᱢᱮ ᱯᱤᱭ ᱥᱟᱜᱩᱱ ᱚᱸᱧᱮᱢᱮ

এ্রেল সামটাওরে মাষ্টার দুর্গাপ্রসাদ হেমব্রম।

সরেশরে — জিৎনাথ, ভঞ্জ পরায়নি শান্তিলতা, সরস্বতী, বাবু সমায়, সমরায়, কিরিঞ
কিরিঞ জানেগুদলী, মাহিগুরুবারি

সেক্রেটারী - নবীন হাঁসদা, ম্যানেজার - কংক, ফিল্ড ম্যানেজার - নিমাই মুর্মু

রাঙ্কী পিরা
তিরলা মাঝাং বুরু
সাওন পিরা
সাওন তন্‌গর
আপেক মাড়াং রে আরশি লেকা ঝালকাও আতেয় — বীনতী বাজোহী
সীতারাম হেমব্রম গমকে তিকিনাঃ চুইহর কলম খদাতে
ছাপাও আকানা রড় লাঁদাতে
লড়ম লড়ম সড়ম আকানা, নেশাঃ বাম্পার হিট - গমহেড় গায়ান
"পানি কেতেল কেতেল বীজু কমর বানর
চুড়ি সেকেজ সেকেজ কাসো লিসয় লসয়।"
দেলা পাঞ্জাএ মেরেএ বাগিয়াম কান
দসার সাপড়াও -
"রিকশা রিগিড় রিগিড় সাইকেল কিচ কচ
তায়ম সিট রেএ দেজাঃ পাছেএ কেচেল এবুরুঃ"
আমদ দুলাড়িয়াম
এটাঃ এনা
ডাইরেক্টর গায়ান বায়ার সীতারাম হেমব্রম আর হরিমহন হেমব্রম গাঁওতে সিদাড় সিকৌরিয়া বানু সিংরাই সরেন

নিউ সিধু কানু অপেরা
সারিগে সাঙ্গাত সারিগে
-ঃ দসার সাপড়াও ঃ-
কোলকাতা সৗগৗই গাং গাডা নৗই
সরেশরে ঃ- গোপাল মুরমু (জাহেরগাড), মহেন্দ্র হেমরম (জাহেরগাড়), রাজারাম মুরমু, তারাপদ সরেন, সাঁওতে জনি লিডার বাবু বুরুগুডুজগন্নাথ হেমরম এমান ক। কুড়ি ক - মৗই ফুলমনি হেমরম পূর্নিমা মুরমু, সুমিত্রা মুরমু, মৗই মুদলী সরেন।
সাডে সাপড়াও রে — সমরেশ হেমরম আর জয়পাল হাঁসদা

রীস্কী সান্দেশ।　　রীস্কী গিড়া।　　মিংটান উন্নান।

২০০৬-০৭ সাল রে উন্নান নাগিং ক সীত সাপড়াও আকান —

শ্রীমান নারায়ণ চন্দ্র সরেন গমকে তাকিনা সরেহ্ থনাং সরেশ উতার গায়ান, রাঃ লাংদাতে পেড়েজ আকান, এনেজ সেঁরেঞ তে গাবান আকান, আঁডিগে আডিতেং হাহাড়াঃ গায়ান পুঁথি -

সারা চেতানরে সাগুন ঠিলি

ডাঃ মঙ্গল সরেন গমকে তাকিনা .হাহাড়াঃ গে গায়ান পুঁথি -

দুলাড় দরয়ারে পোঁড় তাঁয়াং
জিয়ন ঝুড়রে হেঁদে আঁয়াং

আড়তিরে ঃ- **নাওয়া ইপিল অপেরা**

সংকেতেঃ- বিশ্বনাথ হেমব্রম, সুকুমার হেমব্রম, সিতারাম মান্ডি, রমণী সরেন, কানাই মুর্মু আর সরস্বতী টুডু।

হেড অফিস ও দল ম্যানেজার ঃ- শ্রী মঙ্গল সরেন গ্রাম ও পোঃ - কেশবপুর, বর্ধমানপিন নং -৭১৩ ৪২৩ব্লক - রায়না -২

চাঙ্গা অফিস ঃ ধারাণ গোডাউন বাস স্টপেজগ্রাম - ধারাণ, পোঃ - পলাশনপিন নং - ৭১৩ ৪২৪ ডাঃ এম সরেনফোন ঃ (এম) - ৯৭৩২০৪৯৯০৮

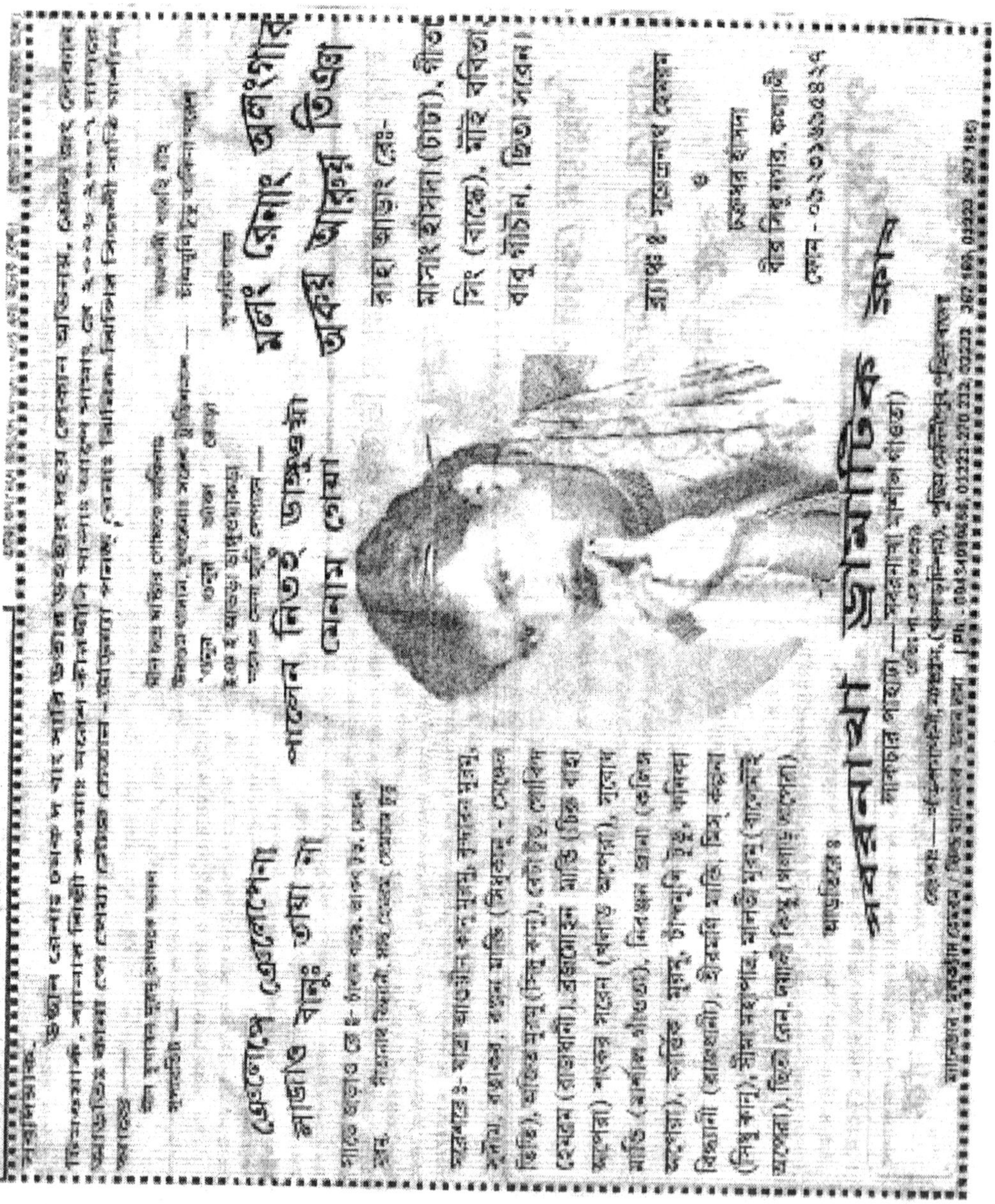